Praise for Nic...

Collision L...

Short-listed for the P...
Literary Sports Writing

"An instant classic of the genre....A triumph."
—Mark Leibovich, *New York Times Book Review*

"Dawidoff has established a reputation as one of the best chroniclers of sports in American life....A deeply nuanced look at an organization—a business—with characters who leap off the page."
—Elizabeth Taylor, *Chicago Tribune*, "Editor's Choice"

"*Collision Low Crossers* is the best book ever written about football and I'm in awe."   —Wright Thompson, senior writer, ESPN.com
and *ESPN The Magazine*

"On every significant American subject there are only a handful of really good books, and *Collision Low Crossers* is one of the best books ever written about sports. Dawidoff takes you into a closed world of interesting men who are obsessed with how to perfect the art of football. The book is closely and boldly observed, frankly reported, ferociously written with both humor and humanity; it teems with wonderful lines, rich and vivid passages. The end result is what all coaches long for, the magical pleasure of watching a perfectly managed game that ends in a great victory."
—Thomas Powers, Pulitzer Prize–winning author of
The Man Who Kept the Secrets and *The Killing of Crazy Horse*

"Nicholas Dawidoff shows us everything television doesn't. By the time I finished *Collision Low Crossers,* I realized that what happens on the field is only a tiny fraction of a football season—and hardly the most interesting. It was a huge pleasure to be led behind the scenes by a writer with such subtlety, wit, and style."
—Anne Fadiman, author of *The Spirit Catches You and You Fall Down* and *At Large and at Small*

NOV 2014

"It is rare indeed that any writer can infiltrate any sports team so thoroughly as Nicholas Dawidoff has done in *Collision Low Crossers*. His access, though, is but the foundation of this sports *tour de force*, for his year in the belly of the New York Jets is so informed with insight and sensitivity alike that it reveals to us not just the season's secrets of one team, but the complicated attractions that trap men in football's mean clutches."

—Frank Deford, commentator on NPR's *Morning Edition* and author of *Over Time: My Life as a Sportswriter*

"I loved *Collision Low Crossers*—it's revealing, engrossing, extremely funny, and about as close as you can come to the NFL without getting a concussion. With expert reporting and an enviably light touch, Dawidoff shows the warm heart beating inside the most dangerous game." —Chad Harbach, author of *The Art of Fielding*

"A startling, year-long, day-in-and-day-out tale of large men and obsessive, outsized personalities. Nicholas Dawidoff is a committed watcher and listener who takes Plimpton's participatory impulse and applies it in his own artful way, creating an entirely original— and thoroughly grand—portrait of an NFL team. Before *Collision Low Crossers*, it's now quite clear to me, I didn't really understand pro football at all."

—Ted Conover, author of *Newjack: Guarding Sing Sing* and *Rolling Nowhere*

"*Collision Low Crossers* is a book that I would highly recommend not just for lovers of sportswriting, but for lovers of intelligent writing that sheds new light on something so universal in the average American's life that the average American might never notice. This is a wonderful book by a talented writer I hope to read more from in the future." —Michael Jones, *Seattle Post-Intelligencer*

"An unusually smart and revealing (and often funny) look at the quirky subculture of pro football."

—Tom Perrotta, author of *The Leftovers*

"Dawidoff also illuminates the inner life of the game.... In a way that is both honest and compassionate, *Collision Low Crossers* is an insightful and witty window into a weirdly insulated world that on almost every level is hard to comprehend from the outside."

—Julian Benbow, *Boston Globe*

"In the hands of a skillful observer such as Dawidoff, the volatile personalities and intricacies of running a professional football team become both accessible and understandable."

—Robert Birnbaum, *Virginia Quarterly Review*

"An exceptionally detailed description of how the coaches of an NFL team prepare for and survive a season that turns out to be a disappointment.... Full of intriguing, creatively chronicled little moments."

—Bill Littlefield, NPR's *Only a Game*

"A rare behind-the-scenes look at what makes a football organization tick."

—Rick Maese, *Washington Post*

"May be the best book I've ever read about football."

—Mike Pesca, NPR's *All Things Considered*

"A fascinating, incisive look at football, written in prose that soars like a perfect pass."

—Marilyn Dahl, *Shelf Awareness*, "The Best Books of 2013"

"Superb.... Excellent stuff.... Dawidoff is as good as they come."

—Jeff Pearlman, *Newsday*

"Dawidoff is a crack writer, saturating the book with the best of a year's worth of anecdotes and lacing it with the backgrounds of coaches and players with an intimacy that begs the question how he got all this sharp and often moving material.... He has a sure hand with the nature of passion, the rancor, and weeping joy that characterizes every season in the most popular sport in the country. Insightful, immediate sportswriting. Readers will feel every bit of the team's frustration and elation."

—*Kirkus Reviews* (starred review)

Also by Nicholas Dawidoff

Collision Low Crossers

Inside the Turbulent World of
NFL FOOTBALL

NICHOLAS
DAWIDOFF

BACK BAY BOOKS
LITTLE, BROWN AND COMPANY
NEW YORK   BOSTON   LONDON

For Kaari Pitkin

Back Bay Books / Little, Brown and Company
Hachette Book Group
237 Park Avenue, New York, NY 10017
littlebrown.com

Originally published in hardcover by Little, Brown and Company, November 2013
First Back Bay paperback edition, September 2014

Back Bay Books is an imprint of Little, Brown and Company. The Back Bay Books name and logo are trademarks of Hachette Book Group, Inc.

The publisher is not responsible for websites (or their content) that are not owned by the publisher.

The Hachette Speakers Bureau provides a wide range of authors for speaking events. To find out more, go to hachettespeakersbureau.com or call (866) 376-6591.

Portions of this work appeared in a slightly different form in the *New York Times Magazine* and *The New Yorker*.

Library of Congress Cataloging-in-Publication Data
Dawidoff, Nicholas.
  Collision low crossers : inside the turbulent world of NFL football / Nicholas Dawidoff.
    pages cm
  Includes index.
  ISBN 978-0-316-19679-6 (hc) / 978-0-316-19678-9 (pb)
  1. New York Jets (Football team)   2. Football—United States.
3. National Football League.
  GV956.N37D38 2013
  796.332'64—dc23   2013030013

10 9 8 7 6 5 4 3 2 1

RRD-C

Printed in the United States of America

"I knew something like this would happen."
"No you didn't," I said. "Not anything like this."

—*James Dickey*, Deliverance

Better pass boldly into that other world,
in the full glory of some passion, than fade and wither
dismally with age.

—*James Joyce, "The Dead"*

Contents

Part I
Before

Part II
During

Part III
After

Collision
Low
Crossers

PART I

Before

Prologue

A FOOTBALL METABOLISM

Success so huge.

—*Philip Larkin, "The Whitsun Weddings"*

Back before it all began, when the 2011 football season was just a lush, sweet section of future calendar for me, it was easy to imagine the path to a Super Bowl victory stretching out straight as a sideline before the New York Jets. A lot of it was that the Jets head coach, Rex Ryan, was always assuring me in his big, warm-blooded, exuberant way that the Jets were "going to win it all." It was Ryan, and the Jets general manager, Mike Tannenbaum, who invited me to spend the year with their team at the Jets facility in Florham Park, New Jersey. They gave me a security code, a desk in the scouting department, a locker, and the freedom to roam. I was hardly any kind of football expert—I wasn't aware, even, that football teams never tackle in practice during the season because it's too dangerous—but I knew enough to be sure that Ryan's gleeful, unbuttoned optimism was something rare in football coaches, a notoriously frowning and tight-lipped cohort. I liked that Ryan was different. I was there because Ryan was different. Nobody in modern professional football had ever let someone like me inside before.

Not very long ago, the NFL had been the cushioned recliner onto which men collapsed, disengaging from life for "the feeling of being alive," as Frederick Exley described his Sundays in *A Fan's*

Notes. Cartoons in the 1970s joked about the football-focused man; in one, he's informed, "There's a family reunion in the dining room"; in another, he dismisses his wife with "I doubt that Pat feels obliged to sit and watch with Dick."

Suddenly now football was the great spectacle of twenty-first-century America, the game of our time. The field's squared-off dimensions, so compatible with the grid of electronic screens, and the stop-and-start pace of play, which accommodated replays and flickering attention spans, made it a better game on television than live. You could miss everything and miss nothing—football was an ideal activity for a distracted public. With every game now of national interest, the networks were doing land-office business. *Sunday Night Football* displaced *American Idol* as the country's most popular broadcast. More women watched NFL games than watched the Academy Awards. (The Jets running-back coach Anthony Lynn had been divorced several years earlier after an eighteen-year marriage. He is now remarried, but he told me that the biggest change he noticed during his second round of dating was that women had come to love football.)

And yet, was there an activity that Americans paid closer attention to but knew less about? That was what made football so different from baseball, the soothingly familiar national pastime. Baseball was nostalgia, past times; football lived in the ongoing moment. Baseball individuated; football, which Ryan always called "the ultimate team game," huddled up and scrummed. Yet for all that exposure, football kept its distance, remained a closed society whose core inaccessibility increased its appeal. It was the national passion, the unrequiting sport—something graceful, thrilling, dangerous, and concealed in plain sight.

That most fans had no idea what the players were doing was something of a point of pride within the game. Tom Moore, who had a long and distinguished offensive-coaching career primarily with the Pittsburgh Steelers and the Indianapolis Colts, tells a joke about an older woman who attended a football game for the first time. Afterward, somebody asked her what she'd made of it. "It was delightful until some crazy guy kicked a ball. I never understood anything after that." The Jets linebacker coach, Bob Sutton, compared players in their helmets and pads to armored knights on horses—"You knew there was somebody in there but you didn't know who the hell it was!" Sutton likewise savored the fact that, to others, a coach was "a kind of mystical person."

The game thrived on mystery. Just as the equipment obscured the players, the mechanics of the sport were such that you were always trying to figure out what the hell had just happened. Half the time you couldn't locate the ball, tucked away as it was like a bean in a bowl of Bartlett pears, and even when it was spotted, each play took place so quickly that in postgame press conferences, the standard coachly response to any request for reflection was that the coach himself couldn't yet say because he hadn't reviewed the game tape. So much went on away from the ball that it was impossible not to assume that you were missing a lot of what was meaningful about football. In particular, what tended to pass by unnoticed was good defense, the intricate countermeans that disallowed the ends. If, like me, you considered defense to be the essence of football, this was a significant lacuna.

The course of play depended on stratagems conceived ahead of time, in the game plan. During games, coaches chose these play calls from sheets that on a television screen resembled the neoplastic grid of black lines and colorful cubes in a Mondrian painting. You could see the design so well because the coaches held them before their faces as a bulwark against opposition lipreading. The whole idea of a game plan intrigued me to no end. I imagined something on the tactical order of Robert E. Lee and Stonewall Jackson drawing up between midnight and dawn the brilliant flanking maneuvers for Chancellorsville. But how a game plan came to be, what a finished plan looked like, I had no idea. I'd heard that all copies were shredded as soon as the game was over.

The sixteen one-hour games that each team played in its regular-season schedule at stadiums were brief interludes from the serious work of football life, which took place almost year-round at the team facility. The facility! The invincible, love-minus-zero / no-limit red-dogging perfection of football terms! There was the image of a secure, vaguely forbidding workplace, a gleaming safe house–cum–laboratory for covert football experiments. True, throngs of journalists covered NFL teams during the season, but at the facility, they were monitored by team officials, led in columns, like state visitors to Pyongyang, into the locker room or out to the practice fields for their few furtive glimpses each week. They saw how competitive the games were; they didn't see how competitive the process was. The real day-to-day passed them quietly by.

So did the terminology on which a playbook depends. Football's was an abstruse, constantly evolving jargon with confidential local vernaculars—a thieves' cant for coaches. "Collision low crossers," for example, was a particular favorite of mine. The phrase, virtually unknown outside the facility, was used in their playbook by Jets defensive coaches to describe players, usually linebackers, making legal contact with any potential pass receiver who was crossing the field within five yards of the line of scrimmage. Beyond five yards, collisioning someone became a penalty. Since football is a game of precise timing and geometry, the point was to disrupt the pass route by diverting the pass receiver from his appointed course. If you knocked the hell out of him, all the better. It was challenging to collision a low crosser because the pass receiver knew where he was going and the defender didn't. Also, most players who ventured into the lowland were nimble, shifty, and moving very, very fast. The real inspiration of the phrase was how instantly it evoked the most basic elements of the game—speed, aggression, the interplay between space and time, plans that likely would not come to fruition, and the essential calamity of what goes on out there. How there was always someone lurking, ready to ruin your life.

In the end, the significance of it all seemed to be that in an age of exposure, the thing Americans liked best operated in almost total seclusion. Maybe the exotic pull increased the pleasure, and perhaps also those who watched were afraid of what they'd see if they got too close.

The tension between speed, design, and aggression made football an exciting sport, but as much as those in football might love the game, love wasn't what gave football its magnitude. This was a hugely expensive undertaking. In addition to the $120 million salary threshold per team for players in 2011, each of the thirty-two teams spent anywhere from twenty to thirty-five million dollars a year on overhead expenses. Airline tickets alone might cost upwards of two million. And as the game grew to a nine-billion-dollar revenue industry, with more to lose, the NFL seemed increasingly uncomfortable with the nature of what it was. Revelations about the long-term effects of concussions had recently tarnished the NFL and made it seem to some like the Big Tobacco of sports. The discovery that the New Orleans Saints had created a system offering cash bonuses to players who injured important opposing-team players left a similar queasy feeling. Were people truly surprised that bounties existed in football? Probably not; more likely, most had suspected something of the sort but preferred not to have it confirmed. Which, in turn, led a wary organization already known as the No Fun League, for its aversion to nonconformity, to grow even more skittish about public perceptions.

Mike Tannenbaum used to worry about my expectations. The Jets general manager supervised Rex Ryan and supplied him with football players, a hiring-and-firing job that, I always tried to keep in mind, required a willingness to be the person others blamed for everything. Somebody had to make the hard calls, the decisions that might not work out. Because Tannenbaum was just enough of a romantic himself to have a gunmetal dread of romantics, he wanted me to understand the full implications of what I was getting myself into with the Jets. "Anything can happen," Tannenbaum warned me in a tone of voice that reminded me he had a law degree. "Things can go very badly."

In football, everything was complicated by the presence of thirty-one other teams that were trying just as hard to win as yours was. In September, no team really knew how good it was. The process of finding out was the season. Since, in the end, only one team won, the dominant culminating experience in the NFL was always disappointment. Probably a lot of disappointment. Disappointment struck me as the foundation stone of football. The emphasis out in the world was on touchdowns and victories, but my strong impression was that the visceral appeal of the game had to do with its relationship to losing.

Loss seemed so prevalent. The average career lasted only three and a half years. "You know what *NFL really* stands for," the players were always telling me. " 'Not for Long.' " If you were put on waivers, released by your team, and unclaimed by another team, you were "on the street." I never got used to the finality of that industry expression for the end of something barely begun. Football had few guaranteed contracts, no tenure, no stable tomorrows. In their perpetual effort to upgrade the roster, NFL pro-personnel directors made their livings by bringing in yet another week's worth of free-agent prospects to sprint around the orange cones, hit the blocking sleds. Walking by these auditions, current members of the roster feigned superior indifference, but they saw. Pro football players live close to their bones. The physical costs are so extreme— the game has a 100 percent injury rate, Ryan always said—that football players are men with an intimate understanding of pain.

When most people thought of the Jets, they thought of losing. Competing in New York against the blue-chip, gray-flannel Giants, the Jets had long struggled to hoist themselves out of forlorn waters—the perception that they were a doomed, even tragic lost cause. Their early years as members of the American Football League, an insurgent association that competed with the NFL, had climaxed in 1969 with a Jets Super Bowl victory that Joe Namath had personally guaranteed beforehand, the Battle of Saratoga that brought credibility to the parvenus. The AFL joined the NFL the following year, and ever since, the Jets legacy had been defeat. This was the team that rented, did not own, that was behind on its car payments, and that felt a little class rage every time it saw the Giants pulling another string to get their kid into private school. The endlessly afflicted quality of Gang Green was something Vivian Johnson noticed in 1999, when she asked her son, Jets receiver Keyshawn, "What's *wrong* with y'all?"

Tannenbaum, who had been with the Jets organization for fifteen years, told me about the wages of football disappointment with reference to Bill Parcells. Everybody in pro-football management was once somebody else's protégé, and Tannenbaum's senior mentor in professional football was Parcells, who led NFL teams to three Super Bowls, winning twice. None of these championships came during Parcells's term with the Jets, in the late 1990s, when Tannenbaum came to know him. All these years later, the two still spoke frequently by telephone, and on occasion Tannenbaum would share with me things Parcells said. "This sport's not for the well adjusted" is among those that made the deepest impression on Tannenbaum. Another was Parcells's revelation that losing football games was a far more potent experience than the satisfaction he got from winning them. Parcells told Tannenbaum that the reason he finally stopped coaching was that he could not handle the losses.

That so much effort went into something likely to end abruptly and painfully was, to me, the signal aspect of the game. By giving himself completely to such a difficult cause, a person would probably lose, but he might also find understanding.

At the moment, however, in early 2011, winning was in the air at the Jets facility. That January, I had been in the stands in Foxborough, Massachusetts, when the Jets achieved their greatest victory since

Namath, defeating the heavily favored New England Patriots 28–21 in an AFC divisional playoff game. The Patriots were the Jets' primary rivals. Just five weeks earlier, in December, the Patriots had humiliated the Jets on the same field, 45–3, harrying their twenty-four-year-old quarterback Mark Sanchez into three interceptions. Meanwhile, the Patriots All-Pro quarterback Tom Brady had thrown four touchdown passes and played with such masterly precision it was possible to imagine he'd solved some deep riddle of the profession.

But here, in January, my seat was on the Jets side of the field, high above the team bench. As the teams warmed up, I watched from that bluff-like vantage, and my eye was drawn to the decision-makers, to the Jets trench-coated general manager, Tannenbaum, and to the team's rotund head coach, Ryan, at midfield whatever yard line he stood near. Across the way was Brady. Even from afar, I saw there was something in his carriage that exuded complete confidence. He was famed for his tuxedo poise.

The game began and I could see the Jets defensive coaches below me substituting groups of players, moving them on and off the field—a fresh down, a fresh corps. Sometimes a group of Jets substitutes started onto the field and then, after a few yards, turned heel and raced back to the sideline. A personnel feint? I had no idea what all the to-and-fro meant, but it was obviously the expression of creative decision-making. Clearly the Jets had devised an aggressive situation-by-situation dossier to redress what had been done to them five weeks before, and just as clearly, the game plan was working. The Jets defenders intercepted Brady once, sacked him five times, and sufficiently harassed him that, from the heights, I could see that Brady looked different than before the game. He was playing raggedly because he was uncomfortable. (Mark Sanchez, meanwhile, displayed a level head and a cool hand, throwing for three touchdowns, remaining "clean"—no sacks—and committing no turnovers.)

What had the Jets done to worry Brady's feet? I'd detected a few clues. A Jets safety, Eric Smith, had spent the afternoon making tackles in numbers usually reserved for linebackers. An actual linebacker—the team's best tackler, David Harris—seemed to have been given a day pass that allowed him unlimited visits out to the shallows of the secondary. It was Harris who intercepted Brady. But what had really taken place down there, I couldn't say. After the game, I watched the Jets coaches walk off the field together, and I wondered what they knew, wondered how, out of the ordinary football metal, they'd forged an intricate mousetrap for Tom Brady. Looking at the coaches together, I saw that there must be a fascinating interior football world they inhabited as they pursued the game at its most competitive level. They had a whole life together, and I wanted to know what it was like.

A month later, I came to the Jets. Even though they'd failed to reach the Super Bowl in 2010, losing in the AFC championship game to the Pittsburgh Steelers, around the league they had respect and cachet. It was a moment when players all over the NFL were telling their agents that they wanted to play for the Jets and, in some cases, that they'd be willing to do so for significantly less money than other teams were offering them. It was fair to say that what made the players want to come to Florham Park was the same thing that had attracted me—the coach. Rex Ryan had become the ascendant figure among headset-and-ball-cap wearers, renowned for his progressive defensive-game theory (which he called Organized Chaos), as well as his swashbuckling dialogue and impressive silhouette (he weighed 348 pounds).

In particular, Ryan had become famed for his pronouncements. In 2009, at forty-six, after ten years as a defensive-line coach and then defensive coordinator with the Baltimore Ravens, he left that hard town by the sea and came to New York for his first head-coaching job. Many people defer to others for a time when beginning a job, taking the measure of things, but no sooner had Ryan arrived on the new waterfront than he let it be known that he had it covered. Up in New England, Bill Belichick, the dour, relentlessly on-message dean of football coaches who had led the Patriots to three Super Bowl wins, was the recipient of these first-day-on-the-job felicitations from Ryan: "I never came here to kiss Bill Belichick's, you know, rings." From afar, I found this raising a dust hilarious. I began to think of Ryan as one of those vivid characters in the great American Out There and to look forward to what he would say next. To me, Ryan was happy hour, a gratifying lift to ordinary moments, especially during the shorter, chillier days of the year. Many others were less charmed. Ryan was rebuked as an arriviste, a buffoon, and, most commonly, "a big blowhard." And those were the professionals speaking.

Everything about the man was big. His voice—flat, stentorian, tinged with the one-horse-Oklahoma inflections of his forebears— was an instrument whose design predated the age of microphones. Standing beneath the media kliegs, which emphasized the astonishing whiteness of his teeth, the smooth flush of his face, the convexity of his configuration, Ryan brought to mind a Coca-Cola Belt politician planted atop the back of a flatbed truck, suit jacket flung at his feet, imparting jubilant election-week promises to the little guy. And yet there was that rumpled fabric of precedent. The Jets had not won all of anything in forty years. Nor would they in Ryan's first two seasons. To vote against such valor seemed the better part of discretion.

But from inside a helmet, the view was different. The essential NFL coaching dilemma is this: When everything seems so impersonal and so fleeting, how do you create a unified sense of group purpose? As the Jets began to consider hiring Ryan as head coach, they had just parted ways with Belichick's protégé Eric Mangini. Like Belichick, Mangini was a graduate of Wesleyan, a young master builder both studious and disciplined. Mangini talked often about the importance of players possessing "good character," but "he made me hate football, how he used to put people down," remembered the Jets All-Pro cornerback Darrelle Revis.

Revis soon came to feel affection for Ryan. A professional foot-ball head coach's daily encounters with players are mainly transi-tory. Somebody's walking toward him down a hallway; somebody's standing next to him during a drill at practice. No one ever got more out of these moments than Ryan. He'd come sidling up to a massive nose tackle, and in no time they'd both have their shirts pulled high, debating who had the "better boiler." He kept up with his players' interests and employed this knowledge in the old male art of faux adversary. Word would come to him that Nick Mangold, a center, had begun collecting California vintages. Whereupon Mangold would soon be confronted with "I hate wine. I like beer!"—Ryan's sideways means of expressing that what he really knew and loved was Mangold. Onward Ryan would amble, though even when he was at a distance, Ryan didn't keep his distance; the just-within-earshot compliment was another specialty. Through the clamor and cry of practice, a feather would drift to Mangold: "He's the prototype center—size, strength, smart as hell, big ass, and he's from Centerville, Ohio!"

The game itself was a series of short, intense interactions punc-tuated by pauses, and that was how Ryan walked the world—he had a football metabolism. It was challenging to keep up with all fifty-three members of a team's active roster, the eight members of the practice squad, and those disabled by injury. Ryan could do it because he was naturally curious. He drew people out, made them secure in revealing themselves. Ryan noticed personality and char-acter traits and then found ways to apply them to football, could foresee players having success, and saw it with such certainty that they believed him.

Ryan's approach to defensive play was the strategic manifestation of his intense personal interest in his players. The signal feature of Organized Chaos was limitless possibility. Most NFL defenses are built from a rigid template and require players to adapt to the mold. The players who fit the system best are the ones who are chosen to play. Ryan's idea was that on any given down, anything might happen.

He rejected the durable premise that offenses are cerebral and determine the unfolding of play, whereas defenses are aggressive and responsive. He wanted a defense that was imaginative enough to take the initiative and yet tough enough to break your face.

All but the very best NFL players have significant limitations as well as pronounced strengths. The joy of the game for Ryan was creating calls and strategic situations that made capital of as many of those strengths as possible—he wanted to find everybody a role. As Ryan conceived it with the Ravens in Baltimore, his defense was a force of relentless, unpredictable mayhem. He began with the proposition that whatever an opposing team's offense did best, "we're going to take away from you." A broad mandate of aggression required adaptability. There are six basic defensive fronts in football. Teams usually play one, typically either the 4-3, with four down linemen and three linebackers, or the 3-4. Ryan featured all six fronts, each packaged with dozens of variations. Probing for mismatches, he often lined up the defense in one front and then shifted to another before the snap. Another thing almost all defenses do is distribute personnel in a balanced left-to-right, back-to-front formation. When Ryan was their defensive coordinator, the Ravens were almost always unbalanced, and pretty quickly so were opposing quarterbacks.

Ryan's game plans were designed to provoke confusion by disguising the sources of the blitzing pressure he sent in waves toward opposing backfields. He sought to create the apprehension that sorties of pass rushers were about to come strafing. Sometimes they did come, in numbers; sometimes they traveled alone; and sometimes it was "simulated pressure," and everybody dropped into coverage. Different calls required players to shift between positions and then from any of those positions take on tasks that defied traditional conceptions of their roles: massive nose tackles floated out of the pit to defend against passes; running backs turned up in the secondary; linebackers morphed inside and out like peppered moths, so many linebackers flying around the flame.

Ryan's girth and bluster belied what he was, a thinking man's defensive coach. Tom Moore had been the Colts offensive coordinator during Peyton Manning's years with the team, from 1998 to 2010. Moore spent the football season by the quarterback's side, helping Manning prepare for games. Moore prized his years with Manning because the player was so curious and so demanding, constantly imagining potential football problems and asking for answers. Their lives became suffused with these football problem sets, to the point where the Jets defensive coordinator, Mike Pettine, said that Manning became "legendary in the NFL for how much of a maniac he is, prep-wise." In the 2009 NFL playoffs, after his team had defeated the Ravens in the divisional playoffs, Manning left the winning locker room and drove straight to the Colts facility, where he began preparing for the Colts' next opponent, the Jets, whom they would play in the AFC championship game. Manning did not start by watching Jets tape. First he went back and looked at film of the Ravens defense from Ryan's years in Baltimore. Moore and Manning admired Ryan because Ryan understood how deeply they thought about things, and Ryan (and Pettine) thought right along with them. As Pettine said, "If we wanted to be successful we had to use Peyton's preparation against him." All the film study enabled Manning to run an offense predicated on his fluent ability to translate his opponent's intentions. Manning routinely made his play calls and set the blocking scheme by standing behind the center and decoding the roles of the eleven defenders spread before him. Against Ryan, said Moore, it was more difficult for Manning to trust what he was seeing: "In protection schemes, you had to figure out who the down linemen were and who the linebackers were, and sometimes they all had linebacker numbers! We were constantly blocking guys who weren't coming." It was a hybrid landscape and a distorted one. There was the unsettling realization that trouble could come from anywhere, and probably would; that you were far from home, in lost country, after dark, without a flashlight and your passing game was in bad decline.

A model Ryan player was the linebacker Bart Scott. Scott came from the slums of Detroit; "It was the Wild, Wild West." Scott said. "Nobody sees any hope. Crackheads, drug dealers, violence, and I was right in the middle of it trying to be normal." Scott received no scholarship offers from Division I college football programs, and, after playing at Southern Illinois, he was not chosen in the 2002 NFL draft. He did receive a free-agent tryout invitation from Baltimore, where he went out and scrimmaged—abnormally. Scott was like one of those remote-controlled toy cars children play with; he spun and careened across the field at skewed, frantic velocities. Scott became a Raven through his willingness to sacrifice himself, to fling his body into multiple blockers, to pulverize the wall of protection on special teams. After hard hits, he delivered hard promises: "Next time I'm gonna knock your punk ass out."

Scott belonged to a category of player Ryan particularly relished: the unheralded, unwanted outsider whose response to indifference was to force his way onto a team by pure effort and excellence. (As is the way with such things, Ryan was drawn to this type of personality because it was more or less how Ryan saw himself.) And so, although Scott was on a Ravens team with many veteran stars, Ryan ennobled him, giving him featured opportunities, calling a personnel package and blitzes after him. Scott, in return, christened the scheme Organized Chaos and never missed a game, despite dislocated clavicles, torn knee ligaments, and a broken hand that kept shattering into more slivered fractures—he shot it up with numbing and painkilling drugs and played on. "I didn't want to let Rex down," he said.

A necessary coaching obligation was putting players in harm's way. What Scott and others appreciated about Ryan was that he valued their bravery and, within the realm of the game, didn't abuse it—he might overrule an injured athlete who wanted to keep playing. "Sometimes," said Ryan, "I make my own decision. 'No, you're not going back out there.' They're not a fucking piece of meat to me."

Scott became a free agent in 2006 and was offered nine million dollars more to join the Cleveland Browns than the Ravens had put on the table. He stayed in Baltimore. Three years later, Ryan left Baltimore to coach the Jets. Scott was about to become a free agent again. At midnight on the day his Ravens contract expired, Scott answered the doorbell at his house in Maryland and discovered Ryan standing there. The coach asked the linebacker to fly back up to New Jersey with him and sign on with Ryan's new team as "my flag-bearer." Scott didn't hesitate. "I would die for that man," he said.

I could understand this, for from the time I met him, I too felt susceptible to Ryan. I found it easy to get caught up in his infectious confidence, considered him among the most appealing and seductive people I'd ever known. The way he talked was vivid and funny, a jumble-up of man-cave comic patter and jive inflection. His dining preferences were always his go-tos, as in "Chips Ahoy is my go-to cookie." The day before a summer softball game Ryan was playing in, he confided to me that he hadn't swung a bat in years but said he wasn't worried: "I don't practice. I just show up and crush!" Ryan's go-to word was "absolutely," the emphasis always on the third syllable. He liked country expressions, and he placed the intensifier "ole" before just about anything, elongating the vowel, as in the "*oooole* bell cow" or the "*oooole* hotbox"—which is what he called the sauna, where he retreated in early evening with several coaching companions to perspire and converse. This was known as the "ole executive workout."

Ryan did nothing without company. He had grown up with a twin brother, Rob, and through college the two were inseparable, sharing one wallet and one set of car keys. After graduation, Rob went off to make his own way in the football world—he is currently the defensive coordinator of the New Orleans Saints—and Ryan spent his adult life accumulating surrogate brothers, many of whom have adopted his expressions as their own. Football is an ideal profession for someone who can't stand being alone.

Sometimes Ryan would tell me with earnest sincerity, "I'm just an average person," which always caught me by surprise, because the language he used in talking about football was outsize and mythic. Football players were "rare dudes," those "mighty men." What he said about "great players" like Ray Lewis and Darrelle Revis and "great teammates" like Samari Rolle and Bryan Thomas felt exhilarating and true to the sport in a manner that was as contemporary as his way of speaking and yet also traced back to something I'd only heard about, never seen—to a world populated by guys called Cookie, Crazy Legs, Night Train, Tank, Bruiser, Bulldog, and Greasy; to the Carlisle Indians, the Columbus Panhandles, and the Providence Steam Rollers; to a soulful old throwback charisma. It was now the great age of passing, and the fact that between-the-tackles football was Ryan's passion seemed only to support my impression that he was one unique dude.

It wasn't just me. To a lot of people who knew him far better than I did, Ryan, who was enthusiastic about playing football but never particularly good at it, seemed to embody the spirit of the dirty, risky sport. Ryan's attitude was "It's a game. Don't take it so seriously," by which he meant that the anxiety associated with football's importance to others should never be allowed to overwhelm a player's joy in the experience. Ryan approached football as the blues of sports, something difficult and emotionally complex and ultimately uplifting, and the night before games, when he spoke to his team behind closed doors, he was inspiring; he lifted them, lifted even the rookie who was supposed to be busy keeping track, for the players' weekly pool, of how many times in the speech Ryan said the word "fuck."

And why wouldn't the Jets win? is what I was thinking as I joined them full-time early in 2011. They'd come very close the previous two years, both times losing in the AFC championship game. The team's defense was, as Ryan would say, "a given." The young quarterback Mark Sanchez, whom Ryan frequently referred to as the Kid, had for two years been restrained by conservative game plans. Now he was a third-year veteran, no doubt more capable of diversifying Ryan's "ground-and-pound" offense. Under Ryan, the Jets were joyful and optimistic, braying and bruiting with an uninhibited elation that proclaimed the bad times were behind them and there was nothing to hide. "What don't we have?" Ryan would ask anybody who came near his (wide-open) door, and who was I to say that one reason people love professional football so much is that nobody has everything.

Mike Tannenbaum knew this as well as anybody. We often sat in Tannenbaum's spacious second-floor office at the Jets facility in Florham Park, facing each other in the well-built custom off-white leather armchairs Tannenbaum had ordered because earlier seats had a propensity to give way and collapse under the ample weight of Ryan. Tannenbaum was, as he put it, "a belt-and-suspenders man"; he was always on the hunt for details that might be overlooked. Since he and Ryan spent most days in and out of each other's offices, it made sense to order the more resilient furniture. It was also important that Ryan's chair be monogrammed with two large cursive *R*s, similar in style to the *L*s that adorned the sweaters of Laverne DeFazio in that 1970s study of oddball friendship, *Laverne & Shirley*. Pro football functions best when it's a buddy movie.

Outside Tannenbaum's west-facing wall of windows there were four football fields, all of them Garden Club Lawn-of-the-Month kempt. The road between the security checkpoint and the parking lot for players and coaches was also visible, allowing Tannenbaum, if he chose, to monitor all comings and goings. Over my shoulder was an unusually large fish tank populated by what I always thought of as the waiver-wire tropical fish. Tannenbaum had bought them for his bedroom, but his wife, Michelle, considered fish inappropriate bedroom décor. Thus the fish were migrated upstream to Florham Park.

Maybe because Tannenbaum's fish tank was the most conspicuous object in his office and served no obvious practical purpose, I began to associate the tank's low, humming sound with its intensely practical owner. Most hours of the year, Tannenbaum was strictly regular in his busy habits: if he went downstairs for a workout in the morning, he left his dress shoes in the same spot close to his desk, but if he exercised later in the day, the shoes were placed in their afternoon location, several feet away. Tannenbaum was a curious and convivial person—he had been the president of his fraternity at the University of Massachusetts at Amherst—who often found it best to restrain his curiosity, subdue his warmth. He was in the habit of inviting people to join him for a "five-minute lunch." When he heard of a new book that really interested him, he might attempt to convince his wife to read it for him and then send in a report. A substantial portion of the books that caught his attention tended to be about either how to run a business more effectively or Abraham Lincoln, but the truth was that Tannenbaum didn't enjoy books nearly as much as he savored reports. He was always commissioning them, and when a new one arrived with an analysis of, say, the reasons premier NFL pass rushers were sometimes slow to develop, he might intend to read it later in the day on the StairMaster and then find himself unable to wait.

Tannenbaum grew up in Co-op City, the massive Bronx mixed-income housing complex, and then Needham, Massachusetts. His father, Richie, worked twelve hours a day, seven days a week, as an electrical engineer, repairing signal lights and switches on New York's and then Boston's subways. Richie was a dutiful man, said Tannenbaum, but "at times he hated his job," and this made an impression. Among his local suburban circle of friends, Tannenbaum came from the least prosperous family, and as Tannenbaum thought about it, he realized that his father probably worked the hardest but could give his family the fewest things. Tannenbaum's great daily pleasure as a child was disappearing at the breakfast table into the *Boston Globe* sports pages, where there lived a parallel world of characters that brought him endless satisfaction and drama. How to join them? Tannenbaum wasn't a good enough athlete to play anything beyond high-school sports, but perhaps there were alternative ways to avoid becoming, as he said, "another Jewish lawyer from Boston." Tulane University's law school, he discovered, offered a degree in sports-management law.

While he was still at Tulane, Tannenbaum was hired for his first (unpaid) NFL job by Chet Franklin, the director of player personnel for the New Orleans Saints. Franklin liked Tannenbaum because—as Franklin said, clicking off the boxes like a scout—"he was confident, competent, dogged, smart, and a good guy." As a reward, Franklin allowed Tannenbaum to sign a free agent. "Toderick Malone," said Tannenbaum. "I offered him eighteen thousand dollars. He signed for eighteen thousand dollars. I'll never forget it. It's like the first time I had sex. I probably remember Toderick better. More exciting to me!"

It was difficult for Tannenbaum to describe how much he enjoyed his job. He tried words such as "unbelievable" and "amazing," and then he offered more and more superlatives, but they all seemed insufficient to him. His fulfillment was such that it poured over the rim and became a source of anxiety that could be forestalled only by greater and greater exertions. "I'm relentless," he said. "I'm going to show up every day almost to an irrational extent. I want to work. Insecurity drives me. Every day. I don't want to go back to Needham. I don't want to be the man in the frozen-foods section of the grocery store, the guy who ten seconds after I pass by with my peas hears people whisper, 'That guy used to be the GM of the Jets.'"

Disciplined as Tannenbaum was, his vigilance was crosscut by looming disorder. The NFL draft, the team salary budgets, and the schedule were all designed to help the previous year's losing teams improve in the next year at the expense of the winning teams. And most losing teams weren't drastically inferior to begin with. While the qualifying standard for joining any NFL roster was rigorous—Rex Ryan liked to say it was easier to win the lottery than play in the NFL—once a player made a team, he found that the difference in the abilities of NFL starters and reserves "wasn't dramatic," as Tannenbaum put it. All of which was to say, the system worked. In recent years, anywhere from half to three-quarters of NFL games had been decided by one score. And sheathed right there in cold, blunt statistic was the murmuring anxiety of Tannenbaum's predicament: the NFL teams had achieved such a level of parity that a form of competitive entropy existed. In any given game, either team could win. Tannenbaum was in command of what he could not control.

During my conversations with Tannenbaum in the off-white armchairs, a phrase often came up to express this low standard deviation of NFL teams: "those slender margins." As the GM saw it, his job was to scrutinize football so thoroughly that he could locate—and then exploit—any inefficiencies in a system grooved with very few of them. He knew that areas of potential advantage did exist. He was also aware that the most pronounced of them depended on something the Jets didn't possess.

Because most people watched football to see touchdowns, and also because head injuries leading to degenerative brain disease in former players had recently become an urgent NFL concern, the game's evolving rules regarding pass protection (increasingly liberal) and physical contact (increasingly restrictive) gave a significant advantage to teams with preeminent quarterbacks—players on the level of the Patriots' Tom Brady, the Packers' Aaron Rodgers, the Saints' Drew Brees, the Giants' Eli Manning, and the former Colts' and now Denver Broncos' Peyton Manning, Eli's brother. A team with a great quarterback in effect drove a car that was more likely to start up on a frigid winter morning than did a team with a still unproven signal caller, like Mark Sanchez.

An exceptional quarterback was a wonderful thing to own, but if you didn't have one, then you'd need a significant compensatory asset. The reason Ryan called football the ultimate team game was that every play involved eleven people. Training eleven large, fast men to the point where they could move as one through exacting choreography with violence erupting everywhere around them required so much time and commitment that football players had to spend almost every waking hour of the year together. Perhaps the most revealing football term was "reps," an omnibus shorthand for repetitions of actions, be they games or practice plays or lifts on a weight machine. There were even mental reps, which required the injured and those not otherwise engaged to watch a given activity and experience it vicariously. It was a game of reps, an over-and-over pursuit; reps made the man. All that montonous laboring could make even an outdoor field feel claustrophobic. The frequently tedious immersion required that people like coming to work. So if a man in Tannenbaum's position could find a bonding agent, some emulsion that promoted a quick-setting and dependable sense of joy in the purpose, that element would be of rare value. In other words, Ryan was a potential competitive advantage.

He was also a potential disadvantage. Tannenbaum supervised the Jets' entire football operation, everyone from Jeff Bauer, the Jets college scout based in Ankeny, Iowa, to Sara Hickmann, the team's Upper West Side psychotherapist who once told me that in a world where everyone walks around with anger and aggression, football appeals "to an unconscious wish that we could drill somebody." Tannenbaum was the sort of boss who tried to keep up with the lives of all one hundred and twenty people who worked at the facility—he would ask how their renovations were going, remembered birthdays and significant life events. Yet it was Ryan who preoccupied the GM. Before the Jets owner Woody Johnson and Tannenbaum hired Ryan, Tannenbaum compiled reports on potential coaching candidates, enough to fill a big black binder. What those reports told him about Ryan fascinated Tannenbaum and also had given him pause—and Tannenbaum wasn't the only one. Over the years, Ryan had interviewed for several head-coaching jobs, including one with his own team, the Ravens, and always he'd been considered too big of a risk. His appearance suggested a lack of control, and so did a police report describing the bloody pulp Ryan had made of a Maryland neighbor's face after an argument on the man's front porch. Was Ryan too emotional to be an effective head coach? Was Ryan sufficiently organized? Could he, a defensive specialist, manage a game when the Jets offense had the ball? Did the pleasure he took in getting along with his players mean he'd be unable to draw the line at recalcitrant behavior? It was one thing for Ryan to urge players not to take football too seriously, but nothing was more serious to Tannenbaum. Tannenbaum worried about everything; would Ryan worry enough?

In Ryan's first months with the Jets came an event that Tannenbaum considered of defining, if inexplicable, significance in their relationship. These being men, it involved a road trip and many hamburgers. Ryan; Tannenbaum; the Jets offensive coordinator, Brian Schottenheimer; and the quarterbacks coach, Matt Cavanaugh, were going to Kansas to scout a potential draft choice: Kansas State quarterback Josh Freeman. Ryan dutifully appeared wearing a spread-collar shirt and pressed trousers, as he had for the many business dinners he'd attended since being hired. This time Tannenbaum told his new coach: "Rex, he's a draftable player. He has to impress *us*." Ryan's eyes grew big. He disappeared back into his office and reemerged in a flowing garment that he referred to as "the dress sweats." The four men flew west, landed, and got their rental car, a pickup truck. Ryan drove, Tannenbaum rode shotgun, Schottenheimer and Cavanaugh sat knees to chest in the back. Ryan told stories of the Great Plains. Soon all four were dusty. Nobody minded. They watched Freeman throw and run. Then, on the way back to the airport, Ryan suggested a visit to a Sonic Drive-In for some refreshments. Most of the items on the menu were ordered, including, for Ryan, a cup of limeade the size of Topeka. The truck shook. Nobody can say why. Possibly it was the many men feasting. The result was that Ryan's cup began to tip. Freshets of limeade poured everywhere. "Oh, no!" Ryan cried.

"The dress sweats!" It became an iconic line, and every time Tannenbaum remembered those words, he felt happiness.

When he came out from behind his desk to sit facing Ryan in one of the matching off-white chairs, Tannenbaum thought of himself as being in partnership with Ryan, not so much a supervisor as a buttress providing the core support that allowed the coach to stand tall against lateral pressures. Reinforcing Ryan was such a significant part of Tannenbaum's job that on days when Tannenbaum arrived at the Jets facility parking lot and could read the painted word *Rex* on the space adjacent to his because Ryan's green-and-black extended-cab Ford pickup wasn't there, Tannenbaum developed a ritual. "I walk around his name. It's my way of reminding myself I have his back, I have him covered." To Tannenbaum, Ryan was like "chocolate. He makes everyone feel better." He was also "the ultimate musician. He won't sit still for long or read binders full of statistical studies, but his game plan for beating Tom Brady is second to none. He's a football savant."

One thing Tannenbaum never had to worry about was my expectations. I just hoped to see a representative NFL season, see the NFL for what it really was. Even in the silver light of February, where all the talk at the Jets facility was of the bright victories to come in the fall, I knew that, while football wasn't exactly subject to the butterfly effect, there were deeply random forces at play. Yet, though I understood that part of what people enjoyed about football was the idea that anything could happen, I thought they also liked that there were men out there pushing hard against that premise — thirty-two groups of coaches and personnel men, all of whom thought that their team could win. That's what I most looked forward to watching, the attempt to impose order on a significantly unstable pursuit. Serious people who thought they could plan well enough to control an uncontrollable world labored under a profound delusion. That was art. That was life. Or maybe it was death.

What defined Ryan was the fullness of feeling. Ryan really believed he could organize chaos. He seemed to think he could overcome the randomness with conviction, as though his wanting something badly enough meant he could will it into being. No matter that Ryan didn't have a Tom Brady or a Manning brother. No matter that he was setting off on his 2011 quest with a strong defense in an offensive age. In Ryan there wasn't any trace of inadequacy. He believed, his belief would be contagious, and everybody else would believe what he believed so ardently that it would come to pass. That was what really drew me to Ryan and his roostering Jets, and what lent them an emblematic quality. They would suppress nothing. They teemed with thermal ambition and powerful desires, and because of the combination, they had more at stake than other teams. Small pleasures would never be enough for them. They were going to be about either the ecstasy Ryan imagined or the despair Bill Parcells had known. I had the sense that whatever happened to them, the Jets were a kind of plumb line. They would somehow go deeper toward football's center of gravity. To be with the Jets promised a real human adventure.

One

COMBINE

He seems very strong. Did you notice his torso?

—*Preston Sturges,* Sullivan's Travels

The year really began in the last days of February, at the NFL Scouting Combine in Indianapolis. The Scouting Combine is an annual invitation-only event at which more than three hundred of the country's most promising draft-eligible college football players gather to audition for NFL teams by running, jumping, lifting weights, taking intelligence tests, and sitting down for private interviews, where each one might be asked about almost anything, including his injured shoulder, his bar brawl, his decision to save himself for marriage, and, as had happened the year before with the receiver Dez Bryant, whether his mother was a prostitute. When Eric Mangini led the Jets, he sometimes began a Combine interview by requiring the ten or so people in the room to introduce themselves to the player, after which the coach turned to the player and asked him to repeat all the names he'd just heard. This did not always go over well. LSU's Dwayne Bowe, now a Chiefs receiver, believed Mangini was trying to humiliate him, and he shut down, producing a lengthy awkward moment that Jets officials still can't recall without shuddering.

The Combine was a spectacle that had elements of other spectacles: it was a football screen test; a football beauty pageant; a strongman contest at a football county fair. Jets receivers coach Henry Ellard, a former NFL star, thought back to his own Combine experience and remembered the queasy feeling of standing on display, "only in shorts," for crowds of men who tugged and pulled at him "like a piece of meat." Ellard, like most Combine attendees and most NFL players, is black. The majority of the people evaluating the players are white, creating a dynamic the Jets coaches warned me I might find disquieting: "It looks like a fucking slave auction," one coach said.

The Combine was also exactly what the word proclaimed it was: an NFL harvester that winnowed the field of ripe young football players and separated them into wheat and chaff. Two months after the Combine, at the end of April, the threshing would be completed in New York, when two-thirds of the contestants would hear their names called at the NFL draft ceremony. For the players, the Combine loomed the way the MCAT did for their classmates who hoped to become doctors, and most of them prepared just as assiduously. These study sessions were often conducted by agents, who helped the players to have ready responses for just about anything anybody might ask them to do or say.

The Jets had been preparing too. In Florham Park, after a season spent living in the moment, coming within a game of reaching the Super Bowl, the Jets coaches and team officials had stepped back, evaluated the team, assessed its deficiencies, decided what had kept them from the championship, and then discussed whom they could find at the Combine to deliver them. Defensive coordinator Mike Pettine, for instance, hoped to discover "a bitch-kitty pass rusher." By this he meant a defensive end or, in a 3-4 alignment, an outside linebacker who would smell a warm quarterback and become an insatiable, unblockable, pocket-infiltrating force of war-daddy bedlam. In other words, a sacking specialist. A fundamental fact of a defensive coordinator's life was that a sack reduced the chance of the opposing team's scoring in any drive to 7 percent. For all their reputation as a pressuring defense, the Jets didn't generate many sacks, leading to the perception that they lacked a real pass rush, were doing it with mirrors. Their basic problem was that there were not many large men capable of accelerating off a mark at high speed and then making a feline curve around the edge of pass protection by dipping their shoulders low enough to the grass that you could imagine them passing beneath a café table without disturbing the vase of tulips on top before raising a little backfield harm.

Attending the Combine was the University of Wisconsin defensive end J. J. Watt and the Texas A&M outside linebacker Von Miller, and either would have been the answer to Mike Pettine's (and Rex Ryan's) prayers. But because the Jets had been the NFL's third-best team the year before, their position for the seven rounds of the upcoming draft was low—they would pick thirtieth out of the thirty-two teams. Watt and Miller would be drafted by other teams long before that thirtieth slot. So Pettine was looking elsewhere. Pettine had watched cut-ups, collections of film footage on a common theme chosen from various games of the college careers of all the defensive players the Jets scouts and front-office people had graded draft-eligible. In his best moments on film, Temple University's Muhammad Wilkerson had impressed Pettine as much as any lineman in the draft. He weighed 315 pounds, had arms that were three feet long, and he looked like a Volkswagen when he sprinted. But Pettine worried that on too many snaps, Wilkerson needed "a little gunpowder in his Wheaties."

For the coaches and front-office people, the Combine was an industry convention. Downtown Indianapolis teemed with contingents from all the NFL organizations. Everybody knew everybody, and there was a reunion feel. At hotel lobbies and in restaurants and bars, you could hear scraps of conversation particular to the time and place: "You can't coach nasty"; "He's only six three"; "Optimal hips!"; "Josh McDaniels thinks he invented football." McDaniels had been hired in 2009 to be the head coach of the Denver Broncos. Only thirty-two and another protégé of Bill

Belichick, McDaniels was then the young NFL coach of the moment. But in December, with the Broncos a 3-and-9 dead horse, he'd been fired, and now there was a different ascendant NFL leader who also happened to be the undisputed king of the Combine—Rex Ryan.

The combination of his coaching success, his charm, and a star turn in the 2010 season of HBO's training-camp documentary *Hard Knocks* as the smack-talking, life-loving profane fat dude with motivating charisma—"Let's go eat a goddamned snack!"—had earned Ryan first-name recognition out in the world: Rex! For him there were now invitations from the likes of Letterman, Sandler (a movie cameo), and Doubleday (a memoir). His popularity had only increased with *Deadspin's* discovery of fetish videos in which Ryan praised the feet of his pretty wife of nearly thirty years, Michelle. Ryan was not only gregarious but also a happily married inamorato! (Around the facility, when the other coaches teased him about this episode, Ryan would retort affably, "I'm the only guy in history who gets in a sex scandal with his wife!") Within the well-insulated facility, one could still believe that things with Ryan were as they had always been. Out at the Combine, it was clear that much was different.

In Indianapolis, as soon as Ryan was free of his long schedule of meetings, he was all over town, as he always was at the Combine. Only this time, everybody wanted to join him for a cheeseburger—or lob one at him. He'd given a press conference in which he'd guaranteed a Super Bowl victory for the Jets.

As for the Jets defensive coaches at the Combine, after hours of asking players to diagram their college base defenses and showing them cut-ups of themselves making good and poor plays on the field—clips chosen to stimulate a revealing discussion, assess the player's football acumen, and measure his responses to uncomfortable situations—the Jets coaches would gather for a late meal or drinks and conversation. They discussed peekers (a player who so badly wanted to please that every time he made a mistake, he looked to see the coach's reaction). They discussed various methods used to defend the back of the end zone (a discreet hand to a receiver's hip to "help him out-of-bounds" was one). They discussed Stanford defensive players ("Buyer beware!"). The coaches worked together closely year-round, so it was understood that, in the interests of group harmony, they would not discuss politics, religion, or wives. The dating exploits of the unmarried coaches were, however, fair game, and questions arose on the order of what was the appropriate interval of time to let pass after breaking up with a woman before one asked her roommate out.

And then there were the ongoing adventures of young Mike Smith. Smitty had been a Ravens linebacker until a severe shoulder injury ended his career. With the Jets, he was still officially a defensive intern, but Pettine deemed him a promising enough coach to lead the Jets outside linebackers. He was a dark-haired Texan with a big, cheerful arm-around-the-shoulder manner, and in a community filled with strong, physical men, there was something sweetly unmenacing about Smitty. The others enjoyed telling Smitty stories in front of him, partly because the stories were so amusing and partly because Smitty's policy in the face of less than flattering personal history was to smile and tell himself, You just have to take it. A year earlier, Smitty had prepared to celebrate his thirtieth birthday, only to realize on the birthday morning that actually he had just turned twenty-nine. Reporting the oversight to Pettine, Smitty used the word "forgot." Another day, Smitty's car was discovered parked at such an angle that it consumed two facility parking spaces, one of them not Smitty's. When confronted, Smitty claimed all ignorance, said he'd left the car perfectly parked. Smitty was a native of Lubbock, Texas, where the gusts were such that sometimes locals seemed to walk at a forward lean. That explains why, on the subject of his askew car, Smitty ventured this speculation: "The wind must have blown it crooked."

At the Combine, Smitty's hotel roommate was Jim O'Neil, with whom he also shared an office at the facility. O'Neil was Pettine's extremely competent quality-control vizier, and he also assisted Dennis Thurman, the Jets secondary coach, which made O'Neil a slow young white guy in charge of some very fast black guys. If this intimidated O'Neil, he never showed it. He had tremendous self-confidence grounded in a belief that his capacity for preparation would always win the day. You looked at O'Neil's big, pale face, jug ears, and upturned chin, and you had the idea that as a kid he must have spent a lot of time down in the family basement lifting barbells while listening to Tom Petty. In another life, he would have been the union boss buying beers for his guys down at a bar called Jimmy O's. Except that he hated unions.

O'Neil's affection for Smitty did not keep him from revealing to the others that his roommate preferred showering in the dark. Or from putting Tabasco sauce in Smitty's can of Skoal chewing tobacco. Or from telling Smitty that O'Neil's Pennsylvania high-school team would have kicked the Texas out of Smitty's. That was a dropped handkerchief Smitty could never resist picking up. O'Neil had played at Central Bucks West, in Doylestown, for Pettine's father, a storied coach who rated aggression above all football qualities—as did O'Neil. Time after time, O'Neil lured Smitty into these debates with assertions whose sheer unprovability seemed to deter neither of them.

O'Neil: "Dude! Our fullback was two hundred and fifty pounds! How you gonna stop him?"

Smitty (*indignant*): "I'd have woodshedded him with my shoulder!"

O'Neil (*going in for the kill*): "Dude, we'd have ruined your shoulder long before you got to the NFL and ruined your shoulder."

And so on.

The Combine was a business trip, and one that had the distinctive energy that develops among a group of work colleagues who are traveling together as a unit. In a sport like football, where people are constantly shifting teams and group identity is everything, this was how they owned their present colors. During one Combine meeting with a defensive lineman, the Jets coaching and front-office contingent was looking at the player's inconsistent film with him, and Terry Bradway, a former Jets GM who had stayed on with the team as Tannenbaum's senior personnel consultant, said that the tackling and effort needed to be better if the lineman was going to play in the NFL. When it was the defensive-line coach Mark Carrier's turn to speak, he said, "I agree with Mr. Bradbury's point." The little malapropism was received with much hilarity; it provided the sort of moment the coaches lived for. Bradway, of course, became Mr. Bradbury for the duration of the Combine and well beyond, and his name was worked into conversations with regularity whenever Carrier was in the room.

The prize moment in that year's Combine meetings involved Ryan. These daily sessions went on for long hours, and to keep his energy up, Ryan ate many snacks. He was working through a stack of cookies while the Jets interviewed Clemson defensive lineman Jarvis Jenkins. At the table, Mike Tannenbaum received a text from someone across the room telling him to look under Ryan's chair. A swarm of ants was enjoying a cookie-crumb banquet. Tannenbaum sent out an e-mail to all the Jets people in the room alerting them to the sudden ant-farm developments; the subject line read "Right Now." Soon everyone was shaking with laughter, except Jarvis Jenkins, who didn't flinch—which earned him high interview marks from the Jets for Composure.

Not that anybody was going to fall too hard for a player because of anything that happened at the Combine. The team's draft personnel were still recovering from the debacle of 2008, when they'd held the number-six pick. Then, as now, they had been in search of a bitch kitty, and during the 2007 college season, an Ohio State defensive end named Vernon Gholston caught their attention. Gholston had just set his university's record for sacks in a year—fourteen—and one of them was against Michigan tackle Jake Long, the lone sack that portcullis of a lineman had allowed as a senior. In Indianapolis, wearing only shorts, Gholston looked not so much sculpted as quarried. Mangini was still the coach, and what he and other Jets executives were thinking after they watched this 266-pound man run a forty-yard dash in 4.65 seconds and bench-press a Combine-best thirty-seven reps of 225 pounds was that they'd just seen, as one of them said, "a Greek god who jumps over buildings."

As so often happens when people look back on the history of how they made terrible decisions, the Jets possessed all the information to warn them away from Vernon Gholston. That information simply didn't prevail. The Jets knew that Gholston had begun playing football very late, as a high-school sophomore; that he was on the field for only two seasons at Ohio State; that half his college sacks were compiled in two games; that he didn't seem like a "natural" football player so much as an "analytical" athlete who appeared to process every action before he committed to it; that Gholston's impressive Combine measurables might indicate only that he was "a workout warrior."

All players have flaws. NFL draft mistakes often come down to the team's inability to know if a football player will continue to display a relentless desire to play and to improve at the game after he's signed a contract for a great deal of money. As soon as Vernon Gholston joined the Jets, put on his pads, and began playing live football, it was clear to many Jets players that the rookie had little feel for the game—that he lacked both a passion for it and "the good awareness," as Darrelle Revis put it. Moving straight ahead, Gholston could charge hard and fast, but football is a game of angles, and sudden changes of direction drained his momentum. As plays began, Gholston had no instinctive ability to limit and refine the possibilities presenting themselves to him. "In football, no matter how fast you are, you have to see before you see," said the Jets linebacker coach Bob Sutton.

When they came to the Jets, Ryan and Pettine had no more luck improving Gholston than their predecessors had. As the Jets defensive coaches evaluated Gholston's practice and game film, his reactions were routinely so stiff, somebody in the room might yell at the screen, "Get the oil can!" It was Jets special-teams coach Mike Westhoff who crushingly observed, "If he touched a hot stove today, he'd scream out tomorrow." Occasionally in practice, Gholston would display the astonishing speed and power that reminded the other players why he'd been a top-ten draft pick. But in 2011, he'd just completed his third professional season, and, as in the first two, he hadn't made a single sack. When the Combine ended, the Jets were going to release him.

Every organization makes mistakes, but this flagrant one was a cautionary tale for the Jets. The most discussed player at the current Combine was Auburn quarterback Cam Newton, and even he elicited restrained commentary from the Jets. They were detached, letting the process play out in full. The Combine was only one chapter, a bewitching spectacle that needed to be treated with skepticism. For all the reports and films and algorithms and studies and formulas and statistics inundating NFL personnel departments, there was no reliable science to predict the professional success of college football players. Gholston, the quiet man who never sacked anybody, was the team's metaphor for the inside/outside existence of the NFL. Out there, in shorts, he was still the picture of an NFL player. Inside, the image blurred.

When the defensive coaches spent after-meetings time together at the Combine, Ryan was never with them. Since coming to the Jets, he'd left active management of the defense to Pettine. To many, Pettine was a man of inscrutable, complicated passions, the dark order complementing Ryan's joyful chaos. In Baltimore, he had been Ryan's protégé, and the two had worked so well together over the years, planning the Ravens defense, that they had become "brothers," as Ryan put it. The past two years in New York, the Jets defense had been either the best in the league or just about. Pettine had run the defensive meetings and done the majority of the defensive game-plan building, and Ryan had asked him to call some of the games from the coaching box high above the field. Now Ryan was making it public that all the game-calling responsibilities would be Pettine's. These had all been Ryan's privileges as the Ravens defensive coordinator, and he wanted to treat Pettine with the same consideration and trust Ravens head coach Brian Billick had given Ryan.

This generosity to a subordinate spoke to another aspect of Ryan's grand ambitions. Not only would the Jets win one Super Bowl, and maybe more, but his coaching staff would go off into the football world and become coordinators and head coaches themselves. Pettine, Ryan believed, would be an excellent NFL head coach, and he thought the same of offensive coordinator Brian Schottenheimer. Such was his faith in the abilities of his staff that on some days, Ryan would name the Jets coaches for whom he predicted leading futures: Thurman, Carrier, and, down the road, Smitty and the special-teams assistant Ben Kotwica. The offensive-line coach Bill Callahan, who had been an NFL head coach with the Raiders, would rise again. By the time Ryan reached the end of his list, he'd named nearly everybody who had a coaching office in Florham Park. Unlike most head coaches, Ryan allowed his assistants to speak with the press. He thought it necessary for their futures that they possess such skills. At the Combine, he said that he expected to "will a championship" from his players, and he had similar confidence about the eventual growth of the Ryan "coaching tree."

The defensive coaches all were very fond of Ryan. They admired the way he'd earned his stripes in the business, spending years crossing the country, working coaching jobs at Eastern Kentucky, New Mexico Highlands University, and Morehead State. They revered his "beautiful football mind." And they owed him: most of them were Jets because of him. Many of them vacationed with him in the summer at a beach house he rented on North Carolina's Outer Banks, and all could list substantial good turns he'd quietly done for them and others. But as the coaches talked in Indianapolis, they turned the conversation to a more somber topic: their worry that Ryan's growing renown was distracting him from football. He had become so adept at the off-field, face-of-the-franchise aspects of the head-coaching job that he seemed to feel obligated to "always be the show" wherever he went. Just now had come word that he was going to appear with Tannenbaum on the TV program *CSI: NY.* Ryan seemed less focused on the team; he had a little less warmth, a distanced quality. The coaches felt Ryan had worked so hard for so many years, he deserved his moment in the sun. Nonetheless, he hadn't won anything yet, and neither had the coaching staff. It was only February, only the Combine, but the coaches were wary.

Another source of unease was the one defensive coach who hadn't made the trip to Indianapolis—Jeff Weeks. Weeks was Ryan's best friend from college, a man Ryan cared so much for that he called him his other twin. As the coaches knew firsthand, there was nothing Ryan wouldn't do for Weeks.

After college, Weeks had spent years coaching at places like Fort Scott Community College (in Kansas) and Trinity Valley Community College (in Texas). Then, in 1998, Ryan became the defensive coordinator at Oklahoma, and he hired Weeks to be an assistant. Weeks slept on an air mattress in the defensive meeting room that year. When it got late, the Sooners defensive coaches turned on music and danced. When the weather was bad, they went looking for tornados. They never found one.

Ten years later, Weeks was divorced, had a young son in South Texas, and was at loose ends. Ryan's twin brother, Rob, then the defensive coordinator for the Raiders, learned that his team had a coaching fellowship available for minority candidates. Rob thought of Weeks, who, he noted, "has got a drop of Indian blood." Weeks lived with Rob that year. In the winter of 2009, Ryan became the Jets coach. Weeks was hired to work as a defensive assistant and given a fine office and a salary to match. When the Ryans bought a house in New Jersey, Weeks moved into the attic guest room, called the Crow's Nest by Ryan. Ryan's thinking was "He's never made a lot of money. Now he can save some. I'd do it for any coach."

As a coach, Weeks was enthusiastic on the practice field with the players, charging around full of brio. His role as Ryan's comic foil made for merriment, good to have on taxing football afternoons. During coverage review, Ryan would scoop up a football, motion Weeks into formation and throw him passes while linebackers tried to intercept them. Footballs sprayed everywhere, along with advice: "Weeks! You got to grow or something!" Mark Carrier said with approval: "When I played, I never saw coaches doing things like that."

But much of the job of coaching in the NFL took place within offices and classrooms, in meetings and on computers. Modern football coaches couldn't have done their jobs without constant reliance on computers, which analyzed every aspect of the game for them and also served as their means for exchanging information. They used computers to break down and dissect the game film of opponents; on computers they built the game plans, and on computers they drew the opponent's best plays after choosing them from the film breakdowns. These drawings were then printed out on cards and run live by the players in practice. Jeff Weeks did not fully understand the new programs that allowed football coaches to do all this. Perhaps he didn't want to. He said he considered computers the "inefficient" tools of "desk coaches," making Weeks at this point similar to a nineteenth-century textile worker railing against automated looms. Nor did he have much regard for the single-mindedness of those around him. "Football's football," he would say. "They're putting people on the moon who work less than us. Guys who operate on brains work less." More than the other coaches, Weeks explored New Jersey; he ventured into the ethnic neighborhoods of Newark and Brooklyn and even started to learn Portuguese. There were those in the organization who thought Weeks was plenty smart and more clever than most people gave him credit for. Others sympathized with him, saying that Ryan had placed Weeks in "a horrible position." But they also said that, given the opportunity Ryan had presented to such an inexperienced professional coach, Weeks ought to be the hardest-working man in the building.

Weeks reported to Pettine. Pettine was all about winning. He thought that since so many uncontrollable variables decided whether or not a football team would be successful, it was vital to control what variables you could. Pettine believed Jeff Weeks was impeding the Jets' chances to be successful. In midseason of 2010, Pettine wrote and distributed a ten-point memo entitled "Coach like a Jet" that detailed his expectations for defensive coaches. These included "Can grade their players bluntly and honestly based on detailed knowledge of each defensive call" and "Completes their weekly scouting report assignment and practice cards professionally and on time." He did this because Weeks was falling short in many areas, and Pettine wanted Weeks to understand what was expected of him. He also wanted to spare Ryan what he knew would be a painful confrontation. Mostly, Weeks concentrated on keeping out of Pettine's way, and in the daily defensive meetings led by Pettine, he refrained from saying a word.

Ryan never deviated from his conviction that Weeks was "a good coach," but he also used Weeks to communicate both his belief in loyalty and his belief that football was foremost a game, and if you removed the pleasure and valued only effort, you were lost. Among the other coaches it was understood that Weeks was in Florham Park because he was Ryan's confidant. Such relationships are common on NFL teams because the top job is inherently stressful, and during the inevitable low times, it's attractive for the head coach to have somebody of unquestioned devotion thirty steps away. Ryan had grown up in a unique way and had uncommon qualities, and the feeling around Florham Park was that if Weeks's company helped make the headman's life better and Ryan wanted Weeks around, then so be it.

Some of these matters were discussed late at night in Indianapolis. It was an awkward, perplexing predicament, and now also worrisome. Weeks was not on the trip because he was taking a little time away from the team to resolve some personal problems. The previous year Weeks had worked with the outside linebackers. In Pettine's view, "suddenness" was not all the Jets lacked at the position. The edge pass rushers needed better coaching. So leading the outside linebackers was now going to be Smitty's job, and Weeks would assist Carrier with the defensive linemen. And Weeks would no longer be living with the Ryans. Weeks was a lively bachelor, and with a teenage son in the house, the Ryans had decided it would be better for their old friend to have a place of his own. As for Ryan, he hoped that when Weeks returned, everyone would just get along. Why can't they? he wondered. It was the NFL. They'd reached the cusp of the Super Bowl in each of their first two years. There was enough here for everyone.

Two

BROTHERS

What strange creatures brothers are!
—*Jane Austen*, Mansfield Park

Mike Pettine came late to pro football. He had played high-school football for his father, Mike Pettine Sr., at Central Bucks West, in Doylestown, Pennsylvania, and Pettine was a strong enough quarterback and student that the finest schools recruited him. He chose the University of Virginia, where he played free safety and graduated with a bachelor's degree in economics in 1988. He earned good money underwriting life insurance and then supervising the hull-manufacturing division at a boat company. Although he was interested in both strategy and risk, Pettine was not a man who saw his life's purpose in an actuarial table or at the bottom of a boat. At work, Pettine found his thoughts were always straying to football. So he took an entry-level football job as a graduate assistant at the University of Pittsburgh and then became a coach at a Pennsylvania high school. He married, had children, and bought a big house. He enjoyed coaching high school, but that felt like being on to something rather than in on the something. He spent his weekends breaking down game film just because he enjoyed it.

In 2002, right after Pettine's third child was born, an old acquaintance, the Baltimore Ravens offensive coordinator Matt

Cavanaugh, told Pettine that the team had an opening in the video department. One thing, said Cavanaugh: the job paid very little. Without telling that part to his wife, "who never would have gone for it," Pettine took the video job, opened a new bank account, and began secretly cashing out his 401(k) fund and depositing the retirement money in his checking account to maintain the balance. This felt like taking two risks in one.

You can't get more entry-level in NFL coaching than third video guy. During the day, Pettine filmed practices from the Trico camera tower high over the field and worked on the techy pick-and-shovel projects that had gotten him through the door. But in the evenings, he lingered. It was around this time that high-level football coaching began to rely on computer templates for making playbook drawings, studying scouting and practice film, and designing game plans. All that was fine by Pettine. When he talked about anything, if a computer was near, it was natural to him to illustrate his thoughts by calling up an image or a map or a clip of video. Word got around that there was a person at the facility who was both football and computer literate. Friends of Rex Ryan, in particular, were hearing about "this dude who knows how to do everything."

As for Ryan, it had to be admitted that he displayed an imposing range of inabilities. Spelling, punctuation, fixing stuff—the whole under-the-hood world was anathema to him. Ryan thought of himself as bad at anything with directions, and yet his enthusiasm was such that he'd open the box anyway, get to the end of the operation and find the damn swing set had been put together backward and there were twenty extra pieces spread around him. His old college-coaching colleague Sam Pittman had watched enough of this to reach the obvious conclusion: Ryan was not very handy. True, Ryan might not be a builder—he couldn't put together a swing set you'd trust your kids on—but he could do other things. During a football game, he could see the whole field in flow—not just where the ball was but where all twenty-two players were and what they were doing. If the left guard sealed the nose tackle, Ryan could see that. If the right end got up too far, Ryan could see that. If the back side was clean, he could see that too. Other coaches told him they could pick up one or two such actions in real time; Ryan could see all three, and everything else besides. Years later, a psychological test revealed that Ryan was dyslexic. That helped explain why he couldn't do another thing: spell. The test also suggested that Ryan had unusual abilities as a creative problem-solver—a great virtue in a football coach. But how it was that Ryan could look out at a big heaving smudge of men and see them stilled into ordered clarity—nothing could explain that. It was his gift alone.

An effective coach was a person skilled at getting talented people to do things for him. After Ryan designed "the biggest kids' fort in the world!" for his two sons to play on in their Maryland backyard, a round-trip airplane ticket from Illinois to Baltimore was purchased for Sam Pittman. Upon arrival, Pittman was presented with a three-level drawing made in Ryan's hand. The two men went out to the yard, and while Pittman measured and sawed, Ryan was right there beside him telling stories about tornados, making work seem like fun.

In Baltimore, Ryan became a football architect, and Mike Pettine his football engineer. The Ravens head coach at the time was Brian Billick, and Billick said that pretty quickly it was evident to him that Pettine would be "a brilliant coach." Pettine had a naturally analytic mind, and on film, football glowed hyper-limpid and comprehensible to him. If in life he preferred to keep a Robert Mitchum–ish sort of distance, from the remove of a football movie-goer, he got in close and could understand the actions of fast-moving men in granular terms that told him not only what every player was doing but also what they were seeing and thinking. Most football coaches sought to correct imperfect results; Pettine tried to teach players to make smart decisions. Players, he knew, wanted coaches who could give them something that would help prolong their careers, make them more money.

Pettine was organized, precise, and, like Ryan, very sure of himself. That was crucial when you hadn't played pro football, hadn't even coached college ball, and were making the jump from game planning for Friday night to working with Ray Lewis and Terrell Suggs on Sunday afternoons. Coaches with the pedigree of Ryan and Pettine were always aware that it would take them longer to earn the trust of professionals than it would take former players. But this often made them better coaches than former players were because they were seeing their team as it was, not through the distorting prism of their own experiences.

Pettine was asked to return for a second year in Baltimore and given a five-thousand-dollar raise. Life continued apace until the final week of the year, when his wife discovered that there was something peculiar going on with the family finances. She was very upset, convinced her husband was having an affair. Let me explain, he said, and he did his best. But what could he tell her—that she was losing him to football?

After Ryan became the Ravens defensive coordinator, in 2005, he promoted Pettine to outside-linebackers coach, and the two began working on the defensive game plan together. By now they were all but inseparable. They appropriated inflections and casual language from each other, each man prefacing his thoughts with "To me," each using convivial phrases like "Oh, my goodness" and "the funny thing is" the way teenagers leaned on "OMG!" On Tuesdays they worked straight through the night; on Mondays and Wednesdays, they'd knock off by midnight. Often, when it got late, Ryan would take his coat, get in his car, and leave the facility so that the assistant coaches and video guys would go home to their nonfootball lives. Then Ryan would circle back to the parking lot and resume work with Pettine. They were so deep in that everything else fell away. It was tiring, relentless work. The Ravens had excellent defensive players, like the linebacker Ray Lewis and the safety Ed Reed, and the coaches felt they were in competition with them and were determined that the scheme should be up to the players' standards.

New defensive concepts were always occurring to Ryan; he kept a pad and pencil by his bedside. Each fresh idea seemed to him miraculous, and he'd come bursting in on Pettine, waving a scrap of notepaper, crying, "It's perfect!" Pettine would remain motionless, glowering at him. Still, it was an intrigued glower. Ryan would stride to the wall and draw his play up on the whiteboard, and then back and forth the two would go, Pettine probing, methodically pointing out flaws, Ryan reluctant to accept that there could be any flaws, indignant at the very idea—"No fucking way!" Now indignation would flame in Pettine, and after an outraged "But Rex!" he would supply logic in complete paragraphs, which had a stimulating effect. "Okay!" Ryan would say, as though they'd seen it the same way all along. "We could do this!" Back and forth some more they'd go, a blade and a stone, until at last, almost casually, Pettine would say with a nod, "That works." The two were engaged in what amounted to an ongoing creative dialogue about defensive strategy and were so comfortable in their process that Ryan came to feel that developing an idea with Pettine was part of having the idea.

The fact that Ryan grew up with a twin brother is fundamental to his personality. Through early childhood, he and Rob were always together, and when they were assigned to separate classrooms as teenagers, each found it deeply painful to have the other out of view. They considered themselves closer than just brothers, had their own twin language. During a low moment, Ryan told his mother, "I'll never be without a best friend. If Rob's not around, I look in the mirror and see him." In a sense, each was always the other fellow, and they grew up thinking about how it was for someone else. That was the very essence of a coach.

Once Rob had his own flourishing career as a football coach, Ryan needed a surrogate twin. In Baltimore, that was how Ryan thought of Pettine. To Ryan, their shared passion for the game was the same, and it went as deep in Pettine as it did in him. Ryan thought maybe this came from having similarly demanding football-coach fathers. During games, when Ryan grew emotional and wanted to abandon the game plan they'd spent so many hours developing, Pettine would be the one to talk him out of it. These mollifications involved prodigious use of the words "mother" and "fucker." "Are you guys okay?" others would ask, and Ryan would always reply not to worry, that this was just how they rolled, that "Pettine is me."

For other people around the Ravens facility, Pettine was a hard man to know, a quiet, self-effacing, intense figure — always vigilant, saying little, smoldering with attention to detail. After a practice, NFL position coaches watched film of what had just taken place and graded each player's performance on every snap. When Pettine graded the practice reps of the Ravens outside linebackers, he wasn't chary about expressing exasperation, as a group of Ravens linemen found when they got a look at Terrell Suggs's sheet and discovered the Pro Bowl pass rusher had been rebuked for playing "dumb ass" football. Nobody talked that way to T-Sizzle.

There was perhaps a lot going on inside with Pettine. His father had coached Central Bucks West to a 326-42-4 record across thirty-three seasons with a leadership style Pettine described by saying, "My dad only smiled on picture day." Mike Pettine Sr. had fevered eyes that kept in constant heedful motion, a deep, booming voice, and minimal tolerance for imperfection in boys. He was the sort of distant, Roman figure who was feared in the moment but years later often thanked by grown men who, in retrospect, were grateful to him for demanding more of them than they would ever have required of themselves. Pettine Senior made practices so challenging that the games were easy. Everything depended upon the discipline of the player's approach — whether or not he got a drink of water during a sweltering summer practice, whether or not a clipboard was broken over his helmet.

As a small boy, Pettine began stuttering, and his mother, Joyce, took him to the doctor. The doctor asked if anybody was trying to make Pettine do something physical the boy was reluctant to do. Well, yes, said his mother. Mike wanted to do things left-handed and his father kept telling him, "It's a right-handed world." The doctor said Senior should cut it out. The stutter went away.

It was more of the same when Pettine made the varsity football team and began playing for his father. To be absolutely sure that his son was treated impartially, Senior was partial to everybody else. One day at practice the entire team had to perform punishment up-down exercises until all of the eighty boys could do no more. There were only three players still rising and sprawling when Pettine reached his limit, whereupon he confronted a familiar shoe and heard, "Get up, you mama's boy." The day finally came when Pettine said, "Fuck this," and walked off the practice field and across the parking lot, stripping off a piece of equipment every ten yards as he went. He was down to his shorts when the senior he was competing with to be the starting quarterback tackled him from behind and told him, "You're not leaving." Pettine became the starter, and a Division I scholarship candidate. Bright and self-assured, Pettine argued every night at dinner with his father about what had happened at practice that day until Joyce banned football talk from the house. After that, on the drive home from practice, Senior would pull off the road into the elementary-school parking lot and father and son would have it out until the anger was spent.

Later, when Pettine was coaching Pennsylvania high-school football, his team opposed Senior's five times and never beat them. When asked whom she was pulling for, Joyce said her husband; she still had to live with him.

As a high-school coach, Pettine had been by turns stern, vocal—"I got after guys"—and funny. You couldn't berate professionals, though, and Pettine mostly adjusted. The adult environment suited him better in terms of both the football—his ideas and expectations had run ahead of what the teenagers he coached could handle—and the camaraderie among men. Pettine was large and laconic; he shaved his skull and wore a mustache and goatee. The affect and the mien were intimidating, and people who met Pettine prepared themselves for "Stone Cold" Steve Austin.

Gradually they'd discover that Pettine was kind and generous, if indirect in his demonstrations. He found ways out of the moment to let people know him. While Ryan's charisma was all body, heart, and passion, Pettine's had to do with standards and distance. You wanted him to think well of you. This was true for football players, and also for women, who fell hard for Pettine.

If you have a father like Pettine's, you can either feel destroyed by him or you can take the best from him. Clearly with Pettine it was the latter, but life is a matter of degrees. Pettine decided that he didn't regret anything about his upbringing. It had made him who he was. But he also thought that maybe he should regret it, that the people who told him he had too hard an exterior might be right. No Jets coach had more of his children's art on the office wall than Pettine. (No other coach had a copy of the Warren Report or a book by Howard Stern's sidekick at the facility either.) Nonetheless, if you caught him at the wrong time, he'd raise his eyes and meet yours with a still, forbidding gaze that resembled the winter in Berlin. "Sometimes I pass in there and see his face and just get out," Smitty told me one day after I thought I'd offended Pettine but wasn't sure what I'd done. "An hour later he's laughing and smiling. He doesn't eat breakfast!"

Ryan's reaction to all this was to go right at it. He'd tell anyone within Pettine's hearing, "Pettine was the high-school coach you *don't* want your kid to have!" Every year at the beginning of a Ravens defensive meeting, Ryan made sure to screen for the Ravens players a scene from Pettine's high-school playing days: Pettine, running for the first-down marker, was blown up by a tackler near the sidelines, and there was his father, telling him he was "a mama's boy," stepping right over him, and calling the next play while standing astraddle his son. The Ravens players would exclaim in amazement as Ryan rewound the film, and Pettine himself didn't mind so much, because nobody better to have as your big football brother than Rex Ryan—who knew all about edgy football-coach fathers.

*   *   *

Ryan was the son of the defensive-coaching pioneer Buddy Ryan. In professional football, a team's offense and defense commonly exist in separate but neighboring regions, and, because they practice against each other every day, the two groups are competitive with each other. Buddy Ryan took this familiar tension to an extreme. His defensive innovations, most notably the 46 defense, were variegated riffs on all-out aggression, and the hatred he encouraged his defensive players to feel for the opposition carried over to the offense of their own team. When he became a head coach, nothing about this appeared to change. The impression Buddy gave offensive players and coaches was that he regarded them with contempt. In January 1994, when Buddy was defensive coordinator of the Houston Oilers, he punched the team's offensive coordinator, Kevin Gilbride, on the sideline during a game. Of that infamous day, Buddy told me, "All I did was say Dumbass Charlie—because all year we're throwing interceptions right before the half. He came at me. You come at me, you're gonna get poked." The Oilers, at that moment, were ahead 14–0 in what would turn out to be their eleventh consecutive victory. They lost in the first round of the playoffs. It wasn't that Buddy couldn't help himself; he didn't care to.

Rex Ryan didn't grow up in Oklahoma, but Oklahoma formed him. His people were Merle Haggard characters, hard-dirt farmers and housepainters, and Ryan absorbed the forbearance of those who stayed, those who didn't put a mattress on the car roof and flee the Dust Bowl for California. Buddy spent his boyhood on an impoverished farm in Tillman County priming the pump, milking the cows, smelling the whiskey breath on his father, "Roarin'" Red Ryan. Most weekends, Red set up a boxing ring, and his four sons would have to fight, starting with the youngest against the third-youngest and on up to Buddy. Buddy could whip them all. Then came the show. Everyone would watch as Red kicked the hell out of

Buddy. Perhaps as a result, Buddy proceeded through life like someone determined to show his father he was tough enough.

Doris Ward was a Phi Beta Kappa homecoming queen and debate champion from Ardmore; she was sitting on a sorority-house porch at Oklahoma A&M when Buddy was introduced to her. Buddy had been on the bloody front lines in Korea and was now playing football like he was still in combat. He hadn't, however, managed to accumulate any college credits yet. Doris soon came to consider Buddy a fine dancer, a fine street fighter, and better than fine company. As for him, once they began dating, Buddy happened to become academic All-America.

Buddy coached high-school, then college, and finally profes-sional football. His basic training approach to football players was the same with teenagers in Gainesville, Texas, as it was with pros in Chicago and Philadelphia: First, humiliate your own, then rehabili-tate them so they can humiliate others. Buddy had contempt for sensitivity in men; he liked players who could handle being called pussy or slob or dumbass or worm while he was making them hit until they bled. Those who could handle it, he was usually there for. Many of them would then go through life telling people, "Buddy Ryan made me a football player."

These testimonials tended to come from defensive players. Quarterbacks, Buddy referred to as pompous bastards, and he meant it; his antipathy for offensive players had the feeling of class rage. He explained his aversion to me this way: "Defensive players are my kind of guy. Guys who spit on the floor and say, 'How much are you gonna pay me?' Offensive player says, 'Please let me play for you, sir.'"

As is the case for most innovators, Buddy's best-known idea was an expression of self. He arrived in Chicago in 1978 to coach the Bears defense and after some evaluation concluded, "We don't have any players." So he devised the 46, which massed as many as nine defenders at the line of scrimmage. Then, went his thinking, "Depending upon how you line up, we're always one more than you got. You don't know who's coming. Might be two. Might be more." You could see what his intentions were, all the taunting elements looming close, probing opponents for weakness and fear. What offensive coordinators like Bill Walsh eventually devised in response was a long spread of receivers who'd run concise patterns—in effect, thrown running plays. In the opinion of coaching authority Bill Curry, Buddy's lasting contribution was the creation of the football auteur: "Because of Buddy Ryan, football evolved into my quarterback versus your defensive coordinator."

Plot a coaching lifer's career on graph paper, connect the dots, and you'll get the outline of the country. Football coaches are like war correspondents: they can't stay away from the action. As a result, every night all over America, sleeping badly on office couches, are overweight middle-aged men with broken marriages. Some people question why football coaches put in such hours, but with men like the Ryans and the Pettines, a game plan is their creative work. Coaches say that even on the best professional teams, only 10 percent of the time do all eleven players perform their roles as scripted. But you always aimed for better.

Back in 1962, while Buddy was somewhere out in the middle of America recruiting players for the University of Buffalo, he telephoned in to Doris to ask how the late fall storm season was back in Oklahoma. In that way he learned he had three-day-old twin boys to go along with their older brother, Jim. Doris eventually divorced Buddy, not because she didn't like him—they remained good friends—but because she was spending her life raising their three children without help or company.

Leaving the twins with her mother in Ardmore, Doris went to the University of Chicago's school of social sciences and got a doctorate in education. She took a job at the University of Toronto, and that's mainly where Rex and Rob Ryan grew up. Ryan believes his parents' divorce didn't affect him much because he was cushioned by his friendship with his twin, but it's true that he and Rob got into a little more trouble than most boys. Doris was concerned enough about them as teenagers that she sent them to live with Buddy in Minnesota, which Rob later decided probably saved their lives.

When Buddy moved on to the Chicago Bears, the twins got jobs with the team: washing practice clothes, painting the goalposts. At training camp, they became favorites of Bears running back Walter Payton, who used their window to sneak out of the dorm at night. Later, Rex Ryan named his first son Payton. Ryan liked football players and admired their courage. To him, courage meant that something scared you, but you went ahead and did it anyway. He felt that way himself running down the high-school field on the kickoff team.

The brothers gravitated to defense because it fit the images they had of themselves: underestimated blue-collar hell-raisers. As defensive ends at Adlai Stevenson High, the twins were tall and skinny and, in Ryan's opinion, "mean as shit. We'd post a guy up and the other guy would wipe him out from behind." Their interests were mainly sports, women, and fighting—and their skill at these pursuits tempered life's difficulties for them. Ryan was a varsity catcher with batting power and fading vision—a problem when he lost a contact lens. "In one game, this guy's pumping fastballs by everybody. I had two strikes. I'm like, 'Time!' I tell Rob, 'I can hit this guy, but I need a contact lens.' Rob gives me one. Two-run homer! Dad had cancer. He was in Sloan-Kettering. We weren't gonna trouble him over a contact. But it's tough playing catcher with one contact. Rob had two. I borrowed the left. All the guy had was a fastball."

There weren't many college options for indifferent high-school students who wanted to play defensive line and weighed a hundred and ninety pounds. Buddy knew the coach at Southwestern Oklahoma State, in Weatherford, and so the twins were admitted to the school and off they went, a nine-hundred-mile drive. The land around Weatherford was flat and dusty, the tumbleweeds as high as a linebacker's eye, and from a sixth-floor dorm-room window, the horizon was so long and uninflected the brothers had the feeling they could just about see Chicago. Coming from a childhood mostly spent in vibrant, cosmopolitan cities, the Ryans were horrified—and lonely. It helped immensely when they became friends with a fellow football player who'd been an All-State wide receiver up north in Bartlesville. Jeff Weeks wore small shoes and had the Cherokee blood, so the Ryans called him Little Foot. The thing about Weeks was that you could call him anything and he'd just shrug and say something affable in the half drawl, half twang that made him sound as though he were from Little Dixie— southern Oklahoma.

Weeks's father had cut meat as a chief petty officer in the navy, and Weeks had a blunt, open face and the conviction that his family was special because they'd stuck it out through the Depression in Oklahoma. To this day, Ryan can't quite explain what it was about Weeks that made the twins so close to him other than the shared experience of being young and on their own. Anything the Ryans were up for, Weeks was up for. The twins' many fights were Weeks's fights too. Road trip to Stillwater? Weeks was in—and by the way, what's going on in Stillwater? "It's almost like we're triplets!" Rex would say. Or, as Doris put it more dryly, "He's my fourth son whether I like it or not."

Ryan marveled at Weeks's uncanny success with women, the thrilling mystery of why great beauties had always fallen for his friend. Even Buddy Ryan remarked on this. "Never could figure it out. Women love him," the old coach said. "He's supposed to be good-looking, according to women." That Weeks was so open to the enthusiasms of others was part of it, but beneath the sheepish grin, there was in Weeks an integrity about pain. Suffering is a huge part of football, and more than most in the game, Weeks had experienced and thought about the condition. Once at the Jets facility, Weeks, at Ryan's urging, told of dating a woman long ago who danced as a Dallas Cowboys cheerleader. Weeks said he'd begun to worry that she was two-timing him and so he had placed a baby monitor in her bedroom and then waited outside with the other monitor to learn the truth. "Don't ever listen to something like that," he warned me. "It'll hurt you too much."

That Ryan was a brawler overshadowed the interest he always took in other people, and even now when he talked about his college friends and girlfriends, they were presented as characters in stories: the One with the Yellow Eyes; the Player to Be Named Later. As they had in high school, he and Rob went through college with their one wallet, carried by Rob, and their one car key, held by Rex. Ryan met the woman who would become his wife, Michelle "Micki" Goeringer, and on the first couple of dates, it was just the two of them. Then it was "Rob's not doing anything tonight. Rob's coming." After that, for two or three more dates, Ryan and Micki were in the front of the car, and Rob was in the back. Finally, it was Rex and Rob in front, Micki in the back. She didn't mind; it was like driving around listening to the *Car Talk* brothers diagnosing football problems. When Ryan required an engagement ring, he and Rob went shopping. Two pieces of jewelry were in contention, and Rob pulled out the wallet and they went for the bigger one. "It set us back two hundred and eighty dollars," Rob recalled. "It looked like a wheelbarrow in the pawnshop!" Said Ryan, "Eventually, I upgraded."

Jeff Weeks remembers the Ryans studying only one subject. They were obsessed with football to the point where they held their own mock draft with each other. Out on the field one day, Ryan had a revelation. His best quality as a player was that he knew what it took to succeed. Opponents hated lining up against him and Rob because the brothers were pests, swarming nuisances who by the fourth quarter wore out the will of bigger opponents. Ryan thought he could get others to play like that.

Buddy was by then the head coach of the Eagles. In Chicago, he'd described the twins to the press by saying, "I've got two nice kids at home but I wouldn't want 'em playing for me." What he did want for them were lives more stable than his had been, and he lined up postgraduation jobs for them with a Philadelphia food-service company. They said, "But Dad, we want to coach!" So it was that on graduation night, the three Ryans holed up in a Weatherford motel, and as Buddy drew up blitzes like Schoolyard and Buddy-Go, this thought passed through Rob's mind: He's teaching us the family secrets, which he invented. Buddy used an easel to explain the pressures and coverages. Then he erased the diagrams and the twins flawlessly explained them back to him. As they did, Buddy had the sense that in that little motel room, he was meeting his children for the first time.

Mike Smith had an empathetic nature, and usually this served as one of his assets as a coach. Smitty was inquisitive about people, wanted to understand them. It helped him immensely that nobody had ever questioned his toughness on a football field. He grew up first on a Texas ranch and then in Lubbock, where his was the rare local father who wouldn't let his son play football. Smitty was small and so good at baseball that in high school the New York Yankees began scouting him. Boone Smith didn't want his son to get hurt. Smitty's mother was the one who gave football her blessing. As a hundred-and-eighty-pound high-school linebacker, Smitty cut through running backs like a band saw. He played college ball at Texas Tech, where his roommate was the future Patriots wide receiver Wes Welker. Smitty's potential professional baseball career ended in a Red Raider football uniform when his left hand became caught in his own face mask as he fell forward. When the hand hit the ground, it bent back over the wrist, kept bending and bending until it snapped. "Sprained wrist!" was the team doctor's diagnosis. So Smitty kept playing.

The untreated break was so severe the bone began to die, which resulted in Smitty needing grafts. Then Smitty broke an ankle and played four games with pain that had him almost fainting on the field. Before games, he'd join the line for injections; of what, he wasn't quite sure. He took bigger injections after he hurt a knee, and even bigger ones after a torn elbow ligament. The wrist was so sufficiently mangled that Smitty couldn't swing a baseball bat very well anymore, but through four seasons as a starter, he missed only one college football game, and on his old Texas Tech film, he can be seen, an undersized linebacker, flattening future NFL stars like Adrian Peterson, Philip Rivers, and Eli Manning.

There were no Combine invitations for Smitty. He watched the 2005 draft sitting on a toolbox in his father's garage, and Smitty stayed with the socket wrenches until the seventh and final round, when at last he heard his name. A Baltimore Ravens scout named Ron Marciniak was retiring from the team, and as thanks for his fifteen years of service to the organization, Ozzie Newsome allowed Marciniak to make the seventh-round choice. Marciniak had seen film of a Texas Tech linebacker who seemed to tremble with hostility as he played. After Marciniak drafted Smitty, it got back to Smitty that the scout had told Newsome, "He's the kind of player, he doesn't look like much, but once you let him on your field, you'll never be able to cut him." Smitty kept that in mind.

The Ravens at the time had six past or future Pros Bowlers playing linebacker. On Smitty's first day in Baltimore, one of those linebackers, Terrell Suggs, looked Smitty over. Suggs was a relentless pass rusher and nearly as unyielding a character. After he'd suffered a painful Lisfranc (metatarsal-displacement) injury to the midsection of his foot, Suggs had reported, "This Anne Frank injury be killing me!" Now, to Smitty, Suggs said, "They're drafting a white linebacker? This team's really going to shit." Ray Lewis wouldn't even talk to Smitty. Ryan called every Raven rookie by the name of his college, and one day he told Texas Tech to cover Oklahoma—Oklahoma being the first-round draft choice Mark Clayton, a receiver so speedy he was a challenge for a defensive back, let alone a linebacker. Smitty shut him out. Smitty played every defensive snap at training camp, and Ryan and Pettine began switching him from position to position. Smitty hadn't studied the playbook for all these roles, of course, so before each play, from the sideline, Pettine mouthed his assignment to him. One day in nine-on-seven running drills, Smitty hit fullback Ovie Mughelli so hard he de-cleated him, knocking him into the air and back into another player, who also fell down. "Okay!" Ray Lewis said to Smitty, breaking his silence. "You're one of us now."

Before the fourth and last preseason game, traditionally an NFL contest in which only rookies and veteran backups see time on the field, Ryan told the players that almost all of them wouldn't make the team, but if they had pride, they should stand up and show what they were made of—everybody in the NFL would be watching. Smitty thought, I really want to play for this guy. Ryan's system, with that array of responsibilities for a smart linebacker, made sense to Smitty, and so did the Ravens surly approach. Like many nice people, Smitty carried around a fair amount of private aggression. On a football field, Smitty wanted to hit people and hurt them. "I was a prick out there," he said. "I wasn't like that anywhere else in life." After that last preseason game, Newsome cut a veteran to keep Smitty.

Midway through Smitty's second season, in 2006, Ray Lewis injured his back, and Smitty started his first NFL game, against the Tennessee Titans. The Titans center was Kevin Mawae, an excellent player with a reputation around the league for cheap shots. Because Mawae was so talented, the late hits seemed especially unforgivable to the Ravens, and, taking note of the huge cross he habitually wore around his neck, they referred to Mawae as the Dirty Christian. On the first play of the game, a run blitz for Smitty was called. What happened next became a favorite Ryan and Pettine story. "You gotta see it!" Ryan exulted the first time he told me about it. In short order, Smitty was collected from his office down the hall and we all trooped into Pettine's office. Pettine clicked into his computer archive, cued up the footage, hit Play, and began narrating. Smitty was wearing number 51. "Fifty-one should be wider," Pettine announced as the ball was snapped. "Not so athletic," he noted as Smitty ran toward the ball carrier. The sudden arrival in the video frame of Mawae was to Pettine indication that Smitty had "showed blitz too early." Smitty neared the ball carrier as Mawae closed in from slightly behind him. Smitty never saw Mawae, as the center went low and cut Smitty's legs out from under him. "You think Ray Lewis misses that tackle?!" Pettine asked. Meanwhile, Smitty's extended right arm hit the ground, and it was planted rigid at an angle as the full weight of Smitty's body followed, driving into the limb. It looked like an airplane landing on the point of one wing, and you could almost see the instant ruin of muscle, socket, and tendon. Somehow, with one arm, Smitty did help make the tackle. Then he was up on his feet, running around, getting ready for the next play, with the dislocated arm sagging weirdly to his side. "I couldn't get it back in!" Smitty said. "The way to get it back in," Pettine told him, "is to pull it out more. It's elastic." (Later, when Smitty described the pain he was in, he made it sound like a coal mine on fire, an underground blaze that burns hotter and hotter.) The teams lined up again. "My last NFL play!" Smitty said. A Titans back went in motion and Smitty, covering him, in effect became the cornerback. The throw went elsewhere, and Smitty came off the field. "Ray would have intercepted that!" Pettine said, and they all laughed. I wanted to know why Smitty had played on with an arm that had nearly been removed from his body, and he said, "I was thinking, I can't let Rex down. That's what all the guys felt. It's very rare. He's like our dad. We don't want to let our dad down. Everybody in Baltimore misses him. Guys in Baltimore who left Rex didn't play as well after leaving him. Rex is the guy you drink beer with on Saturday nights by choice, he's the guy you go fishing at the lake with, he's the guy you've always known, the forever guy. The hardest thing besides not being able to play football is not to be able to be a part of that defense and play for Rex."

During the year, I spent more time with Pettine and Smitty than any other Jets, and that was the closest I heard Smitty come to complaining about his bad fortune. In 2011, he was only twenty-nine; he could have been a Bart Scott—and had a Bart Scott contract—but there was never any indication from Smitty that until recently he had been a promising NFL linebacker. He was all about his new role.

Former players who took coaching jobs didn't always have that ability to move forward, to fully reimagine themselves as coaches, to embrace the grind, as the saying went, and embrace the entry-level money. That Smitty did have it made Ryan and Pettine want to help him with everything from groceries to the extra room in Pettine's town house, which Smitty lived in, rent-free. In return, Pettine, who hadn't had a younger brother when he was growing up, got the closest thing possible to one, as well as an excellent wingman.

Pettine was a very eligible bachelor, and his approach to women was not unlike his approach to football—he thrived on process. The quickening increments of courtship seemed to interest him so much that Smitty came to regard him as a romantic lighthouse whose beam was intermittently intense and alluringly withdrawn. He admired Pettine's poised remove, and so did women. Once Pettine invited a woman he'd reached "a special point with" to dinner. He took her to a fine restaurant located on a promontory across the Hudson River from Manhattan. Their table offered a dramatic panorama of the city lights. (In NFL coaching circles, this is sometimes referred to as a "drop-your-pants view.") The evening progressed as all such evenings should until Pettine realized that after a last-second decision to switch sport jackets, he had forgotten to transfer his wallet. Remaining composed, Pettine remembered that Smitty had recently been to the same restaurant and had gotten along famously with the manager. An idea blossomed. When Pettine's date visited the powder room, Pettine called Smitty, who, in turn, telephoned the manager, put Pettine's bill on his credit card, and supplied the man with some dialogue to recite. The manager then appeared at the defensive coordinator's table and announced,

"Mr. Pettine, it's an honor to have you here with us tonight. Your bill is all taken care of."

Most professional football coaches make it a policy not to become friends with the players they are coaching. Therefore, it's immensely important for the seven or so people in an offensive or a defensive coaching unit to get along well together. Football coaches see more of one another than they do of their own families, and in the most favorable circumstances, coaching staffs develop a familial feeling. As Andy Samberg described the staff of another work-obsessed endeavor, *Saturday Night Live,* "You're not just hiring talented people, you're hiring people you don't mind seeing in a dark hallway at six in the morning." With Ryan, that closeness was, as the coach said, "nonnegotiable." To Ryan, nepotism was a virtue, and so were connections; he wanted coincidences of biography, commonalities of past experiences with those he was going to be living and fighting with. The words he used to describe his relationships with Pettine and Weeks and Smith, as well as the Jets defensive-backs coach Dennis Thurman and the defensive-line coach Mark Carrier, were these: "My brothers."

Thurman, the son of an aircraft-company worker, grew up in Santa Monica in a three-bedroom house with eight siblings. It was a religious household—every Sunday, Thurman wore his clip-on reversible tie to church. (Later on, a large, bejeweled cross always hung around his neck.) Thurman was a magnificent high-school quarterback and shortstop. Major League Baseball scouts called his home promising bonuses if he'd forgo college and football and sign with them, but nobody in his family had ever gone to college, and, Thurman recalled, "My mother said, 'My son's going to college.'" That was also Thurman's choice. "I was better at baseball, but football got to everything inside of me. Whatever was inside of me could all come out."

Both UCLA and USC, the two best college programs in California, recruited him. Thurman said the UCLA people took him to fashionable restaurants in Westwood, and the coach, Dick Vermeil, promised Thurman he would start as a freshman. USC's John McKay sent Thurman off to eat in the dorms and told him he'd have the chance to prove how good he was. "I felt like USC was showing me how it really would be," he said. "I couldn't afford a fancy restaurant. I couldn't go to Beverly Hills or Hollywood, plus if I could come in as a true freshman and start at UCLA, how good could they be? I fit in more at USC. I was a blue-collar kid. There's a toughness at USC. We always felt like that was an edge for us."

In 1978, the NFL draft still had twelve rounds, and though Thurman had been an all-American safety at USC, an injured knee he suffered in a college all-star game dropped him to the eleventh round, where the Cowboys took him. At training camp, there were twenty-six rookie defensive backs and one open defensive-back job. Thurman was the last man standing because, he said, "Nobody outworked me." As for the knee injury, beginning in Pop Warner and through all his years in football, Thurman missed not a single game. A case of strep throat forced him to sit out a junior-high-school practice in 1972. That was the only rehearsal he didn't participate in. If it had been left to him, Thurman would have suited up that day, but strep was highly infectious, and, thinking of the other kids, his coach wouldn't allow it.

The Cowboys moved Thurman from safety to cornerback. Safety was, like quarterback and center, considered a thinking man's position, and Thurman remembers that many pro-football coaches were still skeptical that a black man could be intelligent enough to play it. Cornerback was then a poorly paid position—"The thankless football job," Thurman said. Thurman did something to change that. As Cowboys, he and Everson Walls together intercepted more than sixty balls while playing as a cornerback tandem, among the highest totals in NFL history. Thurman's approach was to learn "the whole defense" and also to go heavy on opposition research. Cowboys coach Tom Landry noticed this. One day Landry called Thurman into his office and told him he could be a coach. "It's a lot of time and it's mentally very draining," Landry said, "but I have a sense that you are a guy who knows how to prepare." Thurman was an excellent cornerback in part because he could handle being out at a remove, on his own, playing a position where the failures are prominent and a measure of success is remaining inconspicuous.

As a coach, "DT" was always hard on young defensive backs, because, he said, "We're looking for guys who can handle hugely stressful situations." During the 2010 Jets rookie mini-camp, Thurman spent most of the three-day session messing with a Penn State free agent named Knowledge Timmons. He referred to the cornerback exclusively as Ka-Nahledge, and during positional meetings, he might suddenly stop his lecture to frown and demand, "Ka-Nahledge, why you always looking at me like I'm crazy?" Timmons would freeze. The room would go silent. After a few beats Thurman would smile and say, "I kind of like you, man." Timmons was among the lowest-rated prospects in the room. He had been given no chance of making the Jets, and he played to expectations. But although Thurman thought Timmons was "tuurrible," as he liked to say, he kept after him throughout the camp because, like Ryan, DT was drawn to the marginal player, always hoping for the outsider. Not that he admitted that. "I keep it simple so people think I'm deep" was his way of deflecting such observations.

When Mark Carrier was ten, his father was partially paralyzed in an automobile accident. Not long afterward Carrier's parents divorced. Carrier and his sisters grew up with a single mother who supported the family by ripping asbestos out of old boats at the Long Beach Naval Shipyard. For Carrier, playing defensive football meshed with his worldview and gave him an outlet. "I preferred to stop teams from scoring to scoring," he said. "I thought it was harder. Everybody wants glory. I wanted to deny people the glory. For me, defense meant I am gonna shut guys down who want to have fun. My fun was to stop fun. I had a sense of the world as a tough place. It was tight at home."

After high school, Carrier made a verbal commitment to attend

Notre Dame. Then he received a call at his mother's house in Long Beach from a very worked-up man who identified himself as Dennis Thurman, USC class of '78. Thurman kept Carrier on the phone—"Notre *Dame!* Not Notre *Dame!* Why you want to go to Notre *Dame?*"—for hours until he'd convinced Carrier to pledge to USC. "DT wasn't as mellow back then," remembered Carrier.

During Carrier's career as an all-American safety at USC and then as an All-Pro safety in the NFL, the Hammer was known for his shrewd in-game management of a defensive backfield as well as for delivering such brutal helmet-first hits that several times he knocked himself out. Owing to such hitting, by his calculations, Carrier retired as the most-fined player in NFL history.

Ryan came to know both Thurman and Carrier in Baltimore, where the two coached the Ravens secondary. To Thurman, Organized Chaos was "a beautiful language, such a beautiful language you don't want to speak anything else." For a man of action, there is nothing more challenging than becoming a man of response, but Ryan didn't see coaching or defense as responses, and neither did DT. DT always stood with Ryan during Ravens games—Ryan trusted Thurman's calm strategic acumen under fire—and DT stayed right alongside Ryan when he was hired by the Jets.

As for Carrier, Ryan had noticed what Carrier would later describe to me as "my secret love for defensive linemen." Since his Southern California childhood, Carrier had been fascinated by traffic patterns, by the obstructed flow of free movement you saw all over LA. It was a similar curiosity that had led to Carrier's line-coaching job; he wanted to understand the intricate solutions enormous linemen found to negotiate their own crowded workspaces. That huge and powerful men could move with Bolshoi agility fascinated the relatively lithe former safety. Gazing at Ravens linemen like Haloti Ngata and Kelly Gregg, Carrier was like a small boy taking in earthmoving equipment. Ryan, in turn, was intrigued by someone who could be interested in the ways of players so different from the kind of athlete he'd been himself. Ryan had the idea that

Carrier might make a fine future defensive coordinator. Mastering another positional area of coaching would make Carrier a more appealing candidate. So in 2010, Ryan invited Carrier to be the Jets defensive line coach, promising to help him learn the techniques. Carrier was trying to do a very ambitious thing: not only coach a position that was new to him but make a two-position jump. The more usual way would have been for him to work first with linebackers, where some of the responsibilities were similar to working with defensive backs. Carrier was flattered but initially unsure if he was up for the job, but Ryan was sure, and he convinced Carrier to come to Florham Park and try it.

Carrier was considered by the other Jets coaches to be a completely decent person, and also proud, which concerned some of them after the moment at the Combine when he'd referred to Terry Bradway as Mr. Bradbury. There were times lately in meetings where Carrier struggled to express himself, striving for long seconds to find the words he wanted, sometimes never locating them. And so while Bradbury was an amusing new nickname, at a point when everybody in football had become aware of the potential long-term consequences of repeated blows to the head, "Bradbury" also made the colleagues worry about Carrier's memory—worry about all those punishing hits Carrier had delivered as a player.

Taking the other coaches in, always from slight remove, was the linebackers coach Bob Sutton. Sutton was to Ryan the voice of reason, not a brother, but a reassuring uncle who'd seen the world and who wanted the best for Ryan, just as Terry Bradway did for Mike Tannenbaum. Sutt had grown up in Ypsilanti, where his father had a business selling paint, and in 2011, at age sixty, with his spectacles, white hair, bright blue eyes, and composed, appreciative nature, Sutt looked like he belonged in a similar heartland domain—as the life-changing teacher at Harry S. Truman High. Among the Jets scouts, Sutt was known as Scoach (a portmanteau of "scout" and "coach") because his player-evaluation reports matched the standard of their own. The scouts spent most of the year on the road, but from time to time they all worked for stretches of days at the facility, and some had never seen Sutt's parking space without his blue car resting there.

Sutt had prepared his wife, Debbie, for that kind of schedule soon after they met in 1975, in a Kalamazoo bar. "I'm about to get very busy and I can only see you on Thursday nights," he told her, and naturally she thought he was dating someone else. He wasn't; it was that, at age twenty-four, he had just become the defensive coordinator at Western Michigan. As his career progressed, he coached in the North, he coached in the South, he coached offense, he coached more defense, and he became head coach at Army, where he worked for seventeen years, defeating Navy five consecutive times. In 1996, he won the Bobby Dodd Award for college-football coach of the year.

Under Eric Mangini, Sutt had been the Jets defensive coordinator. When Ryan arrived with his own defensive coordinator, Pettine, Sutt had coaching offers from other NFL teams, but Ryan's defense fascinated him, and, as a football purist, he wanted to learn it. So Sutton stayed on as the linebacker coach, quietly making what amounted to a personal study of Ryan. He thought what Ryan had in common with all the best football coaches was his comfort with who he was. He noticed that Ryan was self-confident enough to make sure others knew how much he depended upon his subordinates. Ryan almost never drew his office curtains, and during the season's crucial intervals, everyone who passed by the coach's office could see Sutt in there, offering his counsel.

Sutt considered his job with the Jets linebackers to be preparing young men for a dangerous activity. To help him with his job, he kept on his desk well-thumbed copies of various books on American military history and tactics that instructors at West Point had recommended to him. Among his favorites was a history of the Bataan death march, which he liked because "it reveals the human capacity for perseverance under the most difficult and painful circumstances."

Sutt got out of bed every morning at five and usually returned

home by midevening. During Jets vacation weeks, postseason, and in
the summer, he might leave the office a little earlier. After thirty-five
years of marriage, he still didn't know what time his wife woke up.
Winning games, Sutton said, was the emotional coefficient of the
effort that went into them: "It's hard to define the energy in the first
five minutes after you win, but it defines all of us and you're always
seeking it." Losing, by contrast, was so horrible that Sutton would
descend into a state of anomie that he would lift himself from only
when he dug into the next game. Until then: "I'd be so off on my
own." In all the places he'd lived, Sutt had never known his neigh-
bors. A particular sadness was the "events I missed in my son's and
daughter's childhoods that I would have liked to have been part of."
He was intrigued by golf but had never learned the game and knew
he never would.

In the coaching day-to-day, Pettine leaned on Sutton's experience,
and he tried to do the same with DT, who processed football in a
sophisticated way but sometimes required others to draw it out of
him. Even by NFL standards, Pettine believed, the 2011 staff was "a
special group." Pettine loved Jim O'Neil for his eagerness to learn,
the fearless way he'd speak up in meetings in front of far more
experienced coaches, willing to take the chance that they'd dismiss
his opinions. Pettine was sure both O'Neil and Smitty would someday be college or even professional coordinators themselves. He
felt responsible for their careers. One day, Pettine presented Smitty
with a video about chewing tobacco and mouth cancer, and then he
stood behind Smitty's desk chair, hands planted on Smitty's shoulders, until Smitty had taken in every disgusting frame. "Tough
love," Pettine said as the video ended, and then he walked away. In
football, some of the recompense for not spending much time with
your real family was that you watched over the growth of able
younger men and tended to their lives day by day.

Three

TAPE DON'T LIE

His feeling seemed to be almost one of spite, as though
the drawings themselves had offended him and he
wanted to revenge himself on them.

—*James Lord,* A Giacometti Portrait

After the Combine, mornings at the facility began with the coaches turning their SUVs and BMWs into parking spaces that had their nicknames painted on the asphalt. The parking lot was a time card rack for the facility. A quick scan told you who was there, or, really, who wasn't, since just about everybody worked just about always. Football people could be as competitive about parking spaces as they were about most things. Which one someone got and how long his car spent there tended to be noticed. And so each space was assigned with a purpose.

In the hundred-and-eighty-space parking lot, the four spots closest to the facility entrance belonged to, respectively, team owner Woody Johnson; Tannenbaum; Ryan; and the equipment manager, Vito Contento. A native of the Appalachian mining town of Hazard, Kentucky, Contento left his Long Island home every morning at 5:30, drove his Toyota fifty-seven miles, and arrived at Florham Park at 6:30. Contento was a short, stout man shaped roughly like a U.S. Postal Service mailbox with a snapping turtle perched on top of it. Though Contento was only in his midthirties, he had the world-weary manner of a person who had seen far too many reasonably intelligent men toss their dirty shirts into the towel bin. Players and coaches delighted in trying to get a rise out of Contento and were even happier when he, well, snapped back at them. As I watched Contento grimly shouldering his way through the facility in the afternoons, enduring just a little torment everywhere he went, I liked to think of him encountering that beautiful parking space again at day's end.

Before designing the entrance to the facility, the architect had been directed to draw up a lobby that might stimulate an uptick in aggression and focus, might encourage an off-tackle state of mind. The resulting ingress subliminally suggested the stadium tunnels that teams ran through on game days before bursting onto the field, and the lobby may have achieved its purpose. Watching the march of the coaches entering the facility in the morning, I thought of water pouring into a flume.

Here came the offense, always arriving first. The earliest to his desk was Bill Callahan, once a quarterback at Benedictine, a small Catholic college in Chicago, who coached the offensive line and designed the Jets running game. Callahan awoke daily at 4:45 a.m., taught line play like a catechism: "It personifies grinding. It's all minutiae and it all matters." Then the tight-ends mentor Mike Devlin pushed through the doors, shuffling along with his ex-lineman's joints, a self-described "sawed-off guy, whatever," whose torso seemed to call out for a bloodstained butcher's apron. (He had worn one long ago at an Iowa City food market where he and several other University of Iowa students held summer jobs, including the woman working the cash register who became Dev's wife.) Anthony Lynn—A-Lynn, as he was known—had been the best high-school halfback in Texas twenty-five years ago, and the Jets running-backs coach still walked in with newel-post posture that seemed to announce "athlete"; his face was expressionless until his large eyes met yours, when suddenly he might grin. When quarterbacks coach Matt Cavanaugh wore shorts, they revealed a Pitt tattoo alma-matering the former

Panther signal caller's left leg. Nothing about the offensive coordinator Brian Schottenheimer's mood would have told you he hated the first half of the morning. All season long, I never saw a man more capable of keeping his adversities to himself.

The offensive and defensive coaching staffs shared a pod of first-floor offices. The two staffs faced each other across an intern bullpen, much like a Wall Street firm where the partners have the private spaces. No coach had a window to the outdoors in his office; the back of each room was solid wall, and the front was glass, so that everybody looked out only on other football coaches. There was also a kitchen area that was kept stocked with snacks and drinks, many of which had the word "energy" on the label. Across a small lobby was Ryan's large office, and next to it a meeting room where the defensive coaches often gathered.

Ryan had decorated his office with sports photographs and souvenirs. Most of the other coaches placed no personal mementos on the walls of the rooms where they spent twice as much time as they spent at home. Why put up what you might soon have to take down? Learning how to lose your job was part of the job. "It's like joining the navy," said Bill Callahan. "There's elements of risk, but I know this. I wasn't gonna live in Chicago all my life, be one of those guys going to the same job and the same bar. I wanted to go out and experience the world."

The separation between offensive and defensive coaching offices reflected the fundamental football dichotomy. At the facility now, as in Buddy Ryan's time, the team's offense and defense existed as autonomous city-states, regions that operated under independent administrations and merged only at team meetings and games. Because they practiced against each other every day, they were rivalrous. "It's a different culture over there, a different world, the difference between a pirate ship and a ship of the line," Callahan said. "Those guys over there dock anywhere hooting and hollering, drinking island rum. They think we're sitting here, overthinking everything."

Because I had chosen to spend my time with the defense, after the morning procession, I rarely saw the offensive coaches. I spent most of the day in the defensive meeting room or occupying one of the black swivel chairs surrounding the white conference table in Pettine's office. The chair next to mine, the last chair along the near wall, was left empty, in case Ryan came by to participate. Since managing the defense was Pettine's job, most of the time during meetings, the only evidence of Ryan was the empty chair and a gash in the wall behind it. When Ryan did sit in, he liked to rock back in his chair until he was propped against the wall. After he left, along Pettine's floor there'd always be a few more scattered filaments of drywall dust. Pettine detested all forms of mess, especially crumbs. If you walked into his office carrying an unopened bag of chips, he'd glare at the bag, might hand you a pair of scissors so he didn't have to hear you open it. Sometimes you'd catch him looking at the scar in his wall with real pain in his eyes.

For the time being, the coaches had somewhere to go but nobody to coach when they got there. The players were on postseason vacation, and the NFL's labor problems threatened to prolong their absence. On March 11, the players would be locked out by the owners until a new collective bargaining agreement was signed. What the players would be missing were the optional off-season strength and conditioning programs at the facility, as well as football school. In the football-school sessions, the players immersed themselves in the Jets playbook, dressed in shorts and walked through plays out of various formations, and played bonding games, like Jets Pictionary, where a player had once drawn Tannenbaum, who was Jewish, as a sheriff with a Star of David on his chest. In many communities that would have been offensive, but at the facility, neither Tannenbaum nor anybody else considered the star any big deal. In football, everybody was as aware of race and ethnicity as the rest of society. Football people just tended to talk about it all, and since none of them softened the blow for anybody, many differences seemed less different. Around the facility, where everything was joked about, what got you ostracized was the inability to take it. There was simply no such thing as political correctness in a football meeting room. Ryan urged those who worked for him to grow "skin like an armadillo" and advised them that the best way to approach anything was "blunt-force trauma." With the Jets, Ryan imposed sensitivity fines on thin-skinned players and coaches.

Because just about every Jet attended the off-season workouts, Ryan used them to help the players to deepen their understanding of the Jets' relatively complex offensive and defensive systems and as a way for the team to achieve closeness. But this year, with it all in the hands of lawyers and union officials, only the coaches came to the facility, where most of their day, and hence mine, was spent watching film of past Jets games and cut-ups of college players and NFL free agents the Jets were evaluating.

Even during the season, NFL coaches watch football on film far more than they see it live on the field. Tape dominates their days, their evaluation of players the quotidian constant during the season, and after it, in retrospective review. Everything that happened at a Jets game or on the practice field was filmed by sideline and end-zone cameras, which created images of sufficient scope that the coaches could track what all twenty-two players did on each play. Once recorded, the images ended up on a hard drive in the video department, so that during subsequent meetings, Pettine, sitting at the head of the conference table with a laptop in front of him and a remote in hand, simply opened a file and then clicked his way through, showing each play. Some coaches rewound the same play dozens of times, which Pettine considered a path to an unquiet grave. His policy was no more than three times.

I watched several daily sessions of Jets film with the defensive coaches, and at first, the pictures seemed to me to present an indistinguishable convergence of humankind. I'd look at the screen and think about Thanksgiving-night shoppers massed outside an appliance store, awaiting the Black Friday sales. I'd seen only TV broadcasts of football, which tracked the ball, so here, as each play began, my eye went always to the ball, and I missed everything on the periphery, which really weren't peripheral events at all because in football, everything has to do with everything else. There wasn't any audio, so the coaches did the announcing, as it were. By listening to their commentary, I gradually found the turgid football amoeba taking on an individuating clarity.

Here, in the off-season, we looked back at various cut-ups taken from several past seasons of Jets play. Pettine would show each clip and comment, and then anybody else could jump in and offer his own observations. It was a democratic procedure for a democratic form. As Pettine liked to say, "Tape don't lie." Pettine attributed commendable actions using an authorial "by," as in "Good patience by Bart." The less praiseworthy might lead him to growl, "That's fucking porn!" There was thinking aloud: "I see what he's seeing." There were axioms. Pettine: "If you absolutely *have* to give up a sack, boys, put a tight end or a back on a legitimate pass rusher." And there were rules subject to specific conditions. After Darrelle Revis obliterated the Ravens' receiver Anquan Boldin with a block during the runback following an interception by the Jets other star cornerback, Antonio Cromartie, Mark Carrier said approvingly, "The two guys you have to block after an interception are the intended receiver and the quarterback because they're the two most pissed-off people."

It was a tough crowd. When the twice-injured Lions quarter-back Matthew Stafford appeared on the screen, he was called Fine China. After watching a Jets defensive back get badly beaten, Pettine asked Dennis Thurman, "DT, you slow down to look at accidents?" Poor officiating calls that went against the Jets on the film were so loudly and profanely lamented it was clear that, even months or years later, nobody in the room was near over them.

Between evaluating the plays on the screen, the coaches had fun adding narrative detail. Of the nose tackle Howard Green, Pettine said, "Rare to see it, but here overeating had positive results." In October, Green's weight had soared to more than 360 pounds, and

Ryan had told him to come back to the team after the Jets bye, their midseason vacation week, weighing 359, or else. "But he owns a restaurant," Pettine continued, "and when he came back, turned out he'd eaten all the profits." So Green was cut. The Packers claimed him, and Green not only won the Super Bowl against the Steelers but pressured Steelers quarterback Ben Roethlisberger into throwing an interception that was run back for a Packer touchdown.

There was so much to see in the film. Using the "veteran flinch," a heady defensive lineman like Mike DeVito might feint one way then square his feet and surge toward the gap. For a linebacker, the difficult thing to do was aim himself at an occupied spot and trust that the space would be vacated before his arrival. If the linebacker waited for the traffic to clear first, the ball carrier would be long past. Bart Scott approached his destinations at ramming speed, which occasionally meant planking people—"planking" being a term for laying out offensive players derived from the former hard-hitting Bears safety Doug Plank. The veteran outside linebacker Bryan Thomas, with his sure instinct for the tides of football motion, navigated obstacles with far less incident than Scott. Cornerback Isaiah Trufant, all 165 pounds of him, could cantilever and dip himself at high speeds with such a compact turning radius that the coaches liked to imagine things he could run beneath—cars, trains, furniture. Speaking of cornerbacks, Revis tracked receivers' routes so closely on the film that the offensive players appeared to be covering him. "Revis is unbelievable," DT said, for the 49,732nd time in the defensive-back coach's life. It was a game of time and space, a fierce contest for shards of terrain that there were numerous methods of claiming.

Each defensive coach approached the daily moviegoing with distinctive technique and style, imbuing the proceedings with his own critical personality. The three senior coaches, Pettine, DT, and Sutton, were the principal commentators. Thurman was funny, candid at some times and at other times a little mysterious. "This guy!" he was always exclaiming, before analyzing "tuurrible" coverage decisions. Sutton was milder, wry. "He's two sixty, but he's a *light* two sixty," he might observe as a linebacker landed on his back. Or, "He's an altar tackler—gets on his knees and prays."

I particularly savored Pettine's critiques. Everyone did. While most of the coaches were obligated to concentrate on the areas of their personal positional concern, as coordinator, Pettine took it all in. To him football film was a Brueghel painting, a canvas strewn with fascinating little human interactions about which he was now the narrator. With remote in hand, in his droll, opinionated way, he would point out the cheap shots; the humorous bodily contortions; the small running backs who intentionally failed to see (and thus did not have to try to block) the big blitzers—Pettine called this "making a business decision"; the blown assignments; the selfish defensive back betraying resentment that somebody else had stepped in front of him and made "his" interception. Pettine could detect unpopular members of opposing teams: their teammates never jumped up and down for and high-fived them after those players had done something well. Pettine's greatest powers of antipathy were reserved for the soft players who had a habit of arriving on the scene just after somebody else made the tackle. "Tape don't lie," Pettine would say, and there the soft player would be, skidding up to the edge of the pile, peering menacingly into the wreckage he'd once again avoided.

Pettine, the former third video guy, was a football Tarantino. Tarantino had begun his career working in a video store, where he absorbed many genres and styles; these were refracted through the funny, violent, referential films he directed. Pettine had a football-film aesthetic that was grounded in those of his two great football mentors: his hardboiled, detail-oriented father, Senior, and the folksy stream-of-consciousness Ryan, whose theory of running backs, for instance, was "once a fumbler, always a fumbler." What emerged was commentary that was distinctly Pettine, words and phrases from his grandfather's generation—"ass over teakettle"— with a mordant Howard Stern edge. The defensive coordinator had terse wit and an instinct for epigrams. Pointing to a large lineman reversing course near the scrimmage-line scrum, Pettine said the player resembled "a tractor-trailer trying to make a U-turn in an alley." Pettine was self-confident in his film comments, but what he sought to draw from the other coaches was group dialogue. Therefore he usually prefaced his remarks with "To me." The provisional concession encouraged alternative or even opposing views. And the other coaches did follow his lead, freely making observations themselves and often using Pettine's expressions as they did, bringing to mind something the Cowboys coach Tom Landry once claimed was the most crucial part of football leadership: "Make sure your coaches speak your language."

There were a lot of those Pettine expressions, and Smitty and I became amateur Pettine scholars, collecting the coordinator's Pet words and Pet phrases under the rubric Pettisms. Here follows a sampling of the lexicon:

Awareness: Usually employed as praise for a player whose movements indicated that he'd quickly and correctly read the play. Typical Pettine usage was "Good awareness by" with a player's name following the preposition. Related words were "Recognition" and "Eyes."

Be the Hammer, Not the Nail: Philosophical: Play aggressive football; don't allow the opponent to physically dictate to you.

Beat 'Em or Hurt 'Em: Should you fail to defeat your opponent on a given play, at least deliver a tiring blow. Football is a game of attrition and one way to overcome a more talented player was to exhaust him through the course of a game until you'd become, by force of will, the better player. On this, Pettine liked to quote the old Ravens defensive-back coach Donnie Henderson: "You got to get an understanding early."

Big Rascal: A lineman Pettine thought well of.

Bloated Tick: An ineffectual lineman.

Foreshadowing: Early indications from opposing team play callers of a play they were setting up to run later in the game. It could also mean something a team was putting on film for opposition coordinators to see and have in mind, to their disadvantage, "down the road" in a subsequent game.

Glass in the Shoes: A tentative player.

Going Outlaw: A player who ignored the design of the play, acted in a rash, impetuous fashion, and undermined the scheme by taking himself out of position.

Just a Guy: A mediocre player who won't last in the NFL.

Laying in the Weeds: A canny defender who had deciphered the offense's intentions, held his water without attracting attention, and thus was in position to surprise the offense by making the play.

Looks Like Tarzan, Plays Like Jane: An impressive physical specimen who was a lousy pro-football player. Exhibit A: Vernon Gholston.

Not a Lot of Lead in the Pencil: Someone who was willing to hit but wasn't heavy enough to do so with sufficient punch.

Pezzed: A player who is hit so hard his neck snaps back like the head on a Pez candy dispenser: "Eric gets Pezzed here."

Production Breeds Tolerance (or P = T): The better player you are, the more of your bullshit we will put up with.

Scalded Dog: A player moving with extreme urgency.

Special-Delivery Jones: A reference to the professional wrestler who was a career jobber—a competitor hired to lose. In football, it meant a defensive practice player who was often beaten by his man, thus giving the offense some confidence.

Suitcased: A player who had been folded up and packed away by his dominating opponent.

The Bigger They Are, the Harder They Hit: Player evaluation truism.

Truck: A violent, flattening hit.

Yum-Yum: Just a guy.

Pettine liked smart, physical play, and when he didn't get it, as he sat with remote in hand, he was fierce. We heard often from him about Bart Scott's erratic post-snap impulses and safety Brodney Pool's indifferent knowledge of assignments. Football required more study than any major sport; every week new calls were added, old ones reconfigured. In football, where everything was a matter of degree, the leeway for error was so narrow that only by driving your team to improve with relentless, harping critique could you hope for success.

One day we were watching clips from a 2010 game the Jets had played against the Bears on a snowy Chicago afternoon. Jets cornerback Antonio Cromartie kept losing his footing on the slick field. He was wearing the wrong cleats for snow, and the coaches said the reason he had those on was that he didn't like the way the snow cleats looked. "That's the difference between knowing to wear a condom and not," one of the coaches said thinly. Cromartie was a figure of complication for all the coaches. The best athlete on the team, the lanky cornerback stood six two, had legs that seemed to go up to his chin and long arms to match. For a tall man, he displayed astonishing torsion, and that was really only the beginning of his skills. Cromartie could throw a football more than eighty yards, could underhand it more than fifty, could skip a football on one bounce to a target twenty yards away (try it). He was the fastest Jet in both a four-yard race and also one across forty yards. Everybody could see the pleasure Cromartie took in movement, the pure joy athletics brought him.

Cromartie's physical ability made him a football player capable of rare feats. Even Revis said that Cro, not himself, ought to be the best cornerback in the league. In the first half of one game, while playing for the San Diego Chargers, Cro had had three interceptions against Peyton Manning, including a one-handed snare he made by reaching behind his own head with his back nearly parallel to the ground. Among his teammates, however, Cro was known as a tough talker but an indifferent tackler, which made him expendable in San Diego. The Chargers traded him to the Jets after the 2009 season.

The next year, during the filming of *Hard Knocks,* the HBO producers sat Cromartie down on a pile of equipment and asked him to name the eight children he had fathered by six women in five states. It was impossible to watch his painfully deliberate recitation without considering the possibility that Cromartie would forget somebody. He didn't, but the image of him furrowing his brow and appearing to tabulate on his fingers was indelible.

During the 2010 season, Cromartie was at times an excellent Jets cornerback. He was also prone to strange lapses in coverage, especially when he played off the line of scrimmage. It was difficult for the coaches watching film to understand his tendency to drop back several yards before the snap, which allowed receivers free release, since Cromartie's long arms gave him excellent leverage to control his opponents at the line, diverting them before they set off on their pass routes. That somebody could be so good at something and yet so resistant to doing it that he exposed himself to public failure baffled the coaches. You could find very few instances on NFL film when a defensive player avoided contact. You had to look to other sports to find an analogue. As Sutton said, "Cro's like an NBA player who hates to play defense." After watching film of Cromartie ducking a tackle, just as he'd done as a Charger, the coaches, thunderstruck, would say things like "He'd already made his one for the day" and "Cro is a visual deterrent!" In the winter of 2011, Cro was a free agent, and the coaches were ambivalent. They wanted Tannenbaum to sign him back, and at the same time, they dreaded it.

The coaches had enormous respect for anybody who could play NFL football. "Go stand ten yards behind the quarterback and see what they see," Thurman told me, reminding me how tall and wide offensive and defensive linemen were. "You can't see *anything*. And yet they see so much. It's *hard* to play quarterback in this league." The defensive coaches all employed Pettine's style of bestowing film-room credit through what sounded like authorial recognition. The distribution of those spoken bylines—"Good initial burst by Bo!"—felt to me as though the coach were saying that the player had done something beyond worthy there on the film, had created something of lasting significance. In the NFL, a player's game film is referred to as his résumé, and since what he puts on tape in practice is archived by his team, there was tangible truth to the idea that every snap mattered.

Yet within the realm of the game, there were standards for the coaches to enforce, and the one thing they could not brook was submissiveness in any form. At first, their caustic responses to what they saw on the film took me aback. But it was a matter of context. On the one hand, the players were actual people the coaches guided, taught, and came to know and care about. On the other, the players were abstractions, works perpetually in progress for the coaches to edit, improve, even transform. It was up to the coaches to reimagine the familiar thing they saw on film in a new light. This was one of the ways in which the sensibility of football coaches, who drew up plays for a living, had much in common with that of fine artists. Cézanne slashed the paintings that dissatisfied him. Giacometti gasped, swore furiously, and descended into melancholy or anguish as he painted James Lord's portrait, often screaming with rage at the canvas and then scrubbing it and beginning anew. On film, the players were the coaches' creations.

The coaches' (often harsh) way of talking *about* the players was so different from the (usually supportive and encouraging) way they talked *to* the players that there seemed to be hypocrisy. It took me a long time to understand how ingrained it was for the coaches to toggle between these binary perspectives of men on film and men in life. When I began to think of the players in dual terms, it all made sense. This wasn't, in the end, so different from the way doctors spoke to other doctors about their patients, the way teachers conversed in the faculty lounge.

It was likewise true that the coaches put everything of themselves into the games and, unlike the players, had no violent physical outlet. Listening to them through February and March, I realized that this was the time of year when all the frustrations of the season had to be purged so that everything could then recede, making way for optimism as the coaches began to look forward.

Watching film with the coaches deepened the team game for me, showing me the crucial contributions made by players who were not as celebrated as playmakers like Revis and Cromartie were. All eleven men on the field were eligible for the coaches to comment on, and more often than not, the action on which success hinged was something I had overlooked. Once you knew what was supposed to happen, it was fascinating to watch Pettine slow the film down to capture the exact moment when the best-laid plans went astray because one player was slow to a gap or displayed poor footwork or because the play caller up in the coaching booth had foreseen a run and set the defense accordingly, and the offense had chosen to pass. The Jets special-teams coach Mike Westhoff was notorious for insisting after games that the kickoff returns he'd designed "should" have been touchdowns, would have gone for six had this one player just done what he was supposed to do. This was both understandable and amusing to other coaches because that was the truth of nearly every play for offense and defense alike.

One Jets player was so rarely chastised by the coaches I came to think of him as the star of the Jets film dailies. This was the safety Jim Leonhard, or Little Jimmy Leonhard, as Ryan delighted in calling him. It was rare for any player other than a quarterback to learn more than his own positional responsibilities in the various calls. But Leonhard knew the full defensive playbook, with the result that from his free-safety position, he could see twenty-two intersecting dramas and either react or hold his water accordingly. "Nice job by Jimmy—good patience" was the kind of in-absentia praise he regularly received from the coaches.

Leonhard was only five foot eight and was slow-footed by NFL defensive-back standards. Like Eric Smith, his partner at safety, Leonhard was white, and therefore an NFL defensive minority— which was freely commented upon within the team, most frequently by Leonhard himself. Besides his quick mind, he had going for him a chippy drive he used to prove that even at his size, he belonged in the league. Defensive football required understanding the most efficient way to close the distance between two moving points. Leonhard, whose wife was an atmospheric scientist, had superior ability to track both fast-moving men and balls in relation to himself—a neat football analogue to the Coriolis effect. This made him seem faster on film than he was. Leonhard informed this intuition for angles by immersing himself in football detail to the extent that he wrote himself a 119-page PowerPoint document on the Rex Ryan defense. This was, in effect, a literate defender's lecture notes. There were comments on the intricacies of defensive-line stunting and shading; a glossary of coverage terms like "Connie," "Cathy," and "Thumbs"; and a series of reminders such as "We attack, not react," and "Make calls with less moving parts at home because of crowd noise. You can get more complicated on the road with no crowd noise." To plan his path to the quarterback during a safety blitz, Leonhard instructed himself to "set railroad tracks and never leave them." On any blitz, it was crucial to keep in mind that when your target saw you nearing, he might step forward, so "no fly-bys." Leonhard wrote it all down because, he said, "I want to be able to react without thinking." I asked him if, during his three years with the Jets, he'd seen an offense try something he hadn't encountered on a football field before. He thought about it—then: Not once, he said.

Leonhard came from the tiny northern Wisconsin town of Tony, and, at twenty-eight, he still had the face of a kid who had stretched the truth of his age by a couple of years to qualify for that paper route. In 2011, Rex Ryan's son Seth was on the squad at nearby Summit High School, and when Summit had a big game coming up, Ryan liked to joke within earshot of Leonhard about sending his boyish-looking safety over to help the team out. Only by NFL standards was Leonhard anything less than an amazing athlete. As a high-school baseball pitcher, he once struck out nineteen of twenty-one batters, and at the University of Wisconsin he won the football team's slam-dunk championship. He'd become a scholarship player only as a senior at Wisconsin; by then he was well on his way to tying the Badgers' all-time interceptions record. Yet he knew what was to follow: "At the Combine I just waved and walked on by. I know you ain't drafting me!" Still, Leonhard made the Buffalo Bills in 2005 as an undrafted free agent and he impressed Ryan enough during his one year with the Ravens that afterward the coach recruited him to go with him to New York.

In 2010, Leonhard had broken his leg in a freak practice collision right before the big New England game, which the Jets then lost, 45 to 3. That blowout score seemed incongruous, given that the Jets defeated the Patriots in their other regular-season game and would again in the playoffs. To the coaches, the explanation had much to do with the on-field confusion caused by Leonhard's abrupt absence.

In the meeting room, as they now watched Leonhard excel on the screen, the coaches talked of their anxiety about whether his mending leg would be ready by training camp. Not only did the team need him, but Leonhard would be a free agent after the season and could expect to sign a life-changing contract. The coaches wanted that for him. They liked and respected him, thought he deserved it, and maybe it was also that on a football field and on a film screen, the small, studious safety seemed to embody what coaches stood for. He was active testament to the value of what they did.

*   *   *

The bulk of the off-season film-watching subject matter was divided between the ongoing search for a college or free-agent bitch kitty and the laborious reviewing of every single Jets defensive snap from the preceding 2010 season—the effort to get better as a unit. The defensive coaches did the latter not by watching the games straight through but by grouping together all the uses of a given play, looking at them in succession, and then moving on to the next call. So the film skipped around from game to game, creating narratives completely removed from a single game's context. These sequences sometimes led to dramatic emotional fluctuations among the coaches as the calls worked or didn't work. In a call named 3-2 Gibbs 51 Rat, safety Eric Smith hit the Patriots' Wes Welker so hard that the slot receiver's helmet decal exploded off the plastic and fluttered downward like a falling leaf, and the coaches erupted too. A play later, they laughed and laughed as Revis and another cornerback, Drew Coleman, forced a fumble against the Browns and then detoured by the nearby Cleveland sideline to encourage the Browns coach, their former leader Eric Mangini, to congratulate them. Then came a clip of 3-2 Gibbs 51 Rat where the call didn't work so well, leading to a long gain for the Miami Dolphins, and everyone ricocheted into annoyance. A moment later, Jim O'Neil began commenting on something the safety had done, and he confused Eric Smith and Jim Leonhard, which led Carrier to say, "All you white boys look alike!" High spirits were restored. Then Tom Brady threw an interception, and Sutt said, "That's why he's a sixth-round draft choice!" and the movie couldn't get any better.

One purpose of the exercise was to judge how frequently a call could be made without adverse consequences. Max Blow—a call that sounded like the name of an indie rocker but merely referred to bringing as many as four nonconventional pass rushers, such as inside linebackers, and playing man coverage underneath with the support of two deep safeties—was, Pettine thought, a good situational concept that had been overexposed. Max Blow was a minor character who had been given too many scenes in the movie. In the film of games played later in the season, you could see that opponents were ready for Max Blow. "Sometimes we get too cute," Pettine told everyone. "Too much whiteboard coaching instead of just letting our guys play."

So many things surprising to the layman were common knowledge at that conference table, and these details informed the discussions. The coaches knew that until recently, you hadn't been able to trust the sprint times clocked at Penn State pro-tryout days because the school's indoor facility was set on a slope, and trial runs were made downhill. (A college's recruiting efforts were helped when its players were drafted.) They knew that fully a third of Ed Reed's career interceptions for the Ravens came from jumping the same route, the speedo, which is a standard intermediate crossing pattern. "Ed," Pettine explained, was "just out there laying in the weeds." They even knew which opposing lineman had uncommonly large testicles. (The lineman was so proud of this he'd offered proof in the locker room at the Pro Bowl.)

While the coaches watched and discussed the film, soul music played out of Pettine's computer, everybody sipped beverages, DT ate barbecue-flavor sunflower seeds, and several of the coaches spat chewing tobacco into clear plastic bottles. Mike Smith had been dipping since his father had taken him on a fishing trip at age ten. Now Smitty was trying to quit, abetted by the many wagers his colleagues were making with him that he'd fail and by more stealthy Pettine-inflicted deterrents. Smitty would walk into his office, sit down at his computer, and discover that he had a new screen saver—an oral cancer victim's grotesquely deformed mouth. But here now in the film room was Clyde Simmons, a former Eagles lineman, serving as a coaching intern with the Jets and contentedly enjoying some dip down at the end of the table. This put a cruel, contrary look in the coordinator's eye:

Pettine: "Clyde, you're dipping down there! How is it?"

Simmons: "Delicious! Flavorful! Minty!"

All eyes turned to Smitty, whose wincing mumbles fulfilled their hopes.

Another morning, Thurman looked across the meeting-room table and said to Simmons and Carrier, "Clyde, MC, I appreciate you hanging out with me last night when I was lonely."

"Hey, DT, any time," said Carrier. "And if you ever need a kid or a dog…"

A look of concern crossed DT's face and he held up a hand. "All I need is a couple of hours and a cigar, but you don't have to worry about me for any babysitting or dogsitting!"

Divorced, with two grown daughters who lived in Texas, and in his middle fifties, Thurman remained the cornerback out on his own edge. When he had downtime in his office DT played endless games of computer solitaire ("It allows me to compete") and was the one coach who followed soap operas ("I like that everybody's always stirring up some shit"). DT once told me that the only time he had ever given in to coaching peer pressure was trying coffee — which did nothing for him. Instead, he had a desk stash of the Los Angeles candy maker See's peanut brittle and butterscotch lollipops, which he'd liked since childhood and imported from California. At the end of a film review, some of the other coaches planned an early-morning workout for the next day. They invited DT to join them, but per usual, he declined. "You guys keep at it! I want nothing to do with that. For a fifty-five-year-old man, I'm looking fine! Just maintaining. And come summer, you know I'll have my four-pack back!"

After the meetings, the coaches returned to their offices and watched more film on their own. In these moments, I would sometimes look in on the offensive coaches, who had all been doing the same thing — watching film. There was an afternoon when Bill Callahan — who lived for detail, who spent his days out on the practice field yelling, "One more time," who was never satisfied—was evaluating the entire Jets career of his free-agent right tackle Wayne Hunter. Suddenly Callahan came upon a play during a 2009 game against the Tampa Bay Buccaneers that sent the normally laconic coach somewhere toward ecstasy. In the two seasons since the play had taken place, there had been many thousands of game and practice snaps, so now it was as though Callahan were seeing the call fresh. It was a running play known as 20 Mike Draw designed to give the defense the impression that the Jets were passing. Hunter sold the pass by luring the defensive end upfield with three kick steps back and a display of the outside arm that he'd normally use for pass blocking. Then, when the Tampa end took the bait and came upfield at full speed, Hunter clubbed him farther along "like an Olympic shot-putter!" noted Callahan as the Jets running back sailed cleanly by in the opposite direction. The Tampa end recognized what was up and belatedly tried to retrace his steps, whereupon Hunter finished him off, cutting him to the ground. All of it was done so well that Callahan could not think of a single complaint with the technique. That never happened. But there it was—Callahan said he had to admit it, Hunter had been perfect. He seemed stunned. Shaking his head, Callahan said, "That club and cut. It was a thing of beauty."

It was public yet private perfection. Millions of people had watched the play, but it was likely that all had missed what to Callahan was most special about it. Callahan had curatorial instincts, and he wrote down the details in a journal he kept. Now the play was preserved in some tiny form for posterity. If nowhere else, it was forever noted in Callahan's hand that on 20 Mike Draw, in a 26–3 victory over the Tampa Bay Buccaneers, Wayne Hunter had been perfect. "The footwork," said Callahan, his tone of voice still reverent, "was extraordinary."

Callahan thought of coaching as a technical collaboration, and his experience with Hunter the previous year had been unusually satisfying to him. Hunter was one of the increasing numbers of players of Polynesian descent playing in the NFL. He had grown up on the Hawaiian island of Oahu: "Rough neighborhoods, *Bounty Hunter* neighborhoods where the coconut trees don't sway" was how Hunter described them. Hunter's mother held two full-time jobs. "My father was a druggie schizophrenic couch potato who smoked weed. My mom worked and left us with him. I was running around the neighborhood as a five-, six-, seven-, eight-, nine-year-old until ten o'clock at night." The family was so poor that Hunter stuffed plastic bags inside his Converse All Stars, lining them to make them last longer. After his mother left his father, she moved with her children to Waikiki, and Hunter began playing football. He was very large and yet remarkably agile, and he did well. He was also a more than capable student. At first he enrolled at the University of California, Berkeley, but, feeling homesick, Hunter transferred to the University of Hawaii. The Seattle Seahawks drafted him in the third round of the 2003 draft, and Hunter was a reserve on the team for three years. During that time, he was charged with domestic violence. Then he and his brother were involved in a bar fight, and "Seattle let me go."

Every NFL team saw a six-five, 320-pound, fast, smart man out there in Washington and wondered the same thing: Did Hunter have the temperament to remain composed in charged athletic situations? Hunter wondered right along with them. Polynesians, Hunter said, "are aggressive people. Fun-loving, but when it comes to fighting we turn into beasts. Aggression, being hard, is cultural." Football had appealed to him initially as "a good outlet for anything stressful. The game can be rough and I've been raised rough."

After Hunter's troubles in Seattle, his future career seemed in doubt until Brendan Prophett called from the Jets pro-personnel department at the end of 2007 and delivered him to Callahan. Watching offensive skill-position players, with their distinctive forms of athleticism, you can easily see football as an expression of self. But what football revealed in Hunter was, in truth, more profound. Had he played defense, there would have been too much aggression, a complete absence of control. "Because of the way I was raised, and because I've had so many off-field troubles with anger management, I try my hardest not to put myself in positions where I'll snap," Hunter said. "I've had so many fights, it's been such a big issue. It almost ruined my chance to play." Offensive line asked players to yoke aggression with restraint, was "kind of passive-aggressive," as Hunter thought of it. Yet while Hunter was emotionally better suited for the offensive line, he sometimes felt the inherent restrictions were incompatible with his nature. "The aggression of an offensive player is harder. You're waiting for the guy to hit you. Sometimes it gets frustrating, irritating to take the blow. I'm a first-punch person."

As Hunter saw it, ultimately, offensive-line play asked him to confront the central dilemma of his life. It provided him with a managed form of aggression that, if he could stay with it, would serve as antidote to his self-defeating impulses. That tension interested Callahan. Here was a player who needed him as much as any ever had. That Hunter was among the most intelligent and thoughtful players on the Jets team only made working with him more appealing to the coach. Hunter had initially been a Jet reserve. Late in the 2010 season, when the team's right tackle Damien Woody was injured, Hunter became an emergency starter. He played the best football of his life as the team swept deep into the playoffs. Now he was a free agent, and Callahan worried that the Jets wouldn't be able to keep him. There were so many players out there, so many potential teams for them choose from, and also the confinements of the salary cap. A coach, too, had to modulate his desire with distance.

Few people around the facility knew Hunter's story, just as so many details of the troubles and hardships other players experienced as children were not known to most of their coaches and teammates. The players were so young that their pasts were close behind, but the facility and the democracy of tape were havens from all that. On tape was an entirely new autobiography. On tape you could be perfect.

* * *

Right now, in March 2011, building the team's roster was the priority. Who to draft? Who to sign? Who to let go? All over the facility, day and night, people were watching college tape, debating and ranking the players who might still be available to the Jets with their thirtieth choice in the draft. Whatever needs weren't satisfied by draft choices, the Jets would then have to fulfill with free agents. Accordingly, the organization was also ranking all NFL free agents. At various times, the upstairs scouting and personnel staff and the downstairs coaches paused their tape-watching and converged for progress reports. At one meeting, the defensive coaches and pro-personnel staff reviewed every free-agent NFL defensive player. When they got to the linebacker Antwan Barnes, who'd been with Pettine and Ryan in Baltimore, Pettine, low key until then, brightened. "Barnesy!" he said. Barnes wasn't a classic kitty, but he was close, and he would give the Jets the "suddenness" they currently lacked at the position. Not only that: "Everybody has their bitch," said Pettine, and Barnes owned the Patriots left tackle Matt Light.

"We'd blitz him as a safety!" Ryan added.

"We'd invent ways to use him!" Pettine said, getting more enthusiastic. "He's got some coverage ability too. We have too many guys who win on effort. We need some explosiveness." They were pleading their case to Tannenbaum—Pettine really wanted Barnes—and Ryan and Pettine were also warming under the influence of each other, liking Barnes more and more for the Jets, seeing him as a Jet. Rosters changed so dramatically in the course of each year that part of the off-season challenge for a coach was being able to imagine how an assortment of potential players might be integrated to complete the various roles in his scheme. That was really half of NFL coaching—thinking of one's players as characters, each with a set of skills to model in the endless sequence of narrative experiments that sixteen times a regular season became a game plan.

The conversation between Pettine and Ryan pivoted from Barnes to more general musings about the evolving position of linebacker. Instead of "big thumper types" primed to stifle the run, both coaches now preferred "a bloated safety" capable of both pass rushing and covering tight ends and running backs on pass plays. It was nice to dream of a bloat who could also thump but not wise to think you were going to find one. The ground flow would need to be stanched in some other way. So Pettine and Ryan looked at Tannenbaum, and Pettine said, "You get us a dominant big lineman, we'll make it right around him."

To that end, Pettine watched more film of Muhammad Wilkerson of Temple late one afternoon. Wilkerson was now a controversial player among the Jets evaluators. On film he'd occasionally make extraordinary plays, and then you wouldn't see anything from him for long stretches of action. And this against the less-than-imposing Mid-American Conference opponents then filling Temple's schedule. Among the Jets, just about everybody registered a "not sold" on Wilkerson because his effort from play to play was so obviously fickle. But from the start, Pettine had been a Wilkerson advocate, and that he remained. "Guys without great motors scare you," Pettine said. "But at number thirty, that's who you get." Pettine was explaining his theory of scouting—which held that you determined a player's peak level of skill, and then it was up to his coaches to get the player to play to it consistently—when into his office walked Dave Szott, a former Chiefs and later Jets guard who was now the Jets director of player development. Szott's responsibility was player well-being, and in the organization he was respected for understanding the emotional vicissitudes of football players. Looking at Wilkerson on the screen, Szott said, "I see some passion!"

"Eighty-five-inch wingspan is hard to coach," Pettine said. Ryan appeared. "My rankings are way different than upstairs'," he reported, referring to Tannenbaum and the pro-personnel department's read on the draft. Ryan liked "the Missouri guy," Aldon Smith, even though he was deficient on the bench press.

"What's the easiest thing to do in the NFL?" Pettine asked, leaving Ryan to finish—"Add strength!" Alas, there was no chance Smith was still going to be around at the thirtieth pick.

"You can't lengthen arms," Pettine said, steering the conversation back to Wilkerson. The more Pettine and Ryan discussed Wilkerson's arms, the more absorbing they found the subject, until they were calling in everybody who was nearby and lining them up against Pettine's wall so Pettine could measure wingspans. Ryan's was eighty inches, Pettine's seventy-four, and Mike Smith's only seventy-three and a half. Stepping back from talk of individuals, Ryan said it was "a size and speed league," and he was with Bill Belichick, whose drafting mantra was, in Ryan's version, "The bigger they are, the harder they hit." In other words, when in doubt, take the larger player.

"The bigger they are, the harder they hit"—a play on the boxing cliché "The bigger they are, the harder they fall"—neatly expressed the Jets defensive strategy of creating the expectation of something familiar before doing something surprising. The phrase, of course, extolled the virtues of aggression and toughness, and more subtly it also carried with it the echo of its original meaning, the old warning that if you found success, you had to stay true to what got you there or risk sudden destruction.

Four

AN INEXACT SCIENCE

Can't act. Slightly bald. Also dances.

—*Screen-test report on Fred Astaire*

At the end of March, all eyes were looking to the 2011 draft, which was to be held over three days beginning on Thursday, April 28. Here it was, early spring, the players now officially locked out, and even if that could soon be resolved, pro football was still months away from actual football, and yet every day at the facility, one heard the bright hum of volition. The preoccupation had shifted to the things tape couldn't tell you about football players. Tape might not lie, but tape withheld, tape concealed. To look behind the tape, eight Jets scouts had visited two hundred and fifty schools—some of them more than once—and evaluated twelve hundred players in five thousand reports that assessed qualities like personal character, football intelligence, athletic ability, toughness, and competitive nature, as well as position-specific traits. Quarterbacks, for instance, were rated on arm strength, passing touch, pocket poise, the quickness of their feet, decision-making skills, and courage. The scouts had talked with coaches, teammates, professors, and family. Jets coaches had fanned out across the country to attend numerous pro days at big college football programs, where they worked players out, asked them questions, and challenged them to diagram plays. Local players, including New

Jersey native Muhammad Wilkerson, had visited the Jets facility. During his workout, Wilkerson had put Jeff Weeks in physical danger; Weeks was atop a blocking sled, and Wilkerson raised it as if he were a sea creature and the sled a ship full of sailors. I'd watched as Wilkerson went through the drills, and as he responded to each command to sprint, change direction, or smash into something, it became clear that he was a large person who moved like a small person. That was football, the inversion of physical expectations.

All the NFL teams were engrossed in these careful assessments. And yet, at the end of April, many teams would still make mistakes because, said Joey Clinkscales, who directed the draft for the Jets, one quality remained elusive: "If there were a meter on heart, a way to measure how much a guy cares, we'd draft only Revises."

Up in the draft room, football's version of a political-campaign war room, where all the final decisions would eventually be made, Tannenbaum was watching film of draft candidates and thinking about how to measure another person's desire. The walls of the large rectangular meeting space were stark white and emblazoned with green slogans. One of them read "In God we trust; for everyone else we need data." Another said "Talent and character. You can't have one without the other." In front of the ten yards of vast draft board, heavy white stage-style curtains were drawn together, and where the two sections met there was a padlock.

As he watched the film, Tannenbaum said that those skill players who were willing to block indicated they likely had the "urgency" he was looking for. Another possible augury was "guys with no escape clause, guys with nothing else" going for them in life except football. Still, the GM said, you often learned the most about young men by sitting across a desk and asking them questions. In mid-April, every NFL team would have the opportunity to invite up to thirty draft-eligible players to spend a "get to know you" day at the team's facility. (Teams were allowed additional unlimited invitations for local players who grew up or went to college near where the team was based.) Tannenbaum said I should think up a series of interview questions that might reveal something about a person's drive and ambition. If my questions were good enough, I could join him and Ryan when they interviewed potential Jets rookies, and, he said, "We'll let you have at them. We don't have any pride about taking credit for these things; we just want to get them right."

It was ironic that I was suddenly the desire guy. At lunch Pettine and Smitty had been speculating about what kind of driver I was.

Smith: "You're careful. Very cautious."

Pettine: "Ten to two on the wheel."

Smith: "How fast do you go?"

Me: "Oh, very fast! At least seventy-five. Absolute minimum seventy-five. Faster in a speed trap!"

Smith: "Yeah, you're the slow guy ahead of me in the fast lane who won't switch lanes!"

When I got home that night and told my wife about it, she said she wondered if they'd read something I'd once written about learning to ride a motorcycle. "Hon," she said. "Do they know you're the author of 'The Mild One'?"

I wanted to get a feel for how the people who were said to be the most skilled at seeing into players did it, and so I visited with Terry Bradway, the former Jets GM, who was generally credited by Tannenbaum for convincing him to draft Darrelle Revis; and also with Sara Hickmann, the team's psychologist. Bradway now lived a couple of hours south, down near Atlantic City, and even though he said that his current role with the team was to appear intermittently and "stir it up," everybody at the facility looked forward to his visits. Tannenbaum referred to him as "Ray of Sunshine."

Back in 2007, the Jets had held the twenty-fifth pick in the draft. Bradway traveled to see Revis work out at the University of Pittsburgh pro day, which took place in a snowstorm. It seemed to

Bradway that Revis, out on the wet, murky field, could imagine no better place to be. Bradway never saw him drop a ball, and in the movement drills Revis displayed such a gift for the efficient use of space, Bradway called Tannenbaum and told him, "We have to trade up and get this guy." They did, with the fourteenth pick.

Bradway told me about Revis because I'd asked him to. On his own he brought up Vernon Gholston and Trezelle Jenkins, "the two dud first-round picks I've been involved with." Jenkins was an offensive lineman who'd been drafted in the first round in 1995 when Bradway was with the Chiefs and played in only nine NFL games. To keep himself from persistent regret, Bradway said he took to heart the experience of former San Francisco 49ers coach Bill Walsh, the great silver-haired guru of quarterbacks. In 2000, when Walsh returned to the team as its GM, he brought to the 49ers facility for a local workout a slow, gangly University of Michigan signal caller. The kid had grown up right over the hill in San Mateo rooting for the 49ers. When the draft came, in the third round, instead of selecting the Michigan quarterback, Walsh chose Hofstra's Giovanni Carmazzi, who failed to make the San Francisco roster. "Never played an NFL snap," said Bradway. "Now he's a sheep farmer and a yoga guy. Has no TV or phone. There's your exact science." The Patriots didn't know what they had either. They took the slow, gangly Michigan kid, Tom Brady, as an afterthought, late in the sixth round.

Sara Hickmann was a blond former college gymnast who wore muted yet stylish skirt-and-sweater ensembles to work. The players liked to critique her outfits. There were very few women around the team at the facility, and I admired Hickmann's ability to maintain a self-effacing yet distinctive presence there, a keeper of the players' and coaches' private thoughts who brightened in their company. Football players were trained to ignore pain, to never admit weakness and shun those who did, but over the years, enough of them had opened up to Hickmann that she had learned much about the inner lives of football players. After five minutes in conversation with some-one new, she could reliably guess what position he played. She said that the police arrested the Xs more often than the Os because "they're trained to defend, are more reactive and protective—more aggressive." Linebackers were the most aggressive defensive players; cornerbacks exuded conspicuous self-confidence; and safeties tended to have excellent memories and be inclusive people.

Plenty of others besides Hickmann subscribed to this idea of positional personality prototypes. The Jets scout Michael Davis said of wide receivers, "They're always on the edge." Pettine believed that cornerbacks were "the wide receivers of the defense," while safeties typically had "football smarts." Bradway noticed that defen-sive players had the messier lockers. But back in his (orderly) office, DT said he didn't know about all that. "I want playmakers!" he roared. "Give me Ed Reed! Troy Polamalu! You think they're wor-ried about protecting anybody?" All of them were right. Appraising football players was a fundamentally inexact science.

Tannenbaum, more than most people, valued punctuality, and when I arrived late to a pre-draft pro-personnel meeting in his office, I was fined just as anybody else would have been. Tannen-baum gave me a choice: I could pay the standard one hundred dol-lars or roll the dice and cover the cost of the day's draft-room four o'clock coffee-and-treats order from Starbucks. I rolled. Everyone vowed to order half the menu. Then Joey Clinkscales turned his attention to the purple-bandanna headband I'd worn while work-ing out and still had on. He said there were "headband concerns." I was getting used to being evaluated by these expert evaluators. With its need to make many people conform to a unified purpose, football did not prize difference. I was different. In this SUV world, my car was a Mini Cooper. At lunchtime, I was the only one eating beet salads from the cafeteria salad bar. When coaches spoke of a pass route, they pronounced the word "rout," and I kept pronouncing it "root." Too often, when someone extended his hand to greet me with a fist bump, I thought he meant to shake and...ugh. "It's because you are used to the world of business!" said Smitty, trying to help. All my life I had gone by Nicky, but here above my locker the nameplate said "Nick Dawidoff." This was because Nick hit harder than Nicky.

The facility mores were conservative. In the locker room one day I'd overheard someone talking about the television show *The Wire*, specifically about Omar, the badass stick-up man who carries a huge shotgun and preys on drug dealers. "Omar," the person said. "He killed me. He was my favorite until I found out. I couldn't believe it. It ruined it for me." The character of Omar is gay, which was not yet an acceptable thing to be in football. There had never been an openly gay NFL player or coach. Over time, I was sure, this would change, because football always ends up being receptive to anybody who is good enough to help a team. When that acceptance happens, it would be easy to project how a gay player's heterosexual teammates would be: they would make up the wedding party at his marriage and speak out against prejudice. There were a couple of players on other NFL teams who were already supporting gay rights. For the time being, though, the taboo in the game was still such that if teams had an indication a player was "light in the loafers," they were reluctant to draft him because of what the effect might be on the other players in the locker room.

Americans were increasingly accepting of gay rights. Why were gay men still so ostracized here? Like the military, the game required virile men to achieve a level of closeness that felt very intimate. The preoccupation with muscle, strength, and manly deeds amid all that bonding could seem homoerotic, and the homophobia appeared to me to have to do with the worry that the intimacy could go too far and the parallel concern that the presence of an openly gay player might "queer the group," creating distance and unease, infecting the team with a kind of weakness. One day when I took a sauna with the coaches, I was surprised to find everyone dressed in shirts and either shorts or sweats. I asked if they knew that most people around the world wore either no clothing at all into a sauna or else just a towel, and they were horrified. The buffer of clothing was, in its way, really no different from the usual football greeting between two men who hadn't seen each other in a while: the two led with a handshake, and the hands remained clasped between the greeters as they came in for a hug. When the defensive coaches disliked something they saw on the film, they might dismiss it as "gay porn." Truly objectionable play was "gay-animal porn."

During the course of the year, these attitudes would create situations of a like I hadn't encountered since high school. Once, before a defensive meeting, I walked into a bathroom where there were four urinals along the wall. The first and the third were in use, by players. Without really thinking about it, I walked to the closer urinal, the one between them, rather than the one down on the far end. Immediately I could feel I'd done the wrong thing. In such an assertive culture, it was hard not to think about your own assertiveness. This is football, I thought. I have to not back down. One of the two players was the linebacker Aaron Maybin. "Dude," he asked me after we'd washed our hands, "haven't you heard of the one-space rule?"

"Dude," I replied. "I'm a married man with kids and I'm very comfortable with myself and other people. You should learn from my example!" Maybin had studied art and was among the most open-minded of the players. He was vibrant, extroverted, endearing, and, I noticed, currently wearing a hot pink T-shirt. "And dude," I went on, "what's going on with that shirt?"

"Read it! Read it!" he told me, jubilant. The front of the shirt said "Don't Laugh. It's Your Girlfriend's Shirt!"

We strolled into the meeting room, where the eye of Pettine found the chemise of linebacker. "Maybin!" he said. "Somebody give you a Forever Twenty-One gift card?"

Headband concerns addressed, the coaches in Tannenbaum's

office now turned the discussion to how much could be expected from veteran receiver Jerricho Cotchery going forward. J-Co's speed and reception totals had been flagging; he had back problems and dropped-pass problems. He was, however, among the most popular players in the Jets locker room, and his good standing had only improved during last season's Cleveland game when Cotchery tore his groin muscle in midplay, stayed upright, got free by hopping along on one foot, and then hurled his body into a fully outstretched, groin-muscle-shearing first-down catch before crumpling to the ground in agony. Clinkscales, who'd played wideout at Tennessee and then briefly for the Steelers and Bucs, said that the first thing that an older receiver lost was not foot speed but hand-eye coordination. As an example he cited Jerry Rice, the former 49er who holds the NFL record for receptions. Then, considering the unwelcome but perhaps prudent possibility of drafting a J-Co replacement, they all projected how late in the draft the various college receivers they liked would remain available for the taking. Every team ranked players differently, and the trick of winning the draft was selecting players in a later round than you had slotted for them. The men ran through Jerrel Jernigan of Troy University and Jeremy Kerley of Texas Christian, predicting how long they'd last. When they got to Denarius Moore of Tennessee, Clinkscales was effusive about his fellow Volunteer—which raised alumni concerns. Tannenbaum led the charge and then forgave Clinkscales by saying it was a good thing for Tannenbaum there were so few Jewish players in big-time college football. Jets scouts emphasized that one of the things every talent evaluator had to watch for was the propensity to see himself in players, to overvalue in others what he valued in himself.

Visiting days began on April 11, two and a half weeks before the draft, and the college players arrived at the facility for a full day of interviews with the coaches, Hickmann, the strength and conditioning staff, the trainers, Tannenbaum and Ryan, and their "special assistant," me. Tannenbaum and Ryan had invited me to help them assess the characters of the visiting players. Everyone looked forward to finally meeting these players, whose biographies they all had been poring over day after day. More than other sports, pro football was an office job, so it followed that there were these job interviews. Tannenbaum's questions would be disarming, designed to relax the players enough to overcome the buffed gloss of the agent prep sessions that the Jets assumed every player had been through. The GM planned to ask about hidden talents, pet peeves, what the player would choose if he could rescue only one thing from his burning house, something kind he'd recently done for someone else, and the player's most embarrassing moment in high school. I had the idea that before Tannenbaum got married, he was very good at first dates.

Next, Ryan would show the players clips of the Jets in action, including Cotchery's heroic catch against the Browns, and ask the players for their reactions. Ryan would always conclude by telling the player, "What I want from you is everything you got." (They all promised him that, of course, but Ryan swore that by looking into players' eyes, he could sense their souls.) Last would come my questions, mostly about predicaments they'd found difficult to overcome in life or had failed to overcome. I also planned to ask them what they'd do if the Jets followed Google's company policy of allowing employees to use 20 percent of their work time in any way they chose. When the players left, the three of us would grade them with a plus, minus, or neutral. What Tannenbaum and Ryan most hoped for was to find a kid who had qualities that would inspire others—"specialness," as Pettine called it.

The players arrived, and as they made their appointed rounds of the facility, you could see them from a distance, steeples and spires in a low-roofed landscape. Some of the candidates wore designer neckties; a few were dressed in ways that suggested they had never in life been able to afford a discount-store suit. One supremely nonchalant pass rusher wore shorts, which the defensive coaches considered a promising sartorial choice. Most of the players who sat down in the white office chair opposite Ryan seemed disarmingly frank, particularly a couple of self-disparaging linemen. Brandon Fusco, a burly center from Slippery Rock University, talked about his bad luck with women—"I'm not the best-looking guy." Ray Dominguez, a University of Arkansas tackle, evaluated his own draft standing and admitted, "I'm not a hot commodity." When Dominguez described the crowded Georgia household he'd grown up in, Tannenbaum said, "You know what Sanchez told us: You draft a bean, you get the whole burrito!" So Dominguez talked about being a Hispanic kid in the rural Deep South, and how "rough it was to walk down the street sometimes." The insults shouted at him by strangers during his small-town childhood were still, he said, what motivated him.

Who wouldn't root for these kids? I'd have been a terrible GM; I fell for player after player. The Temple safety Jaiquawn Jarrett wore a sharp suit and tie. He said he'd like to have lunch with Jack Tatum, the old Raider safety known as the Assassin, a disclosure that led Ryan to gleefully describe several Tatum secondary brutalities. Jarrett, it turned out, didn't know jack about Tatum, but after he described his own football mind-set as "I'm gonna bury you every time" he earned double pluses all around.

Muhammad Wilkerson was dressed to kill, if the victim was to be an ex–line coach. He wore jeans and an untucked white dress shirt consisting of so much cloth that had you sheeted it up to a spinnaker, it would have luffed just fine. Sure enough, Ryan took one look and announced enthusiastically, "Here's a real one!" Tannenbaum's questions led Wilkerson to say that he'd lived for a while in a homeless shelter and that he had a father who'd been in and out of jail and a mother who was "hard on me," so he would travel a different road. Wilkerson hoped some day to counsel inner-city kids and had recently bought a younger sister some shoes. He raised the heart of the matter himself: "I didn't have a motor on

every play," he admitted, and then declared that his football attitude needed improvement. Ryan, on the player's side by instinct,
told him that Haloti Ngata had said the same thing in his long-ago
Ravens interview. How many years had Ngata been an All-Pro?
Three years running! When Wilkerson revealed that his secret talent was for bowling and that he'd once rolled a 206, the coach was
nearly out of his chair. Full abdication of seat was achieved when
Wilkerson was asked what he most liked to do and he answered,
"Bang into trees!"

The NFL draft had become such an exercise in scrutiny that in the
age of search engines, few crimes were secret. Arrests were not as
common among football players as was their incidence among the
general public, but both the intimate culture of the game and the
fact that NFL players were public figures meant that teams were
tenacious in their character reviews. The peccadilloes of the best
college players could be discovered, and given the salaries paid to
rookies, a team that did not perform its due diligence flew close to
the sun. The Jets scouts were everything casually dressed private
detectives ought to be. They understood what it took to play professional football, and they were aware that in aggressive young men,
impulses were often stronger than scruples.

If you'd helped your family clear out of the Lower Ninth Ward
of New Orleans during Hurricane Katrina and driven them to sanc-
tuary in Texas, the scouts knew it. If you'd failed to pay a speeding
ticket, dated underage girls, suffered from sleep apnea, shoplifted a
DVD, caused a car accident while driving to your DUI hearing at
court, they knew it. If your "extremely hot" girlfriend broke up with
you, they knew why. If your parents were getting divorced, they knew
it; if you were an honors engineering student at a top university but
couldn't remember football plays, they knew that too. If you had a
"sister" seventeen weeks younger than you were and you believed the
two of you had the same mother, because that's what you'd been

told all your life, they knew this. They knew that a top college pass rusher whom the Jets were thinking about drafting had, in anticipation of his big NFL signing bonus, already gone out and bought both a Bentley and a Range Rover. They had seen enough scofflaws, hooligans, tomcats, rabble-rousers, libertines, and second-story men to recognize one at a hundred yards. Taking part in a frat-house brawl might be a virtue or a flaw in a football player, but if you were involved because you'd jumped in to help an outnumbered teammate or because you had drunk too many Long Island iced teas and been the instigating fool, they knew.

Tannenbaum was planning for the arrival at the facility of Colorado cornerback Jimmy Smith, a wonderful college player who'd grown up in gangland California and had had several brushes with the law, including drug infractions. When Darrelle Revis was a college senior, the van driver who shuttled the players to and from the airport said that Revis was easily the most well-mannered player he'd ever met on the job, and Tannenbaum never forgot it. Now he hoped to learn how Smith behaved in those moments during his visit when he thought nobody important was watching.

To more formally assess the backgrounds of high-risk players, the team relied on its security director, a former FBI major-crimes agent named Steve Yarnell who was beginning his fourteenth year with the Jets. With his hooded eyes, pomaded hair, and taciturn gaze, Yarnell was the sort of man who made other people feel he already knew everything about them. He'd been a relentless defensive end for Bill Parcells at Army and liked football players, even as he saw them clear. "The faster they are, the more propensity they have to get into trouble," he once told me. "If an offensive lineman gets into trouble, he's lumbering into trouble. Wide receivers and DBs find it at full speed." Tannenbaum considered Yarnell to be an unusually interesting person. Yarnell was, the GM said, an excellent dancer, and I believed it, even after Yarnell shook his head and denied all. Outside his office, Yarnell left a spread of candy bars. Anybody could help himself, but Yarnell especially enjoyed it when the players he'd once vouched for would stop by and renew acquaintances over a Snickers.

And yet how difficult for anyone, even Yarnell, to know anybody; how faint were the impressions of the players' former selves. And what a strange job market, where aggression was such a virtue. There were not many jobs out there that required potential employers to weigh how much risk they could live with when considering highly coveted candidates, that called for the hirer to imagine how a shattered childhood could be transformed into a flourishing future. Georgia linebacker Justin Houston's home did burn down; he helped family members to escape. During his childhood in the Chicago projects, Illinois linebacker Martez Wilson said he'd made it through winters in an unheated apartment by warming himself with cup after cup of cocoa. In football, nobody held who your father was—or wasn't—against you, and it could well be an advantage to have come up from nothing.

If football's draft was in no way a blackguards' ball, one of its unique qualities was that it inverted so many conventional ideas of what constituted a promising young man. True, those players, like Purdue pass rusher Ryan Kerrigan, who had grown up in two-parent households always mentioned this in their interviews. Tom Brady, Peyton and Eli Manning, and many other offensive stars had, after all, come from "intact" families. That Texas linebacker Sam Acho's father was wealthy, however, made Tannenbaum, Ryan, and, by now, me wary, as did Acho's enthusiasm for Shakespeare and Chaucer. As it happened, Acho won the room with the most sophisticated understanding of defensive football yet displayed in these conversations. "How do you bet against *him*?" asked Ryan later.

Jets scout Jay Mandolesi told me once that the interviews mattered so much because so often player incidents came without context. He mentioned Jets safety Emmanuel Cook, who'd been arrested for possession of a concealed weapon while he was a student at the University of South Carolina. At the South Carolina pro day, Mandolesi asked Cook about it. Cook told him, "Look, where

I'm from, I didn't have a choice. Sometimes you're at a party and a guy wants to show you his gun and you have to look at it." During the brief moment Cook was holding another guy's weapon, the police walked in.

To many out there across America assessing the upcoming draft, Kenrick Ellis was the picture of the thug-life football player. Around the facility, his story was told this way: Ellis grew up in Jamaica and played football at the University of South Carolina, where he smoked enough ganja to fail team drug tests and was invited to matriculate elsewhere. At Hampton University, a friend harassed Ellis's girlfriend. Ellis wished to discuss the situation. The friend brought along his baseball bat. Ellis told him he didn't want to fight, but if it had to be that way, better to take it into the alley. In the alley, Ellis broke the friend's jaw. Felony-assault charges were now pending. All this, but Michael Davis swore by him, and so here Ellis was in Tannenbaum's office, the sort of talented player a team with low draft choices might hope would fall to them because of his "issues."

No players denied any points of biography that Tannenbaum or Ryan asked them about. It was pretty much all out there, after all, and so in interviews, they owned their pasts and used the opportunity to explain. Kenrick Ellis said that when his mother suffered a heart attack, he'd changed his ways. Ellis looked at Tannenbaum. He seemed near tears: "You have to understand, I'm the only member of my family ever to smoke, ever to get in trouble." He said that when his mother had told him, "I guess I'm gonna die and not see you do anything with your life," he was overcome with remorse. Again he looked ready to weep. Once a line coach, ever a line coach: Ryan had easy rapport with all the defensive linemen. He consoled Ellis now by describing the fistfight he had had in Maryland as well as all the coaching opportunities he'd missed out on "because of that." Tannenbaum then looked Ellis right in the eye. "Kenrick, I'm telling you, it's no joke here." Ellis could only nod. After Ellis left, Ryan said, "Very few people on the planet that size."

In walked Edmond "Clyde" Gates, a speedy receiver from Abilene Christian who was raised by his mother and grandfather because his father was in prison for murder during most of his childhood. Gates said his father had recently been released and that the two were "trying to get to know each other." When Tannenbaum asked him if he could remove one possession from a burning house what it would be, Gates said, "I don't have anything that important to me."

My own favorite possession happened to be that Mini Cooper, the first car I had ever owned. The day before, someone had parked up against my bumper and left a deep scrape. When I mentioned this to DT, who prized his sporty BMW roadster, he told me, "You know what, you got to stop obsessing about that car. The stars have aligned and your bumper got scratched. You know what they tell you in Pop Warner? Move on! You're a player now. You have a battle scar. Move on and enjoy that car." Everybody could use a coach like DT.

Joey Clinkscales's man Denarius Moore had arrived, a laid-back country boy from a two-stoplight Texas town, and each question sank him lower in his seat, so by the time I, seated on a couch to his left, asked Moore a question, he turned to face me and rested his chin on the chair's armrest, peering at me like a cat.

UCLA's potential bitch kitty Akeem Ayers wore monogrammed cuffs and said he aspired to go to law school some day. Tannenbaum told him that he himself had been. "How'd you like it?" inquired Ayers. "Lot of reading. Stick with pass rushing," Tannenbaum advised.

Most kids who grew up in Texas want to play college football in Texas. Josh Thomas, a University of Buffalo cornerback, said he went so far afield from his Lone Star home because his mother remarried, and once the stepfather showed up, "things got hectic." He'd found rescue when his grandmother took him in. If his home caught fire, Thomas said, he'd carry to safety the pen his grand-mother used to pay his bills. And if Thomas made the NFL, with his own first check, he planned to fill her house with groceries. Tan-nenbaum decided Thomas was "the most sympathetic figure ever."

Not to DT. Downstairs he and O'Neil were discussing Thomas's struggles with their technical football questions. I told them about his grandmother's pen. DT was appalled: "You want to win football games, you need some gangstas!" DT could hardly wait to meet Jimmy Smith and had graded that interview in advance: "Double plus!"

"How are you?" Tannenbaum asked Louisville running back Bilal Powell.

"I'm good, how are you?" Powell replied in the softest voice we'd yet heard. Powell wore inexpensive jeans and a thin gray polo shirt over a T-shirt.

"I'm pretty damn average," said Tannenbaum from behind his desk. "I eat too much; I don't exercise nearly as much as I need to." Powell managed a smile. He described being raised by his hard-working mother in a rough part of Lakeland, Florida. His father was a drug addict, and Powell eventually joined a gang, the Brick Boyz. He was stabbed and nearly shot before he found a new kind of fellowship in Christianity and football. Powell said he liked the game "because within the rules you can be a good person and hit somebody." The implicit irony, and maybe not so ironic, was that the violence of the sport had saved Powell from a life of violence. His worst experience in football involved a coach who "tried to make me give up my faith." Ryan often celebrated football for bringing together every kind of person. He wanted to know if Pow-ell minded playing with guys who have no faith. Powell said, "Every-body's okay with me."

After Powell left, Ryan and Tannenbaum were very moved. "He reminds me of Curtis Martin," Tannenbaum said, referring to his all-time favorite Jet. The Hall of Fame running back, as a young boy, had watched his drug-addicted father punch his mother, scald her, and burn her hair with a lighter. Martin himself soon found trouble. When Martin was a teenager, a loaded gun was held to his head and the trigger pulled repeatedly. The gun did not fire. "Curtis woke up one day, his grandmother was stabbed, and it later changed his life," Tannenbaum said. "This kid [Powell], in ninth grade he gets stabbed, he changes. That's also a testament to coaching." They agreed that Powell would do very well working with A-Lynn, the Jets running-backs coach.

Tannenbaum and Ryan were two prosperous men talking to young people who came from nothing. Ryan's mother had a PhD. His father owned a Kentucky horse farm. Tannenbaum had grown up in a well-to-do Boston suburb. Neither had been fed with a silver spoon, but they'd always been provided for. And how many football players had they met? Yet over and over, they empathized with people most of whom they very likely would never meet again. They could draft only six of them.

When Jimmy Smith finally appeared, he was, unbeknownst to him, a conquering hero. Yarnell and the scouts had signed off. So had the van driver. Tannenbaum, Ryan, and the coaches couldn't wait to lay eyes on him, and Smith didn't disappoint. He wore loafers, conservative gray trousers, and a diamond in one ear, an outfit that seemed to communicate many things to many constituencies. His conversation had similar complexity. In one moment, he told of how he "got popped" for having smoked marijuana. In the next, he was extolling the virtues of Perry Mason. His pet peeve: "I don't hate to be told what to do, but sometimes I hate to be told what to do." His brother had been in a gang, but Smith hadn't, because "I'm not into getting jumped or jumping people or getting shot or stabbed. I'm scared." What did a kid from the California hood think of Boulder, Colorado? Smith said he liked the hiking.

All this work and preparation, but so often the draft confounded it. You could study a person until you were sure you knew him, and then he turned out to be a different person on a football field. Everybody, said Pettine, "got fooled" evaluating players, first and foremost because "they're still kids. So much depends upon putting a kid in the right system for him to succeed."

The Jets' 2010 first-round draft choice was cornerback Kyle Wilson. Wilson came from a close, well-educated Piscataway, New Jersey, family. His father was a mental-health clinician at a university hospital; his mother taught high-school math. Wilson had badly wanted to play for New Jersey's state university, but Rutgers hesitated, and so he agreed to attend Boise State. Then Rutgers offered him the scholarship. Wilson turned it down, saying he'd given his word to Boise. To the Jets, this had been a sign that Wilson had integrity, could handle himself in life and so likewise would be able to handle it when his job struck back at him.

The job of a cornerback meant a crisis was always in the offing. Everyone who played the position gave up long plays. Good corners had short memories. As a collegian, Wilson was far better than good. He had pliant hips that allowed him to change direction at a sprint, minimizing the wasted motion that allows receivers to gain separation. At top speed he could look back for the ball, and looking back is how interceptions happen and interference penalties don't. An aggressive, trash-talking defender on the field, off it Wilson was humble and well-spoken. The Jets were thrilled when he was available to them with the twenty-ninth pick of the first round.

A few weeks later, at the end of Wilson's (impressive) rookie mini-camp with the Jets, his mother arrived at the facility to pick him up and take him back to Piscataway. Most of the other Jets rookies were boarding a bus for the airport, and right there, in front of everyone, Wilson greeted his mother with a big kiss. Kissing your mom in front of forty football players you've just met is only slightly harder than a fourteen-year-old boy coming in for one in front of forty fellow fourteen-year-olds. The Jets who heard about the kiss were even more certain that the one thing Wilson would never lose was his poise on a football field.

But he did. With Cromartie and Revis in place as the lead cover men, the Jets asked Wilson to protect the slot, where he'd never played before. And when opposing quarterbacks began to have their way with him, he became so demoralized that he lost his ability to react without thinking. Mike Westhoff, the special-teams coach, who had been in the NFL for nearly thirty years, said, "Saturday's a great game too, but Sunday's a man's game and I don't think Kyle Wilson had a man's body yet." Soon Wilson was having difficulty looking back for the ball, flailing in space. There was a smell of burning. Eventually the Jets replaced him with Drew Coleman. Now the hope was that the lockout would end quickly enough to give Wilson sufficient time to remember how to forget.

On Friday, April 15, thirteen days before the draft, with the scheduled interviews concluded, the defensive coaching staff came upstairs to the draft room. By now the sanding had been done, the coats of primer and stain had been layered on, brushed, and sealed, and the time had come to apply the finishing varnish on the 2011 draft board—to pass final review on every defensive player the Jets would consider drafting. Offensive players had received their final review already. Because this process was so time-consuming and labor intensive, once the offensive review was done, the scouts and draft specialists had taken a few days outside the bunker to clear their heads. Now they were back inside to assess the defense. Special teams, as always, would have to wait until last.

Nineteen men in jeans and one in sweats (Ryan) sat around a long, wide, white table that filled most of the space in the draft room. The Jets' eight full-time scouts were all in place, waiting to describe their year's adventures. The defensive coaches and front-office draft people, including Joey Clinkscales, Terry Bradway, and Scott Cohen, were on hand. The floor rug was gray, the ceiling low, and there were no windows, no distractions. A video screen would drop at the push of a button so that a Combine photograph of each player and his draft card could be displayed as he was discussed. There were thick binders everywhere. There was a situation-room feel. A bucket of bubble gum was available to those in need.

The jovial Clinkscales, wearing designer eyeglasses and a cashmere sweater (his mother was a beautician—chic ran in the family), sat at the head of the table and led the meetings. Tannenbaum and Ryan were to his right. Off on the other side of the room, watching the team's back, was Bradway. Bradway had with him two ring binders; two notebooks; a laptop; a stack of internal reports, including the player evaluations made by Ryan, Pettine, and the positional coaches on the basis of all those winter weeks of film study; and memos from outside psychological experts with comments on the order of "Low motivation because believes has no control over events in his life. Raised in extreme poverty. No belief system." Among the coaches, Sutton had the most documentation with him. It spoke well of both Ryan and Tannenbaum, many scouts said, that such fine football men as Bradway and Sutton should accept lower positions with the Jets rather than going to work somewhere else.

The thick white curtain along the front wall was unpadlocked, revealing the draft board itself, a periodic table of college football players consisting of colored magnetized cards ranking the 190 players the Jets considered draft-worthy. Top players (rated 6.4 and above) got purple cards, then came blue (6.25), red (6.0), and green (5.7). There was also a small cluster of black-dotted cards indicating players who, for reasons of health or temperament, the Jets would not consider. Next to one such player's card was a photograph of him brandishing a gun. What a world, I thought, where gangstas are desirable, but a player with a gun is taking the tough-guy thing way too far.

The cards were arranged by positional groups and ranked. As the draft neared, the rankings would fluctuate like political tracking polls. On one end wall was the side board, which displayed the cards of the second-tier players and their free-agent grades. The Jets would attempt to sign them after the draft if no other team took them; the Jets themselves had never drafted a player from their side board. On the long back wall were 224 empty slots, one for each pick in the draft's seven rounds. As players were chosen during the draft, their cards would move across the table from the Jets board and into their selection slots on the back wall.

One way that Tannenbaum signaled his faith in the organization was by his willingness to trade away clumps of lower draft choices for a higher draft choice that would enable the Jets to select a player they'd targeted but feared they might lose to another team drafting before them. The Patriots under Belichick tended to go the other way, trading down to amass extra choices, apparently reasoning that the more tickets they bought in a raffle, the likelier they were to win the prize. Last year the Jets had kept only four choices, drafting Kyle Wilson and three offensive players. This year a trade had left the Jets with no second-round pick. Pettine and the defense were feeling entitled to most of the remaining six. "Linemen," Clinkscales said. "Marcell Dareus, Alabama," and the review began.

Close to an hour of discussion was devoted to every last player, even the most acclaimed stars of the year, like Cam Newton, cornerback Patrick Peterson, receiver A. J. Green, and pass rushers Von Miller and Aldon Smith, none of whom the Jets had bothered to bring in for interviews because all would be long gone before the thirtieth choice came around on draft night. "Is there any hope?" Tannenbaum asked when they got to players like Miller and Robert Quinn of North Carolina, sounding like a Republican presidential candidate talking about the chances of winning Massachusetts. No, he was told, none at all. With Peterson, again the same question, and again the same answer. Ryan's solution to the painful image of another team's uniform on J. J. Watt, the offense-wrecking Wisconsin lineman, was to become his champion, offering the bet of a

Frappuccino to anybody who didn't think that Watt would go in the top ten. "Whoever you get at thirty, there's something wrong," said Tannenbaum, summarizing the predicament. "That's why they're still there at thirty."

On the one hand, Wilkerson had a trick shoulder and that sometimes-sputtering engine. On the other hand, he'd left home for a military academy. Would he play with intensity? Here was a quandary Wilkerson himself had said he couldn't resolve.

Pettine was steadfast. The Jets, he said, needed linemen and linebackers with movement skills because more rules regulating contact were surely in the offing, and they'd only make a fast sport faster: "A boundary-to-boundary video game is what's coming," Pettine said. Ryan agreed. His father, Buddy, once told him never to pass up the chance to draft an "unusual defensive lineman." So now, whenever concerns were voiced concerning Wilkerson, the head coach told all the others again about the young Haloti Ngata.

The room was rife with analogy. Everybody was similar to somebody else, which meant that when the coaches got to the University of Miami's Allen Bailey, his chiseled physique up on the video screen elicited the dread comparison. "Somebody trying to kill him!" a voice from the far end of the table murmured. "Somebody just did!" exclaimed Clinkscales. Tannenbaum shook his head. "It's becoming a verb, to Vernon someone," he said.

During the Kenrick Ellis discussion, Tannenbaum turned to Michael Davis and put the scout on the spot: "You legitimately, sincerely trust this guy?"

"I do," said Davis who before becoming a scout had coached for nine years at Virginia State, a historically black university, like Hampton. Davis had visited Hampton to see Ellis four times. "When his mother said, 'You'll never amount to nothing,' it had a big effect on him." Ellis mentioned his mother so often that Davis had asked what she was like. The scout said he had heard she was a difficult person. Ellis told him, "Mr. Mike, fuck that! My mama's a church lady!"

The draft was a vacillating game of chance featuring sufficient clues and variables to create the illusion that certitude was possible. It wasn't. The Jets didn't know whom they'd have a chance to draft or what the man they did draft would turn out to be like. In a world that was out of the Jets' control, there was comfort only in spending these twelve-to-thirteen-hour draft-room days reviewing more data, dedicating themselves to the process.

There were many moments of indecision about players, and to overcome them, the men fell back on that single reassuring phrase — "Tape don't lie!" — lowered the video screen, and looked at the cut-ups again. But what was on film did not always bring clarity. After watching Wilkerson yet again, Clinkscales said, "The reason we have a debate is half the time he's jogging around." In the end, all they could do was make clearer the potential risks and rewards. A useful way to do so was by comparing players head-to-head. One of these virtual Oklahoma drills featured Clemson's Da'Quan Bowers against Robert Quinn. Bowers, perhaps the most gifted player in the draft, had suffered the dreaded microfractures in his knee, a potentially career-ending injury. Quinn was, after J. J. Watt, Ryan's favorite defender, but he had a brain tumor. Nobody knew what to say; they were all men in need of good horses choosing their mounts from Thomas Hobson's stable. "Quinn!" said Ryan, only because everyone relied on him to go first. "A brain tumor's not something you just tape up," said Tannenbaum, and the impossibility of the choice resonated anew.

Tannenbaum thought of the Jets as an enlightened company where the input of everyone throughout the hierarchy was crucial. Here, he was seeking guidance through dissent that, he hoped, would lead to consensus. Often consensus would not be possible, but the eventual draft choices, Tannenbaum thought, should follow logically from transparent discussions. Somebody had to choose, and Tannenbaum was the somebody, but what the GM wanted was institutional momentum. His lone concession to spontaneity was to "give" one low draft pick a year to Ryan. Last year the coach had selected Kentucky fullback John Conner, who blocked like a crate of bourbon and had receiving hands to match. During the subsequent rookie camp, Ryan would say, "Conner's my fullback until he drops a couple. Then he's Tannenbaum's!"

The scouts respected Ryan's written reports and the way he helped them understand what kind of players would succeed in his system even as he expressed a willingness to find a role for any kind of legitimate talent. Ryan's motto, Play like a Jet, meant tenacious physical play, but even then he loved Cromartie, wouldn't say a word against his tackling. In the draft room, the scouts appreciated that the head coach's opinions were delivered clean and crisp as the snow-white thermal shirts he often wore: "This guy couldn't play dead in a B Western" was a typical Ryan analysis. (Clinkscales, getting into the spirit, said of one defender, "He gets beat like Sunday eggs.") But during the long, tense days inside close walls with Ryan, the former draft-obsessed college student who now got to play for real, there was always a little time for joy. In that regard, they all relied on Ryan's new scheme for shedding weight—a liquid diet. At lunch, he spooned himself meager sips of soup broth and afterward spoke dirges to all the heaping platters of Mexican food—he called it "Rexican"—that were out in the world passing him by—right up until the late-afternoon Starbucks order arrived with a Frappuccino the size of a grain silo marked "Rex." After a long, revitalizing swill he'd report, "That'll jack you up!" When his chair popped a screw, the coach was instantly indignant: "And I've lost weight!" When snacks were brought in on a tray, Ryan would look up hopefully, and if he beheld only vegetables, he'd fix Tannenbaum a look: "Who *did* this?"

Maybe Pettine. A scout slipped Ryan a cookie. "Enabler!" the coordinator cried. Chips and salsa were served.

Ryan: "Yesss!"

Pettine: "Rex, you better go change your shirt."

Whenever the moment called for a digression, Ryan was always there to provide it. He recalled his early days coaching in the impoverished program at New Mexico Highlands University, where he mowed the field himself and then burned yard stripes in with gasoline because paint was too expensive. During discussion of Sam Acho, Ryan engaged in imagining and subsequently handicapping a spelling contest pitting the well-read Texas linebacker against Eric Smith, the Jets safety who had been recruited by both Harvard and Yale. The coach would go with Acho, he said, with compelling logic, because Acho was more difficult to spell.

One afternoon, Ryan was praising Bruce Springsteen's "Darkness on the Edge of Town" as American lyric poetry, and Clinkscales objected: "Can you fill in some of us guys with a darker complexion on what you're talking about?"

"Hey!" said Ryan. "Bruce is for everybody."

Pretty clearly, so was football. In a largely black game (two-thirds of all NFL players), long gone were the days when teams believed black men didn't have the brains to play quarterback, safety, or center—"The thinking man's positions," as DT called them. It still pissed DT off that when he'd played for the Cowboys, it had taken injuries to three white safeties before the team had let him try the position. Prejudice was now so much the enemy of good drafting that the scouts scoured their souls for bias. Many said they struggled not to overrate effort, the try-hard guys. Others confessed soft spots for small-school linemen, offensive linemen who were converted from defensive linemen, players from the South, and even players who were raised by their grandmothers (esteemed for their old-school values). The scout Michael Davis said, "I like the underdog. But I have to fight liking the underdog too much."

Sitting in the unvarying fluorescence of the draft room, a person lost track of the days, the sense of connection to anything but the matter at hand. Toward the end of the linebacker discussion, Nick

Bellore's and Jeff Tarpinian's names came up. Seen on the video screen, Bellore had a huge head; he looked friendly and round. He'd played for the Central Michigan Chippewas, a second-tier program, but no player in college football had accumulated more tackles. Jeff Bauer, the Iowa-based scout, was all for Tarpinian, an Iowa linebacker Pettine had met out at the Iowa pro day. During that visit, Pettine put Tarpinian up at a blackboard and spent half an hour quizzing him about techniques, formations, coverages, and flow. Tarpinian hadn't missed a question. But Tarpinian was undersized and had suffered several college injuries. Tannenbaum shook his head: "Everybody'll fall in love with him and then he'll just get hurt." Either one of those two players, it was agreed, might make an excellent seventh-round choice.

The seventh and final round was traditionally the moment when those in the risk-averse process gave way to gold speculation. Locating an impact player so late in the draft was rare. As an incentive to find one, and following NFL tradition, each Jets scout could designate a favorite unheralded collegian as his "face" or "sticker player." Should that player be drafted by the Jets, the scout who'd supported him would receive a bonus.

Reviewing the cornerbacks took the most time. Across the league in 2011, corners were the most drafted players (thirty-nine). The reason was simple: Corners are football's best athletes. Wide receivers are sprinters who know their destination, and corners must react and keep up. And now what was this there on the video screen, some corner going for a retro look? No! Ryan had found DT's draft card and slipped it in with the others. "Shit," DT said. "If I was coming out today, I'd be so rich I wouldn't know any of you!"

Sometimes during the conversations, interest in a player achieved sudden momentum, as happened with Louisville corner Johnny Patrick. On film he was a stunning athlete—he possessed wonderful body control, tracked pass receivers as though there were a GPS in his helmet—until the ball arrived, at which point Patrick at times seemed to lack the will to make plays. But Pettine believed

Patrick could be the Wilkerson of the secondary. "Look," he said to a long line of skeptical faces. "Revis is so much the exception. With corners, you have to tolerate more. Most corners you'll have issues with." Now Ryan, always in search of objects on which to shine his enthusiasm, discovered he completely loved the kid. Okay, Patrick didn't play like a Jet, but neither did Cro. For such bijous you made exceptions. Tannenbaum was warming to Patrick as well. The team had saved a few of their thirty visiting slots for just such an occurrence. Tannenbaum and Ryan decided to bring Patrick in to the facility. Ryan went bounding out of the room to set up the visit himself. When he returned, the coach was asked if his wife had ordered new guest-room furniture for Johnny Patrick's stay. "Hell," said Clinkscales. "By now Patrick's got a wing in the Tannenbaum house!"

There was an observer effect to the draft—a midstream adjustment of the value of one player meant shifting the room's assessment of other players. Patrick's improving profile raised that of Julian Posey of Ohio University. Posey was a smart corner who'd acted as both on-field tutor and disciplinarian for the rest of his college secondary, praiseworthy qualities Patrick lacked. Alas, Posey had not played well in the game against Ohio State, Ohio University's only elite opponent. But Posey would be brought in too. And Tarpinian.

On to safeties the group went, and UCLA's Rahim Moore elicited pushback from USC grads DT and Carrier. "That Southern Cal, UCLA thing, that's real to them," said Michael Davis. "They mean it. UCLA's the other side—no toughness." Later DT, unsmiling, said, "USC men are tougher and the women are more beautiful." If the Jets drafted a UCLA defensive player, said DT, "He'll have to prove himself to me."

No such obligations for Jaiquawn Jarrett. The Temple safety was lauded as "a hired killer" who would "knock your face in! Pow!" Jarrett got so much love that suddenly the room quieted, the way it did when Jimmy Smith's name had come up the day before. Would he still be there in the third round at pick ninety-four?

*   *   *

On Wednesday, six days in and still eight days before the draft, DT was breaking out the sunflower seeds at eight in the morning. At ten, Johnny Patrick arrived for his interview. He had sweaty palms, seemed fragile. He'd lived with his father since his mother had told him, when he was twelve, that she couldn't "deal with" him.

Julian Posey, by contrast, was friendly and enthusiastic, and he wore a bright green-and-white checked shirt, the only visiting player to think to dress in the Jets colors. His mother was an HIV prevention director in Cincinnati; she'd worked for the Urban League and the State of Ohio. Posey seemed to share that caring part of her nature. In response to Tannenbaum's question about a recent act of generosity, Posey said he had just the day before given away his lunch to a hungry person at the bus station. What did he like about playing cornerback? "I like the comfort of space," he said.

By now various people in the draft room were firmly attached to certain players. Tannenbaum had, of course, been taking note of all these crushes. He referred to Michael Davis as "Kenrick Ellis's legal guardian, Mr. Mike." With a gimlet eye, the GM watched Pettine exhale as the crucial strength-and-conditioning report yielded the words "Wilkerson: 314 pounds of solid muscle." When Posey was described as "a good kid," I thought, "Yes, but he's so much more!" and looked over to find Tannenbaum's gaze fastened on me.

At 6:58 the next morning, with a rolling boatman's walk, Mike Westhoff approached the draft room to make his three-hour case for special teams. The gait was due to a long titanium rod surgically inserted in Westhoff's left leg to replace a cancer-riven femur — one more detail for a figure straight out of a Carl Hiaasen novel. Another was that Westy spent vacations off the Florida coast hunting sharks, his favorite animal. Accompanying him into the meeting was his deputy, Ben Kotwica, a former Army football captain and Apache combat-helicopter pilot who had mastered the West Point swivel that allows a young officer to confidently lead in one moment and be crisply subordinate in the next.

Westhoff was a diva who played small clubs, a grumping, growling peacock with a gift for crusty, old-salt agitation that wore on the busy men who ran the team. "Upstairs," he said a little proudly, "they don't like to see me!" Every man who'd worked a few NFL drafts remembered the present Pro Bowlers he'd touted who had been passed over by the higher-ups. Westhoff remembered them like fresh grudges. He still frequently lamented the Jets' 2002 decision, against his advice, to select Bryan Thomas even though the peerless safety Ed Reed was still there for the taking. (Westy could be fuzzier on the matter of his less successful recommendations.) And while he was strident at times, as special-teams coach, Westy knew that not holding back was his job, and upstairs knew it too. Year after year, they found themselves conceding that the man only wanted to save them from themselves—and he could. Westy was the voice of the easily overlooked, the football dispossessed, and any year the Jets didn't draft players who could be special-teams mainstays, there would be field-position consequences all season long.

Coaching football excited Westy because it was the only sport where you could orchestrate the event as it happened. "Me, as a coach, I take total ownership," he said. "I believe, as a metaphor, I won it or I lost it. Intellectually I know all of us New York Jets do it, but that's how I have to think about it. I want everyone who plays for me to feel that way. I tell them the defensive guys missed the bus; the offensive guys, they ate bad fish and got sick. It's up to us." He said he'd been formed as a person during the years he'd spent in the Pennsylvania steel mills as a teenager, working with grown men, standing over swimming pools of molten metal. "I learned the importance of every job," he said of the mill. "No job was too small." As a coach, he said his favorite players were the blue-collar, no-job-is-too-small athletes at the bottom of the NFL pay scale — "Not the guy everybody knows is a hell of a player. I get to give them an opportunity."

Now, taking his place at the draft table and speaking in staccato beats of snare, he began the meeting with a lengthy policy preamble during which he argued, "I believe you get beat with dumb guys." About kickoffs and punt returns, his opinion was "I think they should all be touchdowns!" Then he said of Jeff Tarpinian, "I'm lying across the table for him." Somebody began reading back the Tarpinian medical report, and Westhoff, who'd survived an aggressive cancer, waved the report off. "Doctors! Don't let 'em scare you. I'm still here."

The man wanted smart safeties and smart linebackers, the versatile position players suited to running beneath a soaring football and performing the unique open-field special-teams tasks. (The intelligence of these players was of crucial importance, because in addition to being on special teams, these players were reserves, had to know the defensive calls despite few practice reps.) Westy repeatedly took off his glasses and put them on again for emphasis as he praised Nick Bellore, who'd impressed the old master by suiting up and playing right after oral surgery: "Football player!" Another linebacker, USC's Malcolm Smith—the brother of Steve Smith, the former Giants receiver—had been, Westhoff said, a problem for him to resolve. Initially, Westhoff had found the young Smith too quiet and shy—not what you want in a linebacker. "But I showed him some stuff. He got into it. I decided, I'll take this guy! Soon as I thought it, he changed. Smiled. Got excited. I don't know."

Then he brought up Akeem Ayers. "I'll be shocked if this guy makes it," he volunteered, before describing how docile Ayers had been during a drill at the Combine. "Is this a guy we'd consider with the thirtieth pick?" he wanted to know. Tannenbaum confirmed the possibility. Disbelief crossed Westhoff's face. He got to his feet. "I'm gonna take a shower," he said. Then he thought better of it and sat down again. "He's not a demon," he said of Ayers. "Thirty years ago I was on the field for that drill. You guys think of me as an old guy. I was on the field." After a long silence, the group moved on to Jarrett. "My number-one-rated guy of anybody," Westhoff said.

"Join the party!" Tannenbaum told him.

"I'm getting out of the shower!" said Westhoff.

Three days before the draft, the personnel men met with Ryan and Tannenbaum in Tannenbaum's office to review the board. Outside the room, Jets employees were checking in with many dozens of players, confirming telephone numbers so on draft night, right before making a choice, the team could check in with those they intended to select to be sure all was well. "What if he gets into an accident the night before the draft?" explained Clinkscales. In the office, the men discussed the bilious feeling a team that drafts late can experience as it prepares to take somebody twenty-nine teams have just passed on. So Ryan told how, in 1971, the Michigan lineman Dan Dierdorf "kept falling and falling." Cardinals owner Bill Bidwill wanted to know what was wrong with Dierdorf, and since nobody could think of anything, the team drafted the future Hall of Fame tackle. As the conversation continued, it doubled back on itself, and suddenly they were finding unsung worth in every player. Ryan said, "This is when you realize we'll be lucky to get anybody." He ordered a large whipped cream with a little coffee from Starbucks. "The diet is off," he declared. "I'm fat and I have to live with it."

Tannenbaum, Ryan's defender even against Ryan, averred: "Husky!"

Then they were betting milkshakes on how good a pro Ryan Kerrigan would be, which reminded Ryan that in 2009, similar terms had been placed on Sanchez. Sanchez had been to the playoffs twice in his first two years. Someone had a milkshake coming to him. Who could it be? "I like Sanchez!" said Ryan smacking his lips, whereupon Tannenbaum gently steered him back to the main course. "Jarrett or Patrick?" he asked.

*   *   *

The relentless, never-ending thoroughness of football men, I loved. To them, an additional hour was never superfluous, one more trip through the film never unnecessary. In the end, the slates might still remain mostly blank, but they were chalk-dusted with informed hope.

Two days before the draft, yet another meeting of the coaches, pro-personnel people, and scouts began. The offensive and defensive lists had been combined and sorted. Boise State receiver Titus Young had sold them all on his ability. Yet many in the room were opposed to the idea of using the second-round draft pick Young would probably require on a receiver because receivers rarely touched the ball for more than a few plays in a game. Which receivers would last to the middle rounds? They hoped for Denarius Moore or Texas Christian's Jeremy Kerley, whom Brian Schottenheimer thought had the sort of zippy movement that would yield big plays out of the slot.

By now the investigation phase was over, and critical theory had given way to the poetry of praise, all of them strenuous in working up odes to those they'd discovered in some hinterland or whom they hoped to coach. "Okay!" said Tannenbaum, shaking his head. "So Titus Young's better than Percy Harvin and Jeremy Kerley's better than Santonio Holmes?" This, I suspected, was the true nature of these men, one so often suppressed. They played hard to get but yearned to fall madly and deeply. Despite all the meetings, when they talked about the short-area foot speed and bending ability of a three-hundred-pound lineman, there remained incredulity and reverence in their tones.

Although some days the meetings lasted fifteen hours, nobody ever drowsed or seemed particularly enervated; there was too much pressure. True, throughout all the many long meetings, Jeff Weeks said nothing, and when, by mistake, he managed to tilt his chair so far back he banged into the wall switch and sent the video screen plunging noisily from the ceiling, it was Ryan who blushed the deepest as he snapped, "Sit on the front of your chair and get into it." In moments like these, I always thought of Ryan as football's Samuel Johnson, the ursine dean of Augustan London who routinely clawed at his old student David Garrick but permitted nobody else the privilege.

Later, in Tannenbaum's office, Ryan and a few others volleyed their preferences back and forth, a process that made Ryan wistful as he considered all the players he'd never get the chance to coach. When Nate Solder lost a head-to-head rankings battle with the Missouri pass rusher Aldon Smith, Ryan looked so sad about losing the big Colorado offensive tackle, Tannenbaum offered to buy him "an emergency Frappuccino." Ryan cheered up at the thought of Mark Ingram, the Alabama running back, suited up in hunter green and white but then was cast down afresh when Wilkerson's name arose. "Gone," Ryan said sadly. "No chance. Gone."

The fallback strategy of forsaking the first round altogether, trading down, and taking Titus Young meant yielding all hope of drafting Jimmy Smith, which, in turn, meant they'd need a cornerback opposite Revis. Tannenbaum, keeper of the salary-cap keys, said in that event Ryan could then try to re-sign Antonio Cromartie. "Fuck it, I'm in!" Ryan said. Bradway took the opportunity to press for drafting a reserve quarterback. Sanchez's backup last year had been Mark Brunell, who would be forty-one years old soon but was regarded by Sanchez as a kind of football big brother. Keeping a less-than-ideal understudy because Sanchez liked him bothered Bradway, who joked that the Jets better not draft Scotty McKnight, a short, slow, but sure-handed Colorado receiver who was not on the Jets draft board. McKnight had great college stats, but in pro football, even a superb numerical past didn't mean so much when your raw skills didn't project. Yet McKnight did have something of intangible value. This was a game where the term "the quarterback's favorite receiver" spoke to the mysteries of connection. Mc-Knight was Mark Sanchez's best childhood friend.

As the men in Tannenbaum's office began to watch more Titus Young tape, the mail arrived, and with it an advance copy of the upcoming Ryan and Tannenbaum episode of *CSI: NY*. They had filmed a joint scene in which they stood on the sidewalk and fended off draft advice from a passing detective who'd recognized them. Immediately, Titus was thrown to the wild beasts and everyone watched the Domination, as Ryan called his TV debut. Then Tannenbaum dialed up the *CSI* producer, put him on speaker, and everyone listened as Ryan made himself available for future thespian employ—"Hello, love scene!" For his on-screen partner in romance, he suggested Heather Locklear, who had been his celebrity crush for more than thirty years. "I'm loyal," Ryan explained to the producer.

The next day at—what else—another meeting, Tannenbaum addressed the West Coast scout Joe Bommarito on the matter of Titus Young. Young was an excellent receiver, but the public record showed that in his time, he'd smoked more than DBs: "Joe, you're signing off on him? When Sanchez wants him here in the building, he'll be here with a smile on his face? Joe, nine forty-one in the morning, you're signing off? This is big, Joe. We may take him. We may have a chance at him because of issues. You're okay with that?" Bommarito didn't flinch. Of course, the scout couldn't guarantee what Young would do in the future; by some accounts, half the NFL runs on grass. But Bommarito had immersed himself in Young's community and believed the receiver could thrive.

"Guys," said Tannenbaum, looking around. "We have a marathon ahead of us."

"Guys," said Ryan. "How many times can we watch *CSI*?"

"Great job, everyone," said Tannenbaum. "Another day and a half until we're picking." Matt Bazirgan, a scout who once played quarterback for Bates College, smiled ruefully at me and said, "In three years, we'll look like fools or we'll look great."

*   *   *

"Happy draft day," Jim O'Neil greeted everyone on the long-awaited April 28. "The Scout Super Bowl," as Joe Bommarito proclaimed it, had come at last, and as the 8:00 p.m. start time approached, the facility was transformed. People walked the corridors in their Sunday clothes: an eggplant-hued corduroy blazer for Joey Clinkscales; Tannenbaum in a pin-striped suit. Only Ryan was resolute in sideline couture. Along a quiet hallway, there were tables laden with chicken Parmesan, cheeseburger sliders, Mexican food, and flatbread pizza, as well as a sundae bar. Around the building, office workers filled out sheets as they tried to predict the draft order, just as office workers were doing all over America. Were these sheets better informed? They were not. Nobody, not Tannenbaum and not Ryan, could really say what thirty-one other organizations were thinking. On the locked draft-room door, a sign was posted: Do Not Clean. Tannenbaum looked as relaxed as I'd ever seen him — he'd done what he could, knew all the roads, and was ready to travel.

The draft room had been dressed up as well. There were televisions tuned to ESPN and the NFL Network and several newly activated telephone landlines, and there were fewer people than usual inside. Fearing distraction, Tannenbaum asked most of the draft team to watch from their offices. The draft itself was at Radio City Music Hall, in New York, where fans, mindful of the lockout, were chanting, "We want football." The Jets representatives there — Vito Contento, from the equipment room, and the video director, Tim Tubito — sat by a telephone, where they would take down the names of the Jets' ultimate picks, write them on a card, and submit it to the league, a horse-and-buggy remnant in an of-the-moment game.

The Jets had to be patient. Each team was entitled to ten minutes on the clock to contemplate its first choice, and most teams would use all that time to invite trade offers. Ryan arrived. "What a spread!" he exclaimed. Looking around, he said, "There's nobody in here!" Turning to Tannenbaum, he asked, "Why am I the nervous one? You're the nervous one." To me, he said, "C'mon, Nicky! Let's get ice cream!"

The evening passed fitfully. From time to time, the telephones on the draft table rang with other teams proposing trades. As players were selected, a Jets scout would move the appropriate cards from the wall of available players to the drafted wall. Ryan, Tannenbaum, Clinkscales, Bradway, and the others watched their competitors make their picks on TV and offered commentary. They grew most animated when other teams' choices wildly diverged from the Jets' assessment of the player, such as Tennessee's drafting of quarterback Jake Locker. After Houston took J. J. Watt at number 11, Ryan was relieved the big Wisconsin defensive lineman would not be a Patriot. New England then selected Nate Solder, and everybody approved; if you possessed as excellent a quarterback as Brady, you had to give him time to throw. Ryan and Tannenbaum periodically picked up the phone and checked in with other teams that had recently made their first-round selections and might want to acquire another one by trading with the Jets: "Great pick! If you guys are interested in coming back up, let us know." Everybody in these conversations was on a first-name basis with everyone else. The only exception was how Ryan addressed Oakland owner Al Davis, the rare owner to make draft decisions for his team. Davis had long been a pariah among the league's other owners, but Davis was a pro-football legend, and Ryan called him Mr. Davis. Jets owner Woody Johnson and his brother Chris sat in for a while, watching closely.

Twenty picks in, other teams had chosen three players to whom the Jets had assigned second- or third-round cards, and one they'd rated a fourth- or fifth-rounder. "Wilkerson, hang in there, baby!" Ryan cried. The team's medical staff was called into the room. Da'Quan Bowers, with his microfractured knee and first-pick talent, had not yet been chosen. Should he be a Jet? Dr. Kenneth Montgomery, the team physician, urged against it. The Redskins

had passed on Bowers, Montgomery said, and their doctors performed his knee surgery.

The telephone rang: Seattle offering to trade their pick at
twenty-five for the Jets' number thirty and the Jets' third-round
choice. Tannenbaum took out a trade-value chart that looked like
something a life-insurance firm would have on the wall. The columns of numbers told Tannenbaum he should counter Seattle's
third-round proposal with a fifth. Thank you, no, said Seattle. The
Eagles were up. Along with the Ravens, the Jets feared, Philadelphia
was most likely to draft Jimmy Smith. But, no, the Eagles went for a
lineman. High-fives were hoisted. Seattle called back. A fourth?
"No," said Tannenbaum. "On our chart, a fifth is fair. Your guy will
still be there at thirty!" Of course, he didn't know who Seattle's guy
was. Seattle went ahead and used their pick to take James Carpen-
ter, rated a second-rounder on the Jets board. Tannenbaum was
speechless. He was sure the Seahawks had, in effect, passed up a
bonus pick.

The Ravens drafted Jimmy Smith. Groans! Curses! A plague
on both of Seattle's houses! "He'll never make it!" Tannenbaum
said, and like that, binder pages turned, time sped, and just after
eleven, the Jets were on the clock at last. Tannenbaum's instructions to Contento and Tubito at Radio City were to write down
Muhammad Wilkerson on the card but do nothing while the Jets
fielded offers. Lowballs were lobbed over the facility wall. Clinkscales called Wilkerson to make sure he was intact. Then he put the
player on hold. Four minutes left. A tasty offer arrived from
Dallas—but not as tasty as 314 pounds of fast-twitching Wilkerson.
Tannenbaum took the phone and greeted his new lineman, and
then Ryan took over: "Everything you got, Muhammad! None of
this bullshit every-other-play!" The scouts poured into the room.
Hugs and handshakes were exchanged. "He'll be a ten-year player
for us," said Tannenbaum. Wilkerson appeared on the TV screen.
"Look at those arms!" marveled Ryan.

The next day, a festival of Wilkerson family members stopped by the facility, looking proud. Wilkerson himself mostly spent his visit quiet and smiling, wearing an expression into which the Jets read profound gridiron truths. "That's a *man*," said Pettine. "I like him even better now!" gushed Ryan. Tight-ends coach Devlin agreed—"He *is* a beast!"—and Ryan seemed grateful. Praise for defensive players always meant most when it came from the offense. Once a drafted player was yours, Tannenbaum explained, "you love him more."

When the second round began at 6:30, the Jets, without a choice, were participants who couldn't participate. On the television the just-drafted were leaping off couches, hugging fathers, kissing mothers, kissing girlfriends. At the facility, there were fruit smoothies available to all, and a smooth operator from another team calling to offer the Jets its second-round choice for three lower picks. The Jets accepted, whereupon the other team asked for more. A bait-and-switch was not an unusual occurrence, and Tannenbaum seethed only a little. With Wilkerson in hand for Ryan and Pettine, he was hoping to trade up and deliver Titus Young to Schottenheimer and Sanchez. Maybe the other team would call back and un-renege. "Come on, Titus, come home," said Tannenbaum. But Detroit drafted Young at pick forty-four. "Plan B!" Tannenbaum announced. "He's dead to us! Come on, Jaiquawn Jarrett!"

Ten picks later, the Eagles took Jarrett. "Really?" said Tannenbaum. *"Really?"* At 9:00, *CSI: NY* appeared live on one of the televisions. "Everybody's an expert!" Ryan was telling the football-fan police detective on the screen. In real life, with the draft seventy-four picks in, Tannenbaum still had five players left he liked just fine at ninety-four: Kenrick Ellis, Bilal Powell, Johnny Patrick, receiver Jerrel Jernigan, and Florida safety Ahmad Black. "We'll get one of them," promised Bradway. At eighty-three, the Giants selected Jernigan. At eighty-eight, with the room's collective abdomen clenched, New Orleans went for Patrick. And then the Jets were finally back on the clock, and the sequence repeated itself—

other teams making offers; Michael Davis calling Ellis; all the scouts pouring into the room to slap the broad shoulders of "Mr. Mike!" At ninety-four, the Jets had landed their forty-fifth-rated player.

Pettine visited the draft room for a polite interval and then retreated to his office to watch tape of Ellis playing games at Hampton. This school's football didn't look like the sophisticated pro-style game they played at Alabama or USC. Here, players launched themselves at each other like bombardiers, hit with delirious aggression. In the middle of the frenzied rough-and-tumble, wading through the cheap shots to make tackle after tackle, was Ellis. In every frame, he was the largest player on the field, a man so big you could imagine his belly full of gravel, rusty cans, maybe an old shoe, a bicycle wheel, and two dozen fishhooks. Pettine found it all hugely entertaining. "Look at this big rascal run!" He chortled. Ryan entered. "The big bull!" he said happily and took a seat. "You know what I always say, got to win in the alley before you win on the field!"

Because of the $120 million salary cap in 2011, NFL teams couldn't afford to keep all their expensive veterans. One reason the Jets' scout face-card-bonus policy existed was that if a scout could find you an impact player in the seventh round, it would help the budget enormously. More than half the players who would be on active 2011 NFL rosters were drafted in the fifth round or later. You had to win at the margins.

For the final four draft rounds on Saturday, each team had only five minutes before making selections. The day went quickly. In the fourth round, the Jets drafted Bilal Powell. On television, an analyst praised this as the pick of the day. Bradway—teasing—said that was only because Tannenbaum had taken the analyst's calls. Tannenbaum said Bradway was probably right. The Jets still sought a receiver as well as linebackers and defensive backs to play special teams. Everyone in the room knew that somewhere downstairs was a displeased Mike Westhoff. They could feel him. After Denarius Moore went off to Oakland—"Fuuuuck!"—the Jets traded up with Philadelphia to be sure they wouldn't also lose out on Jeremy Kerley. The Eagles were also given the Jets' sixth-round pick; the Jets received the Eagles' choice for the seventh. In Kerley, Westhoff now at least had his return man. Philadelphia's GM told Tannenbaum how well he'd been drafting. Tannenbaum had been practicing this same form of back-scratching for three days, but despite himself, he was pleased. "They wanted Ellis," he reported.

Clinkscales, worrying there was still a plan afoot to draft Sanchez's friend Scotty McKnight, shared with Ryan his concern that the Jets hadn't been hard enough on their young quarterback. Ryan disagreed: "You can't win four road playoff games and not be a man." Clinkscales pondered this. "I agree with you, but I don't agree with you," he finally said. When Minnesota took the self-effacing center Brandon Fusco, Ryan sadly said, "They're all going."

As the first of the Jets' two seventh-round slots approached, Bradway reminded Tannenbaum that the Jets had only one quarterback signed for the roster—Sanchez. Bradway loved—adored!—Greg McElroy, who'd led Alabama to a national title with an average arm and advanced-placement acumen. Getting Westhoff linebackers was on everyone else's mind. They all knew that in the end, no matter what, Westy would say, "Fuck it, we'll make it work," but part of Westhoff's skill was his ability to make others wary of offending him. Even the way he dressed—he wore salmon-pink vests over short-sleeved white polo shirts with black slacks—set him apart, made him something singular to deal with. In this way, he could assemble surprising players for his low-priority-but-crucial unit. Now on the board was a linebacker he coveted whom nobody else liked. Tension in the draft room built. What to do? Minnesota took the linebacker! Ryan called Westhoff to console him and remind him that Nick Bellore and Jeff Tarpinian were still out there.

The Jets drafted McElroy and then watched ESPN interview him. McElroy's answers were so articulate and self-assured Ryan said, "I'll just turn it over to Greg!" At Radio City, players from Yale were being drafted while Bellore and Posey and Tarpinian remained there for the taking. Suddenly—what was this? Tannenbaum and Ryan left the room. Bradway followed. Clinkscales looked alarmed. Time passed. Bradway reappeared, his face flushed. Then Ryan returned with Tannenbaum, who seemed—well, it was difficult to be sure of Tannenbaum's disposition, but "pleased" wouldn't describe it. Ryan wanted to use "his" pick to draft Scotty McKnight. The scouts were crestfallen. Clinkscales was furious. Under Tannenbaum, the Jets had never before drafted someone rated below a seventh-round grade. McKnight didn't merit a draft card, hadn't even received a Jets physical. He could have been signed as a free agent. That another team might take him was inconceivable.

Ryan was so deeply lovable that people would forgive him almost anything. During the foot-fetish-video fallout, he'd been moved by the instant support he'd received throughout the organization. But the events of the current moment threatened all that goodwill. It was only a low seventh-round choice, and yet in the draft room, the happiness about the draft had given way to gloom. The coach explained that because of the lockout, the league prohibited coaches from talking to players. For months before the lockout, Ryan and Sanchez had been joking back and forth about Ryan drafting Sanchez's bestie. Ryan had begun to worry that Sanchez thought Ryan was serious, and, said Ryan, "I would never want a player to think I lied to him." He apologized to the scouting department, said he was sorry about the face cards, said he was aware there were concerns about "babying" Sanchez. And yet, who knew what McKnight might become. Wes Welker of the Patriots was perhaps the best receiver in the league. Nobody'd thought to draft him because he was "too small." And chemistry mattered between those who threw and those who caught. "If he's bullshit, it's on me," the coach concluded.

The room's occupants remained quiet and unconvinced. Why would Ryan compromise all their work just to appease one player? It occurred to me that the coach's approach to football inevitably placed unusually strong emphasis on human relationships. I thought again of Weeks. Ryan believed that he was a better coach with his reassuring old friend on hand. Maybe Ryan had looked at Sanchez, inexperienced at being an authority figure, like Ryan himself, and decided the quarterback could also use a trusted sharer of secrets. That Ryan saw football as a game of familial love and passion was what set him apart from so many of the corporate bottom-liners who wore NFL headsets and followed all established protocols.

But would granting one already privileged player such a favor improve the morale of the rest? Everybody knew Ryan wanted only to win. They had to take it on faith that his interests would advance theirs. Bellore, Posey, and Tarpinian had not been drafted. When the commissioner decreed that undrafted free agents could be signed, there was opportunity again for making them Jets. Now, though, everybody just left for home—everybody except Ryan, who had written a memoir and was heading off to promote it.

Outside, the trees were suddenly in bloom. The car radio said there'd been a royal wedding. What a rough business football was. Even this successful draft now felt like a defeat. But the draft and the games weren't really the work. They were the interruptions the coaches and personnel men lived for, yet they were still interruptions. The work was process, the deliberate day-to-day attempt to improve the team. Terry Bradway told me that football executives do all they can during a draft, and then afterward they cross their fingers. The players were so young, and some of them, like Kyle Wilson, hadn't even fully filled out yet. Most people spend their lives hoping for things that never happen. I had begun to see that football was a sport that existed for exultation but was mostly about longing.

Five

THE SOUND OF SILENCE

*I felt that Tom would drift on forever seeking, a little
wistfully, for the dramatic turbulence of some
irrecoverable football game.*

—*F. Scott Fitzgerald*, The Great Gatsby

The lockout meant that with the draft over, the usual rhythm
and texture of a football off-season was disrupted. A strange
time felt stranger to many of the Jets coaches and front-office men
because of the way the draft had ended. Large disappointments
came with the job; football people were used to overcoming far bigger setbacks than the drafting of Scotty McKnight. They did so by
pointing their emotions toward the next crucial date on the calendar. In a normal year, right after the draft, teams attempted to sign
the desirable rookies who had not been chosen. But now, at the
beginning of May, the clocks had been indefinitely stopped, and
teams were forbidden to contact any player. And so, with Ryan away
for a few days speaking about his book, all around the quiet Jets
facility, people dwelled on the drafting of Mark Sanchez's best
friend.

"It was out of the blue," Joey Clinkscales said, straining so hard
to be diplomatic that inadvertently he wasn't. "But tons of free
agents make it. He could be one." Downstairs in his office, the
receivers coach Henry Ellard was watching McKnight's University

of Colorado tape for the first time. "Needs a lot of work," he said in his quiet, matter-of-fact way. Schottenheimer, the offensive coordinator, had never seen McKnight play either, but he'd "heard all about him from Mark!" Schottenheimer himself would have made a different choice, but he was a deeply religious Christian, and one of the qualities his faith had given him was the capacity to move on from what angered or hurt him. Schotty was, like Ryan, the son of a respected professional football coach. He knew this was an unstable, cutthroat profession, and he understood the reassurance a coach or a young quarterback might feel at having beside him someone of unquestioned devotion.

One day, not long after Ryan returned to the facility, I was having lunch by myself, something people rarely did in the cafeteria, when I heard a concerned voice: "What are you doing eating alone?" It was Ryan. Down he sat and proceeded to tell me about his son Seth's recent junior-varsity high-school baseball exploits in such a way that I felt instantly absorbed by the story, invested in whether or not Seth would soon be called up to the varsity. This was a common experience when Ryan talked about his son; Sanchez and other Jets players were always turning up at Seth's games. Ryan's eyes were clear blue, his teeth porcelain tiles, his spirits as infectious as ever, and as he spoke I thought of what a great companion he was, the adult version of the sort of kid you always wanted to be with because he could make anything involving. This was such a helpful quality in somebody who coached a game. He offered the kind of interaction most people rarely experienced in adulthood. Later, as I was driving home, thinking about Ryan's fear that I was lonely, it occurred to me that Ryan enjoyed taking care of people and that one reason he was drawn to young football players, so many of whom came from broken families, and drawn to Jeff Weeks, must be that the players and Weeks needed him. They all were acceptable objects of Ryan's great inclusive sympathy.

The person who took the Scotty McKnight draft hardest might have been Pettine. Winning was everything to the defensive coordinator, and he didn't see how choosing McKnight had made any sense when draft-grade players were still available. The incident was to him a betrayal of football ethics. What did turning a draft choice into a favor for one player say to the scouts and the other players? Why wasn't McKnight simply brought in as a free agent, which to Pettine's thinking would have been favor enough? Pettine worried that it all signaled Ryan had become "day-to-day less connected" with the morale of his staff, that his personal whims were trumping what was best for the group. It bothered Pettine to see people like Weeks and McKnight receiving prestigious NFL positions from Ryan for reasons other than pure ability, reasons of personal connection. Becoming an NFL draft choice was an honor, something Nick Bellore had earned and now would never experience. (It would also cost Bellore financially; seventh-round draft choices typically received a signing bonus of $35,000 to $40,000. Undrafted free agents typically got less than $10,000.) Pettine knew that he himself had worked his way up under Ryan, had busted his ass to earn his place in the NFL, but others thought of him first as a Ryan protégé. Ryan's actions reflected on Pettine. In darker moments, Pettine feared that he and Ryan, who'd once been as close as siblings, who now had everything they used to dream of together in Baltimore, suddenly no longer shared the same football values. The defensive coordinator would think, in those moments, that the time was approaching for him to leave Ryan, to go somewhere else and show how much he knew about football, prove that he was his own guy.

One afternoon, Tannenbaum and I were talking about the head coach, how lovable he was and how that helped him get away with just about anything. Like Scotty McKnight, I said. "Not our finest moment as an organization," Tannenbaum admitted. I never knew Tannenbaum not to take credit for a mistake. "You try to con people, they think you're full of shit," he told me once. The McKnight moment had been very stressful, he said, but he was already past it. These things happened pretty frequently in football, and you couldn't allow a low seventh-round draft choice more significance than it deserved. You had to move on, get the next more important decision right. In the end, everybody in football knew that the talent-level difference between a seventh-round draft choice and a free agent was so negligible as to be nearly arbitrary. I got the feeling, however, that Ryan wasn't going to be drafting anybody by himself again anytime soon.

The real problem at hand, so far as Tannenbaum was concerned, was the lockout. Tannenbaum hated uncertainty almost as much as he hated vacation. He had a surging physical need to be working, to be improving. He put himself out there in such an extreme way that I worried about how he would stand it if the team didn't do well. Even on desultory Wednesdays during these lockout weeks, he'd look at his watch, discover it was 6:40, and think, Where did my day go? Tannenbaum was scheduled to leave soon for a bicycle trip in France with his wife, Michelle, whom he loved so much that he'd agreed to join her for biking in France. Tannenbaum didn't bike. But should the lockout suddenly end, he'd instructed Michelle to have ready the names of the top three people she'd like to replace him for France. In other words, she should create a vacation depth chart.

The lockout wore on everyone. The staff members were task-oriented men of action who were now marooned, isolated, wan, and restless, just trying to push through. They were used to a regimented life. Days when they had to figure out what to do with their time were oppressive. Inertia was the abyss. Jim O'Neil, speaking for just about everyone, said, "I start to get antsy if I'm lingering." So they created projects. The defensive coaches watched film of every defensive play inside their own twenty-yard line—the red zone—in an attempt to make themselves "less vanilla down there," as Pettine put it. O'Neil was so motivated to work that with his wife, Stacy, soon to have their second child, he was planning to use his time at home after the birth of the baby to draw up every common passing route used against all the new red-zone coverages the Jets were considering.

Schottenheimer was feeling just as disoriented by the limbo of lockout. "We're such type-A personalities," he marveled. "Look at us! We're all over the place!" Nobody put in more hours "separated from real life" than Schotty. Seven months a year, he thought of his wife, Gemmi, as a single parent. Through most of Schotty's childhood, his father, Marty, had been an NFL head coach, first in Cleveland and then in Kansas City. Growing up in that kind of household, Schotty became more interested in thinking about football than in playing it. He led his Kansas high-school team to a state title and began his college career as a quarterback at the University of Kansas, but, following advice received from Terry Bradway, then with the Chiefs, Schotty transferred to be a backup at Florida so he could learn a pro-style offense from the Gators' innovative head coach Steve Spurrier. Schotty's college triumphs came while he was wearing a visor and holding a clipboard. Since his first NFL job, as an offensive assistant with the Rams, under Dick Vermeil, Schotty had been, he said, "always driven to be known as myself, not as Marty Schottenheimer's son. I was driven to be my own person."

The lockout also gave the football men time for something rare in their world, reflection on the game itself. As the defensive coaches workshopped the assorted new red-zone coverage ideas, Pettine and DT smiled at each other. They were having the same Ravens memory. "Okay," Pettine said. "We're playing New Orleans, and Ray Lewis calls Red (2) Drop, which means three pass rushers. But he doesn't call the first part, which says who drops and who rushes. So everybody but Ray drops. Ray sees this and he says, 'What the hell!' and he drops too. Looked like recreation hour in a prison yard. We nearly got a pick out of it too! So on *Monday Night Football*, Ron Jaworski shows it and says, 'Eleven-man drop! Rex Ryan is a genius!'

Rex says, 'Don't tell anybody!' Out in Cincinnati, the Bengals begin to practice it and [head coach] Marvin Lewis sees and he yells, 'You dumbasses! It was a mistake!' "

There was a limitless number of things coaches could conceive for eleven players to do, extensive possibilities in the red zone alone. In this way, the coaches' current red-zone investigations continually led them to consider perhaps the central NFL strategic dilemma. You could polish a few calls to perfection, as Vince Lombardi's champion Green Bay Packers had done in the 1960s, most notably with their here-it-comes-try-to-stop-it power sweep. Or you could seek to create a more extensive catalog of looks tailored to counter the particular playing style of every opponent. That kind of opponent-specific game plan, however, risked that the players wouldn't know the newer material well enough. For Ryan, Pettine, and Schottenheimer, part of the joy of coaching was mastering each opponent and customizing game plans accordingly, and they all talked of how hard it was for them to limit the volume of fresh calls, to locate the fine balance.

This spring the coaches had the benefit of some expert companionship to help them think through the football problem sets they were dreaming up for themselves. Every year during May and June, a series of visitors came to facilities across the NFL to talk football with the offensive and defensive coaches. Some of the visitors were college coaches, out to observe and learn, and others were professionals, eager to informally exchange ideas. During the lockout, the Jets welcomed a larger number of these guests than usual, many of them hired consultants. Call volume was a recurrent theme in their conversations. One such visitor was the retired defensive-backs specialist Steve Shafer, who'd been with the Ravens in 2000 when they won the Super Bowl and set a record for least points allowed in a season. Shafer was sharp-eyed and weathered from years of standing on fields in the sun. Pettine showed Shafer film of the Jets defense so Shafer could offer commentary. Throughout, Shafer kept expressing amazement at the skills of Antonio

Cromartie and Darrelle Revis. "Revis is our best practice player," Pettine told him. "Catch a pass on Revis, you don't want to line up on him again."

"I'd come out of retirement if I could coach those two corners!" Shafer exclaimed.

"It's what keeps DT young," Sutton said.

After he'd seen the film, Shafer said that his advice was to resist the urge to overcomplicate things. Pointing toward Ryan's office and smiling, he said, "The guy I used to have to calm down was the big boy over there. He wanted to reinvent the wheel every week." Ryan walked in a moment later, and Pettine, smiling mischievously, greeted him and said, "You've just been accused of trying to reinvent the wheel every week!"

"I'm selling simple," Shafer said, embarrassed. But Ryan was unbothered. "KILL philosophy!" he said easily. " 'Keep it likable and learnable.' "

Shafer now framed the discussion in terms of boredom. In his time, the Ravens had been a defensive version of Lombardi's Packers. The Ravens relied on a few calls practiced to perfection. In the red zone, the Ravens for years relentlessly used but a single call. Eventually the call became so familiar that the players grew blasé about that most threatening defensive situation, and so the Ravens coaches added another look, not so much for opponents as for the Ravens themselves.

During the lockout, Tom Moore was commuting up to the facility from retirement in Hilton Head to serve as a Jets off-season offensive consultant. Sutton said Moore had told him the Colts maintained similar concerns about overfamiliarity while he'd coordinated the Colts offense during all those years with Peyton Manning. The Colts ran a very limited variety of plays, their actual choice dependent on Manning's peerless ability to read the defense at the line of scrimmage and audible the right call. The Colts coaching staff hated it when Manning went to the Pro Bowl and debriefed all the coaches from other teams that he met there, because then he'd return to Indianapolis bursting with fresh plays he wanted to try out. "Let's just stick with what we do," the Colts coaches would implore. Once in a while, Manning would throw a low-percentage deep route when a six-yard out was open, and the coaches would chide him, "Peyton, you're bored."

"It's a game of repetition," said Sutt.

"That's it," DT agreed. "Getting a few things perfect."

"Well," said Shafer. "Now I can go back to California and say that in my time I had it right."

"We appreciate you, Coach," DT told him.

After Shafer left, the coaches affirmed their respect for him as an excellent coach but noted that his simple approach wouldn't work for the Jets defense, which relied on many different options for each player within the scheme. Where Patrick Willis, the Pro Bowl 49ers linebacker, played the same role on every play, Bart Scott had myriad tasks depending on the situation. The Jets defense was the equivalent of the Colts or Patriots offense: a few fundamental features that were, as Pettine would say, "dressed up differently every week."

Meanwhile, the former Super Bowl–winning head coach Jon Gruden had come from Florida to visit the Jets offense. Bill Callahan, who coached for years with the fiery Gruden, had asked Ryan "how honest" Gruden should be with his fellow Jets offensive coaches. "Very," said Ryan. So Gruden was laying into them for overcomplicating their scheme. One problem Gruden cited with having so many calls was that so much "verbiage" was required just to say them. The protracted calls, said Gruden, absorbed valuable pre-snap seconds, sapped drive momentum, allowed time for defensive adjustments, and confused your own players, leading to penalties and blown assignments. "Justify it," Gruden kept saying to Schottenheimer, not quietly. Gruden moved from the snap count to the Jets' ragged offensive red-zone performance, which Gruden blamed on the team practicing it only on Fridays. The traditional NFL players' drinking night is Thursday. "I'd rather stick my head in a car door and slam it than practice red-zone only on Friday," Gruden yelled at the coaches. Then it was on to "How come the Jets screen game sucks so bad?" The Jets defensive coaches, whose first instinct on every day but game day was to be adversarial with the Jets offense, received news of this session with satisfaction.

"Oh, he shredded us!" Callahan told me cheerfully after Gruden's visit. "Which is what you want. Rex talks about having skin like an armadillo, not a deer. We took it all to heart." Although Gruden was now a broadcaster, Callahan said his friend still awakened at four every morning to study the game with the same obsessive rigor he'd been known for as a coach. Now it was as though he were putting together a game plan for the whole league. That level of attention to detail, said Callahan, was the best lesson anyone could draw from Gruden. Callahan agreed with Gruden that the Jets calls had to be delivered faster. "There's more communication in football than any other sport," he said. "You have twenty-five to forty seconds to get a play off. And that's on a normal clock, not in hurry-up. It's intense, it's rapid, it's flying ten thousand miles an hour." Callahan was speaking very quickly now. "Watch the backside end! Heads-up for this pressure! What's the sub package? Personnel substitutions! Get him in. Get him out. Up in the coaching box they're relaying the fronts. It's thrilling. A gas. When it flows, it's incredible. When you put together a plan based on all these situations and your players see you've anticipated it all, you can see that giving them confidence. You predicted it, and now they're making it happen. That's pretty cool."

What Tom Moore had said to Sutton interested me, and I sought Moore out and asked how to square a Jets defense full of hybrid players who performed numerous roles cooked up for them by the defensive coaches with all the criticism of Schottenheimer and the offense's apparently similar impulses. Moore had white hair, a craggy face with recessed owl's eyes, and a deep, resonant way of speaking. Moore said he agreed with those coaches who were leery of trying to give a team too many options to draw from, but he pointed out that complexity was relative. Ryan's defensive system had an array of packages, yes, but, he said, "It's all simple to him and he can make it simple to his players, so they can still play fast. You get to the airport faster if you know exactly how to get there. It's the same with blitzing."

Then I looked in on Matt Cavanaugh, the Jets quarterbacks coach. Cavanaugh had been the Ravens offensive coordinator when they won the 2001 Super Bowl. He'd offered to show me how he made the quarterbacks' play-calling wristbands that were, in effect, the set list containing all the calls in a given game plan. Cavanaugh said that to contain the seventy-five plays the offense wanted available, he created three paper panels each containing twenty-five plays, numbered one to seventy-five. The three pages were then shrunk to size, laminated, and attached with a binding flap to the wristband proper. The call would come in from Schottenheimer first with the personnel group—twelve meant one back, two tight ends—and then the play number, say twenty-seven. The quarterback would open the flap, look down at the second play on the second panel, and see Deuce Right, Scat Right, Seahawk, H-Sneak—a pass call. Everything was written to go right, so if Schottenheimer wanted that same play run to the left, he'd say, "Twenty-seven flip it." I found all the words confusing. Cavanaugh told me not to worry. "Half our guys don't know what it means."

Outside the facility walls, football men tended to close ranks and rarely criticized one another unless they took a network analyst's position. In the meeting rooms, between coaches, however, they were merciless. The league to them was a big family, and everybody talked smack about his cousins.

Don "Wink" Martindale, a former Ryan colleague from the University of Cincinnati, came to the facility. He was there to brief the defensive coaches on the AFC Western Division, whose four teams, Denver, Kansas City, San Diego, and Oakland, would all be on the Jets schedule. Martindale had been the Denver defensive coordinator but he'd been let go after the season. Here, half a year later, he talked openly about how upset he remained with his former boss Josh McDaniels, who was thirteen years younger than Martindale and had treated him, Martindale felt, like chattel. That his pride was still tender, Martindale recognized, even as he kept returning (apologetically) to the subject of the wrong he'd been done: "Take a deep breath. It's over!...I appreciate you guys letting me vent. My wife's tired of it, my dog's sick of it." Despite everything, Martindale had made impressive use of his time off from coaching. He'd lost dozens of pounds and radiated good health.

Martindale hadn't watched tape in six months and was eager to do so. Getting down to the crux of things, he told the coaches about players who were better than they knew (like the Denver linebacker Joe Mays) and worse (like Matt Cassel, the Kansas City quarterback, who, Martindale said, "couldn't hit Black Beauty in a field of white mice"). The Chiefs, he thought, weren't yet sold on Cassel, just as he doubted the Jets were completely convinced by Mark Sanchez. Martindale was a good football man, and one of his virtues was his ability to elicit trenchant commentary from other people. The conversation continued in a similar key as the coaches moved around the league, with everyone now contributing. The Bengals aging quarterback Carson Palmer was "a bee who's lost his stinger," while Cowboys quarterback Tony Romo excelled except under "hot" conditions late in close games, when he'd make senseless mistakes. As for the Broncos, Martindale said he was confident Tim Tebow would be the Denver starting quarterback by the time the Jets played at Denver in mid-November.

This was intriguing. In Ryan's opinion, Tebow "might be the greatest player in the history of college football." During Tebow's second year at the University of Florida, he ran and passed for more than fifty touchdowns and became the first sophomore to win the Heisman Trophy, the award for college football's best player. In Tebow's years at Florida, the Gators won two national championships. During a school vacation, Tebow accompanied his father, Bob, an evangelical missionary, on a trip to the Philippines, where they spread the Gospel, and Tebow circumcised little boys. He was perhaps this country's best-loved athlete. But Tebow threw more like an outfielder than a quarterback, and to this point the Broncos had been wary of the unorthodox motion. Martindale said it was true that Tebow couldn't excel if you kept him in the pocket—"He bounces passes off buildings." But, Martindale warned, once Tebow began improvising, something shifted and he became an entirely different player.

How Ryan should schedule his hour-to-hour time in the off-season was a source of uncertainty to him. Ryan was now, in effect, the COO of Jets football, and COOs were distanced big thinkers, not hands-on detail men. But Ryan was a football coach, not a businessman, and back in his office, isolated from the others, Ryan had ambivalent pangs that he had given up what he loved to do all day. In the offensive meeting rooms, where he could offer no particular tactical expertise, Ryan felt like a trespasser on somebody else's land. And with the defense, where the daily subject was the scheme he had developed with Pettine, there was now a similar tinge of being an interloper. You could tell how some days Ryan really missed the room. He'd enter the meeting at noon ready to get everyone to join him for lunch, take a look at what was running on the film screen, and instantly become involved in it, saying, "Rip off the block! Rip off the block and it's a holding call on the tackle!" Giving others your favorite responsibilities, delegating and supervising: these were aspects of being a head coach nobody told you how to handle.

Ryan's solution was to drop in occasionally on the defensive coaches, always bringing something to share. One day it was a photograph of a lithe, muscular Carrier in his old USC uniform, looking like an action hero under massive shoulder, thigh, and arm pads. "You raid Anthony Muñoz's locker, MC?" Pettine wanted to know, referring to the large and ultra-fit former Bengals lineman. Another day Ryan had with him film of a hit DT had once delivered at full speed to the chest of the six-foot-eight Eagles receiver Harold Carmichael. Carmichael had crumpled like a sling-shotted stork. After they all watched it, DT explained that the pass had been tipped, throwing off his timing so that he couldn't stop. With the receiver looming in front of him, the only thing to do was run right through him, and that he did. "What a shot!" said Ryan. "Okay, that's my contribution for the day. I gotta go dig something up on Sutton!" On a morning I found telling, Ryan walked in to announce he'd just been visiting with Sara Hickmann, the team psychologist, and they'd agreed that everyone in this room, "including Nicky," had "issues," and guess whose were the most acute? Pettine's! "Good bet," said Pettine laconically, refusing to be drawn in.

Various senior Jets coaches were using the lockout time to offer master classes on their areas of expertise for their more junior colleagues, and one day Ryan talked defensive line. Slipping back into his old position-coach persona, he spoke with such intensity you could imagine him out on the Chautauqua circuit. There was method to the magnetism. Practicing defensive-line positions, Ryan said, was incredibly tedious, and it was the coach's job to entertain the players so they'd think their lives were more interesting than the clogged over-and-over of doing the same drills practice after practice. Ryan said that he'd been an inventive line coach because he was such a "shitty" player; he'd needed to come up with insights to compensate. Walter Payton once told Ryan, "I run where the two butts are together," and given that Payton was the finest running back Ryan ever saw, Ryan had dedicated himself to prying haunchy blockers apart by teaching defenders to "club" them, "skinny through" them, or just "penetrate, disrupt, wreck shit." The temptation for defensive linemen was to remain standing too high so they could peek at the action and read the play, but such up-standers were doomed; defensive line was a position of leverage and feel, and you had to stay low to the ground. The ideal man for this job, said Ryan, was "a hired killer. A mean motherfucker. The good ones are big, ugly, and the snot's running out of their nose. Banged-up helmet." Ryan talked hand technique and foot technique and then he talked mystery, how some players just had the uncanny ability to deliver a short, powerful blow, and the opponent was suddenly knocked five yards back. As for the great ones, he said, they were so quick you didn't even notice, and they were gone by.

As much as the coaches discussed the game and watched it on film, nothing could make up for the absence from the facility of those who did the actual blocking and tackling. During the lockout, the league forbade the coaches from having any contact with their own players. What was difficult about this for Sutton was how much he missed the players, especially Bart Scott. Sutton would look out at the empty practice fields and think about the sound of the voluble linebacker, who woke up talking and didn't stop through the morning, afternoon, and evening until, presumably, he went unsilent into the night. Scott often began a conversation by saying, "If you want to be great…" Through the lockout, Sutton tried to honor his player by doing something extra to complete the sentence every day. Sutt still came to the facility by 6:00 a.m. at the latest, even on many weekends. Once there, he followed his curiosity through innumerable football studies. He had done all he could in these weeks to improve, and yet, he said, there was ennui: "I'm looking to meet with somebody, talk to anybody, do something!"

All of the coaches missed the players, and all of them missed Scott. An effect of this was that when the coaches watched the players on film, the usual frisson of interaction now had a heightened intensity. As film frames flashed by with Bart Scott eddying off in haphazard directions, vectoring across the field along angles at steep variance with those he was supposed to take, Pettine proposed setting the commentary on a loop: "Where's Bart going?

What's Bart thinking?" Carrier watched Scott deliver a leg whip and said, "God, I love Bart. Dude makes me laugh." To Sutton, Scott's position coach, Scott was challenging because he kept many coaching points in mind and might apply any one at any given moment. However, Sutt said, the offense had no more idea of Scott's intentions than Scott did, and this allowed Scott to make surprising and important plays. Scott knew nothing of eggshells. He was decisive and did everything at high speed, which was what you wanted in a linebacker.

Once in a while the coaches did receive actual word of the players' lockout activities. Kyle Wilson was said to be spending his time working out with Revis—if true, a very pleasing development. And Bart Scott had been observed in a yellow Ferrari flying along doing ninety in a thirty-mile-an-hour zone. This was comforting news only because it was so normal. In his own way, Bart Scott was near.

One day, during film, the new computer guy arrived to give a quick session on some next-generation coaching software. There were always new computer guys, all of them bearing fresh balms of electronic relief for the inefficiencies of the coaching life. The game was ruled by the relationship between what down it was and the distance an offense needed to cover for a first down. Bill Callahan compared these down and distance groupings to the different rooms in a house. Just as a home had a kitchen, a dining room, a living room, and so on, football game plans were organized by self-contained spaces you entered and left in the course of a game. Those "rooms" found in a typical football "house" included the opening minutes; the end of the half; third down; two minutes left in the game (when offensive teams often ran plays on fourth down instead of punting); red zone; four minutes left with the lead; change of possession after a turnover; backed up (inside the offense's ten-yard line); short yardage; goal line. The game plan described what the coaches considered the best options for filling each of these rooms. The computer could help you measure what to expect from the opposition in each situation and also tell you how the opponent's prior success might guide your ability to thwart him. When Callahan watched a football game on television, he didn't take in the ebb and flow of possessions as typical spectators would. He saw the game as an emerging structure built of either sound or unsound responses to all those situations.

People liked to talk about coaching instincts, those who had a feel for the game, and that was fine. But Callahan knew, as did Schottenheimer and Pettine, that the greatest boon to instinct was foreknowledge: the understanding of self considered in relation to the understanding of others. Brilliant calls came from deep study. Computers were crucial because they organized, refined, and analyzed the data, allowing coaches to envision before games what they wanted players to do during them—to see before they saw. Still, these were football coaches, and when in the presence of a new computer guy, they would have been remiss not to mess with him a little.

Before the meeting began, Smitty took the new computer guy aside and warned him, "Whatever you do, don't look Pettine in the eye. It makes him go crazy." Since Pettine was a computer maven, interested in everything he could learn about the machines, the next hour for the new computer guy, by all appearances a man dedicated to his work, involved strenuous forays into the realms of gaze aversion and neck flinchery. The point of the session was to show the coaches that opposing-team play-calling tendencies in any given situation were now organized and, with a cursor click, available to them on video. If, for example, Carrier wanted to know what blocking scheme the Cleveland Browns offensive line was likely to choose on the first play of the half, the computer would sort the situation by play call, from those plays most frequently used by the Browns to begin the half, all the way down to those they'd tried only once. And alongside each play call, there was the blocking scheme the Browns had used with it. Afterward, Pettine wanted to know what was up with that new tech dude. "Did he think I was gonna Medusa him—turn him to stone?"

As the lockout bore steadily into June, its third month, there were more conversations among the coaches than before about matters unrelated to football. Carrier and I were talking about music one day, and when I mentioned Simon and Garfunkel's song "The Sound of Silence," he said he'd never heard of it. "Really?" I asked him. "Everybody's heard that one. You lived in LA in the seventies and eighties. You couldn't have avoided it!" Carrier insisted that no, he had never heard it. Then, like the great attacking safety he'd been, Carrier went after Simon and Garfunkel. "So, Nick, let me ask you something," he said. "Those two guys get along or are they like all those people who have success and end up hating each other?" I was about to tell him that he was on to something when DT walked by. "Hey, DT!" said Carrier. "Have you ever heard of the song 'The Sound of Silence'?" DT looked at Carrier. Then he looked at me. You could see him considering the situation, noting who was doing the asking, who was standing next to that guy, and what it all must mean. Finally, the most intelligent cover corner of his time replied, "No! I might have been *aware* of it, but I never went ahead and *heard* it!"

Another morning Carrier arrived in the film-watching meeting with a parenting story. The previous day after work, he'd attended his thirteen-year-old daughter's youth soccer-league game where she'd received a yellow card for inflicting violence on an opposing player. Hammer accepted chip-off-the-old-block congratulations from the other defensive coaches. Then he was asked how he'd reacted in the moment. Had he said anything vicious to the official? Carrier said he'd just sat there, cuddling his dog Lucky. What kind of dog was Lucky? Weeks wanted to know.

"The kind of little dog Jack Nicholson had in *As Good as It Gets*," Carrier said.

"That's a nice dog!" Weeks said.

Not to Carrier. "Hell no! It barks all the time, shits all over the house. But it's good traveling and at soccer games."

Pettine roused himself: "Why not leave it in the car except for soccer games?"

Even during the lull, these were coaches, and they were always coaching something. When they learned that at a party for toddlers my son had interrupted some singing to run across the room and tackle a little girl dressed up as a ballerina in a pink tutu, the coaches were thrilled and gave me seminars on form-tackling technique to pass along. ("Tell him lower your center of gravity"; "Tell him hit on the rise.") Another morning, I encountered Sutton in the kitchen area between the offensive and defensive sides of the coaching pod. Here there were two coffee options: A fresh pot of Dunkin' Donuts brew was always available, or you could make your own single cup at the fancy Flavia machine, as Sutton was doing. I'd never tried the Flavia. Sutton said that had to change immediately. Then he proceeded to walk me through it. "Okay, Nick," he began. "Get fired up! Proper procedure is everything, Nick. First, you choose your coffee." I selected French roast, described on the packet as "dark and intense." Sutton continued, "That choice secure, Nick? Okay! Good selection. Now you hit that upper left-hand button and open the machine. Now have your packet ready, Nick. Okay, install that packet. Got it in nice and snug? Good, Nick. Good technique, Nick. We're making progress. Now close the window and—this is key—you must lock the empty cup in under the source or the coffee will not come out." We locked it in and an aromatic smell filled the galley. Sutton nodded approvingly. "Nice job. Good work. Enjoy that coffee, Nick."

In an ensuing meeting, Carrier said he had received some money as part of an injury settlement from his playing days. The coaches had much advice on how to handle such wham. What was "wham"? Was this an old George Michael thing? "Come on, Nick!" cried Carrier. WAM stood for "walking-around money." Smitty, who had never been married, told Carrier that under no circumstances should he inform his wife about this windfall. Carrier, who'd been married for sixteen years, shook his head, disagreeing. You tell your wife about everything, was his view. He and his wife wanted each other to have nice things. Pettine, freshly divorced, agreed Carrier should tell his wife, but on more cynical grounds. Pettine saw football wives and girlfriends as an omniscient quilting circle, and if you failed to mention something like playoff shares or injury-settlement money, your name was soon going to be Doghouse Reilly.

It was a hot day outside. The mention of WAM led to a long group summertime daydream of brand-new convertibles, especially brand-new Maserati convertibles. A local car dealer had loaned Ryan a Maserati as a promotion, and the sight of that car out in the facility parking lot had induced much longing in the others. Carrier shook his head at all this. Noting that during the work stoppage coaching salaries had been reduced, he said, "Hell, if there weren't a lockout you'd see a convertible in my parking space right now." Just then Ryan walked in, freshly shorn. "Is it wrong," the head coach asked, "that I'm driving this Maserati around and I go to Supercuts for an eight-dollar haircut?"

Under the current lockout circumstances, with no players on hand and the roster still undefined, there was only so much useful work the coaches could do. When they were given a long weekend, many traveled to see family. Yet even when separated, they maintained frequent contact with one another, sending streams of texts and also photographs of things they deemed unusual. Because the coaches usually lived in the bubble of the facility, these moments could function as explorations in a world that had gone through changes while they were at a remove, busy working. Upon everyone's return after the long weekend, Smitty told a story of walking through the Memphis airport on his way to make a connecting flight when he espied a man with three cell phones on his belt.

Finding this noteworthy, Smitty pulled out his own phone and snapped a photograph, which he planned to send to the other coaches. Whereupon the wife of Mr. Three Phones tapped him on the shoulder from behind and asked what he thought he was doing. Whereupon Smitty walked away. This led Carrier to hold forth on men who took cell-phone photographs of strange men's wives. Some wives were freaked out by the practice, said Carrier, but he personally thought the women should consider it a positive because nobody was taking pictures of unattractive ladies. This was deemed unimpeachable logic.

Smitty had gone home to Texas to sell his old condo there and gain some cash for his fallow bank account. When he got to Lubbock, he learned that his brother had been laid off from his telecommunications job. So Smitty kept the house and told his brother to move in rent-free.

One of the ideas that Tannenbaum had borrowed from the world of business was an off-season team self-improvement day. Each of the upstairs and downstairs football people arranged to spend time shadowing another professional whose activities might broaden his perspective on his own job. In June, for their day, Ryan and Pettine flew down to Charlotte to talk shop with the former Washington Redskins coach Joe Gibbs, and I went with them.

Gibbs had won the Super Bowl three times, including the one that came after the last NFL work stoppage in 1987. In each case he prevailed with a different, modestly talented quarterback. Always, Gibbs said, he wanted to simplify the game for his side while making it appear complicated to the opposition. Thus, like the contemporary Patriots, Gibbs's Redskins tended to run a limited number of plays out of a large range of formations. The red zone, which he called "the red area," was crucial to him, so he created new plays for his best players, taught them at Thursday's practice, reviewed them at Friday's practice, and then reviewed them one more time at the

Saturday walk-through. The new plays had the added benefit of making the players excited; something was being invented just for them. Gibbs's cardinal rules were to avoid red-zone sacks and red-zone turnovers. To accomplish this, Gibbs tended to use extra pass protection near the goal line and told his quarterbacks to throw the ball away if their two initial passing options were covered. In this respect, he said, perhaps the most effective player he ever coached was Mark Rypien. Rypien didn't have the highest IQ and was by no means an extraordinary athlete, but the quarterback absorbed meeting information so well that he was rarely sacked, and he played efficient football. Like Doug Williams and Joe Theismann, the other quarterbacks with whom Gibbs won Super Bowls, Rypien was battle-tested and hardnosed. Gibbs counseled Ryan to do whatever he could to make life easier for his own still modestly experienced quarterback, Sanchez.

How should Ryan interact with the offense he asked Gibbs. Ryan was a defensive guy; he was of the other world. Gibbs said he had always attended special-teams meetings, sitting in the front row to show the players how important this part of the game was to the head coach. As for defense, about which he said he knew roughly as much as Ryan knew about offense, Gibbs met weekly with the defensive staff. "Make what you're not feel important," he urged Ryan.

Back at the facility, when everybody got together and described their self-improvement days, not a few mentioned meetings with seasoned golf coaches. The explanations for the utility of these consultations were of such persuasive invention that it took everyone else a while to realize they'd gone out and taken a golf lesson.

Smitty, in an effort to lose weight, had been bicycling between Pettine's condo and the facility. Getting daily exercise made him an exception among the coaches. Except for Sutt, recovering from knee surgery but otherwise a committed runner, they were all always in danger of weight gain. "Coaching, it puts on the pounds," said O'Neil, looking at his softening middle. That former athletes working in an athletic setting should forgo activity seemed surprising. The older tennis players still competed, after all, as did the golfers. I'd expected perhaps some excellent off-season lunchtime games of touch football. But the coaches looked at me incredulously when I mentioned this. Football to them meant hitting, and without it there was no point. To have put so much into something for so long and then never do it again seemed poignant, but it also seemed like life.

For the public, the long-term effects of head injuries were a pressing concern, a source of much civic debate. Among people I knew, even those who didn't closely follow football, the subject made for frequent impassioned conversations. Was it acceptable to enjoy something that brutalized the minds and bodies of young men? That impoverished kids became young millionaires by giving their bodies over to a game that might cripple them seemed both wonderful and macabre to people. Here there was no such discussion. The subject of concussions never came up except in the context of regulations. The coaches were aware that they were supposed to have an uneasy relationship to hitting, but to them, physical intimidation was not only how you won at football, it was the point. "It's a violent game played by physical people," DT often reminded me. To play the game well, you couldn't be preoccupied with the risks of injury. The same seemed to hold for coaching. You had to be in some form of denial. Dave Duerson, the former Bears defensive back whom Carrier succeeded as Chicago's starting safety, had committed suicide in February, a death that was blamed on trauma-induced brain disease. Carrier himself had incurred several concussions as a player. When I asked Carrier about Duerson, Carrier quietly demurred. At the annual officials' meeting, senior supervisory officiating representatives from the league paid a call on Florham Park to describe (with video) the rule changes for the upcoming season, and all the major changes they presented sought to limit player injury by penalizing big hits. Listening to the officials, the coaches had worried less about concussions than about their rough sport's physical integrity. "They're taking all the fun out of the game," said Devlin, who'd just had surgery on both hips. "I wouldn't play in this day and age." Sutton didn't think much of incremental rule changes either, and neither did DT. To them, legislating acceptable degrees of hitting was mostly a fool's errand; better tackling instruction and better equipment was the more prudent course. But they offered these opinions only because I asked. Safety regulations were, in the end, the province of the league's medical and legal experts—somebody else's job. At the facility, where the staff's responsibility was to prepare a winning football team, even the rules-change meeting felt like a potentially complicating diversion from the mission—complicating perhaps in ways that the coaches just didn't want to address. "That's an hour and ten minutes of my life I'll never get back," DT lamented.

Thinking about the rule-change meeting, I concluded that during this particularly aberrant off-season, there was already an abundance of change for the coaches, and the prospect of more was simply too much for them to take. Already they were losing moments of preparation they considered critical, and it was no solace that it was the same for the other thirty-one teams. Football coaches were people who thrived on custom and routine; who, as Sutton said, felt lost without a schedule. If Pettine told me once that NFL coaches were "creatures of habit," he said it forty times. This point in the year, late spring and early summer, was ordinarily stopwatch season, when NFL teams celebrated the end of the long off-season conditioning programs by hosting mini-camps where they taught and walked through plays, ran them in live practices, reviewed the film, and had meetings. It was at this juncture that you began to know what you had and, more to the point, what you didn't have.

Instead, out on the practice fields the goalposts had been taken down, and there was only a stray blocking sled. Alone out there against the clear summer sky, the sled seemed magnified in a way that brought to mind a famous Nebraska symbol: the solitary plow standing on the prairie as an image of lonely effort and a certain kind of stoicism.

The long green expanse of empty side-by-side practice fields affected the football men. Those gorgeous football prairies were planted with a rich green bluegrass blend, durable, deep-rooted grass strains that could withstand the punishments of heat and heavy cleated feet. They were meticulously well cared for by Blake Hoerr, the Jets' tanned director of fields and grounds, whose horticulture degree had included a subspecialty in turf science. Hoerr barbered the grass with the same care that the late country singer George Jones had treated his hair, getting it trimmed every day. You'd see the coaches looking out at the grass and at the single, large two-hundred-year-old swamp oak that stood in their midst, and their frustration was palpable. They felt taunted by the landscape.

Nobody admired the oak tree more than Mike Devlin, the tight-ends coach. One day when we were outside getting some fresh air, he began talking about it. "I look at that tree every day," he said. "It's almost a perfect tree, isn't it?" I said it certainly was. "Tree of life," he declared. He liked it, he said, when the air smelled of warm grass, because it meant training camp was coming, and soon enough falling leaves, a chill in the air, football games. He then said suddenly that he knew that the defense was critical of the offense for its multiple shifts and motions and personnel groups. "We'll try anything," he explained. "Same theory as the defense. You can't possibly prepare for all of their pressures." You had to try everything, Devlin said, because it was so difficult to win and everything was riding on wins. It all came down to sixteen weeks, and if you didn't win, you might not feed your kids. "That's a lot of pressure, isn't it?" I said. Devlin said he didn't much dwell on how precarious the football life was. Some things you couldn't control.

He'd been with the Jets since 2006, three years before Ryan arrived as head coach. He felt fortunate that Ryan had kept him on. Most first-time head coaches had a list going back years of fellow coaches they wanted to hire. "My whole focus in life is not to lose my mind," Devlin said. "I'm a steady Eddie." Devlin's cell-phone ringtone was his college fight song; he and his family still lived in a home near the old Jets facility on Long Island. In traffic, Devlin said, despite the fact that he regularly traveled the densely packed highways between Long Island and Florham Park, he'd beeped his horn in frustration only once. He couldn't control the traffic pattern, so why get upset about it? He saw crazy things out there—cars jumping the median on the George Washington Bridge—but nobody could tempt him to try such moves. He just watched the flow and tried to understand it. During football games, Devlin said, he might lose his cool—"because I have a hand in it." And after losses, he admitted, the traffic sometimes nearly got to him. There was too much time to think, and in those moments an idle mind was not a healthy mind.

As Devlin talked about anxiety, it was suddenly possible to move beyond the thrum of his voice to the empty, beautifully groomed fields in front of us and imagine the underlying images of all the scenes that had taken place on them, all the many carefully plotted plays from hundreds of bygone practices, a pentimento reflecting the resilient yet invisibly traced presence of the football past. I could see contrail-like patterns covering the field, lines like those in time-lapse photographs of traffic at night—hundreds and hundreds of interesting lines. It was a dynamic void.

Inside the facility, Schottenheimer was also thinking about the anxiety of the halted moment, missing the sounds of practice, the chattered cadences, the trash-talking, the thud of collision, the clamor of coachly correction. "I love and need this," the offensive coordinator said. He said he'd been pondering his inability to have a life outside football. The defensive coaches, he'd noticed, were better at getting everything done and leaving the building in the evening. One reason Schotty couldn't limit himself, he said, was that he felt so acutely the uncertainty of his world. He lived to soothe the low tremor of perpetual anxiety that says, I can do better, that says, I can do more, that says, I love doing this and they might let me go. As Schotty admitted, "It's the what-have-you-done-for-me-lately of this that excites me."

The present lockout anxiety supplanted the normal anxiety for the coaches, a problem that was winningly expressed by the Jets young college-scouting coordinator Dan Zbojovsky: "This uncertainty is different from the usual uncertainty because it's outside the uncertain framework of what we do."

Later Sutton and I discussed that same topic, that all coaches want security but they're also so inured to the volatility of their world that they—or Sutton, anyway— scarcely noticed that there was anything volatile about it until they were forcibly becalmed, as they were now. Sutton and his wife, Debbie, had just been to the doctor for their annual medical checkups. Debbie proved to have high blood pressure and now had to watch what she ate. Sutton had no health constraints, which he said made his wife a little irritated. "You have the stressful job and you're the one who gets to eat sweets," she'd said, to which Sutt replied that he didn't think the job was stressful. Demanding, maybe, but not stressful.

Six

THE GAME FACE IS ON

You're awake for them even while they sleep.

—*Kenneth Koch, "To Breath"*

Not too long ago, football players and coaches took seasonal jobs in the late winter, spring, and early summer. Matt Cavanaugh worked for a Pittsburgh bank. A-Lynn, the running-backs coach, helped the City of Denver find ways for city bus drivers, who sit all day, to avoid potbellies and back conditions. Then, as football became a year-round occupation, with mini-camps and organized team activities filling the once-idle months, the period from late June through the first part of July became vacation time for NFL coaches. The duration varied from team to team. Some coaches gave their staffs as little as two summer weeks off. Ryan, however, believed that the members of his workforce would do better during the 120-hour weeks of training camp and the season to follow if they were rested and refreshed, so he sent everyone away for a June and July leave that lasted close to five weeks.

In normal years, Ryan rented an enormous beach house on a portion of the Outer Banks of North Carolina that was accessible only if one drove for miles along the sand at low tide. He extended an open invitation to the other Jets coaches and their families to come for a stay, play games like corn-hole toss and washers—a version of horseshoes—take the sun, drink beer, talk football.

Coaches Ryan knew from other points in his life, like Wink Martindale and Sam Pittman, were also welcome. Ryan paid for everything. All he asked was that each family choose one night to prepare dinner for everyone.

Ryan enjoyed traveling, preferably in groups. For years he had been talking with other coaches about visiting Spain to join in the traditional running of the bulls through the city streets of Pamplona. The coach loved bulls. This year, though, the lockout had thrown all such planning asunder. As soon as the collective-bargaining agreement was resolved, the signing of the free agents would begin, so there was no way to commit to a lease. Instead, Ryan headed off to suitably tranquil European locales with his Oklahoma in-laws. He would recover afterward, he joked, in Hawaii.

Smitty was gone to Texas. His father, a hard-liver, had suffered a stroke, after which the father's girlfriend had announced, "I ain't lookin' after you," so Smitty was handling things. Smitty's father did not like to be handled. "This is the hardest thing in my life" was the sort of communication coming out of Lubbock.

Devlin was mostly spending time off the highways and with his family on Long Island, but he did travel to Pennsylvania to give a free football camp for kids who lived in a part of coal country where there was no more coal. He also received league dispensation to attend Jets tight end Dustin Keller's wedding. In the church, a referee's whistle blew and down the aisle trotted Keller's Rottweiler puppy, Achilles, a small box in his mouth. It took Devlin a moment to realize that Achilles was the ring bearer. "Could have gone either way whether the dog would eat the ring" was Dev's recap.

Defensive lineman Mike DeVito got married the year before and had planned to go on a honeymoon this summer, but the coaches had heard he'd backed out because of the lockout. DeVito told his wife they'd enjoyed a lot of quality time together and in these uncertain months, he needed to train. This all sounded like DeVito. Although DeVito was now an established pro, he'd come into the league as an undrafted free agent from the University of

Maine, and in spirit that was what he remained, such a conscientious, worried player that he regularly consulted with DT in case the defensive-backs coach had happened to notice anything about DeVito's interior-line play that DeVito could improve. When the players received grade sheets for their practice reps, nobody took a minus harder than DeVito.

Players like DeVito and Ryan's old Ravens nose tackle Kelly Gregg, another formidable lineman likewise driven by insecurity, were the true "program players" because they were quietly better than solid at what they did, and they were affordable. In the NFL, successful franchises paid good players less than their worth to subsidize the team's best players. If you had enough A and B players making C money, you won.

Pettine had an assortment of vacation plans, including taking the children on a trip to Florida. He was also going to a Phillies game at home in Pennsylvania, and he invited me along. We met up at his parents' house on a quiet road in Doylestown, where his family subjected him to some family. "Michael rarely smiles," his mother, Joyce, said, looking up from her puzzle. Pettine's daughter, Megan, visiting her grandparents from Maryland, chimed in from the couch, teasing her father about being "a dark guy." Then Senior cleared his throat from out in the kitchen. Senior had the sort of voice that naturally carried across practice fields and it did not adjust for the interior life. "You know, I was only a high-school coach," he said, "but I watch these NFL guys and it makes you wonder." Pettine said we had to go or we'd hit the rush-hour traffic.

On the way to the game, we hoped to stop for Philly cheesesteaks at Tony Luke's South Philly emporium, not far from the ballpark, but the shop proved difficult to find. I suggested rolling down the window and consulting a passerby. "We don't ask for directions," said Pettine.

Despite the fact that he worked in professional sports, Pettine retained his strong affection for the Phillies, followed them closely, and like many otherwise somewhat-closed men, was open and emotional on the subject of his favorite team. I thought it was interesting that Pettine could remain such a big fan while also working in the business. He said, "Outside of our sport, it doesn't change. As a Phillies fan, for me it still goes back to childhood."

He thought that baseball was a simpler game, much more by the book. Even the most educated football fan could really hope to follow only the back-and-forth of possessions. What they couldn't see, and what baseball didn't have, were the multifarious strategic options confronting football teams on every play. Pettine told of how the Jets defensive coaches had decided in the 2010 playoff game against the Patriots to lure the Patriots into running, allowing New England a reasonably effective series of runs that distracted the Patriots from what they did best: pass. To a fan, Pettine said, it looked like the Jets were porous against the run that day. But that was intentional, what won them the game. The other strikingly effective strategic innovation in the game had been to present Tom Brady with much more zone coverage than he was accustomed to seeing from the Jets pass defense — usually a man-to-man operation. "In football," Pettine said, "only afterward will people figure out what we were doing, and that's if it worked."

The baseball game began, and soon the Phillies were winning. Between innings, we pondered the mystery of how the 2009 Jets, without Cromartie, had given up only eight passing touchdowns, while the 2010 Jets, with a second world-class corner now paired with Revis, gave up triple that number, twenty-four. Was it possible that Cromartie, so accustomed to being a number-one corner, found it disconcerting not to be the main guy? Had paired man-cover corners made the Jets coverages too predictable? Or was the root of it a less potent pass rush? The difficulty with football problems was that there were often so many potential explanations that causal clarity slipped behind passing clouds of irrelevance and caprice.

The hour was very late by the time we got back to Doylestown and so I went to bed in a guest room. A little after eight the next morning, drumbeats sounded on my door and a ringing voice wanted to know, "You gonna sleep all day?" It was Senior. I was on the road in no time.

Back in Florham Park in July after his own vacation, Tannenbaum scrunched his heavy brows and narrowed his dark eyes into an expression that brought to mind French bulldogs. The GM craved work, wanted to have at problems. That the lockout might end any day was the rumor, and his desk was covered with preparation for that moment. "The game face is on!" he cried. Several Jets, including safety Eric Smith, Cromartie, offensive lineman Wayne Hunter, receivers Braylon Edwards and Santonio Holmes, and the running quarterback and special-teams star Brad Smith, were free agents, and the Jets had to be prepared for the likely event that some of them might join other teams. Tannenbaum was running roster scenarios. One of them involved signing the Raiders star free-agent cornerback Nnamdi Asomugha, the best player at the position in the game except Revis.

Downstairs, Sutton worried about limitation, how much material would be too much to expect the players to learn now that they'd missed both their off-season organized team activities and mini-camp. And heaven help the rookies. "We've got the water," Sutton said. "But the cup's only so big."

Thinking of the young players, O'Neil was reviewing film, finding examples of model defensive backfield play so as to create a "teach-tape." It was a repetitious endeavor. "That's really good by Revis," he said, marking the play with a click of his mouse. And then: "That's great technique by Revis." Click. And: "Look at Revis break the hypotenuse." Click. "Look at Revis!" Click.

Later, in the meeting room, the defensive coaches watched tape of all the free agents available around the league at positions the Jets might need players. One criterion they were evaluating, per Sutton, was whether the man's play suggested he had sufficient football intelligence for him to learn the Jets system by September.

It was now mid-July; Smitty was still in the Southwest tending to his father, and the coaches, missing him, told Smitty stories. They reveled in a new meteorological explanation he'd recently given for his badly parked car. Discounting the strong-winds theory, Smitty now posited that because it had rained while his car was parked that day, and the temperatures had then plummeted, the car had "probably slipped." Or, Smitty said, maybe the water hadn't quite frozen, in which case the car likely had "stationary hydroplaned." Smitty's colleagues noted that Smitty's real thirtieth birthday was coming up soon. All of it led Sutton to say, "Mike is short in only two areas: math and logic."

As for Ryan, also back from vacation, on his right calf there was now a large green tattoo, a Hawaiian tribal marking that Ryan said meant "believe in yourself." Ryan had picked up the new stamp on vacation to show his Hawaiian tackle, Wayne Hunter, how much he wanted him back.

By late July, details of the proposed new collective-bargaining agreement were making their way across the facility transom. One of those proposed changes would limit teams to a single training-camp practice a day instead of the dreaded two-a-days that had been a camp staple for generations. (This did come to pass, as did strict regulations for the number of padded workouts allowed during the seventeen-week season—fourteen—as well as restrictions on how long the players could be on the practice field.) The prospect of less practice time made the coaches very concerned. Football was the only professional sport in which teams practiced more days than they played. Practice was the essence of football, where a team learned and perfected all those plays, where a team became a team. How effectively an NFL team practiced during the week was a reliable indication of how well it would play on Sunday. Carrier and Sutton blamed the necessity for the changes on coaches who'd known no moderation about practice, had overworked their players in the summer and fall so they'd collapsed in December. Now that was going to be a thing of the past.

Over in his office, which, like every coach's office, had no windows facing the outdoors, A-Lynn said the lockout and the new rules all suggested how much more serious a business football had become. When A-Lynn came into the league, as a player in 1993, there were more nicknames, more characters, more pranks. Even the star players on his team, the Broncos, didn't take themselves too seriously. Linebacker Simon Fletcher might well be smoking a cigarette on the field just before practice. During the stretching that began practice, tight end Shannon Sharpe told nonstop funny stories, "so you couldn't stretch, you were laughing so much. Didn't matter, he made you loose with his jokes." The big money, A-Lynn said, had homogenized the game, making it riskier to take risks and more difficult to relax. "You play better when you're relaxed," he said. This also held, he said, for coaches. Looking around his office, he said, "I want a window, baby. I'd feel a little more alive. You can be here eighteen hours and never see the sun." He said that whenever he left the facility, he had to adjust to the "regular world," where different behavior was in order, where his wife sometimes had to tell him, "I'm not one of your players."

Another way football was different now had to do with how sophisticated pass-defense techniques had become. In the defensive meeting room DT gave a master class on defensive backfield play, and a large crowd of coaches and front-office people turned out for him. It had taken a lot of convincing to get DT to address the masses. Standing at the front of the room, DT began with reference to his own playing days. He said he'd never looked at a receiver below the waist or above the chest, and as he ran, he shifted his eyes from quarterback to receiver and back every two steps. What made Revis so good, DT said, was patience. Revis prepared so carefully and then played with such deep concentration that he never panicked;

he could endure the pressure of something being primed to happen that had not yet happened, could exist in an inconclusive state until the man finally committed to his route. Think, DT said, of a baseball hitter who waited on the approaching pitch because he trusted his good hand mechanics to protect him.

DT was putting so much effort into his presentation that there was sweat glistening atop his shaved head, and with that and his muscular torso, he began to resemble an aging middleweight prizefighter. He described a series of eight "help concepts" that defensive backs could call on to avert crises. This included limbo, a technique used by the defensive backs to declare who had whom when two receivers crossed paths in close proximity. For closely paired receivers who cut in the same direction and might afterward stay short or go long, you could sort responsibilities on the fly by calling out for the triangle technique, a distribution prearranged for the nickel, corner, and safety. Triangle was tricky for Revis, whose instinct was never to accept help—he preferred to latch on to his man and never let him go. When he finished talking, DT received an orator's applause.

Later, in his office, DT said that the simpler the passing attack, the more complicated the defense's array of coverages had to be in response; otherwise, a quarterback would simply take what the coverage gave him—as Tom Moore had described Peyton Manning doing. Tom Brady followed the same approach. The Patriots offense was a gyre of surprising actions on television and was also that for defenses, yet to Brady, all the elements of the Patriots offensive scheme were rudimentary. The New England coaches were switching out ends and receivers and backs, making the offense appear different, but from play to play they used identical route combinations out of the different personnel alignments. All this made life easy for the quarterback, who, of course, knew what everyone's role was, and hell for a defense. That's why the defense needed to counterconfuse with those techniques DT had just described. Of the eight advanced-coverage concepts he'd discussed, DT said, he'd been aware of none in college. Carrier hadn't either. This was

cutting-edge, postdoc NFL stuff. And even in pro ball, not everyone believed in them. Al Davis, the very involved Oakland team
owner, would never allow his defensive backs to use the radar concept, which involved moving the safety away from the middle of the
field, where, Davis imagined, the safety's speed could always save
the day. DT thought Davis overvalued speed and pure athleticism
in football players, probably because he'd never had either himself.
Then DT shook his head and said, "Nick, all this and unless you
win, nobody gives a shit." After two near misses in the past two
years, if the Jets didn't win this year, DT said, then everybody would
be over them. Things happened that fast in the NFL.

On July 25, the defensive coaches walked down the hall to watch
film together, and just as they settled in, Smitty returned, entering
the room in new black cowboy boots to applause. Instantly apprised
of the tenor of the conversations involving him that had taken
place in his absence, Smitty reaffirmed all previous denials of cul-
pability in the parking-space saga. He did, however, submit yet
another fresh theory. He'd left his SUV parked there for several
days with the keys inside, so perhaps somebody else had "moved it
on me." Later, discussing golf, Smitty made everyone smile by
describing a particular hole of personal scorecard doom as "my
nemis." Spoken with a West Texas accent, this sounded like "my
nimis." Smitty could tell how much pleasure his shaggy-dog misad-
ventures and malapropisms brought the others, and he was good-
natured enough not to begrudge them that. He was who he was,
and made no pretenses otherwise — the quality players always said
they most responded to in a coach. As Wayne Hunter would tell me,
"Mike Smith is so genuine."

One afternoon at lunch, a couple of people whom I didn't know
well were discussing the Patriots, the one NFL team whose window

of winning opportunity seemed wedged forever open. Life around the New England facility was described in contrast to life at Florham Park as a pure football culture, where casual conversation was rare, and where everyone walked tensed through the hallways, wary of being chewed out for some perceived deviation from the mission. (As a result, Patriots games were beautiful business-school case studies of how to win at football.) In the NFL, victories on the field dictated the righteousness of the Patriots' approach, but of course Bill Belichick, a defensive specialist in an era of parity and passing, owed some significant measure of his success to good fortune. Back in 2000, Belichick, like everyone else, had had no idea how good a quarterback Tom Brady was. In a compensatory sixth-round draft choice, the coach had found his offensive double: a player of lethal brains, talent, and ambition, a supremely prepared athlete who strode the facility hallways in the same frame of mind as the head coach. In 2001, because of an injury to Drew Bledsoe, Belichick was forced to play Brady, and when Brady began winning NFL games by the dozen, a magnificent defensive coach became a magnificent head coach.

It was a restive time, everybody working but not doing the usual work, everybody ready for the resumption of the usual, preparing for the usual, while the usual remained elusive. When the defensive coaches watched film of free-agent defensive backs, it reminded them—as if they needed more reminding!—that it was approaching August and they still didn't know who their safeties or their starting cornerback opposite Revis would be. Evaluating yet again the free-agent candidates for these jobs, the defensive coaches were like skilled carpet traders at the souk: in every player, they could identify some kind of striking deficiency. Among the flaws they named were low self-confidence, overreliance on painkillers, poor technique, "not a trained killer," "has some Bob Sanders in him," "a pit boss," and "lousy teammate." A non–trained killer was a reluctant tackler.

Having the Sanders gene meant that, like the former Colts star safety, a man played so hard and so recklessly he was going to get hurt every year. A pit boss was too much of a gambler, took too many chances on the field. What did it mean to be a good teammate? Pettine had examples at the ready. After a touchdown was scored against the defense, the usual procedure was for the position coach to gather his defensive players on the sideline and make a correction. Then the coordinator might add something. But during one Ravens game when the safety was beaten for a score, the head coach Brian Billick, whose expertise was on the offensive side, interceded with the defensive backs. Seeing this, the cornerback Samari Rolle told his head coach, "Get out of here! You come talk to us after we give up a TD? Either talk to us all along or just stay out of it." A good teammate also covered for the mistakes of others. When various Ed Reed improvisations led to big plays by the opposition that seemed to be Rolle's fault because he was the only person left in the area that the safety, Reed, had vacated, Rolle accepted the public blame, never sold out Reed. And after Wes Welker took it upon himself to hit the Ravens defensive back Corey Ivy late from the blind side, it was Rolle who saw the cheap shot and on the next running play hunted down Welker and delivered a blow to his mouth. Pettine and Ryan had film of all these moments and were always finding reasons to show them to their players and to watch them again themselves, as if to reinforce their own standards.

The lockout made for months of frustration, but I never got the sense that people thought it was any more damaging to the Jets than to other NFL teams. There was confidence among the coaches that they were making the best of a trying situation, and during the lockout, optimism about the coming season pervaded. The optimism around me was so staunch that, after six months with the Jets, I myself was at a point where I could imagine only success for the team. This despite the Jets franchise's long, dreary record of failures, despite the fact that the team lacked a proven player at the game's difference-making position—quarterback. Optimistic was the way you were supposed to feel within a football team. Confidence was crucial to winning, and the long off-season spent walled off from your opponents was designed to create the necessary air of your team's invulnerability. As the weeks passed, it was easy to imagine the Jets doing well. What grew difficult to picture was the lockout ever ending.

And then, in late July, it did. The long holding pattern, the daily uncertainty, the thwarting anxiety, the reduced paychecks—abruptly, all that was gone. It was as if snow that for months had obscured everything in a white cover of silence had melted overnight to reveal the bright-size life of the world. Once the lockout was over, all memory of its inhibiting inconvenience slipped forever out of the minds of the organization. Industrious as everyone around the facility had seemed during the lockout weeks, they had merely been burning off secondary energy, enduring a longueur, making a tolerable new life while pining for the old one. Now they were rejuvenated by just the promise of seeing the players again. "I can't wait to get with my guys," said Pettine, speaking for everyone. Callahan was equally excited. "You do realize what you'll be dealing with?" he asked me. "These are rare cats. Freakish athletes. I had a guy in Oakland, Mo Collins. He'd hit you on the back and it was like an anvil was in his hand. Boom! My wife would see me, and she'd say, 'What happened?,' and I'd say, 'Oh, Mo Collins saying hello.'"

PART II

During

Seven

TRAINING CAMP

What is difficult becomes habitual, what is habitual
becomes easy, what is easy is beautiful.

—*Constantin Stanislavski,* Stanislavski on Opera

Early in the afternoon of July 25, Tannenbaum was preparing
for the undrafted-free-agent free-for-all. He drew up a seating
chart for the long draft-room table and installed phone extensions
at each spot. Laminated lists of the Jets' targeted players and their
agents' telephone numbers were supplied to those who'd be doing
the calling—Jets coaches and a few front-office people. Some
teams were rumored to have been talking with players throughout
the lockout, but not the Jets. The league had forbidden contact
with any undrafted player until precisely 6:00 p.m. on July 25, and
Tannenbaum had been a terrier about compliance.

Sanchez's and Revis's salaries alone cost nearly a quarter of the
Jets' salary-cap-enforced budget. So to complete his roster, Tannenbaum, like all NFL general managers, had to rely on cheap,
undrafted free-agent rookies, who made the NFL minimum of
$375,000—the late bloomers, small-school stars, and undercele-
brated members of high-profile college-football programs. Out
there, if you could find him, was a player who might turn out to be a
Fred Jackson, who'd risen from being undrafted out of Iowa's Coe
College to his current status as featured running back with the

Bills. Or even a Jim Langer, an undrafted linebacker from South Dakota State who signed with the Dolphins in 1970 and was gradually transformed into a Hall of Fame center. Every winter, undrafted free agents were named to the Pro Bowl, fanfares set in counterpoint to the springtime march of the first-round debutantes at Radio City Music Hall.

The undrafted free agents were of particular concern to Ryan. That he'd gone to Southwestern Oklahoma State and spent his early coaching career at those way-upriver football logging camps in Kentucky and New Mexico and had worked as somebody else's assistant for twenty-five years before he became an NFL head coach had made Ryan feel like an undrafted free agent himself. It was no accident that when he took the Jets job, he'd brought the undrafted Bart Scott and Jim Leonhard along with him as his "flag-bearers."

So it was that at 5:59, Ryan's eyes fixed on the digital clock on the wall, his finger hovering above a landline keypad, the first eight numerals of Nick Bellore's telephone number already dialed. The small, slow-seeming linebacker whose unusual aptitude for the game had made him a prolific college tackler—a poor man's David Harris—had unique value to the Jets. He was reparation. If Ryan got Bellore, his drafting of Scotty McKnight wouldn't functionally have cost the team anything.

All around Ryan, the other coaches were similarly on their keypad marks. The hour turned and everybody was talking at once. "You're my guy," Ryan told Bellore. The Jets hadn't drafted him, he said, because "you're not the quarterback's best friend!" Ryan inquired as to what jersey number Bellore might prefer. Soon Sutton, who'd attended Eastern Michigan and coached at Western Michigan, was greeting the Central Michigan linebacker. "Nick! Long time." Down-table, Pettine told Bellore's agent, "If the kid can hear thunder and see lightning, he's gonna make the team."

Meanwhile, DT was talking with Julian Posey, the Ohio University cornerback. Ryan took the phone from DT midstream and introduced himself to Posey: "Do you know who we drafted? We took a receiver from Colorado. He's the childhood best friend of our quarterback. My quarterback wanted him, I said, 'Okay!' We do the right thing by our players." Every player Ryan spoke with, he told about Scotty McKnight. The players, he knew, had all heard about the cruel, impersonal NFL. Here was proof that in Florham Park, things weren't that way. In bringing up McKnight, Ryan also seemed to be talking to those assembled around him, telling them *semel in anno licet insanire*—once a year a man was allowed to go a little crazy.

The scene itself was manic. The players bargained for time to sort out their offers, while the Jets, and every other team, tried to get them to commit. From the players' perspective, it was deluge after a drought. Posey asked for thirty minutes "to think about it." DT gave him twelve. To Jeff Tarpinian out in Iowa, Pettine was retailing the hybrid linebacking roles available to a smart linebacker in the Jets defense. Tannenbaum was giving "my word" to somebody's agent. Five coaches were working on Posey. Excelling on special teams was the typical way for a player to make an NFL roster, and Ryan wanted Tarpinian to know "Westhoff's crazy about you!" Then Ryan explained that the Jets had no depth at inside linebacker; unlike all those other coaches, Ryan didn't just want Tarpinian, he needed him. DT was on the phone again with Posey, who was agonizing. "Dude," DT said. "I can't keep calling you back. Trust your gut. Your gut is telling you to say, Yeah!" DT listened. He frowned. He fingered the large cross around his neck. Then he said, "You put the phone down for twenty seconds and then pick the phone up and tell me what God said." Pettine looked at me. "Feel like you're on the floor of the stock exchange? Sell! Sell! Sell!"

On it went. Ryan was asking Tarpinian's agent why the player was hesitating. Courtney Smith, a South Alabama receiver who'd visited the team in April, quietly signed on. Tannenbaum assured Bellore's agent that the linebacker would be coached and developed with care. Then Tannenbaum was smiling. "Great news!" he said. Hanging up, he told the others, "Got him! That was the big one." It was 6:41.

In the midst of all this, Jim Leonhard happened to call Jim O'Neil, his assistant coach. "Hey, Jim," O'Neil greeted him. "We're in the draft room trying to sign some Jim Leonhards!" Ryan asked DT about Posey, who turned out to be yet again on the clock. "He's got until seven," DT said. Ryan consulted his contacts sheet and dialed the number. "Posey," he said. "This is God!" But Posey remained agnostic. Tannenbaum status-reported that Tarpinian was "fifty-fifty between us and New England."

Ryan and Tannenbaum ordered in huge victory steaks for their supper to celebrate the signing of Bellore. Posey was proving a slippery commodity. It was as though he understood that as long as he held out, he maintained some control in his life, but once he committed, he'd again be just another face in the football crowd. At 7:00 and one second, Posey told DT he wanted to sleep on it. Ryan again took over and made a long and impassioned case for the way the Jets defense suited Posey's style of play. The head coach didn't, however, offer more bonus money, because the Jets had a hard ceiling of seven thousand dollars per player. Ryan listened to Posey and then he said, "Yeah, well, nobody else drafted you either." Posey conceded that was true, but other teams had been calling him right through the winter, pledging their interest. Where had the Jets been? Tarpinian had said the same. Ryan explained that the Jets had held back because those were the rules. Rules, said Posey, hadn't stopped other teams. "Well, how do you like those ethics?" Ryan asked Posey. Then Ryan began telling the cornerback about his future position coach. Did Posey realize that DT had taught the great Ronnie Lott how to play? That Troy Polamalu had gone to USC because of DT? And where else could Posey watch and learn from Darrelle Revis at practice every day? Posey said his mother was calling on the other line. "This guy!" DT exclaimed. "DT's had to work harder to get Posey than he did to get Polamalu for USC!" O'Neil chortled. Ryan couldn't resist: "That's because he has less money to offer!"

A few minutes later, Posey called back. His gut was leaning

toward the Chicago Bears. "That's a safety-oriented cover-two defense," DT said. "Corners get lost in that defense. I can hear it in your voice where you really want to go." Posey was no lock even to make the Jets practice squad, and Ryan had never seen him play, but there had been nothing resembling real competition for him for months, and Posey was the present grail. Unable to reach Posey's agent, Ryan was talking with the agent's assistant. "He belongs here!" And then, indignant, "What do you mean, five corners? We only got three!" A moment later, multitasking, Ryan left Tarpinian a message telling him that the Patriots were already "four deep" at his position and that he'd be buried on the New England depth chart. Soon Ryan was dialing up the assistants to assistants. Sutton said it was a good thing Ryan wasn't a college coach. He was so competitive that once he got up a head of recruiting steam, there was no telling what regulations he might inadvertently trample.

Tarpinian chose New England. Brian Ferentz, son of his Iowa college coach Kirk Ferentz, was on the Patriots staff. "We'll knock him on his ass!" Ryan vowed. "How quickly it turns!" cried O'Neil. Tarpinian called Ryan to thank him. Ryan wished him luck and then warned Tarpinian he'd better "strap it up" when he played the Jets. At 8:40, Ryan got off the phone with Posey's agent—"We're still in, I think."

A team typically takes ninety players to training camp. Only fifty-three will make the active roster. So the Jets were also trawling for what were known as camp bodies. "I got a guy from Villanova who will kill people as long as they don't go to the left or right of him," one personnel guy offered. Ryan pulled out a telephone number. He knew and liked the coach at Monmouth, a local college. The Monmouth coach had put in a word for his center, whose name was Tom. Ryan wasn't sure of Tom's last name (it was Ottaiano) so taking it to the zenith as always, Ryan referred to him as "Langer." When Ryan reached "Langer" the head coach told him that each year, he claimed one draft choice and one undrafted choice, and this year Langer was his undrafted guy. "You ain't gonna beat out Nick Mangold," Ryan told the player amiably. "But go out and buy a Jets hat and talk shit and don't be nervous."

At midnight DT called Posey to wish him good night. Revis also telephoned out to Ohio with some honeyed words, and so it was that at 8:19 the next morning, despite his agent's worries that the Bears would never want to work with him again, Julian Posey became a Jet. "What we just did was we got ourselves a couple of draft choices!" Pettine whooped. Watching DT accept congratulations for his recruiting work brought back memories for Carrier. He began telling everyone the story of how Dennis Thurman, USC class of '78, had convinced him to renege on Notre Dame and go to USC. "You know," said Carrier, "I never beat Notre Dame." Everybody was now calling Ryan "Goose," after the former New York Yankees relief ace Rich "Goose" Gossage. Hell, he's Mariano Rivera, said Terry Bradway, invoking the finest closer of them all. The Jets had just signed three players they had thought about drafting.

All day, as these signings were being completed, the under-contract Jets players were drifting into the facility, and the building filled with back-to-school high spirits: in the corridors and offices, there were many shout-outs, many man hugs. The players wore casual clothes—work clothes, exercise clothes. Some of them made a great deal of money, lived in luxury homes, and drove designer cars, but inside the facility, there wasn't much evidence of anybody's wealth. The veteran who carried a Louis Vuitton satchel to meetings was the exception. Most players had student backpacks. Revis's was a subdued plaid. Everybody blended.

DT's TV was tuned to a soap opera for the strife he required, but he was paying more attention to the hallway, where "it sounds like it's supposed to sound—guys making noise!" He and the other coaches scanned the faces of the players, looking for signs at the chin or flank that might indicate somebody had been relaxing and drinking a lot of beer. Most of the Jets appeared to have come through the interregnum lean and fit.

Dwight Lowery, the moody defensive back known as D-Lo, looked into Pettine's office. Smiling, D-Lo said that he was now married and that love had changed the air for him. "My head is good! It wasn't always right last year." In a mellow state of mind was the longest-tenured Jet, Bryan Thomas. "I missed y'all," BT told Pettine and Smitty. "My old lady was getting sick of me."

The All-Pro center Nick Mangold, an alp of a man with a woolly blond beard and long blond locks, generally regarded the world with detached bemusement. But today, even Mangold was excited. When he saw Pettine he stretched out his enormous arms, cried, "My favorite mean guy!" and enveloped him.

Pettine, meanwhile, was beginning to contact the NFL free agents the Jets might be interested in. His first call went to Antwan Barnes. As a boy in Miami, Pettine said, Barnes had been so poor that he'd sometimes gone searching for meals in garbage dumpsters. Pettine had a lot of affection for him, which he now expressed by asking, "Hey, Barnesy, does your agent know who you are?" Many unsigned defensive players were calling Pettine and Ryan, promising they'd take less money to come to New York, proclaiming how fit they were. "I look like a superhero!" promised Trevor Pryce, once a dominant lineman but now five years on the "wrong side of thirty," as the coaches would say. Kelly Gregg, just released by the Ravens, told Pettine, "I'll wash the jocks, I'll play for the minimum and beat up all day on that long-haired center of yours."

Later, stopping back in Pettine's office, I discovered Mark Sanchez, the starting quarterback, sprawled across a chair, bantering with Pettine. It was like Sanchez to visit the defensive coordinator and try to soften him up. An NFL training camp is long weeks of rivalry between offense and defense; for the next month of practices, Pettine would be trying to raze Sanchez's hopes. Pettine seemed mildly disarmed. With his dark curly hair, sloe eyes, beauty marks, and pouty mouth, Sanchez could have been one of the soap stars on the TV down the hall in DT's office. Being that good-looking, Sanchez was initially a startling presence in any room he walked into, but then he settled everyone down with his good nature. He was a carefree Californian who called most people "dude" and saw the world optimistically: there was little in life that wasn't "sweet!" or "sick!"

These qualities had been in evidence when a Jets contingent that included Tannenbaum and Ryan went out to meet him in Los Angeles before the 2009 draft. On that day, Sanchez threw for them with prototypical passer's form. His classic, tightly spinning balls stuck in receivers' hands like broadheads in a tree. There was, the Jets people noticed, a much larger crowd of local receivers volunteering their time for Sanchez than was usual at such workouts. People liked him. The Jets took Sanchez to dinner at a Mexican restaurant in Los Angeles, and then afterward, as they walked through the parking lot, Sanchez said good-bye and hopped onto a motorcycle. The faces in the Jets group froze. "Kidding!" Sanchez cried, and he climbed off and walked on to his car.

Sanchez's father, Nick, an Orange County Fire Department captain, sought to bring up Sanchez as a poised all-American. Nick devised simultaneous intellectual and sporting challenges, quizzing Sanchez about math, chemistry, or American history at the same time that Sanchez was hitting baseballs or throwing footballs. During batting practice, to develop his son's toughness, Nick would pelt him with fastballs and make him shake each one off and keep hitting. Sanchez had taken up football late for a quarterback, in junior high school, and while he was a gifted, dedicated athlete, he had played only three years at USC, just one as a starter. Nick urged him to remain enrolled for his final college season. Sanchez's college coach, Pete Carroll, advised the same.

As it happened, most people in the 2009 Jets draft room were with Nick Sanchez and Pete Carroll. Those Jets evaluators preferred Kansas State's taller, more experienced Josh Freeman (now with Tampa Bay) and, in any case, disliked the idea of trading the strongbox of players and draft choices required to move up high enough in the draft to secure Sanchez. Making such a trade also meant a substantial long-term organizational commitment to an unproven man. The playful charm that drew other young athletes to Sanchez didn't necessarily mean he'd be a commanding leader capable of holding grown men accountable. The one quality his USC teammates hadn't admired in Sanchez was that during games, they could always tell just by looking at him if things were going against the quarterback. NFL players wouldn't respect such pique. On a football field, Tom Brady and Peyton Manning were hard people. Each was absolutely dedicated to football and emanated the composure necessary to make the right choices under stress.

As a college player, Sanchez had of course also not yet proven his aptitude for panning the line of scrimmage and decoding the sophisticated intentions of a modern NFL defense. And after the snap, he rarely looked off defenders, meaning his intentions were too often apparent.

Ryan believed that you lost football games most quickly at two positions, quarterback and cornerback—especially at quarterback. Upon taking the Jets job, Ryan had no viable starting quarterback, and to his eyes, Sanchez was the best one available. Tannenbaum agreed. After the Jets dealt three players and two draft choices to the Browns in exchange for the fifth choice in the draft, Sanchez arrived in New Jersey to sign the most lucrative contract in franchise history. Looking up from the document, Sanchez said to Tannenbaum, "Wonder what my dad thinks now!" Tannenbaum considered that a promising moment.

The Jets quickly made Sanchez their starter, and in his first two seasons he led them to the AFC championship game—or perhaps they led him. In Sanchez's young career, the Jets had carefully protected the "Sanchise," emphasizing his virtues, limiting his playbook, minimizing his job competition, posting a media-relations staffer by his locker whenever he gave interviews. All this served to make Sanchez seem, from afar, like a football prince and reinforced the impression that Sanchez, although playing the leadership position, was still a kid. While he flashed the potential of some day becoming the polished, dynamic professional Ryan and Tannenbaum foresaw, he was still erratic, and so mostly he was a restricted element in a conservative run-first offense stocked with able veterans who gradually, over the course of the game, wore down the opposing defense. In the modern NFL, however, it would be too difficult to consistently win playing against the grain. And so now, after two years, the Jets hoped Sanchez was ready to begin his ascent as an efficient passer. Brady, after all, had begun as the caretaker of a Patriots offense filled with veteran talent. That the Jets still had no clear idea how good a quarterback Sanchez would become was nothing surprising; it pointed again to the difficulty in predicting the futures of football players and was part of the game's mystery.

Now that the undrafted free agents had been signed, the NFL teams were in negotiation with free-agent veterans. A football team employs many people, and most of them, coaches included, are unaware of personnel transactions the team is considering until the decisions about signings or trades are made at the top of the command chain. Ryan and Tannenbaum spent their days walking up and down the stairs to each other's offices, speaking behind closed doors, seeding their plans. The other coaches talked of having no clue about what's going on. They'd ask just about anybody, including me, "You got any idea?"

The coaches were normally so busy that they rarely took the opportunity to hear or read media commentary on their own team. Now, during the crucial signing interval, however, everybody along the facility hallways had an ear or an eye alert to what the radio, the television, and the Web knew. When the Jets re-signed their enigmatic top receiver Santonio Holmes, plenty of front-office people learned about it via news reports.

Eventually word spread that the team was in pursuit of Nnamdi Asomugha. This was really Rob Ryan's fault. During the five seasons Rob had coached the Raiders defense, he and Asomugha had grown close. NFL tradition holds that when a player makes the Pro Bowl in Hawaii, he brings his coach to Honolulu as his guest. Even after Rob left the Raiders for Cleveland, he remained the coach Asomugha invited to the Pro Bowl. Because the Ryan brothers spoke at least once daily, Rex Ryan by now had heard many things about Asomugha, things that made a man covetous—even a man who already had Darrelle Revis.

Ryan's thinking was that if you took away the opposition's two best receivers without allocating double coverage to either, you could then use your surplus personnel to unleash a terrifying pass rush. The problem was that plenty of other teams also wanted Asomugha, including Rob's new team, the Dallas Cowboys.

With all Jets defensive free-agent decisions contingent on what happened with Asomugha, even DT took a break from his usual sources of television companionship and switched over to ESPN. So it was that one morning when Sutton stopped by, he found his colleague in an apoplectic state. An ESPN expert, contrasting the skills of Revis and Asomugha, had described the free agent as the more aggressive press corner. "It's awful!" DT seethed. "Awful! This guy's just wrong. Nobody's ever played like Revis. The number-one thing he does is play physically after the receiver takes his first step." He began drafting an e-mail to ESPN. What distinguished Revis, DT wrote, was that while Revis trailed the opposition's best receiver wherever he went, Asomugha lined up exclusively on the right side of the field. That allowed opponents to place their number-one receiver free of the flytrap, on the left. The e-mail grew longer, taking on a heavy ballast of statistics.

Sutton loved that in support of his player, DT was willing to go all Marshall McLuhan on the ESPN man, showing up from nowhere the way the philosopher had appeared out of the mists in Woody Allen's *Annie Hall* to tell a windbag McLuhan scholar: "You know nothing of my work!" But Sutton's years at West Point had taught him about picking one's battles. There were a lot of media messengers out there, Sutton said, too many for even a Lancelot like DT to conquer. The thing to do was switch the channel and rise above. "You're right," said DT. He hit Delete and started up a game of solitaire.

The first day of training-camp practice would be August 1. A winning football team, Ryan believed, depended on the elusive unity that came from bucolic immersion and so he preferred to take the Jets away for training camp to the SUNY campus in Cortland, a slow-moving small town between Syracuse and Binghamton. There, players spent a few weeks in college-dorm beds—"It's like a huge man trying to sleep on a matchbox," Bryan Thomas said—eating dining-hall food, and, for a big night out, visiting the local fish-fry. But this year's labor truculence had made it impossible to confirm arrangements with the university, so the Jets players would train in Florham Park, and (except for the hotel-bound rookies) would sleep in their own beds. With two-a-day training-camp practices eliminated by the labor agreement, everything felt strange to the coaches, and easier. Football was, the coaches all thought, an argument for difficulty. To them, in a time of parity, difficulty was their advantage. So now, in their new collectively bargained world, they worried.

Under the rules, until August 1, the Jets players could work out on their own at the facility, in plain view of the coaches but without their supervision. They could approach the coaches and ask questions, but the coaches couldn't approach them. A rookie defensive back, playbook in hand, visited O'Neil for some early clarification. Clarification received, he looked at O'Neil and said, "Man, if we ran some of this shit in college, we'd have been niiiice!"

Looking through the facility's second-floor windows to the turf field just below, you could see camp bodies wearing minimal Lycra, stretching and sprinting and taking quick glances up toward those same second-floor windows, hoping to find someone standing against the glass noticing how ripped they were. It was a team sport, but out there the camp bodies were a bunch of guys who'd driven in from somewhere, local heroes just trying to punch their way in. Most had been astonishing college athletes, and almost all didn't stand a chance with the Jets.

Each camp body had put so much into football. What would happen to them when they ended up out on the street? They had all been to college, and no doubt the future would go well for some, but not for many others, for whom the rest of life would sink into anticlimax after the thrill of the game. A recent *Sports Illustrated* report had found that nearly 80 percent of players encountered financial stress within two years of departing the NFL. The Hall of Fame former Ravens tackle Jonathan Ogden told me, "As soon as you get into the NFL, you don't think about life after football. The job demands focus and energy; you can't plan for life after it. These guys are twenty-two years old. The typical career is three and a half years. They don't realize what it means to live off their interest. They buy big cars and they don't fly JetBlue. A lot of guys go broke." For some players, life after the NFL had commonality with the struggles of soldiers arriving back home from military combat. Ryan himself knew former NFL players who got depressed after their careers ended and took to drugs. During an off-season trip, he'd encountered one of his former Ravens defenders, a top draft choice now in such financial disarray that he had no coat for the cold weather. Ryan stripped off his own coat and gave it to the man. "There's a million of those stories," Ryan said. "Some of those guys get taken. Or they just blow it all."

Growing up, many players had found the structure of football to be its greatest advantage. The Jets, like every NFL team, had many players who had experienced severe trauma as children—a mother who died in childbirth, a father who died of an overdose. There were Jets players who had been shot at, stabbed, abused by relatives, jailed. It was a world of peril out there. One person who would be late reporting to the team this year was the Jets reserve defensive back Marquice Cole, a Northwestern graduate with liquid eyes and a penchant for hooded sweatshirts. Cole's brother had been shot multiple times and killed outside Chicago, and Cole was back in Illinois for the funeral. Later during camp, the undrafted rookie defensive back Davon Morgan, who'd been raised in Richmond by his grandmother because his father had been murdered when Morgan was two months old and his mother was a drug addict, would learn that his cousin had been murdered. Morgan and the cousin had grown up, he said later, "as brothers," but he didn't return to Virginia for the funeral. "I didn't leave because if I left, I knew they weren't bringing me back. They'd just bring somebody else in." The Jets team doctor Kenneth Montgomery told me that in all ways football players were naturally selected to endure pain.

Football was often seen as an outlet for aggressive young men. Among the players, a more commonly expressed attraction of the game was the company of coaches and teammates, who offered some of what was missing at home. It was up to the coaches to provide consolation to these players, around whom they spent most of their waking hours. This was a reason that Tannenbaum valued the warm presence of Ryan; of sturdy men like A-Lynn, Devlin, Sutton, and DT; of mature Jets players like Bart Scott, David Harris, Brandon Moore, Bryan Thomas, and offensive tackle D'Brickashaw Ferguson. The NFL life could quickly give way to the slipstream beyond the facility, and a GM needed to establish as many sources of manly stability as possible.

Out on the field, Sanchez led some passing drills with the receivers, including Scotty McKnight, a diminutive figure crossing from the slot to hug footballs to his chest in a way that made you think someone had just tossed him a sack stuffed with groceries. McKnight ran precise patterns and hauled in everything thrown near him, yet I kept expecting a can of San Marzano tomatoes to drop from his arms and go bouncing along the turf.

The players couldn't see them, but from time to time there were front-office people and coaches watching from behind the second-floor curtains. Invariably, each of them rooted for those he'd championed through the draft process. In Terry Bradway's office, he and Schottenheimer spectated as Greg McElroy completed a pass to the free-agent swingman Josh Baker. "McElroy to Baker for *another* Jets first down," called Bradway, who'd advocated for both. A play later it was Jeremy Kerley accelerating into the open for a catch and Schottenheimer exulting, "And Kerley has that extra gear!"

"I'd give anything to be the worst guy out there," said Bradway. Not Schottenheimer. He felt born to coach. In any case, something he'd noticed had been nagging at him—the way Sanchez seemed to be redesigning playbook routes to get the ball to McKnight, as though the two of them were back in sixth grade.

The Jets hadn't yet signed any notable free agents because they were waiting for Asomugha to decide what team he'd play for, and Pettine was annoyed at the way the cornerback's indecision was costing the Jets. Antwan Barnes had just given up on Ryan and Pettine and signed with the Chargers. Maybe a guy like Asomugha wasn't really interested in sharing the field—and the attention—with Revis? Down the hall, DT was watching *Cold Case* and thinking dark thoughts. "Come on, Nnamdi," he called out. "You're holding up progress."

Westhoff wasn't happy either. Was Westhoff ever truly happy? I encountered him in the hallway one day. "Hi, Mike," I said. "How are you?" His gaze was long. "Tortured, as always," he replied. Now, as Asomugha deliberated, Brad Smith, whose photograph had pride of place on Westhoff's office wall, had joined the Buffalo Bills. The belief in the Jets front office was that it was unwise to commit too much money to a player who was rarely on the field, even such a dynamic athlete as Smith. "I'm gonna miss Brad,"

Westhoff said. "I love that kid. Love him. He offered to take a million a year less than Buffalo offered, but I don't think they even noticed. The offer was not noticed."

Such was the budget that the team asked Bart Scott to accept a salary cut. Perhaps "asked" was not quite the word. Sitting in Ryan's office, the linebacker agreed. Money was never the defining factor for any decision Scott made. What was a million dollars less to stay with a coach you'd lay down your life for? That was also Scott's way on the field; he emitted an aura of sacrifice and danger, disrupting the point of the blocking scheme in the same reckless way that he used to forfeit his body on kickoffs. "I wouldn't do that for somebody who didn't have my best interests at heart," Scott said of Ryan.

Many players took salary cuts or signed on with the team for less than they were offered elsewhere. Some were given reduced offers and then put on a timer by the team, to be cut if the clock went *beep-beep*. All were praised afterward by people in management for being "pros" about the money. The players felt provisional. They were all for a better team, they wanted to win, and yet their careers might end tomorrow. They were eager to see how the money saved on them was spent.

Jim Leonhard was hanging out in Pettine's office with Pettine, O'Neil, and Mike Smith as Pettine's television displayed a news crawl about the new contract the Chargers had given their safety Eric Weddle; his signing bonus alone was more than all the Jets safeties combined were earning. "White DBs are getting paid! Nice!" said Leonhard. Then he smirked and joked that the salary must be related to Weddle's off-field charitable activities—"Now we'll hear he's really great in the community or something." On the Jets, where white players were in the minority, where the atmosphere was open and people were blunt when they talked about race, Leonhard was always making jokes about his white man's lack of speed—a syndrome the white coaches called Caucasianitis. Scott referred to himself and David Harris as "lineblackers," since he and Harris were African American but neither of their backups was. Kenrick Ellis, who'd attended Hampton University, was asked in a meeting for details about an exotic defensive formation, and when he answered correctly, another lineman (black) said, "That's that black-college education." One day, some outside linebackers and Pettine had a discussion about white guys' alleged aversion to dancing, a conversation begun by Jamaal Westerman, who was black.

Westerman: "Y'all are bar guys."

Garrett McIntyre (white): "That's like saying all black guys club!"

Bryan Thomas (black): "I'm a bar guy!"

Brandon Long (white): "I like to dance. I churn the butter!"

Long was blockily built and had been unable to practice because of a leg injury more or less since his arrival at camp, so this seemed especially funny. As everyone laughed, Pettine said, "Yeah, you churn, with the white man's overbite and the random finger-point!" More laughter.

One day, Marcus Dixon, a young black lineman, and I were talking about race. As much as any Jet, Dixon had thought about the subject. Dixon was a child in Rome, Georgia, when his father abandoned him. His mother was a drug addict and had been in jail. His grandmother cared for him until he was eventually taken in and adopted by a white couple, Ken and Peri Jones. After the Joneses did this, Ken and his brother stopped speaking, and his mother moved out of the house. The Joneses always referred to Dixon as their child and believed he was a boy of rare abilities and exemplary conduct. His 3.96 high-school grade point average and football excellence won him a scholarship to Vanderbilt. In 2003, when he was an eighteen-year-old high-school senior, Dixon and a white fifteen-year-old sophomore had sex in an empty classroom. Soon he found himself charged with rape. Many commentators believed Dixon's case would not have gone to trial had he not been a young black male in Floyd County, Georgia, who had had sex with a white girl. He was acquitted of rape, but the prosecutor also charged him with statutory rape, a misdemeanor, and aggravated child molestation, and Georgia's sentencing guidelines for child molestation applied even when the two parties were teenagers close in age. Dixon was, in effect, convicted of having consensual sex with someone two years behind him in high school. When Dixon was sentenced to the standard amount of prison time for the charge—ten years—his jurors were aghast. He spent over a year in prison before he was set free by the Georgia Supreme Court. Dixon eventually went to Hampton University, where he was three times the captain of his team and made the dean's list. Dixon said that on a football team, all the racial back-and-forth brought black and white players closer: "When people joke about race, it just makes us realize we're all brothers here."

As for Leonhard, everyone understood that attitude was Leonhard's edge. The scorn he displayed in conversation translated to the defensive secondary, allowing him to seem unimpressed even by the fastest NFL receivers. He was supremely confident on the field and played his best in big games. Leonhard would be a free agent after the season, and more than ever the coaches were hoping he'd get a big contract like the one Eric Weddle had just received from the Chargers. Partly this was because Leonhard was such a pro, so generous with help and advice for young teammates. For Jim O'Neil, who worked with Leonhard and the other safeties, it was also because Leonhard compensated for what he wasn't with preparation, intelligence, and will. In Leonhard, O'Neil saw himself.

Mo Wilkerson was sitting with Pettine, who was telling the Jets number-one draft choice that his Temple film had reminded a lot of Jets people of a young Trevor Pryce. Then Pettine described the way that Pryce in his All-Pro years as a defensive lineman could "make himself skinny" and fit through crevices in the offensive battlements, and the way Pryce's feet never ceased moving. Every defensive meeting began with a posting of the depth chart, where,

Pettine told Wilkerson, he would be a day-one starter. Still, he'd draw competition from Ropati Pitoitua. He wasn't as physically gifted as Wilkerson, but "Ropati's relentless—nobody plays harder than he does. He gets the most out of himself, and that's true of the whole unit. I hope that won't be a problem for you." Wilkerson had a peaceful way about him. He'd just been taking it all in. Now he said it wouldn't be any problem.

Just then a whoosh of energy shot through Pettine's door. It was Bart Scott, his alert round face looking as full of life as ever, despite his lightened pockets. Pettine told Scott about Marquice Cole's slain brother. "Chicago!" said Scott. "That shit's crazy. If Quice is like me, back home it all falls on him." Scott made some terrible decisions in the midst of play, and the coaches referred to the propensity as "Bart losing his mind." This football quality was noteworthy to me, because off the field no Jet made keener, more imaginative assessments than Scott. He said playing football was like serving in the army: you inhabited a separate, extreme life. The months away from the facility required "disconnect" from football and a process of "reentry" into normal life. Scott had formulated this transition. When he returned to Detroit every year for an off-season family visit, he went first to the Eastland Mall, bought himself an orange slushie and some cheese nachos with jalapeño, and then he ate, drank, and watched the soft parade: "I see ambitious kids that used to be me. I see people it's not working out for. I reengage with life. The ghetto's crazy. Then I go to my grandmother's house and sit on the porch. I'm not the biggest guy. Wearing a polo shirt, eating nachos, I could be anybody."

At the facility, things began to happen fast. Asomugha surprised everyone by joining neither Ryan brother, instead choosing the Philadelphia Eagles. Since the Eagles already had two fine cornerbacks, the Jets coaches thought this was an odd choice, and they thought the same thing about Philadelphia's decision to promote the offensive-line coach Juan Castillo to defensive coordinator. That was like asking a navy captain to lead an army's infantry regiment—two different careers. With their big money unspent, the Jets now signed Plaxico Burress, a former star Steelers and Giants wide receiver who'd just spent nearly two years in prison after carrying a concealed handgun into a New York nightclub and accidentally shooting himself. Eric Smith was re-signed to play safety and special teams, placating Westhoff, as were the defensive back Donald Strickland, former Ravens receiver Derrick Mason, Antonio Cromartie, reserve quarterback Mark Brunell, and Callahan's (and Ryan's) man Wayne Hunter. The arrival of Burress meant nothing good for Jerricho Cotchery, who, to the dismay of his teammates, asked for his release and then signed with Pittsburgh. Cotchery wasn't a receiver in the dynamic class of Holmes and Burress, yet on the team, J-Co was admired for what a first-rate person he was and for being the sort of comradely professional who brought out the best in others. "We're all replaceable and sooner or later we all will be replaced" was Sutton's reaction to the Cotchery news. Then Sutton was talking about practice, how some players tended to see it as something to get through on the way to the game, whereas in his view, it *was* the game. Sutton believed that if you watched someone practice, you'd see what he was as a player. No offensive player had practiced with more dedication than Cotchery.

Training camp began at last on the final day of July, the first order of business a series of meetings in the team's clean, well-lighted rooms. With their ample whiteboards, sleek AV equipment, and terraced seats and tables, the rooms could have been modern university classrooms. The players moved from meeting to meeting dressed like undergraduates, in shorts and T-shirts, and with backpacks slung over their shoulders, completing the feel of a college quad in miniature. (Pettine and others often referred to the facility as "campus.") In the main team meeting room, everybody chose a seat and it was somehow understood that now that seat was his for the season. (The veterans and coaches kept the same seats from year to year.) The quarterbacks all sat together up front. Plaxico Burress and running back LaDainian Tomlinson were toward the rear, just in front of Sutton, A-Lynn, and, between them, me. Various Jets officials addressed the players on the danger of concussions, on treating the attendants on team flights with respect, and on playing "like a bad motherfucker." That last was Ryan. He spoke spontaneously, without notes. Searching out rookies in the room, he said, "I'll cut you on the spot if I don't see you smiling." He seemed miffed at the idea of unhappy faces. "Guys!" he said. "Have fun. Talk shit! It all goes so quick. When guys poke at you, it's because they like you."

At the first defensive gathering, the players sat in the reverse of their on-field formation. Linemen filled the back, linebackers were ahead of them, and the defensive backfield was up front. I took a chair against the wall next to BT and not far from Smitty. Across the room was Revis, angled slightly forward in his seat, just as he stood on the field. Even at rest, the great player had something about him that claimed the eye. He seemed to gleam with posture and intent. He looked carved from a tree. He looked like an Egyptian king. "How many guys in here have a Super Bowl ring?" Pettine asked. None did. That settled, Pettine said that exertion was expected—"We don't coach effort"—and so was (here was that phrase again) "skin like an armadillo." Players who took themselves too seriously would receive sensitivity fines. Fights happened on football fields during training camp, and Pettine's (and Ryan's) rule in those situations was that defensive players were allowed to pull only an offensive player away from the fray.

They went outdoors and ran conditioning races, all of which were won by rookies. The rookies always won for the first few days. Tannenbaum was there, looking very Soviet Bloc penal colony. His eyes were crimson and his face was puffy. During the player-signing period, he'd spent thirteen out of fourteen nights sleeping on the couch in his office, alongside his humming fish tank and glowing telephone. Because of the business coming through the latter, he'd done very little sleeping. "It's good to be outside," he said, rasping.

The daily practice schedule was always distributed to coaches and front-office people at least an hour in advance. All the play calls and down-and-distance situations were printed on them, though the offense and defense were not supposed to see each other's scripts. A few minutes before a session's start, the coaches would put on shirts and shorts (their lockers were stocked with official green-white-and-black gear). Then they'd pass through the bathroom, where there were big, sweet-smelling jugs of sunscreen. Following liberal application, they'd run out onto the field, Ryan usually in the lead, sometimes in black Converse high-tops. When they reached the field, the offensive and defensive coaches would fan out to await their players, who were stretching as a team. Pettine often wore black overshirts on even the hottest days, and whenever he did, so did Smitty. A year ago Pettine had bought a North Face vest, and a few days later, there was Smitty in the freshly purchased identical garment. "Little brother," explained Pettine.

After stretching, the players retreated to positional groups for drills, the defensive linemen driving at their padded buckboard blow-delivery drilling sled, kicking up clumps of sod like bison, hitting the buckboard again and again with such rapid urgency that from a distance, you might think you were hearing an old Teletype machine. To instill in their linemen the need to keep low, the coaches had them run at a crouch under a mesh-covered device that resembled a huge bed frame on wheels. Interception practice for the defensive backs was footballs fired at them at close range by Thurman and O'Neil. A drop meant ten penalty pushups. Though DBs were said to play the position because they were receivers who couldn't catch, drops were rare.

The kickers, punters, and long snappers were ceded their own field, and the sight of them over there, like deer on a neighbor's lawn, emphasized that they were something apart, not really football players, as Ryan liked to tease Nick Folk, the incumbent kicker. Westhoff believed in annual kicking competitions, so there were two kickers, two punters. Eventually the punters would be called over, and you could hear the velvet corner-pocket *thwock* as returners Kerley and Leonhard secured punts against their chest pads. Sometimes a returner held a ball in one hand and fielded the punts with the other—one-handed. One day, Antonio Cromartie joined Kerley and Leonhard in this, and as the punt descended, he threw the ball he was holding up into the air, caught the punt with one hand, and then resecured the second ball with the other. It was a remarkable thing to see.

On a field full of gifted athletes, Cromartie fascinated everyone. People were always comparing Cro to long, slender, arresting things: an antelope, a principal in the Paul Taylor Dance Company, an oboe, with its fragile reed. To Revis, Cro was "the most athletic freak of nature. He's six three, two hundred pounds, can run like a deer, can jump like Kobe Bryant. He's a creation! A player on Madden!" On the sideline, Cromartie would stretch his long legs by kicking them over his head, Rockette-style. Out on the field, when he started moving, there was a sound to it, like the rustle in the woods just before a bird in the underbrush bursts away to safety. He'd accelerate, and it was a blur of long strides. How fast did the Cro fly? "I let everybody else talk about how fast I am," he said. "I don't know how fast I am. I don't know my true speed. Nobody knows!"

There was something frangible in him, making it surprising to many that Cro was a defensive player. He grew up in Tallahassee with a single mother who worked multiple jobs, and the family "moved so damn much from age five to sixteen I went to twelve different schools. We were evicted, couldn't pay the rent, the lease was up—always something." I asked him once how often he went back to Tallahassee, and he said, "Never. I'm not going back there. Life for me was better anywhere else. Why would I go back home?"

He could play cornerback because for such a tall, long-legged man he possessed an unusual ability to change direction at high speed. But to watch him live was to see that the tape hadn't lied, that he didn't relish rough contact. When he drifted back before the snap instead of crowding the line of scrimmage and using his long, sinewy arms to disrupt his receiver's pass route, the coaches couldn't understand it. "He should play angry," they would vex. "The way Revis does. Revis plays *angry*." But it was rebuke that made Cro seethe. He didn't take male criticism well, except from Ryan, who periodically would try to explain that the coaches were on his side; they just wanted to help him improve. "You gotta swallow your pride a little bit and be coachable."

Even if you hadn't seen Cro haltingly naming all his children on *Hard Knocks*, to be around him for any time was to sense that his life away from football must be very complicated. He just wanted to play. More than any Jet, he exuded a love for practice, an unwillingness to leave the field. He thought of football, he said, as "a getaway. Football is a different, more relaxed home. You can be comfortable with yourself, stepping into a better world."

The daily defensive meetings featured what were called installs; a series of defensive calls from the playbook were projected, one by one, onto a movie screen and explained to the unit by Pettine while everyone followed along in his playbook. The room smelled faintly of chewing-tobacco mint—the players would spit into water bottles that slowly filled, the way sap buckets did under tapped maples. There was a lot of football jargon, like "tango," "poison," "reduce," "rip," and "liz," and full sentences where I had no idea what was being said. The more Pettine installed every day, the more the complex pathways of football spread out before me, like a diagram of the subfamilies of some Finno-Ugric language. Then would come something that opened up the game a little more: "You have to know the location of the quarterback at all times," Pettine told his linemen. "If he's under center, it's going to be quick and short. You don't do slow-developing rushes. You knock 'em back and get your hand up. This is a thinking man's game. You've got to make decisions quickly and communicate them."

Every year, Pettine reinstalled the entire defense. For masters of the system, like Leonhard, BT, and the signal-calling inside "Mike" linebacker David Harris, this was redundant, but they understood that Pettine and Ryan wanted all of it to be second nature to everyone. You could hear Leonhard and Harris murmuring to young teammates, untangling confusions. After the installs, the players would divide into positional groups with their coaches, who'd explain the finer points. Then they'd walk through the calls in shorts. They'd lift weights, eat lunch, get taped, dress, grab their helmets, and go out and stretch. Finally, at the afternoon practice, they'd run the calls live against the offense.

It was a life of meetings for the players and even more so for the coaches. After practice, while the players showered and ate, the coaches would review the film of what had just happened, grading every player's performance on every snap with a plus or a minus and a comment along the lines of "good pop" or "soft shoulder." Then the players would watch the film with the coaches. Pettine narrated, mixing instruction with quips and badinage. Dressed in black, wielding his red laser pointer, Pettine's affect seemed to imply, I'm on your side, but only as long as you don't fuck up too much. He could be very sarcastic. Kenrick Ellis was told, "If you're gonna be this bad, just fall down. Maybe someone'll trip over you." The coordinator was always a little gentler with Cromartie's mistakes: "Cro, every year we put together a clinic tape on pressure rushes and that one's not gonna make it."

Since football was taught by daily correction, it was essential for Pettine to have a player who could demonstrate how to take criticism. That player was Bryan Thomas—BT. Pettine liked to call BT "a blue-collar football player." Out there on the fringe, not quite a linebacker or a lineman, BT did the understated jobs that made the unique Ryan scheme flourish. He knew how to shed blocks so as to hold his ground, forcing the flow back toward Harris in the middle, and he knew how to tackle in space. Three receivers would line up close together in a so-called bunch, and BT would get his hands on each of them in succession, disrupting the timing of three routes. This was a crucial skill. Pettine and Ryan had discovered that because their reputation was for pressure, opposing quarterbacks tended to get rid of the ball early against them. The result was few sacks and few completions. With the receivers jostled off course, those hurried passes tended to land harmlessly.

What Pettine admired so much about BT the other players also respected—that he was a good-natured character who didn't take himself too seriously and was "country-smart." He'd sit there squinting at the screen and then be taken to task for being a big, ugly, old, bald half-blind man who was *still* too vain to buy glasses. BT would giggle and in a rising tone of voice that made everyone laugh, he'd admit it was "all true, baby." One minute after the meeting start time, if Pettine hadn't begun speaking, BT would tell him, "We on the clock." If the meeting went one minute too long, he'd noisily rustle papers. One day, BT was a minute late. "Penny holding up a dollar," Pettine said as BT hurried in. "BT, I should do to you what my dad used to do to me. He'd turn the projector off and say, 'Stand up and explain to your teammates what you were doing.'"

"That's degrading!" BT said, horrified.

"Now you know why I'm so twisted," Pettine said, an admission he made for everyone's benefit, and one he'd have made for no other player.

"That's how everyone's dad was," said BT. Moments like that were how you "built a room," as Pettine liked to say.

BT had been brought up by a single father. Stanley Thomas was an Alabama coal miner in the pits near Birmingham. "He used to beat me, mostly for grades," BT told me once. "But I appreciate

everything he did for me. He'd come home, a cold in his chest."
Stanley hadn't wanted his son to "go down there," and BT never did.

Every practice field had a scoreboard, and the various practice periods were all governed by the blinking red minutes and seconds on
the scoreboard clocks. Each time the clock wound down, the equipment manager, Gus Granneman, would sound an air horn, and the
team slowly assembled in larger and larger configurations until the
offense and defense were complete units. Whereupon they ran
plays, sometimes in shorts and helmets and some days in full regalia. Most players, with the exception of running backs, wore no
body protection other than helmets and shoulder pads, even in
games. Leg pads, they claimed, inhibited speed, and as David Harris explained, "If you're an NFL player, you shouldn't get hit in the
legs." Though players grabbed at and collided with one another in
practice, they did not ever make full tackles; the risk of injury was
too high. Once in a while, somebody couldn't resist throwing an
opponent to the ground, and while the coach's reproof was instant,
it wasn't always convincing unless it was somebody like Santonio
Holmes or LaDainian Tomlinson who had been planked. You had
to be pretty worked up to hit a quarterback. They all wore red noncontact jerseys, and the penalty for tackling a quarterback could be
expulsion. I never saw it happen.

Standing along the practice sideline, you could hear the every-
dayness of football life. There was always pre-snap commentary
from Scott: "You scared, motherfucker? You so crazy. Kill yo'self!"
When Greg McElroy, late of the University of Alabama, took his
snaps, Scott would scream, "Hey, Fourteen, this ain't NASCAR, this
ain't no SEC Roll Tide, this is faster." He'd even call out references
to the movie *Any Given Sunday* to the Alabama rookie—"Goddamn
it, Cherubini, quit flinching!" The defensive backs also communi-
cated with their adversaries: "Where you going, baby?" Then came
the tectonic *boom* of the initial padded collision. When receiver

Santonio Holmes made a difficult catch, he might explain to the defense, "You gotta make it look easy." Reaction came from Pettine (to a linebacker: "If you ever get blocked by a wideout on the edge, go sit on their sideline. They're a bug on our windshield"). And reaction came from Schottenheimer (to Pettine: "I'm in your head, Pet!"). And then the positional coaches swarmed in with their own thoughts. They were like studio art teachers, those coaches, making their way through the group, taking care that everyone's work was critiqued. At the end of every practice, the team gathered around Ryan at midfield and he offered his own assessments. Then he'd call on someone, usually a player, to break the team down, leading everybody together as they all yelled out something on a three-count, such as "Jets!," "Team!," or "Family!"

Even without tackling, football was a very rough game. During one practice, linebacker Calvin Pace hit Matt Slauson so powerfully the huge guard toppled and landed hard, like a glass bottle falling from a high countertop to a stone floor. "That shit hurts so much it goes straight to your legs," said DT. To many of the players, the game was elemental, a way to explore yourself in terms of force—what you could inflict, how much you could take. Because football was so permissive of violence, it did have qualities of being in a state of nature, a place where you could be someone else, feel immortal. Even though helmet technology improved every year, some veterans continued to use the headgear they'd worn when they came into the league. They claimed the new models resembled space helmets, but beyond the stylistic concerns, and as with the disdained leg pads, there was the belief that conceding anything to safety meant conceding also some sense of self.

One player who felt that way was Scott. "I'm a classic old-school guy" was his explanation. "I don't need that crazy-kazoo satellite helmet. I'm in proper tackling position. I have a twenty-inch neck. I never had a concussion because I know what I'm doing." He said that he'd always been aware of his vulnerability in the world, and how he dealt with it was to hit back. "Everybody gets at least one shot to define themselves," he said. "I came from Detroit, the most dysfunctional place in America." When he got to the NFL with the Ravens, he said, "It was the Harvard of football. I went a hundred miles an hour, outworked everybody." His eyes grew large at the memory. "The biggest statement you can make is to be physical. You knock the shit out of somebody, everybody's excited—it's the slam dunk, the knockout punch. People love football for the physicality. One guy gets three picks, another guy knocks the shit out of somebody, it's, Did you see *that?* Football reveals you. My introduction was hitting the Detroit Lions legendary wedge. They had all linemen up there. I was the first man down and I took out two of them." He pointed to the fullback John Conner, who by Ryan was called the Terminator and known for the punishing blows he inflicted. "Why'd Rex draft a fullback last year? He went to Kentucky to see a linebacker, saw that guy hit, and said, You come home with me."

Not everyone was as reckless as Scott. "Part of the game is to look past a lot of it," Jim Leonhard told me. That said, while it was still crucial to prove your bravery to your teammates, Leonhard observed, there were now limits. "Used to be, you got a head injury, you were a pussy if you came out. Now it's the opposite, the worst thing. In the old days it was seen as the easy way out—my head's not right. It's a huge thing now and that's great because it's not worth it." Greg McElroy had the same impression: "At Alabama, the training room was a sign of weakness. I never said anything about aches and pains. I didn't want to be considered soft. Here, guys are smarter about it. Do what you need to do to get your body healthy." Such incremental concessions were, as the players said, new within football, and they carried significance. Out in the world, many people thought that if the game could not find a way to mitigate collisions, it either was doomed altogether or, at a minimum, would go the way of boxing, once perhaps the USA's most popular sport and now in decline, banned in some countries.

These conversations with Leonhard and McElroy took place

during off-hours. Matters of gravitas were not for the practice-field sidelines. There, many people talked about the weather. The summer was hot enough to remind the defensive lineman Marcus Dixon of his Georgia home — "I love the humility," he said, winking at his pun. The close air brought Ryan back too, to Oklahoma, where once, after a rainfall, he and his brother Rob were outside jumping in puddles when his grandmother came out and grabbed them both. As the screen door whanged behind him, Ryan looked back and saw the enormous cone of a tornado. The house had no basement, so Ryan's grandmother had the boys lie down in the bathtub. Now Smitty was remembering a slow, steamy boyhood day in West Texas. Smitty's brother lit a caterpillar on fire. (Smitty pronounced it "caller-pitter.") The animal made a sound "like a human scream," and Smitty couldn't sleep for nights.

Only twenty-two players could scrimmage at a time, leaving most of the team gathered along the sideline yard hashes, watching and talking. Always, they divided by unit. I stood with the green-shirted defense, where topics of conversation included toughness. There was Ravens guard Marshal Yanda, who played on despite all manner of gruesome injuries. But his reputation in this regard was really clinched the day when someone brought a Taser into the locker room and Yanda agreed to be shot. After absorbing a bolt to the chest, Yanda cried out, "That all you got?" Then he accepted two more. Said DT dryly, "It's supposed to stop your heart, but it didn't seem to affect him." Yanda had grown up on an Iowa dairy farm where the electric cattle fences built up his resistance. Another Iowa farm boy was Jets lineman Matt Kroul, who had a tough mom. In their part of the state, there were hay-bale-throwing competitions, and both mother and son were champions.

One day the nose tackle Sione Po'uha described in detail how to cook a horse Polynesian-style. You dug a pit, lined it with banana leaves atop hot lava rocks, and roasted the horse for many hours. Then you marinated the horse in coconut milk, chili peppers, and spices. "You'll love it," he promised. Po'uha was the only Tongan on the team. The other Polynesians were of Samoan ancestry. Something else separated him from them: The last time Po'uha spoke with his father, the father had touched Po'uha's hair, and when his father died soon thereafter, Po'uha had decided not to cut his hair again in paternal memory. It flowed out from the nose tackle's helmet like a shroud, and when Po'uha felt himself to be in stressful circumstances, he touched it.

Every day at training camp, there were guests along the sideline. Team owner Woody Johnson, an heir to the Johnson & Johnson fortune, might bring along several guests, men and women who were dressed as though for a regatta in linen, straw hats, and sundresses. Kenny Chesney, the diminutive country singer, visited practice one day. Ryan asked Donald Strickland if he knew who Chesney was. BT didn't give Strick time to answer. "Rapper," said BT. "Little Kenny."

I watched several practices with Senior, Pettine's dad, and we'd sometimes talk about his time coaching his son. The day Pettine had quit and then stripped off his equipment and clothes as he walked through the parking lot, Senior said, he'd looked at his speechless assistants and told them, "Guess I better change my approach." After that, he said, "things got better." During the season, Senior often sent Pettine critical memos on the defense. He brought them to training camp as well, in an envelope. "Good toilet reading," said Pettine when he was in receipt of one. And yet Pettine also would say, "My dad's in the stands with sixty thousand people, I hear his voice. It's a frequency thing."

Presiding over it all was Ryan. Wherever he was out on the practice fields, Ryan was hard to miss. All the diets (and lap-band surgeries) later, he remained an immense man whose thick foothills of neck and haunch swelled into a spectacular butte at the midsection; he possessed a personal geography that, from first-and-ten distance, assumed a form that followed his function—Ryan looked like nothing more than an extra-large football. By nature appreciative, the head coach meandered through the panorama of players, marveling at these "big uglies," these "mighty men." He thrilled to be the one on their side when others were in opposition. Upon taking the job, he'd been told that BT was a problematic person, and Ryan delighted in contradicting that: "He's been one of this coach's favorites from day one." Marquice Cole wore his practice shorts so low on the posterior that they appeared to be a gravitational anomaly. Some, said Ryan, objected to this sort of look in a football player, but not him: "Hell, he's a great kid. Funny eyes: half-closed. Looks like he was up all night or something. Smart! Northwestern!"

Now Ryan watched his new receiver Plaxico Burress. A machine flung footballs at Burress, and he absorbed them; it was like seeing a row of nails being gunned into drywall. Ryan was excited that he now had three receivers who wanted the ball in crucial situations. On the field and around the facility, Burress was a distant presence, always out wide and alone. Because he was not in shape and day after day missed parts of practice, others were critical of him, calling Burress Plaxiglas and Plaxitive. Receivers were considered the prima donnas of football, but this behavior was a little extreme. Maybe, Ryan thought, prison had made Burress wary of adults. He'd noticed how comfortable Burress seemed around children.

The one Jet Burress clearly liked was Santonio Holmes. Holmes was small for a football player and had such an innocent way about him that you'd find yourself thinking of him as Little Tone—until suddenly such an experienced expression crossed his face that you'd catch your breath. He claimed to have learned his position by playing video games, and sure enough, he could emerge so abruptly from a series of cuts that there was the temptation to look for the joystick manipulating him, to check and see if he'd left his shoe behind with foot and ankle still inside. One day Ryan watched Holmes go by and shook his head. "Amazing, that kid, where he's been. Belle Glade, Florida, is the AIDS capital of the country. It's swamps and cane fields and incredible poverty, but he made it out of the sugarcane."

Holmes himself described a horrific childhood, a bullet-riddled apartment, without enough beds, that was constantly broken into; the sound of police sirens every night; a dead body outside the window. "It was according to who you decided to be around which allowed you to survive," he said in his soft voice. "The friends I started out with are still in the same spot standing on the same corner just happy to be alive, with no ambition." Belle Glade is famous for its "muck," the rich, ink-dark soil in which the sugarcane thrives but not much else. "There's no opportunities for jobs in the area," Holmes said. "There's just a lot of guys who want to be in gangs. Nobody wants to be an individual. I was too busy taking care of my little brothers. I watched the kids and tried to keep them out of trouble." In the summers, Holmes traveled north with his mother, babysitting his siblings while she worked in the cornfields of Georgia from midnight to 11:00 a.m. as a migrant laborer on the mule train, a massive, moving staging area for sorting and packing. One year Holmes joined her; his job was lifting boxes. He drew me a picture of the mule train. Beside one tiny figure he wrote, "Me." The work was arduous—too much for a boy.

Sports for Holmes were "my way of seeing something other than the streets." In high school, he said, he took AP calculus and biology. Ryan always talked about how smart Holmes was. Ryan knew that as a Pittsburgh Steeler, Holmes had had brushes with the law. But the coach remained all about the present. He was expecting a lot out of the receiver, felt that by virtue of his large new contract, Holmes could no longer "lead from behind" but had to be "out in front." Holmes, he said, "has responded." During training camp Ryan told Holmes he was going to name him a captain and that he'd retire with a C on his Jets jersey. "The kid had tears in his eyes. By making him a captain, it's about making him accountable."

Seated near me in the daily defensive meeting was linebacker Brandon Long, who, since he'd quickly sustained that leg injury, had never practiced. Long always brought a capacious sack of sunflower seeds to the defensive meeting, which annoyed Pettine because of the noise the plastic bag made whenever Long touched it and, probably even more, because it was hard for Pettine to watch someone who did not play enjoying snacks in his meeting. Long always had his monthlong training-camp schedule with him, and every day he'd make a big *X* through the current date. He was a perfectly inoffensive fellow, provided a daily hillock of seeds to anyone who expressed interest, but the Jets seemed suspicious of him. A common NFL phenomenon was the injury settlement. Because a team couldn't release an injured player, and because players lost via injury counted against the salary cap, all NFL teams were leery when someone who obviously wasn't going to make the team got hurt during training camp. Every player who was cut from a team was required to sign his health release, and some players would take that opportunity to bargain for a financial settlement. At times, their afflictions were legitimate; at times not. So what the front offices did was retain a player, treat his injury, and then play him at practice just long enough to get his healthy movements on tape. Then they'd release him.

When teams signed players who'd previously been injured, sometimes these players agreed to waive parts of their body, meaning that if they reinjured those areas, they wouldn't hold the team responsible. One linebacker on joining the Jets waived over half of himself.

Through the early days of camp, the offense seemed generally out of sorts. A source of discontent was the loss of Jerricho Cotchery. Ryan was aware of this and met with the players to tell them that Cotchery had requested a trade and then, when there were no takers, his release. The Jets had very reluctantly accommodated him. A great guy, Ryan told them, a guy everyone loved who wasn't any longer the player he wanted to be.

The concerning issue for the offense was that day after day, the defense was manhandling them. "You want to be physical, we'll be physical, and you'll have a long camp, bitch," Scott would yell across the line. The Jets new strength coach, Bill Hughan, just hired from the Atlanta Falcons, was incredulous: "I've never seen a defense so totally dominate an offense. The O needs to get it together."

No defense wanted to add its own team's offense to the year's list of opponents, but there were first-down markers out there, and on every play, somebody won. Pettine was a ferocious competitor. "Hammer," he might say to Carrier, "is the D-line ready to stem yet? That way we can fuck with them." (He was asking if the defense was familiar enough with one another and with the offensive cadences that they could smoothly shift from one front to a confusing new presnap look.) In the film meetings, he and the other defensive coaches took pleasure when the cameras caught the offensive coaches wincing during that day's beat-down.

Competing against one of the best defenses in the league, the offense was—well, what was the problem with the offense? For one thing, the quarterback wasn't playing effectively. If a defense allowed even an average NFL quarterback to set his feet, follow through, and lift his back foot off the ground, he could pass with impressive accuracy. Not Sanchez. The quarterback threw interceptions in seven-on-seven drills, typically dominated by the offense. His two-minute drills lacked urgency and precision. "Hey, somebody better settle down Sanchez," Jim Leonhard yelled on the sidelines one day. "He's confused out there." Sanchez made so many feckless decisions that when he finally sailed a pass far and safely out-of-bounds under pressure from DeVito, Leonhard said, "If he's throwing it away, that's a big step for him." Some of this discontent with the quarterback was taken out on Sanchez's friend Scotty McKnight. When the rookie receiver made a mistake in a drill, Westhoff shouted, "You're still here? It's a miracle you even got here."

Among the team members, there was an ongoing Sanchez dialogue. It went something like this:

He's just a guy.

He won four playoff games in his first two years!

He's an immature kid who did it with training wheels.

He beat Peyton Manning and Tom Brady back-to-back and he's had a better first two years than Eli Manning.

And so on.

That Ryan had named Sanchez a team captain bothered some people, those who considered him neither a proven player nor a leader. What constituted a football leader? I asked Ben Kotwica, Westhoff's assistant, who'd studied leadership at West Point, about some of the preferred qualities. He listed prior accomplishments, skills, the respect of others, and the ability to inspire teammates to a higher level of play.

But if there was tension between offense and defense, it was hardly all Sanchez's fault. Offensive players barely knew their defensive teammates, and during training camp and the season, the coaching staffs tended to be similarly Balkanized. Greg McElroy called it "the natural tension in all of football. Players get frustrated with the other side. It's natural; they're so divided." This was an ongoing conflict in the history of the game: one aggrieved group on a team feeling that the other group wasn't carrying its share of the burden. It was possible to be successful under these circumstances. The Chicago Bears won the 1986 Super Bowl with defensive players who told their head coach, Mike Ditka, "I don't play for you." Those players answered to the team's defensive coordinator, who happened to be Buddy Ryan. When Rex Ryan, Pettine, Thurman, and Carrier coached the Baltimore Ravens, their defense collectively seethed in the same way. So did John Rowser and his Pittsburgh Steelers defensive teammates in the early 1970s: "With our offense, anything we got was a bonus," Rowser told the writer Roy Blount. On the Jets, where the defense was not only tough but original, there was the growing feeling that Schottenheimer and his offensive players were holding the team back from winning a championship. In 2010, the Jets had begun their season with a game against the Ravens and lost, 10–9. The Jets offense was one for eleven on third down and secured a franchise-low six first downs. The game had been personal to the former Ravens coaches on the defense, and before it they had given Schottenheimer many suggestions regarding the Ravens players they used to coach. None were taken. Afterward, Pettine was so upset he could barely speak. "We *knew* them," he kept repeating.

Ryan was aware that the reason the Ravens hadn't hired him as their head coach was that they considered him one-dimensional, purely a defensive coach. Every head coach specialized, but most head coaches had offensive backgrounds. Among the reasons was that if one unit was going to intimidate the other, it would be the defense doing the bullying. Ryan believed that to the offense, he could offer "my presence," could engender a joyful team-wide sense of purpose, toughness, and physicality. And yet, it was now two years into the Ryan administration, and much as offensive coaches Callahan, Devlin, Matt Cavanaugh, A-Lynn, and Schottenheimer liked working for Ryan, the head coach himself admitted that he was "uncomfortable" with the offense because "they're different." Feeling not a part of things in the offensive meetings, he retreated, ceding everything to Schotty. And by giving Schotty the room, Ryan gave himself license to feel the old pride in the defense he had created.

During training camp, he'd walk into Pettine's office and tell him, "I think we gave up a first down today!" Watching film one day after another defensive pummeling, he mused, "We should probably give the defense a day off tomorrow."

"Because the offense took one off today?" Sutton asked.

"Imagine if this happened to us," said Pettine.

"We'd be here until two in the morning," Ryan said.

The defense's superior attitude, Pettine knew, "chaps some asses across the hall," but this was the way football teams worked. It was an emotional, aggressive business, and if Pettine gave too much quarter, his defense would slip. He liked Schottenheimer, considered him "a great, great guy," and he knew that with a young, erratic quarterback and such an accomplished defense, "Schotty's in a tough spot." If Pettine had been the head coach, he might have sought Schotty out, tried to help. Pettine hoped someday to be a head coach. But now he was the defensive coordinator, and "I never want to farm somebody else's land. That's how you get in trouble."

A few NFL officials were assigned to every team during training camp for some live preparations of their own, and the contingent of officials who were to spend time with the Jets held a meeting to introduce themselves and explain their priorities: safety and fairness. They cautioned against players launching themselves at one another and decried blows to the head. Eventually they asked for questions. There were none. The officials would have liked questions. It was their appreciation for the game that had put them in stripes. Watching Revis in coverage drills, one of them shook his head: "It's all true. He's glue."

When you saw the players practice every day, you sometimes forgot how rare were their abilities. Many were learning their place in the scheme, and because all were marvelous players, there was a leveling effect. This was not true with Revis. Everyone enjoyed watching the cornerback practice to see the combination of unmatched skill and unmatched intensity. Said Leonhard, "Rev's not only the best player I've ever seen — day in day out, he's the best practice player I've ever seen." Even on a hot summer Tuesday, Revis abhorred the idea that any of the Jets receivers should catch a pass against him. They seldom did.

During one-on-one passing drills, which were refereed, a receiver pushed off Revis to create space, and he made a catch. When no flag was thrown, Revis exploded. He followed the official as the man tried to continue his adjudications, arguing, "He was pushing me! *We* can't do that!," then expanding his appeal to whoever would listen, protesting on statutory grounds, ethical grounds, and finally philosophical grounds: "They're trying to make it an all-offensive game!" Giving up the discussion only when it was his turn to drill again, he lined up against Santonio Holmes. At the snap, Revis roared into Holmes, pushing him, beating him, administering such a marauding martial flurry that Holmes never left the line of scrimmage, three flags fell to the ground, and everyone, including Holmes and the official, burst into laughter. Everyone except Revis.

Revis was intense even about the daily noncontact walk-throughs in which, like actors pacing off their stage blocking, the players slowly rehearsed the plays they had just learned in the classroom. The cornerback used the time to master his position in relation to the yard markers, the sideline, and the other players so that, always, he had a perfect sense of where he was on the grassy districts of the grid and where everyone else was and could soon be. His peripheral vision was such that walking along the facility hallways, he'd appear to have his head facing forward and yet greet you when you were still steps behind him. On the field, most defensive backs, including Cromartie, had to slow to look over their shoulders and find the ball in the air. Revis could look back both left and right while sprinting, but he never did it unless he was within a step of the receiver, which was the proper technique.

His movements were not liquid, like Holmes's, but carbon solid. On a field he was canted low and slightly forward, and he gave the impression that he was running without ever placing one foot in front of the other, that he was moving, somehow, in a single full-body-forward thrust. As a result, on film the receivers sometimes appeared as though they were covering him. When they swayed, he swayed. What the coaches most appreciated was that playing his high-stress position, Revis did not panic. Even if he bought a fake, his recovery was instant because he was in rhythm, had an inner quiet, *sprezzatura* even. He was a cruising instrument securing the perimeter.

On a field Revis was all business, and yet he never seemed to be putting himself above the others. Far down the sidelines, you could hear his head-thrown-back laugh, and after practice he sometimes played invisible football, pantomiming the game sans ball with Cromartie and Leonhard, each successfully completed play culminating in leaps, bounds, and celebrations. "You can do amazing things in invisible football," he said.

To the others, Revis was the consummate team player, a modest virtuoso playing defense, the less decorated side of the ball, who expressed the pinnacle of the sport, an action hero in a football suit. Wayne Hunter, the introspective tackle, said, "As a player we put him so high on a pedestal because the guy can live up to it. I never saw a guy on the number-one receiver every game, never heard of it. He's Michael Jordan!" Leonhard thought similarly. "I've never seen anything like it," the safety said. "If he struggles, he's truly hurt. You always hear about Michael Jordan, how ultra-competitive he was. That's Rev. Guys don't want the number-one corner diving during practice. It's that he wants to win so much. I've been around a lot of truly great players, Ed Reed, Ray Lewis, and I've never seen anything like it, a man so physically gifted with all the intangibles. It's the craziest thing I ever saw. You just don't expect anybody to catch a ball against him." The coaches were in agreement. They wanted to hold him in time.

I used to ask the coaches if it was possible to invent a play or a pass route or a defensive look that nobody had ever seen. Mostly they were dubious about the possibility and claimed it had all been done before, under different names, in slightly varied iterations. Still, they were always trying for invention. In this way, a coach was like any creative person taking on a legacy of masterworks; as Goethe had said of Shakespeare: "He gives us golden apples in silver dishes. We get the silver dishes by studying his works, but, unfortunately, we have only potatoes to put into them." One person who always wanted to devise new lines and directions for football players was

Ryan, and that was because, when it came to football, he had an artistic temperament.

Often when Ryan entered Pettine's office, creative things seemed to occur. The two men were collaborative by nature. One morning before practice, Ryan was messing around with Smitty in Pettine's office, playing pepper with a tiny souvenir Phillies bat and a golf ball, when suddenly the head coach put the bat down, went to the whiteboard, and drew up a way for a safety to relieve an outside linebacker of coverage responsibilities in an early-down pressure called Under Bear Fire Zone. "Save that," said Pettine, and he got up and circled it for emphasis. Frequently plays came to Ryan in the middle of the night and so he kept the pad and pencil on his bedside table. He'd learned, over time, to make sure he was awake enough to write the notes legibly.

Another day in Pettine's office, Ryan declared a training-camp weight-loss competition among overweight coaches. Their names and weights—Smitty: 240; Pettine: 256; O'Neil: 232; Ryan: 292—were listed on Pettine's whiteboard, circled for safekeeping, and the salad days began.

Everyone called training camp a grind, and it was an exhausting experience. The first meeting of the morning began at eight and often the day ended well past ten at night. Those hours made it difficult for me to travel back and forth to my home in Brooklyn, so often I stayed at Pettine and Smitty's place. Pettine lived like the bachelor coach he was, in a sparsely furnished town house. We'd come home, go instantly to bed, and awaken with just enough time to make it back to the facility. I slept on the couch in the living room, beside a tall, dead brown plant that I developed a fondness for. That famished plant seemed to say it all about the life, more even than the stove on which no meal was ever prepared or the refrigerator whose only contents were a few condiment jars and a couple of forgotten beers. The football immersion was such that

Smitty and I relished our one-mile drive to work together when we could listen to the radio. He may have been the only NFL coach who began his day with folk music.

One night, the late meetings were canceled, and Smitty and I decided to go to the movies. Outside the theater afterward, a demolished-looking man was asking everyone for food money. Nobody gave but Smitty; he reached into his jeans and produced a fistful of bills. "I don't know what he'll spend it on," he said. "Probably booze. But at least he'll have one nice night." Smitty, making an intern's wage, with a sick, broke father back in Texas, in winter had given five-dollar tips to the men who filled up his car at gas stations, explaining, "It's cold and rainy out there."

Smitty's attempt to quit chewing tobacco gave him a constant headache and also, at times, a balky stomach. In a meeting, Pettine looked at him. "Did you burp?" Smitty frowned and denied all. Five minutes later Pettine told Smitty, "Get out of here."

"What?" said Smitty, eyes wide.

"Five minutes ago you said you didn't burp. And now I just heard you burp and it smelled the same as five minutes ago, so leave."

"I didn't know I burped five minutes ago," Smitty protested. He was permitted to stay. Nobody could resist Smitty.

By the middle of August, David Harris, the linebacker, could no longer keep track of what day of the week it was. Much as they liked to play football, the players thought of training camp the same way coaches did—something to endure. "It's a blue-collar sport," the guard Brandon Moore said while walking off the field one day. "Got to bring the lunch pail. You do a lot of things you don't like to do. Uncomfortable things." Moore's father had worked in a Gary, Indiana, steel mill for forty years: "Wake up every day, one hundred and something degrees in the casting room. Come home dog-tired." Watching that, Moore said, had prepared him for football.

"Nobody loves practicing. It's repetition—over and over. Besides Sundays, the fun is the one-on-one battle, doing your job and winning more than you lost." Like Moore, David Harris felt that his father's work—he was a die-caster at an auto-parts plant in Grand Rapids—had in some way readied him for the sport.

Halfway through August, the fields were looking worn, and so were the players. Sometimes their eyes grew heavy in the afternoon meetings, and if Pettine saw that he'd say, "Get up and throw a couple of jabs if you've got to. Fight it." Scott, who claimed that he'd missed only three practices in his life, sat one out. "My legs are getting tired standing here," he said. "I'm dehydrated. Bees are stinging me. My mind's not right. I can't take it!"

Football was, as the linebacker Jamaal Westerman put it, "a job, but you don't want it to feel that way."

Of all the coaches, it was Jeff Weeks who found the eighteen-hour training-camp days the most trying. He considered them "overkill" and "unnecessary," said he couldn't understand why, "when they didn't do a thing all day against our defense, we'll have to be here until ten at night." Weeks thrived in the football outdoors, and sitting hour after hour in the unremitting meetings where he almost never spoke, he seemed trapped.

One night Ryan canceled all the evening meetings and announced that he was taking the entire team bowling. The offense would roll against the defense. When linebacker Calvin Pace learned of this, he couldn't wait. "You can give football players so little, make them a T-shirt, and they're so happy," he said. "That's something Eric Mangini never understood, how important it is to bring players some happiness."

Tannenbaum wouldn't be going bowling. The GM had promised his children that he'd come home that night and tuck them in. Tannenbaum said that not seeing your family was a suffering that football people "got used to absorbing." Such choices, he said, were "very tough—football's not all roses, not even close," and that phrasing seemed perfectly to express the GM. Ryan would go bowling, and—you could count on it—he'd wear a colorful shirt, woof about his skills, give out "gutter-ball prevention tips," and have the time of his life, and everyone around him would too. For Tannenbaum, it would have been work, partly because around Ryan, Tannenbaum somehow seemed stiffer than he really was.

The GM often stood alone on the practice sidelines, rocking back and forth, scowling balefully, shifting his weight, a dealer in costly commodities vibrating with wary anxiety. Every day is the opportunity to improve, was the sort of thing you could see he was thinking during a messy practice. Why aren't they taking that opportunity? Tannenbaum inevitably wanted more from people, would sometimes stroll alongside a younger player and give him an impromptu playbook quiz or offer him admonitions about working hard. Tannenbaum was the boss in the organization, the authority figure who made people nervous when he walked into the room. There was the sense that he liked the role but that he might have wished not to project his authority so emphatically, that he did so because Ryan left him no choice. It was in Ryan's nature to get along with everyone, to exude a sense of well-being, and that relentless conviviality left Tannenbaum the role of de facto taskmaster, the dogged one, the one who worried.

Cuts had begun almost immediately. Three days into camp, the team decided to part ways with Tom "Langer" Ottaiano after practice. When the session ended, before anyone from management could approach Ottaiano and lead him upstairs to the pro-personnel director Brendan Prophett's office to receive the bad news, Ottaiano went over to the family area to visit with what looked like his parents and girlfriend. Watching this from the second floor, the pro-personnel guys were horrified. The last thing they wanted was to embarrass a player in front of his family. When the girlfriend gave Ottaiano a big kiss, everybody winced. And then when a local reporter strolled up to him and requested an interview, there were groans of "oh no!" Joey Clinkscales spoke up. "I don't feel bad for him," the chief of scouting said. "He got to play pro football for three days." When Ottaiano was finally brought upstairs, he didn't quite see it that way. He was angrier than any cut player Prophett could remember: "Are you shitting me? Three fucking days is all I get?"

Cuts were part of the game, and most of the players accepted it. Some of them might say "No hard feelings," and a few even looked relieved when they were released. One of those was a linebacker who'd worn a T-shirt that said "Running Sucks" to meetings, which was deemed by the defensive coaches to be the worst camp-wardrobe decision in anyone's memory. Most, of course, were there to make the team, and they worried a lot. Martin Tevaseu, a friendly three-hundred-pound nose tackle known to all as MTV, said, "We have no idea what they say about us in meetings. We come out here, and we love football, but we also hate it because it's so stressful. You never know what they see."

In the middle of August, the coaches began emphasizing how soon the first game—on September 11, against Dallas—would be upon them, which meant that reps for players competing for the team's final roster spots, like MTV, would be sparse. He was an unlikely player, loose and boxy (he looked somehow like a dresser with its drawers left open), with long, flowing black hair and a far-seeing expression. MTV's unpromising appearance first worked against him, but then from his nose-tackle position he'd make a rat drop, retreating into low coverage looking to collision somebody, and the sight of him hurrying across the field would bring cheer to his coaches. Day after day, his grade sheet was filled with pluses: he was difficult for blockers to dislodge, he played hard, and he knew his responsibilities, making him, said Pettine, "found money."

That was also Nick Bellore, who quickly learned the playbook and, unlike most of the other defenders, also mastered the reasoning behind the calls. He was the player who, in a defensive meeting, could answer a Pettine question by saying, "Motions and shifts primarily happen in the first quarter because offensive coordinators script the whole quarter."

Ellis Lankster, a physical cornerback who had spent his two years since college on the penumbra of pro football, living on and off NFL and Canadian teams, was a new favorite of Westhoff's. Everybody could tell this because Westy called him Lancaster. Lately Westy had been calling Marquice Cole Maurice, another good sign. To the German—as Westy called the rookie linebacker Matthias Berning, who'd grown up in Germany—he said, "The way you're playing now, fifty years ago you'd have been killed." This was thought not to be a compliment, though nobody was sure. Still, it was better to be the German than simply "my man," Westy's way of referring to those who remained only a face to him. Since the roster had been filled and camp had begun, the special-teams coach was in improved spirits. "I'm loyal," he said. "Hell, I fight and fight, but once it's done, I work with what I got."

In the heat, with players desperate to make an impression on the coaches, things between two players could get "salty," as the coaches liked to say, and fights would erupt. You'd hear a cry, and the organized scrum of football would devolve into a different kind of violence, loud punches banging off the hard plastic of helmets until the combatants were quickly tackled and restrained. Then, as everyone milled around, running back Joe McKnight would dart among the huge bodies and slap BT's helmet before dashing away. This was very amusing to watch on film in the meetings, and the players loved it, especially the day when BT responded with a blind mule kick that missed Little Joe by two feet.

A reserve offensive lineman named Rob Turner, who had an important role on the team because he could play many positions, had a reputation as an impressive brawler, which suffered after he appeared to get the worst of it in practice bouts with Kenrick Ellis and Ropati Pitoitua. After several days of this, Ryan told the team, "Okay, guys. We've had enough fights. Somebody's gonna break a hand."

One day soon after Ellis and Rob Turner fought, the coaches noticed that the two were now buddies, working out together on their own. "That's what happens," said Ryan. He said he'd heard that among Polynesian kids in Hawaii, there was competition to be the so-called bull of the school, the toughest fighter. The bull of the Jets would be either Ropati or, he thought, Wayne Hunter because of his "switch." Sometimes when tempers rose, Ryan said, you could see Hunter turn away and put his head down to avoid the angry impulse. As an offensive player, Hunter was an exception, Ryan said, because "offensive guys get the high Wonderlic [an intelligence test] scores, but defensive guys are mean, nasty, violent sons of bitches." As Ryan was speaking, Smitty came up. Ryan put the question to him. Wayne or Ropati? "Well," said Smitty, weighing Hunter's fearsome temper against the six-foot-eight Pitoitua's strong resemblance to Chief Bromden in *One Flew Over the Cuckoo's Nest*. "It would end with both dead, ears scattered everywhere," he decided.

The training-camp days had scarcely any downtime scheduled, and what there was sometimes resulted in antics that were sophomoric at best. A player would open his playbook and encounter a cardboard dildo inscribed "I've missed you." Bumper-sticker raids were carried out in the parking lot and vehicles plastered with messages like "I Stop for Gay Bars" and "I Like Gay Porn," adornments that sometimes weren't discovered (and removed) for days. It was the sort of thing that so many people I knew expected of football players. Pettine once asked me if I considered football people to be the worst homophobes I'd ever met. I told him my theory on the subject, and he nodded and said that football culture was homophobic but that when gay players began identifying themselves as such, they'd be accepted and the sport would lurch forward.

So much that went on in August was about achieving group closeness. Because Garrett McIntyre had played in Canada after his college career at Fresno State, people at first thought he was

Canadian and that his name was McIntosh. Even when his biography was clarified, he continued to be known in the defensive room as O Canada, just as Matthias Berning, who really was from Duisburg, was called the German. Gradually it became clear that McIntyre had, as they said, "the good awareness," and he was also tough and physical. As he proved himself to be one of them, O Canada fell away and he became Mac. Berning, not quite as good a player, remained a foreign element, the German.

When the players had a night off coming up, which was rarely, you could hear them talking with excitement about Manhattan, the trendy meatpacking-district dance clubs, the upscale hotel bars. The team's staff did what they could to keep the players informed about and safe from the trouble that could find them in the big town, even providing a telephone number for no-questions-asked transportation home at any hour. And every day, there walked Burress, living proof of how badly a night out could go. Still, for them, young men of means posted to the tranquil Jersey suburbs, the city loomed out there, glimmering and dangerous.

And then there was Revis. Usually he went home and slept. One night an uncle of his, former All-Pro lineman Sean Gilbert, went with him to a movie. Nobody recognized either of them.

The defensive coaches had different kinds of leisure dreams. A huge Powerball jackpot led each of the men to speculate what he'd do if he won that much cash. O'Neil would rent out a resort and take all his friends. Not DT. "I'd be long gone," he said. "None of you would ever see me again. You'd never be able to find me. I'd be somewhere in Africa, where I'd blend in. I'd put a bone in my nose and a big earring!"

O'Neil said, "But what if I have a question about press coverage?"

"All of my materials would be right here for you!" DT told him.

Nobody believed a word of this. DT was the sort of coach who printed up T-shirts for his players that said "Keep Yo' Eyes on Yo' Work."

DT, DT, DT—there was nobody quite like DT. Before a rookie and second-year defensive-backs meeting, DT was teasing me about how football was turning me into a negligent father. "Your child won't remember you," he said.

"You sound like a man speaking from experience," I told him.

"That's it!" he cried. Then he faced the seven corners and safeties in the room and continued working the theme. "Do what I tell you, I'm like your daddy!" he said. "I got seven kids! Maybe soon only six." Then he looked at a baby-faced cornerback and suddenly became literal. "How many kids you got? Three?"

"Just one, Coach."

"That was my way of finding out!"

"I know it, Coach."

One of the seven young defensive backs was Julian Posey, the undrafted free agent for whom the honeymoon had indeed ended as soon as he'd signed on with the Jets. In the meetings DT gave him constant corrective advice, and it was the same on the practice field. "Son, stop fucking holding," he told Posey. "You develop bad habits, you'll bring them to the game, and we can't have that. Use your eyes and your feet." Whenever DT rebuked him, Posey's huge, round eyes would get big as soup bowls, and he'd nod furiously at everything, make affirmative sounds, affirmative notations. Sometimes in the face of all that, DT would have to turn away so Posey wouldn't see him smiling, occasionally even shaking with laughter. Recovered, DT'd growl, "Okay! Get your minds right. Don't be looking at your damn phones. You all need to improve."

Even as a coach, DT remained a cornerback. He was tough and charismatic, yet he was also a loner who was very comfortable on his own in a far corner of a bar, sipping a drink and thinking his DT thoughts. To the players, he was what they wanted out of a football coach. "DT, I love him to the bottom of my heart," said Revis. "He's gonna tell you the honest truth. He bites his tongue for nothing. He'll say, 'I'm fifty-five, why lie? Did it in the past, but why?'"

Standing in front of a roomful of rookie defensive backs, the large cross hanging from his neck, DT would slip into ministerial elocution: "Playing pro football is harder than anything you'll do in your life. You are playing to stay in the NFL. You all ought to die trying to get it. You know what Shannon Sharpe said when he was an undrafted rookie free agent out of Savannah State? 'Me not making it is not an option.' That's you. If you're not gonna commit to it, don't play. Because of the sacrifice you make to play, I hurt every day when I get up in the morning. It's from this game." He paused and looked out at them. "That's my first speech. My next one will be a Come-to-Jesus. As far as you're concerned, I'm one of His disciples."

Suddenly we were two and a half weeks into camp and it was time for the first exhibition game, a trip to Houston to play the Texans. Ryan gathered the team after the last practice and told them all to wear sweatpants on the plane and be on time for the team bus, "because we won't wait for you unless you're a really good player, and if you're not sure if you're a really good player, you're not."

At the Florham Park field house, TSA officials set up and supervised a security screening checkpoint: players and staff walked through and then boarded buses that drove, with a police escort, directly into a hangar at Newark Liberty International Airport, where they boarded their charter. The players and coaches got on first, and then, once they were settled, everyone else followed. Sutton had warned me that if I brought my playbook with me, I shouldn't leave it in my hotel room because "they have a way of disappearing." The fine for losing your playbook was nine thousand dollars, and the shame far more expensive. On the flight, I sat beside one of the Jets security men, a former New York police department organized-crime task-force member who told stories of setting up fake chop shops to bust Mafia figures. "Hey, Carmine! Next time, don't forget the fucking cannoli!" they'd yell at the mobsters once they had everything on tape.

During the flight, food was served more or less constantly. Chips, cheese, fruit, and pretzels were waiting on our seats, and then came burgers; chicken fingers; beef fillets; grilled chicken; more chips, cheese, and crackers; a snack tray teeming with everything from chocolate to Slim Jims; trail mix; a final chips reprise; and a steady supply of Gatorade and water to wash it all down.

In Houston, a group of hotel ballrooms was reserved for the unit and team meetings. Everyone took his seat, as always, in a positional cluster. Standing before his team, Ryan, so mellow through all the camp afternoons, began speaking in a sudden rush of intensity that I was unprepared for. It was as though, like an actor, he was suddenly in character. Glaring out at the room, he said that not everyone would make the Jets or the NFL, but they had better fucking do their best to. Their job was to beat Houston's ass and make his and Tannenbaum's decisions difficult. It was crucial that they score a lot of points to serve notice, because the rest of the league would be watching.

At breakfast on the morning of the game, some of the coaches were discussing the early days of steroids, how bad some players had smelled when they sweated. It was understood that the league had mostly moved on from the juice to human growth hormone and that some number of players were probably taking a lot of HGH to aid their recovery from injuries and help them stay on the field. Across the league, such was the supposed prevalence of HGH that when you heard of a player recovering from a severe injury in no time or when a hard-hitting career lasted well beyond the usual duration, it was impossible not to wonder if He Got Healthy because He Got Help. But who on the Jets might be doing it was only a matter of speculation. Around the facility, where the Purell stations were plentiful, the training staff urged the players to put only safe, approved substances into their bodies, but the players weren't telling the trainers anything about their experiences with the darker aspects of football medication. The coaches occasionally had their suspicions; they assumed the players discussed HGH among themselves behind closed doors, but the players never brought it up with the coaches.

At the stadium that night, I watched the game from the coaching booth, where Pettine called the defensive plays with O'Neil and Brian Smith on hand to assist him. The booth was up on a suite-level concourse, high above the field. Pettine liked being in the booth for its lack of distraction; there he could be sealed off from the sounds and the emotion he'd experience if he stood on the sideline. Schottenheimer preferred to call the offensive plays from the sideline — he wanted to feel the currents of the game. Mike Devlin and Lance Taylor from the offense were always up high to provide Schotty with a longer view. Scott Cohen, Tannenbaum's efficient, observant deputy, was also there serving as the team spotter, calling out the Texans' personnel groups so the Jets could counter if they wished to. Everyone wore a headset. Offense and defense each had an open channel for its own unit and a second, private channel the coordinator could switch to for conversations with individual assistants. Ryan was on both the offensive- and defensive-group channels. There were also telephone lines connecting the field and the coaching box. If the telephone receiver was picked up on one end, it rang on the other. Should Pettine or Devlin up in the box want to talk with a player after he came off the field, he'd tell whoever was monitoring the bench telephone to send word. The other tools of their in-game work were sheaves of statistical charts and an abundance of colored pens and energy beverages. A video assistant provided intermittent still photographs of the game.

Pettine made his calls by radioing them down to DT, who relayed them out to the inside "Mike" linebacker—David Harris when the starters were in. (Harris, like Sanchez, had a microphone inside his helmet.) Before and after calling the plays, Pettine carried on a conversation with Ryan down on the field. Sometimes he switched channels or picked up a telephone with a sideline connection and spoke with other coaches and occasionally even players. Most of what was said related to mistakes. What was most impressive was how quickly Pettine saw the game. The Texans would come to the line: "Alert Woody Boot," the coordinator would cry, and sure enough the backs crossed, and the Texans quarterback sprinted out opposite the blocking flow and flipped a pass to the back. "Are you fucking kidding me?" Pettine would cry when a long gain ensued, and then he was past it. The linebacker's responsibility was edge containment, either to collision the back or drop off and cover him, but once, then twice, neither of those things happened. The third time the Texans' Woody Boot worked against the Jets, Pettine waited until the players came off the field and then called down by telephone for outside linebacker Jamaal Westerman. When Westerman got on the line, Pettine told him he was better than that.

Mostly the offensive and defensive coaches in the booth ignored each other, concentrating on their jobs. When the former Arizona Cardinal kicker Neil Rackers lined up to attempt a fifty-yard field goal for Houston, Pettine predicted he'd miss because "he's got some Cardinal in him." Rackers made the kick, and Devlin, who'd played for Arizona as well as Buffalo, said, "Hey, Pet, what do you mean, he's got Cardinal in him?"

"Dev," said Pettine. "You've got way more Bill than Cardinal in you."

After all the months of waiting for live action, the game went rapidly past, a 20–16 Jets loss. When late in the game the defense finally stopped the Woody Boot, Pettine cried, "Hey!," and Lance Taylor, his eyes still on the field, said quietly, "Halftime adjustments."

Before I took my first football road trip, I imagined them as adventures for the players, youthful forays for small-town boys to exciting new American places. That was the way it often was for baseball players because they traveled so often and remained in each city they played in for several days. In football, road games were modern business trips, and the stays were brief and tightly scheduled. With all of the meetings and curfews, few of the players saw anything of Texas except the hotel and the stadium, where the sudden encounter with Houston summer air after all the time indoors came as a thick, hot welcome to NFL competition. When games ended, no matter how late, the Jets always flew home through the night. After the Houston game, we landed back in New Jersey shortly before dawn. Rob Turner had broken his ankle during the game, and as he crutched his way off the airplane, you could tell how important to him it was to do it without assistance, and that such was expected of him.

Back at the facility, the defensive coaches brewed coffee and went to work, watching the game film. What they saw was sloppy, so sloppy that there was the same line repeated: "An NFL player's got to make that tackle." The coaches invoked the league so many times—"Now, that's an NFL throw!"—that with a little change in the wording, they could have been a group of Princeton admissions officers: "He's certainly good, but he's not Princeton good!" Ellis Lankster had played so fiercely he'd become Lancaster to all because, said Pettine, "He's been great since Westy malapropped him." Posey—now known as Buster, because every rookie needed to be known by something other than his given name—had been singed by Houston receivers. The consensus was that the cornerback needed a year on the practice squad to get NFL tough. Posey himself said later that the most shocking part of the experience for him was that when the long-imagined, long-awaited, long-rehearsed-for first NFL game finally came, there was no time to think, only react.

The coaches assessed as a unit the things they'd done well and the things they'd done poorly, then sent the two columns of information on to Ryan and Tannenbaum for the after-action meeting they held with their top assistants the day following every game. Then Pettine instructed his staff to do what they could to help the offense. "We'll wear ankle weights, let them get some success this week," he said. "It's all about the team."

Eight

DIME SPIKE 1 (VEGAS)

Life is to be lived, not controlled.

—*Ralph Ellison*, Invisible Man

A week later the Jets played the Cincinnati Bengals in MetLife Stadium, the neon coliseum in the New Jersey Meadowlands that the Jets shared with the New York Giants. The night before every home game, the Jets checked in to the team hotel near the stadium. The offense had been sluggish in the barbecue air of Houston, and they had remained that way all week in practice. At the hotel, in the meeting room the defense used the night before every game, Pettine discussed the Bengals and then offered some thoughts on the Jets offense, as if to emphasize that the offense should not become a second adversary. "There are some issues over there," he said. "It'll take them a while to work some things through. Let's be the rock-solid foundation that this team rests its Super Bowl hopes on."

Yet it wasn't in the defense's nature to nurture anybody. The defense players excelled because they aspired to hurt you "right in the feelings," as DT put it. All week during practice they were as vehement, scowling, and ornery as ever, full of feistiness, sending backs and receivers sprawling in shorts-only drills; taunting Sanchez when, under pressure, he made wildly inaccurate throws by yelling, literally, "Ha, ha, ha, ha"; talking relentless smack. You could see it all getting to the veteran receivers, who were used to a more even competition. "I'm not saying anything," Derrick Mason told Sanchez after a play went terribly wrong. "I just want to know, what did you see?"

"That defense is pretty good," Greg McElroy said to Tannenbaum along the practice sidelines.

"Better than Auburn?" was the GM's thin reply. Welcome to the big leagues, son.

No players on the offense would have enjoyed the thought that the defense was spending preparation time talking about them. During the Texans game up in the coaching booth, you could feel the resentments between the offensive and defensive coaches who were there together. In the elevator down to the locker room, the coaches said nothing, and the tense lack of conversation spoke all. The defense seemed to want to have things both ways, enjoying its practice-field dominance over the offense and yet growing impatient with the offense for struggling. To be rivals with shared ambitions was a delicate proposition.

The offense played better against Cincinnati in a 27–7 win. When the team did well in a preseason exhibition, the coaches didn't spend time afterward thinking over the game. In the Jets weight room, a countdown clock displayed, to the second, how much time there was until the regular season began; the Cowboys were the prize the players' and coaches' eyes were on. Most of them said they thought of preseason games as "glorified practices."

Not BT, who questioned the minuses on his grade sheet. BT's grade sheets were rarely without a couple of WTF comments, like "Be more disruptive" or "Fake it, dummy" or "Release more violently," because of Pettine's belief that players had to be pushed and pushed or they'd regress; that the better they practiced, the better they played; that it was crucial for the older players to show the younger ones that a high daily standard was necessary if they wanted to play well on an NFL Sunday. For all his outrage, BT was the only player who left his grade sheets behind after meetings so that anybody could look at them.

As it happened, for many of the coaches, the highlight of the Bengals game had come afterward. Ryan always received a police escort out of the stadium after home games, and so, following this one, a squad car, lights flashing, parted the thick postgame traffic to make way for the head coach. Though it was not Ryan's sleek green-and-black truck that appeared next but a battered compact Toyota with Jeff Weeks, its owner, at the wheel and Ryan, knees scrunched to chest, riding shotgun.

I spent the last week of August with the offense. I was greeted with suspicion. There were comments about my being a "mole for the defense" and doubts about my stamina: "Don't fall asleep," Schotty warned me. The defense regarded my defection with contempt. "You'll be bored to death with the offense," Bart Scott promised. It was, sort of, all in fun. The loyalties to one's unit were so tribal and immersive that on my first day "over there," when I looked through Schotty's office window and saw Sutton and DT walking by in the hallway, to my surprise I found I missed the defense.

Offense was, said A-Lynn, "a different planet." One world made something and the other tore it apart. The Jets defense was intense and they put in hard days, but Schottenheimer's men were triple-shift piecework laborers, insomniacs kept awake by "performance" energy drinks, fresh cups of strong coffee, and Schotty's committed desire to provide his players with a solution for every predicament. Tom Moore said that when he first saw the Jets offensive playbook it made him feel that in Indianapolis, he and Peyton Manning had run "a mom-and-pop operation." Longer offensive play calls typically designated passes and went like this: "Twins Right Middle Gun Scan Right F Yogi X Oklahoma H Balloon." Westhoff was horrified by all the words: "It's catastrophic. It's another language.

Like the Dead Sea Scrolls." At the beginning of the week, with things not going well so far for the offense, A-Lynn knew what that meant. The running-backs coach looked over at Lance Taylor and me and said, "Bring yo' pillow!"

Jets employees who'd worked for the Giants' Tom Coughlin, famous around the NFL for treating his staff like first-year law-firm associates, said that even Coughlin put out his candle before Schotty did. For the offense, there were no mid-film bathroom breaks, as Pettine gave, and far less levity. And in contrast to Pettine's rule that when watching film, you rewound a play a maximum of three times, at three looks, Schotty was just getting started. This was partly due to the difference between a defense that was "fully built" and the inchoate state of the offense. "We're trying to do what the defense is doing," said Matt Cavanaugh, the quarterbacks coach. "But we have a lot of young players."

The offense divided its primary responsibilities. Schotty handled the skill players, leaving Callahan to devise the runs and the protection schemes. Thus the offense comprised two player units that rarely met together. That division worried Ryan, who also wondered if the offense had brought in too many free-agent "individual contractors."

The offensive coaches did all come together to watch practice film, either in Schotty's office or in the main offensive meeting room. Cavanaugh had told me, "This is a much more complex and difficult world. Defense, you can have ten guys screw up and one guy makes a great play. Offense, everybody has to be together." He was saying that the offensive approach had a more speculative feel than the defense's steel certainty about what a call should look like and whether or not the players had met their obligations. The truth behind that observation was evident as we watched a screen pass that Scott disrupted. "This one had a chance," said Schotty. "Hell of a play by Bart." Callahan agreed. "If Slauson takes care of Bart, it springs." Over in the defensive room, had Slauson played for them, the coaches would have talked about Slauson's failure, and the conversation would have been tinged with derision.

The distribution of blocking assignments in a protection scheme called Midway was debated. Callahan could see "clear as a bell" how it all ought to look.

"Dev, you okay?" Schotty asked the tight-ends coach.

"No," Devlin said. The linebacker designations that the call relied on to tell the offensive linemen who to block were confusing to him. "It's like we're making the Mike the Sam, and the Sam the Jack." The Mike and Will are the strong-side and weak-side inside linebackers in a 3-4 formation. The Sam and Jack are the strong-side and weak-side outside linebackers. Such designations differed around the league; the Jets defense called the Jack the Rush. But Callahan and Cavanaugh were not confused and they didn't think Devlin should be either.

"Will you let me talk?" Devlin said to Callahan. "I played seven years. How many you play?"

"Ohh!" everyone cried.

"Coached thirty-four," said Callahan. "You?"

"Ooh!" swelled the chorus. Soon Callahan and Devlin were comparing how long they'd been married, to much laughter.

"We've got nine minutes left," Schottenheimer interceded. "Do we have to watch the runs?" Like most modern offensive coordinators, Schotty was immersed in the aerial game.

"Yes!" said Callahan, who devised the handoffs.

"Wake me up when it's over!" Schottenheimer told him.

"Ooooh!" said Devlin.

Listening to them, I suddenly saw a band trying to compose a song, saw the guitars, the possibility in all the strings and frets, the shouting difficulty of making something new and pleasing out of nothing, how rare a thing was a standard. Devlin's point was that if you couldn't agree on the key, there was no harmony and everything immediately became destabilized. Even if you could agree, it very likely would still fall apart. That the offense was always vulner-able was the nature of the game's design. You could never tell whether you had something until it was finished and you put it out there. A good blocking scheme had logical integrity. A really good one had integrity and also rubato — expressive feeling.

Early in the week Sanchez had a fine day of practice, completing nineteen of twenty-five passes. In the quarterbacks' meeting that followed, the Southern California–bred starter wore shorts, flip-flops, and bracelets made of rubber and yarn. On the wall, some-body had scrawled "19-25!" They were discussing a 5:30 a.m. text Sanchez had sent McElroy informing McElroy that he needed to take a shower before arriving at the facility. McElroy deemed the morning shower excessive since they showered at the facility after every workout. "I don't want you coming in here all scuzzy like everyone else," Sanchez explained. I'd been told that Sanchez's belief in proper hygiene was such that in the locker room on game days he applied deodorant before putting on his uniform and that at halftime he brushed his teeth. In the history of athletics, this made him just one more guy with a ritual. Revis's uncle, the retired NFL defensive lineman Sean Gilbert, was spending some time at training camp as a coaching intern, and Gilbert talked often about the necessity of becoming a different person to play professional football, that when you changed into the uniform, you had to change yourself: "Everybody in football has a split personality. It's a switch. The light goes on and you have to think, Kill! Kill! After-wards, you have to turn it off. You can't go to the mall thinking, Kill! Kill!" Yet in the bedlam of a game, players also had to remain collected, especially the quarterback.

Sanchez clearly considered McElroy to be *his* rookie. In the time-honored veteran way, so did Mark Brunell, the forty-one-year-old backup. McElroy was always being asked to fetch smoothies or omelets from the dining hall. They'd watch him enter Schotty's office, watch him settle into his chair, watch him thinking maybe this time they'd give him a break, let him see a little of the film Schotty and Cav were showing, let him imagine that finally he was going to learn something he could use, and then it would come—"Hey, Greg"—and off he'd go, on the trot.

McElroy had led Alabama to a collegiate national championship by being the sturdy vinculum binding more gifted elements. At the facility, everybody knew that he'd been an excellent student at Alabama; that he'd completed his degree in three years and graduated from the business program, where athletes rarely ventured; that he'd then pursued his master's; that he'd been a Rhodes Scholarship finalist; that on the Wonderlic intelligence test, he'd scored a very high 43 out of 50. (Sanchez had scored 28; Brunell 22.) Although McElroy could throw a football into a trash can from forty yards, his arm was considered weak by NFL standards, and he presented no evident threat to Sanchez or even Brunell.

Even so, Sanchez seemed preoccupied with him. After viewing some practice film of McElroy scrambling, Sanchez asked, "Greg, what did you run at the Combine?"

"Four-eight-four," said McElroy. "Why? Do I look slow?"

"No!" said Sanchez. "You looked faster than I thought you'd be." He paused for many seconds. "I ran a four-eight-eight," he said.

Sanchez's completion percentage in his first two years had been low for an NFL starter, only 54 percent. To go with it, there had been thirty-three interceptions, only twenty-nine touchdowns, and a surfeit of fumbles—nineteen in all. In the absence of Brad Smith and the Wildcat option packages he'd run so effectively for the Jets in 2010, Schottenheimer was using Jeremy Kerley, who'd been a Texas high-school quarterback, to take snaps out of the formation. The idea was to snap the ball directly to one of your best athletes, and, as Schotty said, "Let him make plays." The Jets called their version of the Wildcat Seminole, after the team's first practitioner of it, Leon Washington, who as a collegian had been a Florida State Seminole. No team that had full confidence in its quarterback took him away from center for a Leon Washington, a Brad Smith, or a Jeremy Kerley. Now when Schottenheimer scripted long-pass plays for Kerley to throw that were not in Sanchez's play list, Sanchez's reaction was to exclaim, "Oooh. Fifty-four percent passer!" In fact, Seminole was being installed only for the Giants exhibition game and then would be taken out—a ruse for the Dallas coaches so they'd see it on the film and waste time preparing for it. The Jets coaches weren't telling their players this, in case Dallas claimed one of them after the team made its cuts at the end of training camp. How Sanchez felt about the prospects of an option package, he made clear through caricature. On Schottenheimer's office whiteboard there appeared a Sanchez-drawn portrait of Tom Moore, still serving as Schotty's offensive consultant, captioned "Tom Moore zoning out during a discussion of Seminole!"

Schotty always talked of Sanchez with affection, the kind of affection a parent displays for a teenage son: "In the morning, his head is down; he can't find his notebook. He doesn't have a pen." By evening Sanchez would be commenting freely on everything. Looking at some Cowboys preseason film he'd notice, "Sweet handwarmer! It's August, dude!"

"At least Mark's straight on the things he's supposed to be watching!" said Schotty.

Cavanaugh broke in. "What was the coverage, Mark?"

"Three deep!" And so it was.

On the field, Sanchez completed a little hitch route against Revis to a journeyman camp-body tight end named Keith Zinger. After the play ended, Sanchez was so excited he ran upfield to congratulate Zinger. Revis looked like he wanted to throttle him, but Devlin understood that Sanchez was thinking of what the moment would mean to Zinger: "No matter what happens in his life, this kid Zinger can say he caught a pass on Darrelle Revis."

Sanchez was an enthusiast. The quarterback had a range of interests that were unusual for an NFL player—he liked to sing and play the guitar, took teammates to Broadway musicals on off nights, monitored the progress of the Libyan civil war ("What's up with Gaddafi?" he'd inquire), and might approach you in the facility hallway with a matter of urgent concern along the lines of "What are the Seven Wonders of the World?" His sense of humor was unique—a form of dry, deadpan repetition. Somebody in a meeting would observe, "Man, that quarterback has a hose!," and Sanchez would say, "Yeah, he has a strong arm too." If Schottenheimer said, "We suckered the shit out of Wilson," Sanchez would come through with "He did bite hard on the play fake!" His expressions were comical. He had a way of glancing at people with hilarious severity, and when they laughed, he'd say, "Yesss!" Sanchez was also self-deprecating. "I'm a five-year-old," he'd say. When bored, he'd begin writing amusing remarks in his notebook for others to discover, such as "Greg going bald!"

He and McElroy were very different. Sanchez walked into early meetings carrying juice and a big box of Golden Grahams, a sugary breakfast cereal that wasn't available in the cafeteria. Nobody else brought food from home. McElroy breakfasted like a coach, starting his day with eggs, coffee, and dip. About football, the rookie was all business, learning his playbook first by drawing the patterns and then by taking five-step drops at night in his bedroom while describing each play aloud to himself, in detail. As McElroy was telling me about this, Sanchez ran up behind him and pulled his shorts down. "Very mature," said McElroy, re-hoisting.

Schottenheimer, a man committed to his Christian faith, seemed to believe that all would turn out well for the offense if the players gave enough of themselves. "It's just concentration, men. It's gonna get us beat. We're asking you guys as professionals to solve the problem."

A person didn't have to spend much time around Schotty to appreciate his dogged capacities. The huge whiteboards along two of his office walls now looked like pages from the *OED,* dense with lengthy, meticulous lists of primary and secondary plays, running plays, passing plays, protections, a full cache of screens, options for the various downs and yards-to-go, the calls that were game plan–specific. If he didn't close the blinds in the window that faced the hallway, anybody could see the coordinator at work. There was no need to imagine Schotty at his desk in a hooded robe and scapular; the blinds were rarely employed. People passed back and forth, they stopped to chat out there, they fixed themselves snacks in the nearby kitchen. Ryan would even slip in through Schotty's door and remove a couple of treats from the glass candy jar on Schotty's conference table. None of it appeared to distract Schotty. Schotty told me once that the South's Civil War generals fascinated him, and though in all the months I saw him every day, I rarely heard him digress from the topic of football, the knowledge that the campaigns and engagements of Lee, Stuart, Forrest, and the rest were of interest to him made a sort of sense. The offense wasn't any kind of lost cause, but in Jets country, it was the unsympathetic side, the undermanned side, the side causing all the trouble. The future stability of the union was up to Schotty.

Schotty remained patient with his players as the Jets defense had its way. "Here's the beautiful thing," he'd tell the offense. "It ain't getting any harder than this. You guys should be glad you play against this every day. How would you like to be [Lions quarterback] Matt Stafford with that Tampa Two shit? Challenge yourself to pick this up." When he and the other offensive coaches watched film, they were curious about and admiring of the defense. "This is a great blitz by Revis," Schotty said. "I never saw it before." They were pleased that Muhammad Wilkerson had begun to play well. Only one subject seemed to try the coordinator's patience while watching film, the presence of Scotty McKnight. "Amazing Mark didn't throw to Scotty here," Schottenheimer would say. "He always throws to Scotty when Scotty's in."

Sanchez, susceptible to distraction, was very different from Schottenheimer. At times Sanchez's optimistic nature seemed to try the coordinator. When plays broke down, Sanchez sought to find something redeeming, whereas Schottenheimer, mindful that Manning, Brady, and Drew Brees never took kindly to failure, would have preferred his quarterback to be more brusque in holding others accountable.

Still, the defining quality in Schotty—as in all the coaches, offensive and defensive—was his caring for his players. As Callahan put it, "I love 'em all. They're my sons." The way Schotty spoke of Sanchez was the way A-Lynn spoke of Joe McKnight, the young running back from New Orleans. During McKnight's rookie year, A-Lynn had lost sleep over McKnight's debilitating insomnia and finally discovered that what was keeping Little Joe awake were the terrifying things he'd seen in the aftermath of Hurricane Katrina. The dead bodies floating through his nightmares were so traumatic, McKnight had come to fear sleep. No wonder, said A-Lynn, that McKnight struggled to remember plays in the afternoon. Devlin likewise felt sympathy and affection for the tight ends he'd coached over the years, for the one who'd been abused by his father and then refused to go to school so people wouldn't discover the bruises and send him to foster care; for the one whose father died of a drug overdose; for the one who had rare ability and no confidence. When one of his tight ends did something well during a game, Devlin, up in the coaching box, radiated with pride.

The night before the third exhibition game, this one against the Giants, Ryan gathered the Jets at the team hotel and told them the game was being postponed because a tropical storm was bearing down on New York. "Hey, don't worry about it," the coach said. "We don't care. We'll play anybody anytime. Just be safe." The facility would be locked and all entry pass codes deactivated so coaches wouldn't try to drive through the storm and keep working. Film would be made available online so they could access it from home by laptop. Immediately, some of the offensive coaches began plotting to go straight to Florham Park, ahead of the storm, and stay there, locked in through the hurricane, bedding down under their desks. The mere idea of unexpected free time was dreaded—they feared not working, because working all the time was the only salve for the anxiety-driven nature of the job.

An extreme version of what coaching could do to you and what could happen if you didn't have the job anymore was the recent plight of former NFL coach Corwin Brown. Some of the Jets coaches had worked with Brown and described him as a first-rate person but too dedicated a worker. After, at most, a couple of hours of sleep, he'd be awake and back to it. Gradually, Brown had begun to lose control. The Patriots, his last team, let him go, and he soon became hard to locate. The old telephone numbers went out of service, people stopped hearing from him, and then he was in a stand-off with a SWAT team outside his Indiana home. Brown held his wife hostage and, eventually, shot and wounded himself. The talk of Brown among the Jets coaches was the rare intrusion at the facility of the world out there. It wasn't that the coaches were dull men. When you work all the time, the other aspects of your identity recede until they seem to have disappeared.

The storm turned out to be Hurricane Irene, a killing disaster of high wind, hard rain, power outages, and worse, so it was wise that the Jets had boarded up the windows and taken down the practice-field goalposts. Schotty waited out the storm at home alone, sleeping and overseeing the offense as best he could, and Pettine likewise was "bunkered down in my place." The Ryans lost power and checked in to a hotel.

Two days later, the exhibition game with the Giants was finally played. Steve Weatherford of the Giants had been the Jets punter the previous year, but Westhoff had declared that he didn't do the job and let him go. Out on the field before the game, Weatherford angled a practice punt toward his old mentor and just missed him. Meanwhile, a young Giants coach was busily making notes, and Smitty walked over to say hello. Looking down, Smitty saw that the coach's notes consisted entirely of scribbles. What was up with that? Smitty asked. The young coach confessed that that he had no idea what coaches did on the field before a game, so every few minutes he'd take out his pen and scribble thoughtfully, just in case Giants head coach Tom Coughlin was watching. Coughlin was a fabled perfectionist, and nobody ever knew what would get him worked up.

Supposedly, according to the New York tabloid newspapers, the Jets were filled with antipathy for the Giants, the team with whom they shared a stadium and a city. But the Jets coaches didn't feel that way. They respected Coughlin and many of the Giants players. The two teams would play in earnest at the end of the regular season, so the coaching tactics on display during a 17–3 Jets victory had a restrained feel; both teams' staffs were holding back for the appropriate time and place—except for Coughlin, it turned out. While watching the film the next day, the Jets defensive coaches were amused to see many shots of him at a characteristic boil, looking like a guy whom the dry cleaner had just told, "Sorry, sir. Six suits you say? Never heard of them."

Since no Jet player had generated anything remotely like a bitch-kitty pass rush so far, Tannenbaum went looking out in the street and brought to camp Aaron Maybin. The linebacker had been a first-round choice of the Bills, but his two years in Buffalo had been marked by his inability to record a single sack, and now the Bills had cut him. Maybin's first-round background made him a curiosity to the others. Players and coaches took in his loud speaking voice and his high-strung way on and away from the field and were at first put off. There were denigrating rumors that Maybin didn't know how to drive, denigrating nicknames like Megaphone, and denigrating assessments like "one-trick pony." Maybin just went about his high-pitched business and ran, said Pettine, "like a gazelle with an Achilles." Standing still, he was in a hurry.

"In the two years we've been here, we haven't had a guy who

could explode off the edge like that," Pettine said. He told Smitty to pay extra attention to Maybin. After that, everywhere that Smitty went, Maybin was sure to go. If you closed your eyes during their impromptu tutorials as Smitty told Maybin, "We don't coach effort. This ain't Buffalo," you could mistake Smitty for Pettine.

One more preseason game remained to be played, against the Eagles. To an NFL team, the last exhibition was virtually meaningless. Starters were held out for fear of injury, and the only people who prepared much for it were the young players striving to make the roster. Final cuts would come after the game. Beforehand, Ryan told them all more or less exactly what he'd told the rookie Mike Smith back in Baltimore days: "The truth of the matter is that for some of you, this will be the last game you ever play in your life. This is the cold, hard facts. It's the business. So make sure you're going out representing whoever coached you, your parents." Then Brian Smith, who'd nearly made the 49ers ten years earlier, stood before the players and described the dark moment at home after San Francisco let him go, when he sat on his couch and realized "the game I loved all my life was gone for me." Looking out at the players, B-Smitty, the quietest of the Jets coaches, talked with feeling of how much he envied them. B-Smitty worked long, uncomplaining hours and seemed bashful around his superiors. He was a minister's son, a studious *cum laude* graduate of the University of Massachusetts. Then I saw him away from the facility, and it turned out he had a switch of his own. He greeted me merrily as Nicky Barnes—a reference to the Harlem drug kingpin who was Mr. Untouchable, until he wasn't.

The last preseason game mattered so little that Pettine intended to give the other defensive coaches the experience of calling a play series under live conditions. The day before the game, each of them received a call sheet. "Nicky," Pettine told me, "study up." He handed me a color-coded glossy piece of paper with calls from the playbook listed under the various personnel groups and then divided further by the down-and-distance situation. "Be ready," he said. "You'll be in control of a multimillion-dollar machine." Immediately there was a sense of panic. From the installs, I had a vague understanding of some of the plays. I had no confidence I'd remember them under pressure, much less know how to select them in relation to the strengths and weaknesses of young Eagles players I'd never heard of. Still, who could resist? I began to work up mnemonics to memorize calls like Odd Wolf Fire Zone, 3-2 Crown 1, Nickel Dog 1, and Dime Spike 1 (Vegas) — calls that were, of course, mnemonics already.

Invariably interesting was the etymology of the call names. Zip Double Field was for Jason Taylor, the former Jets pass rusher who'd played his college ball at the University of Akron, whose team was the Zips. Squirrel dated back to the Ravens and referred to the linebacker Jarret Johnson, whose rural, small-town southern childhood was said to involve squirrel hunting and maybe also squirrel eating. The players thrived on these little recognitions. With the calls, the point, of course, was to create names the players could easily remember. For instance, the first two letters of the call Snake signified a safety and nickel blitz. Many of the calls were variations on one another. A pressure called Cable, dreamed up for a game against the Raiders and named for then Oakland coach Tom Cable, had since yielded related calls like Comcast and others, all named for cable-service providers. As for Dime Spike 1 (Vegas), it had its origins in a pass coverage drop Ryan had created in Baltimore for a big defensive lineman named Keith Washington who'd played his college football at the University of Nevada–Las Vegas.

The usual way for Schottenheimer to install his game plan during the season was across three days. First- and second-down plays would be addressed on Wednesday. Thursday was for third down, and on Friday came the red-zone calls (money-zone, in Schotty's personal terminology). But none of that for this week. McElroy would play quarterback against the Eagles, and so Cavanaugh was preparing him by asking questions about the offensive playbook. After McElroy finally answered one incorrectly, he said, "I'm sorry."

"You don't have to say you're sorry," Cavanaugh told him.

"You're demanded to say you're sorry at Alabama," McElroy explained.

"Are you at Alabama?"

"No."

"I'll get tired of hearing 'I'm sorry.'"

In the locker room at the stadium for the Eagles game, we all put on khaki pants and matching green and white Jets polo shirts and caps. I slipped my folded call sheet into my pocket. Then I removed and unfolded it several times to make notes, reminding myself of things. Golf carts drove us through the stadium tunnels to the elevator, which then delivered us to the coaching box at press level. There weren't enough chairs in the box so I stood behind the coaches, as I'd done each week. In that little glassed-in room, even though there were spectators right there in adjoining boxes or in seats below, you felt removed from the enormous crowd around you, felt you were sealed off in a capsule that was its own little mind space. In the second quarter, McElroy, following through on a throw, slammed his hand down on a lineman's helmet, breaking his thumb. He thought it was dislocated and tried to pop it back in and keep playing—he would have done anything to keep playing—but then Schottenheimer called another pass, and McElroy discovered he could not grip the ball to throw it.

Up in the booth, coach after coach had his turn calling defensive plays, passing them down to DT who sent them out to the Mike linebacker. At the very end of the third quarter, with the Jets losing a listless game, 21–7, Pettine looked at me. My heart shifted. "Nicky, you ready?" he said in that even voice of his. Jim O'Neil was going to call the first- and second-down plays of the drive; the third downs were mine. O'Neil, excited, said something about "Let's do this, buddy."

I took the seat beside O'Neil and retrieved my call sheet. covered now with so many notations that some calls were illegible. I put on the headphones, thick and warm as earmuffs. On the open defensive channel I could hear Ryan and DT talking down on the sideline. Ben Kotwica, who'd flown night missions in those Apache helicopters, had told me what to expect from the headphones: "We've got six people on five radios and it's just like Baghdad—that headset chirps as much as any radio frequency I was ever on when I was flying. Rex talks to Pet, DT tries to call in the defense, Sutt doesn't usually say shit, O'Neil a little bit, but mostly Rex, Pet, and DT." Kotwica believed that "if you packaged it right, it's the number-one show on TV. It's comedy. Should we challenge a call or not? Trying to get eleven guys onto the field. That fog of battle. Everybody's got a game plan, but things happen and the enemy's got a vote."

Pettine showed me which button to push to speak. Behind me, Scott Cohen was calling out the personnel groupings. What looked orderly and matter-of-fact when Pettine did it now felt as though it were happening very, very fast. I looked at my sheet, trying to follow as O'Neil made his calls, doing a nice job of backing up the Eagles to third and fourteen. "All yours, Nicky," he said, his voice thrilling with accomplishment. I had no idea what to call. I blurted, "Nickel Dog," a five-man pressure. I liked dogs! Then I watched my nice Nickel Dog leave me, trot smoothly through the wires, stop to get a pat and a command from DT, and then dash out onto the field, where the Eagles second-year quarterback Mike Kafka—smart!, Northwestern!—showed my nickel dog a trick, completing a twenty-yard throw for a first down. My face was scarlet. How can I explain? There was the feeling that Pettine had loaned me something rightfully his, something valuable, something I had no business touching. It was a borrowed sports car I'd wanted to return without scratches and already it had a big dent.

The Eagles drive continued. Again O'Neil got to third down—third and two. Again he said, "All yours, Nicky," his voice a bit less enthusiastic this time. I'd always liked the sound of Dime Spike 1 (Vegas). The call meant that the dime, or sixth defensive back, should blitz. As the dime sprinted toward the line, the defensive tackle would spike, or suddenly switch from the B gap between the guard and tackle on the line to the A gap between the guard and center, leaving the B gap free for the dime to pass through. Meanwhile, another one of the defensive linemen—in this case, Marcus Dixon—would bluff a rush and then make a Vegas drop into short area pass coverage. Quarterbacks didn't expect a lineman to be prowling around back there, and, if the call worked, they wouldn't see Dixon. Dixon was a large figure, nearly three hundred pounds, but quarterbacks were like most people: under pressure, they surmised, noticing only what they had seen before.

Pettine was right. All the sounds around me fell away and it was intoxicating to be in control of these fast, powerful men, to make what was about to happen on a field far below take place. I felt a little like a puppet master: I spoke, they moved. I called for the blitz, garnishing it with the Vegas drop. And then something amazing happened. Kafka, under pressure, threw over the middle, right where Marcus Dixon's long left arm could reach. Dixon tipped the ball, enabling the defensive back Ellis Lankster to intercept the pass and return it sixty-seven yards for a touchdown. In the box, as Lankster zoomed toward the end zone, everyone was yelling except me. I was incredulous and now felt like a drug kingpin who'd been sampling some of his own product. In the aftermath, I was struck by how purely happy the coaches were. The play had worked to perfection, just as its designers had imagined it. Dime Spike 1 (Vegas) was such a beautifully conceived football idea that rookies and free agents could succeed with it—I could succeed with it. I thought that even as I was completely dumbfounded by the utter luck of it all.

After the kickoff, Pettine told me, "You call a pick-six, you get to keep going." Everyone was joking about my "hot hand," about my getting them "another quick score to tie it up," about the Jets having finally found an offense in me. Instead, I efficiently drove the Eagles down the field for a game-sealing field goal. When my calls failed, I could hear the coaches on the wires lamenting the missed assignments of linebackers, and now a small part of me wanted to agree with them.

The next day, I began what would be my routine for the season, attending the daily 8:00 a.m. quarterback meeting in Schottenheimer's office and then rejoining the defense for the rest of the day. I was one minute late to my first film session back with the defensive coaches. I'd never been late before. As I took my old chair between DT and Sutton, DT said, "He spends a week with the offense and look what happens." Then Pettine said, "Guy calls a pick-six and thinks he can make his own rules." The walls of the meeting room were covered with the numbers and initials of players who might be cut from the roster. On the bubble were names like MTV and Posey and Lankster and, also, Maybin, who'd twice sacked the Eagles quarterback.

All afternoon, there was the smell of gunpowder in the air. A succession of players with gloomy faces trudged upstairs with their playbooks to visit Brendan Prophett. They were young men at the pinnacle of their abilities, and already what they most wanted to do in life was over for them. Some told Prophett they'd been expecting to hear from him; others had no idea, were floored. One linebacker walked into the office before Prophett could send for him and, said Prophett, "cut himself." Prophett thought that most were "melancholy, forlorn." They all asked Prophett why. A few, including Scotty McKnight, promised to prove the Jets wrong. It was rare, Prophett said, that anyone did.

Lankster was cut. Two days later, Aaron Maybin was cut. He sobbed, completely devastated. Davon Morgan, the Virginia Tech safety whose cousin had been killed, said he "expected the best and prepared for the worst." He was in the cafeteria when he was summoned to the office of JoJo Wooden, a senior personnel executive who was sympathetic, knew what this day felt like. After playing linebacker at Syracuse, Wooden had been to training camp with the Arizona Cardinals only to be cut, while his brother, Terry, had had a long NFL career. Wooden told Morgan, "We wish we could keep you, but there's not enough room."

"If you really liked me you'd make room," Morgan told him. Then, "I gritted my teeth and got out of there." The lockout, Morgan believed, had kept him from gaining the sort of familiarity with the playbook and other members of the secondary, which would have allowed him to show the coaches what a smart, decisive player he was. Back at home in Richmond, he said, "At first I was in the slums, confused and hurt. I was lost. I never had nothing. I worked for this all my life." But Morgan also felt that "it's easier to hold on to remorse, to hold on to pain," and he decided that such would not happen to him. "Nothing could take the taste out of my mouth for football," he said. "That's what I love." He found a job but worked out every day—"I'm prayin' on a shot."

Posey and MTV and Josh Baker were among those assigned to the practice squad—a group of up to eight young players who practiced with the Jets but did not dress for games and whose presence with the team did not count as part of the fifty-three-man roster. Meanwhile, defensive back Dwight Lowery was traded to Jacksonville. D-Lo had wonderful skills, but the coaches felt that he hadn't progressed beyond the player he was when he joined the Jets in 2008. In the NFL, if you weren't going forward, you were left behind.

McElroy, despite the cast on his hand, was chipper. He would stay with the team and learn the pro game—he was already calling this "my NFL red-shirt year." He had plans to study and improve his arm strength with dedicated exercise and also read biographies of Ronald Reagan. After football, he was thinking he might be interested in Alabama politics, making him the first player I'd heard discuss professional plans for life beyond football. McElroy liked Alabama, he said, but as a person who spent most of his life around black football players, he recognized the state still had old failings. In a group of white men who'd taken him hunting were people who told him they celebrated Martin Luther King Day as James Earl Ray Day. Shaking his head, McElroy said, "They have no idea it's 2011."

With McElroy hurt and Brunell suffering from a calf injury, there was no backup quarterback to lead the so-called scout team of reserves who simulated the opponent of the week's offense every day in practice for the Jets defense. Someone suggested Cavanaugh do it. "I don't want to depress the defense," Cav said. Then he admitted that his fourteen NFL years had left him with constant knee pain. "How bad is it?" Sanchez wanted to know. So bad, Cavanaugh said, that he planned to have knee-replacement surgery after the season. He'd no longer be able to run, but he would sleep again. During years past, there had been times in the spring when Devlin and Dave Szott were pressed into practice duty. "Don't tell my wife," each would say and they'd suit up. Schotty recalled that Pettine had Matt Kroul "so revved" for his day of opposing Devlin, his fellow Iowa alum, that "snot was pouring out of his nose." Sanchez, a rookie then, said he'd watched Devlin take "a horrible beating. I was thinking, This is the NFL?"

Smitty's thirtieth birthday was celebrated at his favorite local restaurant. Many libations were brought to him ranging from lemon drops to vodka tonics to tropical rum punch to eighteen-year-old scotch. Soon Smitty began to look like four lanes of bad Amarillo highway. Someone mentioned what a fine player Nick Bellore was for an undrafted free agent, and O'Neil, with a subtle look in Smitty's direction, said loudly that Bellore was "unbelievable." Immediately, Smitty, who took all references to long-shot linebackers personally, corrected O'Neil. "Jimmy, he's *good*," said Smitty. "Unbelievable!"

repeated O'Neil. *"Good,"* Smitty insisted. Back and forth they went, until an assortment of desserts arrived on a plate that was inscribed in liquid chocolate, "Happy 30th Birthday AGAIN." As even Smitty realized, it was futile to hope you'd convince people of things at a party commemorating the birthday you'd forgotten. Better that the defense should rest.

The quarterback meetings were now all about the Cowboys, the first team the Jets would play that season, and in one of them, Schotty told the quarterbacks that Nick Mangold had confided that "things are getting confusing," and because "Nick's a smart guy," Schotty had decided to simplify the offensive package a little bit.

Every game week, the Jets pro-personnel department prepared an opposition scouting report so thick with information that Schottenheimer referred to it as *War and Peace.* After the coaches read the report, the person who'd written it (in this case, Scott Cohen) sat in with the coaches, briefing them. Cohen believed the Jets were clearly superior to the Cowboys, but "the thing about the NFL is, the first game, it's always a mystery." The difference, Cohen thought, between the NFL and college football was that in college football, the better team virtually always won. In the NFL, "weird things happen."

A week before the Dallas game, Pettine had his game plan 90 percent finished. It was "heavy volume," he said, because they'd practiced so many calls through camp. As the season went on and the team developed its personality and its play preferences, calls would drop out of the rotation. Five days before the game, on Tuesday night, when NFL defensive game plans are traditionally completed, the defensive game plan being built in Pettine's office still featured fifty calls. An ideal number was somewhere in the low thirties. "Pet, you got too many calls in?" Ryan asked him.

"They've all been repped so much," Pettine said.

"It's all bread and butter!" Ryan cried. "The back of our hand!"

Ryan looked across Pettine's conference table at me and said that in Baltimore, "Pet and I did the whole game plan, just the two of us. We were never home. You wonder why he got divorced." Ryan stretched and got up. It was very late. "As my father used to say, I don't know what else to tell you."

In his third year as a head coach, Ryan was still defining his role. He had given Pettine the same full control of the defense that Schottenheimer had with the offense, including play-calling, but the head coach hadn't quite thought through how he should spend his own hours during the season. When he'd hired Carrier to coach the line, Ryan had promised to help the former safety, but somehow he hadn't got around to it. He occasionally dropped in on the various defensive-position group meetings, but again, it wasn't in his nature to hover over coaches he believed knew their jobs. Ryan had also meant to look in more frequently on the offense, but those meetings still felt alien. It was the classic NFL problem Ryan had taken up with Joe Gibbs, how the master of one side should assert himself to manage the other.

Ryan sat in at the defensive-game-plan install meeting on Wednesday morning, listening to the coaches talking with the players about not letting Cowboys quarterback Tony Romo set his feet, promising them that Romo would eventually get flustered and make a mistake. Sutton compared him with former Packers quarterback Brett Favre: "Another gunslinger. There's no play he doesn't think won't happen." Pettine told the defense the game plan was broad and would be trimmed down across the week. "Any play you're not comfortable with, it's out. We want to play fast. It'll be an emotional night. We'll be geeked up, but a controlled passion. We can't go out of our minds." He paused. "Bart!"

"I can change!" said Scott.

The Cowboys pass-catching tight end Jason Witten was a player they feared, and because, said Pettine, Witten was a "build-up-speed guy" who preferred "finesse" football, the plan was to place rugged obstacles in Witten's path as he sought to accelerate. For Romo there was Jet Mike Mix, a heavy pass-rush bluff that would be used in an obvious pressure situation. The call, if properly applied after a sequence of blitz calls from similar formations, should worry Romo enough that he'd hurriedly throw into what was actually thick coverage. "Don't be the safety who bails early from the look," Pettine warned.

At practice, Ryan was still his old self. Tannenbaum had brought in for a tryout Mardy Gilyard, a shifty receiver the Rams had just cut. Gilyard had a grille full of gold teeth, and Ryan told him, "Hey, you make some big plays, maybe I'll cap my teeth." Then he rolled up his pant leg, displayed his calf tattoo, gestured to Wayne Hunter, and said, "See this? I got it so Wayne would come back. Hell, I'll do a lot to get a good player."

During the defensive walk-through in the late afternoon, Revis and Cromartie were excused to watch tape on their own in the inside linebackers' meeting room. Cromartie ran the film from the back row. Revis was up front. Cromartie's immersion in the game was complete. He'd studied Romo's pump technique and how he looked off defenders, noted Romo's preference for throwing outside the numbers. Jim Leonhard stopped by. "You guys doing extra credit?" Revis's eyes didn't leave the screen. "Just trying to win," he said. Cromartie was feeling optimistic. "Playing against somebody as big and quick as Plax and as fast as Tone means that when we play other guys, it slows down for us!"

DT's response to all this was "Show me Sunday, Cro."

Some of the players liked to wear their best clothes when they went to the stadium on game day, and already on Thursday they were discussing haberdashery. Jamaal Westerman noted that wide receivers generally dressed well. "Bart's pretty good," Calvin Pace countered.

"Except for the problematic Thurston Howell ascot," said Pettine. Having grown up in the shabby Detroit slums, Scott wanted to surround himself with beauty. Outdoor landscaping was important to him and so was cloth. His closets contained more than a hundred bespoke and designer suits made of fine fabrics from wool to linen to a silk of such luminous sheen that in it, he resembled the interior of a conch. Scott favored accessories such as pocket squares and Yves St. Laurent red-and-tan high-top sneakers. How would Scott describe his sense of fashion? "I like to wear things my teammates don't wear and don't know about," he said.

During Thursday's practice, the young reserve tight end Matt Mulligan, who was running Jason Witten's favorite patterns off the coaching cards for the defense, scored a touchdown and proceeded to celebrate. But in order to break open, Mully had deviated from the assigned Witten route. O'Neil said something about Mully being a "card killer." Mulligan offered something tart in reply. Instantly, Pettine was screaming at him. The words "slapdick who has done nothing in this league" were used. DT was likewise outraged. He said the rule for NFL rookies and backups, whom DT called ROYs, was "Be seen and not heard." What did "ROYs" mean? "Rest of Y'alls."

After practice, DT walked up to Posey and told him, "Hey! I haven't heard you asking me to stay late after practice and work on your man coverage!" Posey, who had been staying late on his own, was thrilled by this offer. "Time for him to take ownership of his career," DT purred.

Smitty spent much of the day downcast. A computer hacker had infiltrated his private e-mail accounts and his voice mail, sending it all into disarray, and now the hacker was leaving him triumphant, taunting telephone messages. Finally Smitty called up "my hacker" and told him, "Okay, dude. You got me. Look, it's 9/11 on Sunday. My father just had a stroke. This is America! Let's come together." The hacker was moved. "Dude, I feel bad," he told Smitty. "I'm sorry. I'll restore it all for you." And he did. It was noted that only Smitty would befriend his hacker. Had Smitty offered the hacker game tickets? Smitty said he might have if he'd known where the guy was.

Ryan received an unexpected communication also—a big, flat package roughly the size of a picture window. After unwrapping it, he discovered an enormous signed and framed photograph of Heather Locklear, still and forever "my celebrity crush." Up it went on Ryan's office wall. Pettine came in to inspect. "Only one thing missing," he mused.

"I know," said Ryan. "She has her shoes on!"

Thursday evening, after the last heavy practice of the week, is traditionally when NFL players go out. How these evenings are spent, "we coaches don't want to know," said Pettine. "It's a don't-ask, don't-tell." I never heard about these adventures either. Life inside the coaching area of the fluorescent-lit facility revealed little of the bright lights beyond. "Listen, Robert Frost," BT informed me once, "you have to tell it like this. Make it all drugs and prostitutes or nobody'll read it. Don't worry about the football. You got to have hookers and cocaine in there!"

The favorite work day, other than Sunday, was Friday. The game plans were installed, the hay was in the barn as people liked to say, there was everything to look forward to, the game to imagine, and Friday practices were light and full of Ryan fun. The position groups held little contests, the big defensive linemen running routes catching passes and also competing to see who had the fastest hands, raising their hands from the grass to touch the buckboard drilling sled. I was asked to judge this contest one week; it was nearly impossible to tell whose hands rose from the ground to the board faster. A guest kicker—someone who was not in any way a kicker—was always invited to try a twenty-yard extra point in front of the entire team. If he made it, he tried a twenty-five-yarder from his chosen hash mark on the field. Ryan offered a small reward for making the shorter kick, like a better seat on the team charter, and a double-or-nothing wager for the longer try. This day, Jim Leonhard made his first kick, then attempted the second and missed. After practice, the veteran defensive backs, along with Pettine and DT, stood thirty yards from a goalpost and competed to see who could throw and hit the crossbar first. Rookies like Posey were positioned beneath the goalpost to retrieve the errant throws and throw the balls back to the competitors. They played three rounds and took this very seriously, keeping track of the season standings. Invariably, DT was the man to beat.

Up in Prophett's office, Mardy Gilyard was receiving a plane ticket home. In his chair, getting the bad news, he looked completely diminished. Down on the Jets practice field was Isaiah Trufant, all five-foot-six and one hundred and sixty-five pounds of him, claiming a spot with the team again. By football standards, Trufant was not just a small person—he was a micro-person. Still, he had, as the players said, mad hops. One day while he was a student at Eastern Washington University, Trufant had passed by the court in the gym where students were dunking basketballs. Trufant was wearing flip-flops at the time, but they did not interfere with his ability to walk out onto the court and slam home a reverse. During his brief 2010 stay with the Jets, he'd been a water bug, a pond skater skimming all over the field on special teams. And when he hit you, Trufant carried a surprising payload. As the coaches liked to say, he hit you Tru.

After lunch on Friday, the players scattered, and the defensive coaches reviewed the practice film. In one play, offensive flow to the right had lured Bart Scott away from his responsibilities covering the young Jets end Jeff Cumberland, who was playing Witten on the scout team, and Cumberland then leaked out underneath and across to the left to receive a swing pass for a huge gain. "This Bart guy!" Pettine burst out in frustration. The call was known as the Oh Shit—for what the linebacker thinks when he sees what's been done to him. "I love Bart," said Carrier. "But he keeps you coaching." Later in the film, there was Trufant leaping up after an end-zone play and putting his hand over the top of the crossbar. He looked as though he'd bounced off a trampoline, and Pettine ran it several times as the coaches marveled at the little player soaring so high. For them, even with the first game approaching, film was an ongoing conversation, their way of taking in the world.

The Saturday before the Sunday-evening Dallas game, there were midmorning offensive and defensive gatherings and a new look for Revis. All week Revis had played harder and harder. In meetings, his eyes bored deeper and deeper into the film. During training camp, he had allowed his hair and beard to grow thick. Now that hunting season was about to open, he'd been to the barber and was cut high and tight. When the defense watched the practice film with their coaches and saw the Oh Shit, BT put a towel over his head because he was giggling so hard, and Pettine made a reference to "Bart chasing rabbits." Scott stayed buried in his playbook until Pettine moved the film to the next play. Then Scott said, "I can change."

After the meeting came the Saturday-morning team walk-through in the field house. Music played as Sanchez rehearsed his calls. Up on an observation balcony stood a group of hard-looking men with tattoos and piercings, their caps askew. They were Hunter's friends from the old neighborhood in Hawaii. Taking them in, Sione Po'uha said, "Wayne comes from the Compton of Hawaii."

Since D-Lo had been traded to the Jaguars, I hadn't heard him mentioned. He'd spent three years with the Jets. "Cold as it sounds," Leonhard said, "that's the business." Sutton offered a kinder take. "I think of the NFL as a corporation with thirty-two branch offices," he said. "He just got transferred to Jacksonville." Replacing D-Lo among the Jets defensive-backfield corps was Andrew Sendejo, claimed off waivers from the Cowboys. Sendejo had attended Rice University. Any player who'd gone to a fine school like that was assumed to be smart and slow. The Jets had heard that their claiming Sendejo had led Rob Ryan, down in Dallas, to junk his whole game plan, a rumor that gave Rex Ryan much satisfaction. That was the point. Even so, the Jets had debriefed Sendejo on the other Ryan's defense, which could make a man feel just a little mercenary. Sendejo, no matter how smart he was, couldn't yet contribute much in New York because he didn't know the Jets system. So he stood and watched the walk-through.

Even though there was a game the following night, running through Sendejo's mind right then was the fact that the younger Dallas head coach Jason Garrett had been "much more old-school than Rex." As the players along the sideline sang along with Archie Eversole's "We Ready (for Y'all)," Ryan, out on the turf, was keeping things loose by stepping in for Sanchez at quarterback to throw passes to the receivers. He also practiced his punting. It was impossible to watch Rex Ryan bend over a football, study it, and then stand and unfurl his vast leg without smiling. "There's nobody like Rex," said Sendejo.

Nine

THE WORLD CHANGES

I'm a steady rollin' man, I roll both night and day.

—*Robert Johnson*

In a football season where each of the sixteen games is the brief and fraught climax of a long waiting, the first game, months in coming, is only more so. Ben Kotwica compared the prelude to his experiences in the military. "That was the thing about the army," he said. "The endless battle drills, the occasional feelings of what am I doing all this for, and then suddenly the world changes."

Even by the usual fervid standards, the Dallas game was suffused with strong feeling for the Jets. They regarded playing as New York's home team on the tenth anniversary of 9/11 as a serious civic responsibility.

All football teams, even one as relaxed and player-friendly as Rex Ryan's Jets, maintain their composure through rigorous adherence to routine. Because football people know that they are spending their lives at the mercy of random events, their intense relationship with schedules and plans is what keeps them from thinking too much about the inevitable chaos to come. You can only control what you can control is the sport's tautology, and as game days approached, members of the Jets spoke it with frequency.

By early Saturday evening, every Jets team member had checked in to the hotel near the stadium, all of them ready for a familiar medley of meetings that, year after year, were always held in the same rooms. There were separate chapel services available to any Protestants and Catholics who wished to worship, and these were followed by quarterback and special-teams meetings. At the latter, Westhoff used an overhead projector to display a series of return and coverage diagrams on a screen while narrating in one continuous riff. He was an overhead-projector bluesman playing his slides, the inimitable Westhoff cadences now oddly soothing. You could hear them as free verse:

> *We could pop one right away.*
> *I don't know.*
> *We could do it.*
> *We could.*
> *Be smart.*
> *Make a move.*
> *Or knock 'em right in the face.*
> *That's fine.*
> *We got a million things we could do.*
> *Kickoff return.*
> *Hell, they're not gonna score many times anyway.*
> *The whole package.*
> *I feel good about.*
> *Should feel good about it.*
> *Just watched the film.*
> *I think they're cute.*
> *Cute is what I think they are.*
> *Hit 'em right in the face.*
> *Bam!*

On it went, and on, seamlessly, until it was time for the offensive and defensive meetings.

The defense came together in a small, airless room with the

players in sweats and their chairs jammed so close together that the linebackers and linemen had to adjust their flanks to squeeze in. A Jets banner no bigger than the kind that might decorate the bedroom of a sixth-grader hung on one wall, and a few photographs of the players had been tacked up as well. It was a long way from the spacious, modern lecture halls of the facility. The stripped-down rec-center closeness was a reminder that the players had nobody but one another. In the back, I sat next to Tannenbaum, who bit his nails. Fridays through Sundays were the worst for him. There was nothing left for him to do. Pettine, at the front with his laser pointer, said he didn't want to get "the room too lathered up." The way to control yourself out on the field on such a big night was to take the meeting room to the field, everyone in place, everyone communicating. He talked of possible Dallas gadget plays, screens, long vertical passes, told them there'd be no surprise looks from Dallas—"We've seen them all." He told them they were the best defense he'd ever stood in front of. He showed them a photograph of a championship ring. "Yes!" breathed Sione Po'uha, unaware that any of us could hear him.

Then the defense repaired to the team meeting room. It was a bigger conference space, though again stuffy, and short of chairs, forcing some of us to lean against walls, turning our torsos at angles to fit everyone in. Ryan, in blue dress sweats, believed in the Napoleonic battle theory that held you should never ever praise your opponent because it hurt the morale of your own side. Accordingly, Ryan told the Jets they had more team character than Dallas. He related a recent conversation he'd had with the star Cowboys pass rusher DeMarcus Ware, who'd told Ryan he was going to lead the league in sacks if Ware's coordinator, Rob Ryan, gave him enough opportunities. That, said Ryan, was putting yourself ahead of your team and it was a losing way to think. The Jets would win because, unlike the Cowboys, they were there for each other.

Then it was downstairs to the dining area for the same array of food stations, from pasta to stir-fry to Mexican, that were there every week, right down to the bags of popcorn and the bottomless bowl of gummy bears by the door. Ryan and I were among the last to leave. As we did, I told him what Pettine had said to the defense about how good they were. Ryan said that the best defense that he had ever coached was the 2000 Ravens, who were "the best defense in history!" He looked at me and asked, "You think they bought that conversation with DeMarcus Ware?" Then he winked.

Up in his room, Revis did what he did the night before every game. He watched a movie, chatted on the telephone, and then went to bed. The next morning, he opened the hotel-room blinds and said, "It's a great day for football!" Before the pregame meal, he would take a hot shower, put on a custom Astor & Black suit, and then, "I'm ready to go!" That night he would run out onto the field between flaming torches. "Football," he believed, was "like the old times, like the gladiators. Fans chant for their favorite team or person and if you're not their favorite, they want you dead. Kill him! Crush him!" He couldn't wait. But because he had to, in the interim, he put on a *So Fly* T-shirt and sweats and went to breakfast and then to a defensive walk-through Pettine held in a ballroom normally used for wedding receptions and the like. Revis was taking pictures of people in the room and laughing. Around him, they were all in T-shirts and sweats, all of them laughing, each player seeming as he always seemed, right down to Marquice Cole, who had the hood of his sweatshirt on because, he explained, "that's just the way Quice is. Quice keeps it close and covered!" Looking on, Nick Bellore said that the difference between college players and his Jets teammates was that "in college everybody was so anxious. The coaches were freaking out. Here, they're so relaxed."

When Devlin had played college and pro ball, on game days he'd been the farthest thing from relaxed. He described himself as a player who had to give more to keep up with the others. He arrived at the stadium before everyone else, got his ankles taped, taped his fingers, and put on his shoulder pads, everything at the exact same time in the exact same order every week, and "by the end I was in such a frenzy, I was crying." When he joined the Bills, who were in the midst of a run of four consecutive Super Bowl appearances, in the Buffalo game-day locker room he saw "guys watching TV, guys reading *Playboy*, guys discussing *Playboy*! What stood out to me was when Marv Levy [the head coach] walked in and shut off the TV, the room went completely silent. They flipped a switch and got ready for war. I'd never had that switch." Instead, Devlin became unable to talk with his wife from Thursday night until the game was over.

Clyde Simmons thought of a team in its locker room before a game as an orchestra assembling in the pit: "It's a building up to a beginning. Building...building...building...into the moment." The mood in the spacious Jets accommodation—thick rug, wooden lockers—was purposeful. Most players wore headphones. There were few smiles and no long conversations. Pure quiet was best, thought Nick Mangold; it got you "in the mind-set." Plaxico Burress circled the room, touching every teammate's helmet. Pettine also made a circuit, leaning in to whisper something private to each of his players. DT was back in the coaches' dressing area, reviewing the game plan. When he'd played, he'd laugh a lot before games. "You're getting ready to get involved in physical combat. It's gonna be intense. So cracking jokes was a way of relaxing for me. There's no right or wrong way." Ryan gathered the team, they prayed together, and then Ryan told them, "Our city. Our game," and into the tunnel they went. There were American flags everywhere in the crowd, so much emotion.

After all that, the first half passed as quickly as Kotwica had said it would. I watched for a while in a team box with injured receiver Logan Payne. He thought first games were difficult because you had no current film and thus no idea of your opponent's tendencies, so you couldn't channel your expectations. This game was apparently not difficult for Tony Romo. The Cowboys quarterback was having success against the Jets secondary, while Sanchez, as Callahan told the linemen at halftime, endured "too much fucking heat." The Cowboys led 10 to 7 at the half. The more senior coaches gathered briefly around Ryan. He wanted to make wholesale changes, bring up the free safety in a zone look to "take away" Jason Witten, but Pettine reminded him that the defense couldn't "change into what we haven't prepared."

The Cowboys increased their lead to 24–10 early in the fourth quarter; the Cowboy receivers were having a wonderful game, primarily at Cromartie's and Scott's expense. And then came a series of miraculous occurrences. After a touchdown pass to Burress, a goal-line stand notable for the playmaking of Scott and Mike DeVito culminated in a Romo third-down fumble on the Jets three. Then Joe McKnight blocked a punt just as Westhoff had scripted it, and the ball was returned for a game-tying touchdown by the recently arrived Trufant. On the next Dallas possession, Scott again stuffed them on third down and short. After punts by each team, with less than a minute left, the Cowboys had the ball with the game still tied, and Pettine finally called Jet Mike Mix. Here was that rare moment when all men did their jobs exactly as the play diagram indicated, and the opposition responded just as the defensive play caller wished them to. Safety Brodney Pool showed low pressure and then dropped deep. At the same time Revis appeared to be retreating to cover for the blitzing Pool but then stayed shallow, and Romo never saw Revis lurking. Revis intercepted Romo's pass near the sideline and returned the ball to the Dallas thirty-four, close enough for Nick Folk, three plays later, to kick the fifty-yard field goal that would win the game for the Jets. By then I'd gone to the locker room, where I watched the end of the game on the equipment-room TV with the equipment-room staff and Tannenbaum, down early from his box so that he could greet the players as they returned to the locker room—which he always did, win or lose. At present, the GM was running around in happy little circles, hoarse from saying "Trufant!"

Afterward, there was brown-bag food for everyone, a gathering outside in the players' and coaches' parking lot, and then, for Smitty and Pettine, a trip back to the facility, where a case of Bula had been left in the coaches' kitchen. Bula was the new kava-root health drink Sione Po'uha was marketing. It was supposed to have ancient-Polynesian tension-reducing effects. Pettine and Smitty each cracked one open—it tasted like grape soda—and watched the game tape deep into the night, and when they got to the blocked punt, Pettine smiled and said, "Westy! That crazy bastard!"

Carrier said that on Saturday afternoon he'd arrived home, ready to spend his first free afternoon all week with his wife and children, only to discover that nobody was around. He didn't know where they were. "So I just chilled alone." As he did, he realized, not for the first time, that his family's lives were going along without him. O'Neil liked to say that coaches' wives were "single mothers for six months a year." It was most difficult, he said, when a coach took a new job in a new town. "When we first arrived in Ypsilanti, Michigan…" He shook his head at how hard those first months had been for Stacy.

I now knew a little of how they felt. To my own family, my existence seemed to consist mostly of unsatisfying transitions, all arrivals and departures. It was easier for them to have no expectations of me. When, for the first afternoon in weeks, I had time for a walk around my neighborhood, I felt out of season. Over the course of the year, while I always knew what day of the week it was, I often had no idea of the date; on the third, I might notice that the month had changed. I was amazed that a person could lose a sense of familiar moorings that quickly. Then it occurred to me that if I'd really been a Jet, it would have been imperative by now for me to feel a belonging with them. Inside the nest of the game, there was no time for the real world; that came only after football was done.

With the variedness of the days, so many people and tasks competing for attention, and always that need to forestall football's creeping sense of impermanence, a to-the-minute week's schedule was a crucial necessity. For the next sixteen weeks, the team would follow the in-season daily calendar that all NFL teams adhered to, with only modest variations.

On Mondays after games, the facility training room resembled a busy auto-body shop. Only two or three players made it through a year without some injury, and that didn't, of course, count turf burns, cuts, bumps, and bruises. Mondays for the coaches, meanwhile, meant coming into the facility early to watch and grade the game film. The game was so fast live that much of what the coaches now saw was a surprise to them. Often players they'd supposed had played well had actually been "tuurrible," as DT liked to say, and vice versa. The players were just as uncertain about what had gone on. To them, the tape was their professional standing around the league, and as they soaked out the soreness by switching between the big communal tubs of very hot and very cold water, they wondered how it all looked between the frames. (To take their minds off this anxiety, some of them competed to see how long they could remain submerged in the cold water. It felt like the ocean off the coast of Maine and, within seconds, staying in there became excruciating.) By late Monday morning the coaches would assemble in their two staff groups and watch and discuss the tape together. There would be a team meeting during which Ryan addressed the just-played game by narrating a series of play-like-a-Jet highlights. Then in offensive and defensive meetings, the coaches reviewed the film with the players and afterward walked through any significant corrections with them. In football, all the corrections were done in front of the entire unit so everyone could benefit from them and to emphasize that everything was about the team, not the individual, that linebackers were accountable to nose tackles and safeties as well as other linebackers.

In the late afternoon and evening on Mondays, the focus shifted to the next opponent. The coaches all watched film, everybody scrutinizing at least four of the opponent's prior games, trying "to unearth things," as Pettine put it. All had assigned weekly research tasks: the opponent's down-and-distance tendencies (O'Neil), the preferred plays used with various personnel groups (Sutton), favored running concepts (Carrier), favored passing concepts (Thurman), and any precedent for gadget plays (Sutton). "Concepts" meant a family of run or pass routes. Levels, for instance, are routes in which crossing receivers converge from both sides of the ball and must run along parallel paths so as not to collide. Some players studied every page of this intelligence. For others, said Sutton, "It doesn't fire their imagination." Revis wanted all of it. "The information is key," he said. "Sometimes you hear Rex and them during a game yelling, 'It's third and eight and you know what's coming!' and it's a cool feeling." Weeks filed no reports. His task was to make some of the cards, the drawings of preferred opponent plays, for the scout team to use in practice. Somehow, Ryan eventually ended up doing them for him, to the annoyance of the offensive and defensive coordinators alike.

Tuesday was the players' day off and the longest day for the coaches, who had no time off during the entire week except for the Saturday afternoons before home games. For most of Tuesday morning and afternoon, Pettine and Schotty continued to "slow-cook" their game plans, as Pettine put it. The *War and Peace* advance scouting reports were presented by Scott Cohen, Brendan Prophett, or someone else who came downstairs from pro-personnel. The pro-personnel men labored over their reports like students writing term papers, and they seldom received much feedback from the coaches. What did the coaches think? they wondered. Everybody wanted to contribute. Pettine welcomed suggestions from his subordinates, just as Ryan had in his Ravens years, and all day they were received. Once in a while a player submitted an idea. At night, as Schotty worked alone, O'Neil and Smitty faced each other across the conference table in Pettine's office, drawing the plays on their laptops as Pettine supplied them. Most extant calls received weekly modifications. Pettine did not believe in all-nighters, but the endless possibilities of combination and countercombination were tempting enough for him that it was O'Neil's job to hurry Pettine along so the job was finished, just as it had once been Pettine's job to do that for Ryan.

Eventually, Pettine would signal that he was ready to print the rough draft, called the ruff. There was around the league a lot of mystique about NFL game plans, but Ryan and Pettine didn't respect coaches who valued them over what intuitive players could do out on the field. You could win with a bad game plan if you had superior talent, Pettine believed. Or, as DT put it, "Playmakers will do things that schematically cannot be accounted for." On Tuesdays, Ryan was typically gone by eleven. Pettine slept on the mattress in Ryan's office closet. O'Neil would be on the camping mattress he set up in the defensive meeting room. The O'Neil bed was in evidence during the Wednesday-morning meetings, his red pillow and the blue-and-green blankets still retaining the shape of O'Neil's form, as if, after his three hours of sleep, O'Neil had startled awake and left so quickly that the blankets hadn't realized he was gone.

On Wednesdays, the quarterbacks met with Schotty at 8:00. During the team meeting at 8:50, Ryan previewed the next game's opponent, and then there were offensive and defensive game-plan-installation meetings. (The actual defensive game plan had different sectors of calls for different personnel groups, all squared off in primary-colored boxes. New calls were rendered in bright red. Football design inevitably seemed to recall the great abstract modernists.) A long "man's day," as Ryan liked to say, followed the installation meetings. Thursdays were similar to Wednesdays, and on Fridays, the pace slackened. If the team had won the previous week, Ryan awarded game balls at the Friday team meeting, sailing them out to each recipient as he encouraged Sanchez to notice his deep-ball accuracy. Then came the lighter practice. Saturday mornings the team did the walk-through, which was followed by either road-game travel or a few hours of family time and then the drive to the hotel. No downtime for the younger coaches. They'd spend Saturday afternoon looking ahead to the next opponent, breaking down four more weeks of game film and drawing their practice cards. At the entry level, the workload was crushing.

Going forward, I would experience all of it not as individual days but as a long car trip in which days were absorbed by days and everything happened at an accelerated clip. There were a series of destinations along the way (the games), and getting to each one involved the punctuated routines of the journey: buying gas, stopping for coffee, seeing an interesting billboard, hearing something good on the radio, encountering heavy traffic or heavy weather or a speed trap or a good road turned to swale, all the days blending because they never stopped, went constantly forward—every day many dozens of small occurrences and interactions whose cumulative import I would be able to discover only at the end, looking back. In the moment, to those immersed in the work, every last thing seemed urgent.

The day after the Dallas game was a victory Monday. For the coaches, there were victory magic bars baked by Michelle Tannenbaum, and victory chorizo-and-egg tacos made by Kotwica's Mexican American wife, Christina—touches that seemed in homely contrast to how public and extravagant the spectacle of the games was. Christina had been married to a fellow helicopter pilot of Kotwica's, a man named Jason, who was murdered by a gang of teenage burglars at his home near the Fort Hood, Texas, base. In the aftermath of the tragedy, Kotwica and Christina got to know each other, and eventually they married. Now her children called Kotwica Dad, and he and Christina had two children of their own. It wasn't, Kotwica thought, anything a man could have predicted for his life. Early on, Kotwica had made a point of treating Jason's children the same way he treated his own, but such effort wasn't necessary. His good heart was smitten with all of them.

While the defensive coaches met, Bart Scott, so stout against the run but a liability in pass coverage, was outside running sprints. If he wanted to remain a three-down linebacker, he knew he really would have to change. The defensive coaches were happy they'd won but displeased with how many big passing plays they'd allowed. "I think," said DT at the meeting, "we need to ask the question, What the fuck are we doing?" But there was also plenty of praise around the table for Tony Romo's ability to complete "incredibly difficult" throws right up until "he fucks up at times you can't fuck up—he's got a little black cloud following his ass." They talked about what winning coaches in the NFL say to their just-defeated opponents, debated what the losers liked to hear least. It was agreed that "Hey, good luck the rest of the way!" was a step up from the chuffing "Hey, you guys played hard!"

"We did cover the shit out of the Oh Shit!" noted Pettine. That settled, the coaches went to the dining hall and ate layer-cake-size victory burgers for lunch.

In the meetings, the need for improvement was stressed. "We won the game and I'll just stop there," Pettine began. As he watched a languid walk-through afterward, Ryan said, "Everybody's tired today. After emotional games, that's the way it is." Ryan hadn't been able to sleep, so he and his wife had climbed out of bed and gone to an all-night diner. JoJo Wooden, the even-tempered former Syracuse linebacker in the front office, had watched the game with Tannenbaum in the GM's box. Wooden said the boss had become so excited at one point he'd bull-rushed Wooden and bloodied his nose. All the scouting people had such Tannenbaum-box stories. Clinkscales had once nearly been shoved out the window. Since I planned to watch the Jacksonville game with Tannenbaum, I asked him if I was in danger. I hoped so; it seemed wonderful to watch alongside such passion. "I'm not proud of how I act and I apologize in advance," Tannenbaum said. "But I can't help it."

*　　*　　*

The defensive coaches spent the Tuesday after the Dallas game piecing together their plan for Jacksonville, a team with a gifted running back, Maurice Jones-Drew—Ryan called him Pocket Hercules—and an inexperienced quarterback, Luke McCown. The Jaguars relied on a predictable carapace of conservative, ball-control running but would abruptly slip on a different skin and throw long passes, often to their tall (six-foot-six), fast (forty yards in 4.8) tight end Marcedes Lewis. (To Ryan, he was plain Hercules.) Ryan was for bulking up the box with extra linemen or as many as five linebackers, enticing the Jaguars to throw more than they liked to. "If they can run it, they've earned it," he said. Pettine began shuffling through old computer files, retrieving Ravens run-stopping formations from 2005. "That's some good shit," said Ryan, looking at the old drawings. "Sumbitch used to work. We had some balls then!"

"We never actually put them in," Pettine told him. Ryan, undeterred, said, "Well, we had some balls in the meeting room!" Tannenbaum leaned in. The Patriots had cut Jeff Tarpinian. Interested? "No way!" Ryan responded. "He said no to us." Gently, Tannenbaum reminded Ryan that Tarpinian had been Jeff Bauer's draft-day sticker player and that the Patriots had paid Tarpinian more than twice the signing bonus the Jets had offered. "Rex, you have scar tissue because he said no to us."

"Absolutely," said Ryan.

"We'll think about it" was how Tannenbaum left it.

That night, Pettine, with help from Ryan, Smitty, and O'Neil, made the Jacksonville defensive game plan. A candle was lit, the (old) computer guy's balls were busted, a brief trip was made to the hotbox, cans of Bula were consumed, shoes were removed, the songs of the Hawaiian singer Israel "Brother Iz" Kamakawiwo'ole were played. Listening to Brother Iz sing "Starting All Over Again" was a weekly defensive-game-planning ritual; it knocked the coaches out that a man who was so large—at one point he weighed more than two nose tackles (over 750 pounds)—could croon with such dulcet sweetness. Across the hall, as Mike Devlin drew up the week's blitz protections for the offensive line, he had the film *Friday Night Lights* playing—"for ambience."

Pettine had discovered a new run stunt, used against the Pittsburgh Steelers on Sunday by Baltimore's Terrell Suggs, in which Suggs looped around the interior lineman Haloti Ngata, charged straight up the middle, and sacked Ben Roethlisberger. After drawing it, Pettine went to Callahan's office to see what he thought. "That's an unbelievable stunt," Cally said. "Please don't use it against us in practice." Soon Pettine's whiteboard wall grew red, green, blue, and black with new ideas. Some were Ryan's. His role was generative—and then to insist every play would work. Pettine's was to play the skeptical product-development chief, to say, "That gets you beat if they run the boot." O'Neil's was to wait until Ryan went to the kitchen to spoon a mouthful of peanut butter straight out of the jar and then ask Pettine, about the just-proposed play, "You want it?"

Late in the evening Ryan asked, "Are we putting in too much stuff?" Pettine replied, "The fact that you're wavering tells me to keep it simple and play football." But simple was unappetizing to both of them. Ryan began proposing ideas about how to stop a favorite Jones-Drew run. The running back lined up split left behind the quarterback, broke left as if to begin a pass route, bent back right to take the handoff, and then cut behind the guard while the linebacker retreated in pass coverage. "I'll draw 'em up real quick!" Ryan offered, reaching around for something to write with. "Pen or pencil?" Smitty asked. "Pen!" Ryan said. A moment later, Ryan said, "Got any Wite-Out?" Pettine offered him a pencil—"They have these things on them called erasers, Rex." As he headed off to his office at midnight to draw, Ryan sang "My Eyes Adored You." Across the hall, Schotty toiled alone.

*   *   *

The Jets freshly signed veteran receivers Derrick Mason and Plaxico Burress were nine or more years older than Sanchez. Both expected to be frequent pass targets, as did Santonio Holmes. Sanchez had to figure out how to lead the older men, make them feel sufficiently on his side that they'd develop an on-field rhythm, stay with him, and not become disgruntled during games when the bulk of the action went elsewhere. The Jets, after all, were known as a run-first team. One approach was to go right at the situation. All the starting receivers attended the Wednesday quarterbacks' meeting. Derrick Mason strode in wearing a black-stitched wool hat with a gold 85 on the back. Sanchez playfully attempted a de-hatting while telling him, "Don't wear your Baltimore shit in here!"

Mason, laughing, said, "Man, it's not Baltimore, it's Tennessee!"

"That's even worse, that crusty old thing you were wearing when I was on the couch in junior high watching you in the Super Bowl."

DT was worried that the Jets defense lacked aggression, lacked the necessary toughness. He was irritated with the way they'd played against Dallas, irritated with too much player bitching about play calls, irritated with poor fitness, irritated with how many pass completions his secondary was allowing in practice, irritated that when an offensive-scout-team player ran lazy routes, nobody was stepping up and telling him, Run the fucking route right because I'm getting ready for Sunday and I don't care if you like me! He told them that good football players didn't have many friends. They had teammates who respected them. In this way, DT was following his old coach Tom Landry's theory of coaching, which held that you should be harder on your team when it won because the players were more receptive then. After losses, they were too busy "getting their swag back" to heed much rebuke.

Speaking of attitude, word out of Dallas was that after battling Revis all night, the Cowboys receiver Dez Bryant had been too sore to practice on Wednesday. Revis was out there, though, as usual wearing extra layers of sweat clothes in the late-summer heat to make himself as uncomfortable as possible. He said that during the game Bryant had cussed and trash-talked him in ways "there was nothing funny about" until the end, when, abruptly, Bryant told Revis, "I respect you!" A man Revis respected was Sutton, he said, because, no matter what, Sutton kept up his daily fitness running.

"Only a moron could fuck this fabulous game plan up!" is how Schotty began the Friday-morning quarterbacks' meeting before Sunday's Jacksonville game.

"Hi! My name's Mark!" said Sanchez.

Everyone was in high spirits. Part of it was the first-week win and part of it was Kev. Days before the Dallas game, Tannenbaum had signed Kevin O'Connell to replace McElroy as the team's third-stringer. If you were writing a movie and needed a stock character for the groom's best man, Kev was your guy. He was bright, diligent, and friendly to all. Schotty's good cheer also had to do with the end of a long, eremitic week. "Men," Schotty said. "My wife's coming in today at eleven forty-five. Get out the way!" Since she seldom saw her husband during the fall anyway, Schotty's wife, Gemmi, was spending the season with their children at the family home in Nashville. "I'm really fired up," Schotty said. Soon he was teasing Sanchez about parts of the Jacksonville plan, "Mark, you're not good enough to do this!" Then he looked at McElroy. "Men, I'm hungry. You want anything?" On Schotty's computer, the new screen saver was a photograph of McElroy flat on his back after being sacked during the Houston exhibition game.

"I'm gonna miss the good stuff," lamented McElroy. He looked at Sanchez. "You want anything, Mark?"

"How about, 'Can I get you something, Mr. Sanchez, please?'"

After that, it was one long string of Schottenheimer sentences that began, "Don't forget!" Many of these reminders involved the Jaguars fine linebacker Paul Posluszny. "Take *that*, Posluszny!" Sanchez would say in reply to each point Schotty made. The meeting ended at 8:49 and seventeen seconds. They took the main corridor at a trot and were easing into their seats when Ryan began the team meeting at 8:50.

Working in the New Jersey suburbs meant everyone on staff drove to and from the facility. Many of the coaches were fascinated by the road habits of New Jersey drivers and would talk about the subject in ways that seemed to redound to football. During the Friday practice, Kotwica discussed signature New Jersey driver moves, like tailgating at eighty-five miles an hour; meridian jumping to escape traffic jams; ninety-mile-an-hour cutoffs; lane-to-lane slaloming; and going slowly in the far left lane and refusing to move over for a faster car but then speeding up when the faster car slipped into the right lane and attempted to pass from there. "I don't know how much they think about risk," the former attack-helicopter pilot said. "It's like a football player going for a fumble. Total disregard for the body: That's mine! Same thing out there: It's my lane!"

Amid the Friday practice enchantments of the defensive linemen running their weekly pass routes and making one-handed catches, their buckboard fast-hands competition, the guest-kicker contest, and the hitting-the-crossbar game, hearts were light. Cavanaugh warned me that the scene was deceptive. "It's always happy when you win," he said. "When you lose is the test. You see who they are, how they handle their confidence."

At the team hotel near the Jets stadium on the Saturday night before the Jacksonville game, the quarterbacks sat around a table in a suite that felt like a living room. They all had copies of the large call sheet of plays that Schottenheimer would work from. Sanchez read each call aloud and they discussed some of them. Schotty was, as always, thorough and engaged. With the big play sheet in his hands, he looked like a young architect visiting his building site. Some coordinators scripted the entire first quarter. Not Schotty. After the first play, which would be a run by the halfback Shonn Greene, he went by "feel"—which was the primary reason he liked to be down on the field during games rather than in the box.

The receivers arrived. Derrick Mason was mourning his college team, the Michigan State Spartans, losing to Notre Dame. "What's up, people," he greeted everyone. "I'm just happy that I get to come to a job that I love even though it's been a bad day for Spartan Nation." After the meeting, the players headed downstairs to the offensive meeting room, where, through the wall, you could hear Pettine addressing the defense, telling them that against Dallas, "We didn't play like us."

Schotty gave his offense an efficient summary of the plan, and then everyone converged to hear from Ryan, who began, "I'm so fucking jacked up I don't know where to start!" But, he said, he hated to "sweep anything under the carpet," and he called out the offense for the failure to score a touchdown in sixteen consecutive first quarters, dating back to the previous season. Usually when the Jets won the opening coin toss, they elected to kick rather than receive, a sign of faith in the defense. Tomorrow, Ryan said, if they won the toss, they'd receive, and he wanted the offense to "show me why." Ryan's thinking on pregame speeches was that when the player's head hit the pillow that night, he should have no doubt in his mind that his coach believed the opponent was in every way the lesser team, so Ryan followed his opening remarks with a profane panegyric to the Jets offense, the Jets defense, and even Ryan himself. Of the Jaguars coach Jack Del Rio, a former colleague of Ryan's in Baltimore, Ryan said, "I coached with that guy. He can't hold my jock!" Afterward, everyone stopped by the dining area, and the coaches lingered after the players went up to their rooms, eating sundaes and sipping nightcaps of family-recipe Mississippi moonshine poured from a bottle given to them by David Harris.

During Friday's team meeting, as he did every week, Westhoff had previewed the officials who would work the game, a job he took very seriously and that was obviously necessary but whose actual utility seemed improbable to me. In real time, would players think to adjust their play because of a zebra? Nobody wanted to commit penalties. This week on Friday, however, Westy had mentioned that one of the Jacksonville game officials had played high-school football in Doylestown, Pennsylvania, for Pettine's father, Senior. That could go a number of ways. So now, down on the field before the game on Sunday, Ryan approached the official, Scott Green. "You're not gonna hold it against us that you played for Pettine's dad, are you?" Ryan asked him.

"Well, he did break a few clipboards over my head," Green said.

In the locker room, Schotty gathered the offense. "Men," he said, "we've been challenged. Let's do what champions do. Answer the challenge."

Tannenbaum greeted me as I entered his box by saying, "Nicky, don't fuck it up or you'll be out." He had a yellow legal pad in front of him and was already scrawling thoughts. Bradway and Prophett were also there, wearing suits. The box had four televisions tuned to games around the league, stadium seats upholstered with buttery brown leather, and enough varnished-wood cabinetry that it felt like a law office. The Jets won the toss, elected to receive, and were driving down the field when the play clock wound down and Sanchez had to call a time-out. "Fuck! Not acceptable," Tannenbaum cried, making furious yellow-legal-pad notations. Moments later Sanchez threw a touchdown to Holmes, and Tannenbaum was thrilled that Sanchez was now completing passes he wouldn't have tried two years before. There followed a safety, and then a field goal. The score was 12–0 Jets. On one of the televisions, Dane San-zenbacher, a rookie Bears receiver Tannenbaum hadn't been impressed by during the draft, scored a touchdown. "Hey, Terry," he called to Bradway, whose Sanzenbacher opinion had been more positive. "Why can't we find receivers like that?" Tannenbaum was much more comfortable describing his mistakes than his victories, but he was shrewd. I'd learned recently that he'd made a team-by-team study of the personnel transactions of every NFL GM. There were some opposition front offices whose year-by-year record on releas-ing or trading their players spoke to such savvy that Tannenbaum didn't do business with them.

On the field, Wayne Hunter was struggling at right tackle for the second consecutive week. "We have to help him," said Tannen-baum to his legal pad. Then tight end Dustin Keller missed his block on a linebacker and was thrown into Nick Mangold, who limped off the field. The Jets defense distracted everyone from these concerning developments by intercepting pass after pass. Cromartie snared two, and there were others by Eric Smith and reserve linebacker Josh Mauga. On the ground, the labors of Mau-rice Jones-Drew were to minimal effect. For D-Lo, all this meant extra bad news. His new team was getting its stables cleaned by his former team, he himself was not playing terribly well, and from the sidelines Ryan, an inveterate in-game trash-talker, was keeping him abreast of every development: "Hey, D-Lo, how'd you like that catch? And that one!" The final score was 32–3.

"There aren't many like this," Tannenbaum said. He went down to the locker room, where Santonio Holmes's reaction was "Nice job, defense. Pretty fucking average, offense, but we'll take it." Schotty agreed. "We're great in flashes and shitty in flashes and we've got to get more consistent." To the coaches, the expansive vic-tory was deceptive; nothing about the offense satisfied anyone, and many, like Schotty, were quietly worried. "Nick," Sutton told me, "treat victory and defeat for the impostors they are."

*　　*　　*

According to the official NFL stat sheet distributed to the coaches, the Jets defense had held Jacksonville's Luke McCown to the lowest opposing-passer rating in Jets history, 1.8 out of a possible 158.3. During the entire year, I never met any player or coach who knew how to calculate this convoluted statistic. (It takes into account attempts, completions, yards, touchdowns, and interceptions.) That the Jets didn't know what passer rating actually was in no way interfered with their happiness at the passer-rating accomplishment. This seemed to me, in its way, a perfect little metaphor for a game intently watched by millions but truly understood by very few.

Troubling news was that in this week's game, the Jets would oppose the Oakland Raiders and their powerful defensive line without the fulcrum of the offensive line, Mangold, whose injury had been diagnosed as the dreaded high ankle sprain. The loss of the center, Pettine told the defensive players on Monday, meant: "Gotta put it on our back. We'll gladly accept that." Julian Posey wasn't at the meeting. He'd just been cut. He had been late to a couple of meetings and grown drowsy in others. On the field, the coaches and personnel people thought Posey needed to prove himself to be "more than a pretty-boy corner."

Playing the Raiders in Oakland, said Pettine, was going to be "like fucking Halloween come early." Many Raiders fans dressed up in ghoulish costumes and treated the stadium stands as a mosh pit. The field was shared with the Oakland Athletics baseball team and so it would have dirt instead of grass across the infield skin. Oakland halfback Darren McFadden's passing ability was yet one more unpredictable element to look forward to.

By Tuesday evening, the game plan was in process, and so was the peanut butter plan. That Ryan had been spooning prolific amounts straight out of the communal jar had led the defensive coaches to set up a trap for him. They'd superglued the top of the peanut butter jar shut and set up an iPhone camera to film Ryan's

efforts to open it. The code phrase for Ryan going in search of peanut butter was "spider in the web." Ryan, meanwhile, was in his
office making a tape to boost Wayne Hunter's self-esteem. "His confidence is shot," Ryan said. The head coach's plan was to invite
Hunter into his office and tell him, "I want you to play like this guy."
Then there'd be a video featuring a few dominant frames of the
Hall of Famer Anthony Muñoz, followed by a seamless segue to several dominant minutes of Wayne Hunter.

Around midnight, the spider headed for the web. O'Neil and
Smitty turned on the arachnid-cam and then ran away so Ryan
wouldn't hear them giggling. Pettine kept his head down. Watching
the web film together afterward, the coaches saw Ryan struggling
with the jar, muscling and tugging at it. Eventually he began murmuring, "I don't need to do this." He kept trying for a while longer
and then he put the jar down, told himself, "The thing's too hard to
open anyway," and walked away. "Sometimes you get these flashes
of brilliance," said Pettine.

As for the other game plan, the Raiders used a fairly similar
scheme to what Jacksonville ran, so there were only six new Jets
defensive calls, which Pettine referred to as "tendency breakers." A
blitz that had worked well was removed because Pettine guessed
the Raiders would be too ready for it. Most other Jacksonville calls
would be up again on Pettine's call sheet, including several that Pettine had put in the Jaguars plan and then not used. That frequently
happened with new calls because in the moment, he'd think back
to practice and feel unsure that the players had mastered them.

On Wednesday morning, Schotty told the quarterbacks and receivers that Al Davis had been running the Raiders in the same way for
years. Davis always wanted huge pass rushers ripping up the field
toward the passer while sprinter-fast DBs glided along in coverage.
Sanchez was sitting there in Schotty's office hooked up to several
mobile electronic-stimulus machines—he ached all over. Schotty

and Cav asked him what hurt the most, but Sanchez refused to address the topic. He wanted only to talk across the table with his favorite receiver, tight end Dustin Keller, about how they'd exploit the Raiders over the middle.

As Schotty ran through the game plan, Mark Brunell noticed that the coordinator looked wiped out. He had been in the office deep into the night, door closed, like a lonely scrivener in his garret, fueled by chips and chocolate. "Was your dad a grinder?" Bru asked. "Yeah," Schotty told him. "They called him Roadblock."

The receivers left. "Boy," said Sanchez as he reflected on all the material Schotty had just introduced to them, "the receivers are really into it. If we asked them one question, they wouldn't get it."

"That's just receivers," said Schotty quickly. "Don't let it affect you." Time and again through the year, I'd see evidence that the stereotype was true: receivers and cornerbacks were the most difficult players to coach. As for tight ends, somebody in the meeting now mentioned Dustin Keller's lackluster blocking. Sanchez spoke up loyally: "If he misses a block, he'll just score later in the possession, so who cares!"

At the 8:50 team meeting, Ryan announced that Cro had been named the AFC defensive player of the week, and the team gave him a hand. In one week, Cro had plunged and then soared. As Pettine liked to say, that was life in the NFL.

Out at practice that day, Callahan predicted that with help, Nick Mangold would be back quickly from his painful ankle sprain. Callahan said that he sometimes dropped in on the training room before games to see the injured players lining up to take pregame injections, saw "the veteran guys hesitating, yes, no, okay, I'll do it. It's amazing what they'll do to their bodies." Most of the shots were anti-inflammatories and not casually administered. The NFL was vigilant about its drug protocols, keeping all medications under frequent review, and Jets team doctor Ken Montgomery was considered by the coaches to be an especially caring professional. A tall, amiable Californian, Montgomery shared Callahan's admiration for the ability of Mangold and other players to endure their injuries. Like anything else, the doctor said, playing well with an injury required experience.

Early Thursday morning, Schotty was talking third-down alignment principles with Sanchez and the other quarterbacks when Ryan appeared. "If I could just interrupt," he said. "They're motivated by the hot-dog incident. How funny is that?" The last time the Jets had played the Raiders, the Jets had been so far ahead that Sanchez, then a rookie, was taken out of the game. He was soon captured on camera eating a hot dog on the sidelines, an action the Raiders considered disrespectful.

For Sanchez, life was good. The team was 2 and 0. His pal Scotty McKnight had just been re-signed to the Jets practice squad. There was in front of him a fine McElroy-catered breakfast of steak and eggs slathered in A1 sauce. At practice, as he often did, the quarterback ran extra sprints during his rest breaks.

On the practice sidelines, I listened to Bart Scott claim he had never had the flu in his life, had never tasted beer, and had never seen the like of Nick Bellore's large head. "It's so big, he's evolution!" Then Scott began naming the NFL all-melon team. Peyton Manning was the squad's (heady) quarterback.

As for DT, the man was feeling puckish. For the upcoming long flight to California, he instructed Carrier to "tell the old lady to bake me some cookies."

The team traveled to California on Friday so as to have a day to recover from the cross-country flight. To encourage rehydration, there were coolers filled with Gatorade and other drinks installed in the hotel's meeting rooms and near the elevator banks on every floor. On Saturday, after a walk-through at a local high school where Sanchez, the native Californian, ran around barefoot, Ryan,

Weeks, and I visited Alcatraz. Ryan, after hearing that no prisoner had successfully escaped the island, surveyed the San Francisco Bay's watery swells and declared, "Hell, I could swim it, no problem. The old sidestroke!" Schottenheimer telephoned Ryan during the drive to say that A-Lynn's son, D'Anton, a Penn State defensive back, had been carried off the field during a game against Eastern Michigan with a spinal injury. Ryan immediately called A-Lynn and urged him to fly to his son. It turned out that D'Anton was not as severely injured as had been feared, but Ryan got back in touch with A-Lynn and told him, "Either way, you should go. He'll be scared." Right there was Ryan in full, absurdly self-confident and deeply and feelingly good-hearted.

The game did not go well. I watched with Tannenbaum, who pointed out that Burress offered the time-honored leaving-the-huddle clap only on pass plays. During his three years with the Jets prior to joining the Patriots, Bill Belichick had taught Tannenbaum to notice details like that. The Jets went ahead by ten and were positioned to score more, but Sanchez threw an interception into the Raiders end zone. Given the chance, the Raiders rallied. At halftime, the Jets had outplayed the Raiders but were tied with them at 17, which the GM considered a troubling harbinger. He was right. The Raiders running game surged through the usually implacable DeVito and the other linemen. By game's end, Cromartie had been charged with four penalties and had fumbled a kickoff, missed tackles, and, finally, hurt his chest. Down on the sidelines, Mason lost his temper, confronting Schotty about the play-calling, screaming, in effect, that he wanted more balls thrown to him. After the 34–24 defeat, Cromartie, accompanied by the trainers, passed through the cramped visitors' locker room, picking his way around strewn luggage, his eyes wide with suffering and fear. There was a damp, anxious smell in there. Young Jeff Cumberland had torn his Achilles tendon and was on crutches. It could all go to shit so fast.

*   *   *

On Monday morning, following a long, brooding return flight, the defensive coaches were trying to understand what had happened, what had been done to them, how the Raiders could have failed to convert a single third down and still won the game. Most NFL games boiled down to four to six crucial plays that either went your way or didn't. After a close win, teams simply moved on. After a close loss, everything was questioned, as happened now. The coaches berated what they saw on the film. Jets had loafed. Jets had failed to react. Jets had overreacted. Jets had panicked. What had caused all this? The coaches themselves had caused all this. They were babying the players. As a result, the players were out of shape. The players were distracted. The players needed urgency. "Fucking awful," said DT. "Little bit of tough love coming this week," said Pettine. By the time the film was over, the coaches felt better enough about life that the outcome of the game was no longer taken personally. They could go and meet the players in a constructive frame of mind.

Ryan told the assembled team that they'd been soft. Better not try that again this week. The Ravens were the same sort of tough, physical team as the Raiders but much better at almost every position. And then after the Baltimore game, the Patriots awaited the Jets. Ryan smiled. He said these two weeks would be "a great challenge," one for which he personally couldn't wait. How about them?

"It isn't going to happen just because Rex says it is," Pettine informed the defense in their meeting. On film, time and again, the players watched themselves loping in pursuit or simply freezing while opportunity sped past. BT made soft groaning noises. Cromartie's arm was in a sling. He looked years younger, simultaneously meek and resentful. It occurred to me how unusual it was to glimpse vulnerability on the face of a football player. It was difficult even to see Wilkerson's face behind the cairn of ice bags the rookie had strapped to his shoulder. Leonhard sat there wondering how some players could play to their peak ability every game while others fluctuated from week to week. By now, upstairs and the coaches were agreed that the season would probably hinge on whether the crucial trio of Sanchez, Hunter, and Cromartie played well. When they did, the Jets were formidable. When they didn't, the Jets were something less.

The games quickly came and went, and so did players. The lower end of the fifty-three-man roster was a mass of shifting parts, as was the eight-member practice squad. You were either getting better or getting worse and getting gone, everyone said. The team brought Aaron Maybin back from the street and also Julian Posey. Revis took Posey aside and told him how serious football was. "Don't be late," he warned. "They're not so invested in you that they'll let it slide." The aspiration for the week was "tempo." That was the point of Maybin. The team didn't, of course, know how he'd been spending his time out on the street. If Maybin was fit, that dude was the full agitato. If he wasn't fit, they'd cut his ass, allegro.

Cromartie's character was a source of fascination around the facility. Each week, the superlative athlete was a different player. At the moment, the severity of his injury was a topic of internal conjecture. Would he play against the Ravens? Building the game plan, the defensive coaches had to assume not, and they began to construct calls that would protect the less skilled cornerback who'd man the position in Cro's absence. How glad they all were to have this to do. The urgent challenges of the near future relieved the coaching tendency to perseverate over the recent failures.

In a building filled with competitive people, Pettine was on the ferocious end of the spectrum, and the desire to beat the Ravens consumed him more than it did for any opponent. The year before when the Jets had lost 10–9 to his old team, he'd come out to the stadium parking lot where the coaches always gathered with friends and family to picnic and unwind after games. Pettine had been so disappointed he couldn't talk to anybody. He climbed into his car and sat there alone staring at the steering wheel. Right now he would do anything to beat the Ravens, but with such motivation came the risk of doing too much. This week, the Jets defensive players hoped for fewer calls than the forty-eight they'd had in the Oakland plan. During the Raiders game, Smith and Leonhard had reported to their coaches that the defense was feeling overwhelmed. Part of Pettine realized he probably should cut back. But it was the Ravens! He knew their offense intimately, had opposed that offense with Ryan for years on the practice field, and had developed antidotes for everything the Ravens offensive coordinator Cam Cameron might try. Pettine's intelligence had made him discussed around the league as a rising NFL coach, but right now too much insight might bring ruin. Pettine couldn't bring himself to shrink the plan, because anticipating every explosive play the Ravens might try and providing defusing responses was what he had to offer. At the moment, on Tuesday, the new defensive plan had forty-eight calls.

Bart Scott, who had looked slow and tired in the second half against the Raiders, was going to lose reps this week. Smitty worried about the effect on his old Baltimore carpooling companion, wondered if they shouldn't create a new package for Scott to respect his pride. "Listen, Sara Hickmann," Pettine said, "just make the depth chart." Smitty sighed. He was feeling overwhelmed by life. The staff at the clean, brightly lit nursing home where Smitty had arranged for his ailing father to stay had called. His father was "acting out," and if things didn't improve, he was going to be asked to leave.

Pettine was watching tape, and he discovered a middle blitz Buffalo had used to good effect against the Ravens. After modifying it to his own personnel, Pettine thought about the name for a while, searching for a distinctive M word to communicate "middle." He settled on Megan Double Field, after his daughter, who was at home in Maryland that day turning seventeen.

*　*　*

With so many former Ravens around the facility, suggestions from all points arrived with frequency at the Schottenheimer unloading dock. He and Pettine met—it was unusual for either to cross the bullpen, but these were no ordinary times. Ryan provided thoughts. During the quarterbacks' meeting, so did Derrick Mason, who said that with his ex-team, it all came down to knowing where Ed Reed was. "Ed! Freestylin', doin' what he wants to do," replied Schotty. He looked at Sanchez. "They're all confident because they know they've got him lurking and they've got a good pass rush. If they get to you, which they will some, say uncle! Throw it away."

The receivers left. Then the door reopened and Mason returned. Looking at Schotty, he apologized for his outburst during the Raiders game. "Thank you," said Schotty. "I appreciate it, but it's not necessary. We're thrilled to have you here." What he didn't say was that he couldn't solve Mason's problem, which was that the man still thought like a number-one receiver instead of what he was, the number three on a team that ran a lot because of the limitations of its young quarterback. Had Schotty been up in the box during games calling his plays, he would have been unavailable to Mason. "I would never want to avoid the receivers," Schotty said. "I want to deal with it head-on." Later he would tell me, "There's dysfunction at times when you're losing. There's anger. But once the game's over, you watch the film, you come together, and you move on. You don't want the players to see you change."

It was Wednesday and Pettine's plan still had forty-six calls— he'd killed two darlings. In a normal week, you'd want at least ten fewer. Pettine told his players, "If there's a call you can't play fast, tell me and it's out." O'Neil believed that the worst quality in a coordinator was "to be boring" in front of the players. Now, Pettine reviewed the Ravens offensive personnel with the defense, and when he got to the center Matt Birk, he said, "He's declined physically, but he gets by because he went to Harvard and might throw a book at you!" When he described Megan Double Field, he explained that the call name was a birthday present for his daughter, adding, "The play looks goofy because she's goofy!"

During practice, Cromartie tried wearing a Kevlar vest to protect his chest. He ran sprints, lowered his shoulder a few times against a padded goalpost, threw a ball around. Many silently questioned him. If he could do all that, how hurt could he be? Cromartie looked like a man who could tell what the others were thinking. "He'll play," Pettine predicted. "He's sensitive. We'll build him up." And then, even as the coordinator spoke, there went Derrick Mason and running back LaDainian Tomlinson over to Cromartie, teasing him, making him laugh as they yelled, "He'll play!"

At the end of practice, Ryan gathered the team around him on the field, as he always did, and told the defense he was cutting the plan down to thirty-six calls. "Same for the offense," he went on. "A hundred and twelve down to—" I laughed. Schotty, standing next to me, said, "You think that's funny, Nick?" His voice was tense. He'd slept two hours.

"Yes," I said.

"We don't have that many calls," he said.

"Of course you don't," I said. "He was just joking." I hoped it had been funny. My only role was to behave well. I'd had all of four hours of sleep each of the last three nights. I hadn't seen my family. It was stressful to be around the team after the loss. I looked up to discover O'Neil taking my measure. "What you're finding out is that you could never be a football coach," he said.

Late in the afternoon, Cromartie and Revis watched film. Cromartie pointed out that the way the Baltimore running back Willis McGahee positioned his feet told you whether it would be a run or a pass. After Revis left, I asked Cromartie what he thought about before the snap. "To stay under control," he said. "Slow yourself down. I don't ever think about a receiver. There's never a need to. If the technique is right, he can't beat me." On filmed play after play, he identified the route to come within an instant of the snap.

After the season Cromartie would tell me he'd severely bruised his sternum in the Oakland game. "The entire year, it was hard to hit," he said. "I shied away. You can't breathe. You can't lie on your side or your stomach. It was hard. It was straight hell. It was painful. I don't wish it on anybody."

On Thursday, the loss had receded and everybody was suddenly feeling better, especially the linebackers. A linebacker named Eddie Jones had just been signed to the practice squad. Jones shaved his head in such a way that he closely resembled the intimidating appearance of the Jets Mike linebacker David Harris. Bart Scott said, "I wouldn't let either of those guys within twenty-five yards of a school." Westerman's ear had somehow been sliced inside his helmet, an opportunity for him to peeve that "they don't make Band-Aids for black people. Just another way the white man holds us down." BT began making jokes about Megan Pettine, so Pettine told him he'd lost his privilege of deciding what time the outside linebackers' meeting would begin. "I'm sorry, Michael," BT said. Then he tried again. "I'm sorry, Mr. Pettine." Soon the two of them were giving me advice on raising my own children. They said it was crucial to make my wife get up in the middle of the night when the baby cried. The way to do it, said Pettine, was to develop "a convincing snore." BT suggested giving her "a direct order." My thought was that I'd try, "Honey, would you do it? I'm so tired because these crazy football people keep such insane hours." They liked that.

Cro sat through the defensive meeting attached to a curative blood-flow-stimulating device the size of a small blast furnace. Afterward, at practice, he made two astonishing interceptions, which led to much commentary. "His arm looked like it came out of that tree he got up so high," DT said. "Is he hurt? Is he *hurt*? Hell, yes! His *feelings* are hurt!" Cro, meanwhile, stalked the sidelines, windmilling his arms with intent.

Baseball's Boston Red Sox were completing a disastrous September collapse, and Ryan took note. He believed something was rotten in the state of Red Sox and the team should clean house. Several of the new Boston players obviously couldn't handle the pressure of playing for a big-market team. That's why, he said, he'd preferred Sanchez, coming out of USC, to Josh Freeman. Freeman was a Midwesterner. Sanchez had Hollywood glamour, would know how to handle New York.

Later, Revis and I discussed the fact that because of film, football players knew better what they looked like as they did their jobs than any other professionals except possibly actors. Most people had ideas of their professional selves that rarely coincided with how others actually saw them. Football players had the chance to know exactly what they were. "You don't think about being filmed," Revis said. "You watch yourself get better and better and you can see that." He was sweating copiously from wearing the several layers of sweat clothes over his football uniform. Throughout practice, nobody had caught a pass on him, as usual. He'd swarmed his receivers, bullying them from all sides, it seemed, like a cloud of insects tormenting a miserable heifer. I asked him why he wore so many clothes. "I want to be hot," he said. "I want to fight through hard situations. Guys are so strong and fast in this game, you gotta prepare yourself for the worst. Playing football is a tough, hard life we have. There's a lot of long days, a lot of repetition, a lot of perfectionists, a lot of people with high tolerance for pain. Then when your number's higher on the scoreboard, it's the best!" Revis practiced so energetically, people worried he might injure himself or wear himself down, taking years off his career. Revis had never needed any kind of surgery, and as for the overdoing it—without practicing the way he did, he said, he couldn't play at the level he aspired to: "Practice doesn't make perfect. No! It's a perfect practice that makes perfect."

Carrier was looking forward to watching DeVito play the line after his poor performance against Oakland. For good veteran players like DeVito, a game like that often indicated a health problem.

And indeed, before playing the Raiders, DeVito's shoulder had been bothering him so much that for the first time, he had accepted a soothing injection. "We all have fallbacks," Carrier said. "His is power. His shoulder will never be better because of what we do. So for him, it was his first time taking a needle. It bothered him, and mentally he wasn't right. Now he'll be better because he's gone through it." Some players, Carrier said, got a trial shot for the Wednesday practice, so they'd have the experience behind them before they got the needle for a game.

At the Friday linebackers meeting, it was the job of a selected rookie to supply the veterans with outside refreshments. This time, the linebackers required fried chicken, and Nick Bellore arrived with several boxes from Popeyes and a contribution to the field of aphrodisiac studies: "I must have been hit on by six black ladies!" said the white linebacker. "'Hey, where you going? You smell *nice!*'" Everybody cracked up. "That chicken!" Bart Scott cried.

The game had completely changed in its relationship to race, and Westhoff had that in mind one day when he showed me his old yellow-and-black Wichita State helmet, from his college playing days in the late 1960s. His team had black players, and on the schedule were Southern schools that he said still didn't have them. In 1969, Wichita State played at Arkansas, and Westhoff remembered that he wore the helmet every moment he was in the stadium because the Arkansas fans were hurling bottles and other missiles at the Wichita State team. Westhoff's helmet was patched and looked rickety, a jalopy compared with the Humvees the players now used. "This piece of shit," said Westhoff fondly. "A wonder we didn't get killed." Then he said, "It was a different time."

Sanchez threw poorly in Friday's practice, annoying the defensive coaches, who continued to believe he was being babied by the organization. A problem for Sanchez against Baltimore was there'd be no Mangold again. It would be the rookie substitute Colin Baxter in the middle. Tannenbaum had claimed him off waivers a few weeks before.

On the practice sideline, Bart Scott was excited about the game against his old team. He planned to mess with the Ravens by calling out signals from their own defense that were meaningless in the Jets scheme. Scott was going to be crucial in this game, Sutton thought. Ray Rice, the Ravens running back, was their best offensive player, and if the Jets could stop him, they'd win, because Ravens quarterback Joe Flacco was such a low-percentage passer.

DT and I had begun a private after-Friday-practice crossbar-game competition that one of us—not him—had named the Main Event. This day I hit the bar from thirty yards twice before he did, which, combined with Cro's injury, nearly exploded DT's head, because I threw, he said, "the ugliest ball you ever saw."

Everyone was as loose as ever at the Saturday-morning meetings and walk-through, moving Leonhard to remark, "You'd never know that this is a very big game and that we lost last week. That's not good or bad. Just the way it is." What the safety said was true. Yesterday Eric Smith had made three interceptions in practice, a very rare event. Watching film of these three picks led the black players to rename him Smit-Dog and posit that if one cut Smith open, he'd be black inside. Mulling over the broader implications, Pettine said thoughtfully, "Might be the opposite of you, Westerman."

David Harris, man from Michigan, had just bought his parents a new house in Grand Rapids. His family had moved there in the 1960s because there was no work in their poverty-stricken part of Mississippi, whereas in Michigan, Harris said, "You could lose a job in the morning and find one in the afternoon." Harris's country-boy uncle still grew okra and greens and made the moonshine that the coaches had enjoyed so much before the Jacksonville game.

Among the Jets, Harris was considered Revis's equal as a serious professional, the caller of the defensive signals and "a tackling machine," as everyone always said. He'd just signed a lucrative new contract, and they all were happy for him, giving him an ovation in the defensive meeting room on the day it was publicly announced, though nobody ever knew how landing the big money would affect a player.

After the walk-through, the team traveled to the Newark railroad station. The chartered Baltimore-bound train they would ride was six coaches long. At the quarterback meeting in the Baltimore hotel, I was awarded a rookie nickname by the players.

"*Hook*worm?" I said in dismay upon hearing it. "*Book*worm," they yelled. And just for that, they shortened it to Worm.

This settled, they began discussing that day's Florida (Schotty's alma mater) versus Alabama (McElroy's) college game. At Florida, Schotty recalled with a wry smile, as the backup quarterback who stood on the sidelines during games, "I was the signalman. Everybody has a role." Then he looked at Sanchez. "Say something," he said. "Say something. We'll run the ball all day long!" Because the Ravens played tight coverage, "squatting on the sticks" to prevent first downs, Schotty planned to move them back by throwing deep on the first play.

When you were awaiting a Sunday-night game, the hours passed slowly, and Pettine had urged the players to go for walks rather than spend the day lying around their rooms "getting stale" watching football. Revis, with his sweatshirt hood on, moved so slowly through the hotel hallways, he seemed like an elderly druid with sore joints. Rev was saving it all for the game. In the locker room, Callahan brimmed with enthusiasm, eager for the game to begin, impatient to show that the loss of Mangold could be overcome.

When at last the game started, the inexperienced center, Baxter, could not hold. Neither could Mulligan, the tight end who'd been inserted to provide extra blocking. On the Jets first offensive play, Sanchez faded to throw his deep pass, did not think uncle, did not sky the ball out-of-bounds, was sacked, and fumbled. The Ravens recovered and took it in for a touchdown. It was a violent way to begin, and the violence bore in on Sanchez again and again. The Ravens defensive players would confide in Jets coaches afterward that they thought some of the Jets offensive players had looked "scared" out there. Baltimore's defense played with propulsive ferocity, pummeling through the Jets' weakened line, cuffing Sanchez, jarring him, making him appear a small boy gone off to sea too young. He fumbled four times in the game and threw an interception that was returned for a touchdown—the dreaded pick-six. The Ravens defense would score three touchdowns.

Where the visiting GM sat was at the discretion of the home team, and the Ravens gave Tannenbaum not a box to himself but a seat with the press, where he kept silent except to pound the table surface at every new adversity as all around him New York reporters reveled in the massacre.

At halftime Schottenheimer was livid, threatened to bench the long-faced players in front of him. Mason, the former Raven, was equally angry and again railed at Schottenheimer about the play-calling.

Lost amid the 34–17 disaster was how well the Jets defense played. Many of the things Pettine had imagined for his defense, they achieved. The Ravens quarterback Joe Flacco was held to 10 for 31 passing by Cromartie (who did play) and the others. In the second quarter, Flacco threw ten times and completed not one. DeVito and his fellow linemen limited Ray Rice to only 2.6 yards per carry. The Ravens offense scored only one touchdown. These were Pyrrhic victories; they seemed only to increase the defense's frustration with the offense.

Afterward, as Tannenbaum and Jets owner Woody Johnson greeted the team at the locker-room door, Callahan kept apologizing to them, his long face stricken, while across the room, Pettine looked like a gull who'd flown into a window. He was crushed. He hadn't seen any of it coming, especially not the loss of the player he most depended on. During the first quarter, BT had fallen to the ground, his Achilles tendon torn, his season ended. Ryan consoled the team, told them things would improve, promised they'd see the Ravens again in the playoffs. Unlike most NFL coaches, Ryan urged his players to freely express themselves because, he said, they were "men," and because he trusted in the reciprocating goodwill of those who were on his side. Thus, as Ryan tried during his press conference to explain why Sanchez was the man for his job, Holmes was telling other reporters that such a loss "starts up front with the big guys," while Mason was describing "cracks" in the Jets' sense of well-being. These were quickly forged ingots of opinion that, after the heated moment, might have just as quickly been melted back down. Instead they would gain a virulent traction within the team.

It was a shaken contingent that walked through the Baltimore railroad station well after one in the morning. Limping down the steep platform stairs, shouldering into the train, they seemed attenuated, reduced by their recent experiences from what they'd been two weeks before when they were 2 and 0. I'd heard many songs about the railroad blues, and words from them kept coming into my mind on that late-night ride rolling back from Baltimore. Although the Jets' humiliations had just been watched by millions on national television, I was their witness, and it's hard to be witnessed when somebody just took your baby, when all your love's in vain. When you ain't had nothin' but bad news, you got the crazy blues. So I closed my eyes and pretended to sleep. Not that there was anything much to see as the silent train went north.

Ten

DISPATCHES FROM A LOSING STREAK

I find the games you lose are the ones you can't forget.
Victories fade, but defeats bite their way into your heart
and stick there.

—*William "Pudge" Heffelfinger,* This Was Football

Football people often talked of big losses feeling like deaths, and the requisite periods of mourning had to follow. Others—wives, outsiders—might expect (or dread) defeat, but football coaches never did. The conviction that they would find a way, no matter what, was part of what made them football coaches. The statistics and the clichés bore out this attitude. Well before Allie Sherman, the Giants' inventive coach of the 1960s, had put it in so many words, NFL coaches were committed to the proposition that on any given Sunday, any team could win. The losses were excruciating because they always seemed to come as a surprise. The game had been successfully played and replayed so many times on paper before the spectacular high of kickoff that the disappointing realness was a steep dive. "You can remember every loss" is what Rex Ryan, perhaps the most optimistic man I have ever known, told me. "I can tell you what happened. I can't do that with wins. Look at all the time you lost with your children. You never get it back. You have to win or it's not worth it."

The morning after the return from Baltimore, many of the defensive coaches sat before the film and went directly to Kübler-Ross stage two—anger. They blamed Sanchez: not tough enough, not a leader, an "immature Californian." They blamed Schottenheimer: he should have simplified the game for Sanchez. They blamed the officials: "How can you miss two guys moving before the snap?" They blamed shanked tackles, missed interceptions, deficient edge setting, poor alignment, Bart Scott's declining speed, and less aggressive play, and they blamed the offense for not accepting enough counsel, for failing to score a touchdown across two games in two years when taking on "a system we have *intimate* knowledge of." They even blamed Mike DeVito for not blaming anybody. "Does he ever get mad?" Pettine wanted to know. Most of all, they blamed themselves for putting their players in poor positions to succeed.

Then they accepted and moved on. There was sympathy for Bill Callahan, who spent so much of his day working with reserves who "don't belong in the NFL," sympathy for BT, whose severed Achilles could mean his career was over.

And finally there was praise. Cromartie had played inspired, physical football. Joe Flacco was given his due: his percentage had been awful but he had threaded important completions through the narrow eye of rush-hour coverage. Joe McKnight not only returned a kick for a touchdown but had been inserted in at cornerback for a play and had harried Flacco into throwing a pick-six to David Harris. Calvin Pace was a linebacker who'd moved like a back, shadowing Flacco all game long. As for Revis, in two weeks he had not given up a single reception. Had they not seen him do it, the coaches would have refused to believe a cornerback could accomplish that playing man coverage against NFL receivers.

The coaches walked down to the meeting room to listen to Ryan go through the same range of reactions. At first he was irate, as though he'd been bilked, persecuted. "Lot of smart guys coach in this league," he said. "I'm not the smartest guy but I'm observant as shit. Don't think I don't see what's going on. Somebody doesn't want to do it our way, they're gone. We are going to run the fucking football. This team used to knock guys off the line. We are going right back to where we were. We're gonna have our identity back." This now out of his system, Ryan smiled and became again his genial and certain self. "I fucked up. I will fix it. We will never get beat like this again. Guys will have to sacrifice. Tone. Plax. We may not be able to throw it ten times this week, but we will be who we are."

I found the rawness of some of the things the coaches said unnerving. Nobody else in the meeting rooms seemed so affected. When Ryan called out Schottenheimer or the defensive coaches groused about him, Schotty said he aspired to overlook such aspersions. Schotty saw criticism as one more challenging part of the game he could choose to handle well; he believed "losing tests your mettle." As for the players' take on the defensive coaches' frustration with the offense, Jim Leonhard explained that coaches were of the game, not in the game, and that players accepted that the coaches had to burn off their aggression the way airplanes did extra fuel before the soft landing. The offensive and defensive players, Leonhard said, were always competitive, and yet amicable.

I felt for Schottenheimer. He was a man who lived to plot and scheme residing in a moment that checked the imagination. Schotty had a young quarterback who was regressing right in front of him. He had three temperamental playmaking veteran receivers who wanted the ball—a good thing, except that if Schotty played them all, as Ryan had asked him to, that meant fewer running plays and also no extra lineman. His injured line was a broken fence, meaning you couldn't throw deep, and if the defense knew that there was no risk of verticals, they cheated on short-route coverage. So now the receivers were feeling spiteful. Ryan was outraged. And what was the answer to every one of the Jets' problems? Tom Brady! Whose Patriots happened to be the next Jets opponent.

After the team meeting came the Monday defensive meeting

where BT's seat was empty. "It's crazy," said Calvin Pace, missing him. Several of the DBs had their sweatshirt hoods on. Pettine told the room they'd played a magnificent game and urged them not to worry about things they had no control over. He was just as guilty of that as anyone, he said. It was natural. But the only thing they could do to help the offense was "be as tough on them as we can. We can't allow frustration to affect what we do." Then he offered them the time-honored way to redeem themselves after a defeat. "We have a great challenge," he said. "A great opponent. We built this room to defend New England. We'll have a great plan. It'll be radically different from anything we've done." Then he saluted the absent BT: "We lost a true Jet."

Two mornings later, everyone was still sorting through what had happened in Baltimore. The team meeting began with Brandon Moore rising to his feet at his seat near the front of the auditorium, facing his teammates in their terraced rows of cineplex-style seats, and telling them that recrimination did nobody any good. Moore had a big, round, expressive face with high eyebrows that when he tilted his head back looked stoical and appraising—the old guard. He said that all he could think about these days was his inability to make the running game better. Letting LaDainian Tomlinson and Shonn Greene down by not creating clear paths for them—"It pains my stomach," Moore said. So he implored them all, while gazing at Holmes, to support the team, not to run anybody down in the press or anywhere else. Later, the receiver Patrick Turner would explain that Moore was speaking to "a code of conduct within football. Your team's all you have. Respect everybody to the fullest. That's more important than money. That's from growing up."

Ryan stepped briskly up to his podium. He first read a series of sneering headlines from the local press, and then at the end revealed that all of them had been written after Jets losses at similar low points last year. Next he spoke to the players about the next game, first critiquing the Patriots, describing with nonchalant precision all the ways that various New England players might be vulnerable. Then suddenly he was analyzing his own players, telling the Jets it didn't matter about the opponent, that all that really mattered was them, telling his players to be no more than who they already were, telling them they'd be fine, telling them to "lift up your teammates and you'll be fine," his cadences calm and soothing in their repetition, the conviction in his voice so peacefully reassuring that you could feel a complex shifting of emotions. Even I, who hadn't lost anything, who was just supposed to be watching, had the experience of feeling different, feeling in better spirits, feeling ready for new things, and as I made this discovery of what Ryan had just done, Sutton, who was beside me, leaned over, touched my arm, and said, "Nick, you can't go to school for that."

In 2010 the Jets had defeated the Patriots twice by "wearing the dog out of them," as Sutton put it. Receivers near the line were "affected" by corners and linebackers as they set off on routes. The assumption was that what had worked before, including a game plan that invited the peerless passer Brady to hand the ball off for runs, wouldn't work again. The NFL, Pettine liked to say, "is a copycat league," and NFL coaching was all about "adjustments."

The new defensive game plan assumed that Brady succeeded because of his ability to decipher the weaknesses in any given defensive formation. If he saw the same look with frequency, he'd recognize it and exploit it. The Patriots created an extensive offensive call sheet for every game, dense with provisional sections, which they'd use or ignore depending on what they saw from the defense. New England could do this because Brady could handle so much call volume. Sutton's typed summary of his thoughts on Patriots' screen passes alone was a full page long. The way to beat Brady was to offer Brady so many defensive looks he couldn't trust what he was seeing. Thus the Jets would play an assortment of personnel packages, with the responsibilities within each look assigned in ways Brady couldn't predict. Eric Smith, for instance, would play five different defensive positions. "Don't show stuff too early" was Pettine's plan. "Be a great actor. Get him thinking, rattled, moving around." In a sense, this was again a version of Brady's offense, which featured a core group of plays he'd run countless times but that never felt predictable to defenses because Brady ran them out of many personnel groups and formations.

Brady was an easy man for an opponent to dislike. He seemed to have it all: talent, success, good looks, a supermodel wife, and those big eyes rolling petulantly skyward whenever things didn't go precisely his way. So pretty and so good—how could you not want to knock him around? But that was really hard to do. The Jets coaches admired how prepared Brady was, right down to his personal fitness. Since his Combine, the slow, gangly Michigan grad had made the most of himself as a pro and succeeded to such an extent that "you wouldn't think it's him, that's how much his body has changed," as one Jets defensive coach put it. Peering across the line, Brady was a defense analyst; his release was rapid and sure, making even mediocre NFL offensive linemen seem staunch, and his arm was strong and accurate. The coaches all looked forward to the challenge of trying to beat Brady as well as his coach.

Bill Belichick was the only NFL coach who won consistently, year after year, even though, just like everyone else, he was restricted by a salary cap that meant he was always losing good players when their success made them too expensive to keep. And while it was true that Belichick had won mostly in the company of what the Jets coaches considered the finest quarterback of his generation, all NFL seasons were the triumph of experience over hope. Teams found out across the season how good they were. In Charlotte, Joe Gibbs had told Ryan and Pettine that coming out of training camp, he could never tell if his team had enough to win the Super Bowl: "What makes a Super Bowl team special is a process, an evolution during the season," he'd said, adding that what he most remembered about his three championship seasons with the Redskins was not the winning but the getting there.

Belichick's ability to reimagine his team's approach with new players and new assistant coaches every year was what made him the modern apotheosis of the profession. Around the league, people talked about him as the Ur-coach, the impossible model. Belichick's secretive ways contributed to that reputation. Was there any leader who stood in public more and revealed less? At the press podium and along the sideline, he was at remove, a man whose present distance allowed others to discuss him in the way artists spoke of their own quarter-lit masters—the way jazz musicians thought about Buddy Bolden, actors about Stanley Kubrick. To the Jets coaches, Belichick was a relentless white whale up there in New England for them to pursue. People had faulted Ryan for the brash statement about Belichick he'd made when he arrived to lead the Jets, but Ryan doubted Belichick saw it for anything other than what it was, a compliment. To Ryan, Belichick was "the best," and the Jets hadn't won a championship in decades; Ryan believed you changed a moribund culture by lifting its ambitions.

Bill Parcells, who coached with Belichick for a dozen years, had teased Belichick, called him Doom and Gloom for his perpetual dissatisfaction, and that visible discontent was exactly what Ryan most admired in Belichick, because it meant "he's true to himself." The former Belichick assistants who received promotions elsewhere typically weren't successful with their new teams. Ryan wondered if perhaps each one tried too hard to be another Belichick. Sutton thought the same: "One of Bill Belichick's greatest strengths is that as much as he learned from Bill Parcells, he didn't become Bill Parcells." Belichick's pursuit of football perfection was cold and unsentimental, but it also made him less wary of eccentricity than most football men were. One imaginative hire was a longhaired vegan shredder who got around the hippie town he lived in by bicycle. That was Thomas Dimitroff, who eventually became Belichick's college scouting director and then, in 2008, the Atlanta GM, where twice in his first three years Dimitroff was named the NFL executive of the year by the *Sporting News*. Players believed that Belichick's confident intelligence would help them improve and win. Coaches appreciated the clairvoyent beauty of his game plans and passed around stories of his occasional private displays of warmth. For instance, shortly after losing his head-coaching job with the Raiders, Callahan had received a surprise call from Belichick during which the Patriots coach told him not to lose faith, he was good at what he did.

In Florham Park, they all respected Belichick—with one reservation. Belichick had been the Jets defensive coordinator for three years before being named the Jets head coach, a job he then quit at his first-day press conference with a scrawled note that read in full: "I resign as HC of the NYJ." Revis was one of many who'd noticed that Belichick never spoke of his Jets years and had gone so far as to expunge any mention of them from his official Patriots biography. What led a successful man to behave like that? When Eric Mangini, a former Belichick protégé, had been the Jets coach, the Patriots had illegally videotaped the Jets signals. Nobody could explain why Belichick would behave so badly. They all wanted to win, but perhaps, some thought, his darkness was that he wanted to win too much.

In responding to consecutive losses, Ryan believed, "You can't flinch." As for Mason, who'd yelled at his coordinator during games, Ryan said that in Baltimore, he and the defensive lineman Sam Adams "used to go at it all the time. It happens all the time. You got to be combative. That's part of coaching." Others, however, considered Mason to be over the top, and Ryan did take measures. His office was briefly a woodshed after Mason was invited in. Then, at practice, Mason played with the backups on the scout team, running Wes Welker's routes for Revis from the cards O'Neil had drawn up. Meanwhile, when Brandon Moore arrived at his locker to dress for practice, he discovered a fresh captain's *C* sewn on his shirt. For Sanchez, the coaches had a new air horn, which they were ready to sound at practice whenever Sanchez was too slow to release the ball on a play.

Four weeks into the season, there were many Jets players not practicing because of injuries, and so Carrier asked me to help fill out the huddle as the defense walked through Patriots running plays from the cards. This lasted roughly two plays. Even just walking through, I was too slow. Carrier himself relieved me, saying, "Nick, we love you. Get out."

Pettine's daughter, Megan, had been absorbing a hard time from Ravens fans at school in Maryland, so he employed paternal license, stretching the truth by telling her that David Harris's pick-six against the Ravens was on "her" call. That was Pettine, who fired hard from the hip and then, always in passing, revealed a soft heart.

As usual during the Wednesday-afternoon walk-through, Revis and Cro were excused for their private film session in the linebackers' meeting room. Today they studied Wes Welker's routes. Welker was the best slot receiver in the sport, and although he wasn't notably fast, he seemed it because he could maintain full speed through a series of sudden directional changes. It interested the cornerbacks that the Patriots were throwing more downfield routes to Welker than they had in the past. Most quarterback-receiver combinations created and betrayed expectations in the course of a game. Welker and Brady were working two careers' worth of information. They also had such understanding, Cromartie said, that Welker could make his cut to the opposite of whatever side the cornerback leveraged his own body, knowing that Brady was seeing the same thing.

After a while, as was his habit, Revis left the facility to go watch more Patriots film at home by himself, "in the crib." Of his weekly preparation, Revis said, "I follow the same routine since I've been a rookie. I'm very mental about the game. What I do when I watch with Cro and when I look on the TV in my living room at home is I see the same thing over and over. To remember, I have to keep replaying it in my head. I watch the [receivers'] body language and the routes. Then, when you're in the game, the crazy thing is you see it and the light comes on. Ding! Crazy! I just saw it all week. I can make a play on this one."

Copies of a completely new Patriots game plan were distributed at the Thursday defensive meeting, and the two-day-old ones were collected and shredded. Ryan and Pettine were growing more concerned about defending against an empty backfield and the resulting twin platoons of bunched New England receivers. Pettine then put up on the screen a photograph of Mike DeVito as a boy dressed up for a party in a three-piece suit and fedora. The players loved it. "Where that tommy gun at, Mike?" somebody yelled as DeVito blushed. "You're not mad at me, Mikey?" Pettine asked him afterward. "No, no, no!" DeVito said. Pettine looked almost disappointed. Later Carrier told him, "Mike, I want that guy this week, the guy in the suit and hat!"

After a loss, it seemed to take until Thursday before the team had purged the bad experience. At practice, the defense was rollicking; you could see why Callahan had thought to describe them as pirates. Po'uha did a Samoan dance after he'd all but uprooted a runner. When Revis defended passes, he yelled, "I don't think so!" Sanchez was feeling harassed. Every few plays, the new air horn blared at his indecision. Afterward, I walked to the facility with Brunell. In his two-decade-long NFL career, Bru said, this was the best quarterbacks' room he'd ever been a part of, everyone so supportive of Sanchez, Sanchez himself such an unusual and appealing person. As for the disaffected receivers, he pointed out that receivers and quarterbacks tended to bond in the off-season, but because of the lockout, Sanchez and his new teammates were still strangers. Of the defense, he said, "This is the most creative, aggressive, complicated defense I've ever gone against. You do well here, you can do well against any defense." Except that the Jets offense wasn't doing well here. It was surprising, this wonderful defense that might have been raising the offensive level of play and yet somehow wasn't. It occurred to me later that nobody on the defense ever said such supportive things about the offense.

At the Friday quarterbacks' meeting, Schotty had so many plays drawn, the whiteboard looked like something you'd see in a physics lecture at the Institute for Advanced Study, a few towns south. That's how I thought of this facility: it was the Institute for the Advanced Study of Football. One of the theories among his critics on the defense was that Schotty's solution to any problem was invariably more calls. So much of something more meant that the unit was in constant redefinition rather than confidently asserting an identity. There was probably only some truth to the theory.

Schotty had much to overcome. He was taking on the NFL's best teams with an injured line and an erratic young quarterback. During the two-minute end-of-game drill that day in practice, on third down Sanchez would at last cry uncle and throw a ball away under pressure, except that against the lethal Patriots, the cry-uncle rule had to change. You never wanted to stop the clock at the end of a close game, which would give Brady time for another possession. He could take his team down the field in seconds.

It was a Friday, but that didn't mean Aaron Maybin, whose license plate read "Mayhem," was going to be any different than usual on the practice field. Maybin didn't wear a mouth guard because, he said, of how hard he breathed—"I'm a frantic!" He'd bit through his lip and deep into his gum before. As for the way he moved on a football field, the coaches referred to Maybin now as Baby Colt. "He looks like a turnstile," said DT with a smile.

I asked Brunell about the defense's complaints about the

overdetermined offense, and he praised Schotty for creating this week a crisp, concise plan relying on quick-developing plays. As we were talking, O'Neil walked by. "Hey, Mark, how's the game plan?" he called.

"I'll tell you Monday," Bru replied. The veteran quarterback knew Belichick would see a team with a weakened line and a faltering passer, and the Patriots coach wouldn't prepare for a wide-open attack.

One of Ryan's personal complexities was that he wanted to give his subordinates the autonomy he'd enjoyed in Baltimore but felt betrayed when things subsequently didn't go well. It was in his nature to believe that what he wanted to happen was going to happen, and he believed with such conviction that he made others believe as well. This was a compelling quality in such a competitive, emotional business, where a team's confidence was often the difference between victory and defeat. Yet when there was the inevitable disconnect between what Ryan declared would happen and what actually happened, he could be outraged. Ryan was a loving man and not confrontational, with the result that he stewed a lot. What people really wanted in those moments was more of his confident yeoman's presence. And yet there again, he was reluctant to impose. The quarterbacks still didn't know that the idea for the air horn at practice had been his.

Now, with his offense in crisis, Ryan began on Friday afternoons to meet with Schottenheimer and Sanchez to review the offensive game plan. These sessions were called Like It—Love It, and only the plays all three loved would be used. Such formal interventions were really not Ryan's style. His football brilliance was intuitive—he just saw things others didn't see. He preferred to work off the cuff, ad-lib, on the fly. Similarly, his gift for camaraderie was best expressed in the flow of life. Every young head coach discovered challenges of a sort he couldn't have imagined before taking the position. Bill Belichick had failed at his first job in Cleveland, one of his former players thought, because he had been so introverted, he failed to engage with and motivate his players. For Ryan, it wasn't always going to be easy to use his spontaneous personality to lead such a rigorously scheduled activity, but all over the organization right now, there were people hoping he'd find a way to do it.

At the relaxed Saturday walk-through, the starters went through the call list out on the turf in the field house, and everyone else stood along the sideline and had real conversations. Julian Posey said that after he was cut from the Jets, he returned home to Ohio, where he worked out and thought about how he'd "cherished" the chance to play professional football and how much he'd give for another opportunity. He said that a quality of professional football he'd never expected was how anxiety-producing it was. Everything was, he thought, accelerated for both players and coaches, and everyone had to get better "right now or forget it, it's over."

Practice-squad players didn't travel with the team, so after the walk-through Posey went home, and the team passed through security and flew to Providence, Rhode Island. During the week, the receivers had been as subdued as I'd ever seen them. Mason was especially quiet. At the team hotel in Providence, sitting around a boardroom-style table in their T-shirts waiting to begin their meeting with the quarterbacks, the receivers all became suddenly light-hearted. Then the meeting began. When Holmes didn't know his role in a play, Schotty was quick to explain it to him, but the small moment was freighted with reproach. Everybody looked forward to the games. But as the coaches were always saying, every game was built on a week of practices, and lately Holmes did not always run his practice routes at full speed.

Pettine told the defense to be ready for a rapid-fire battle of personnel groups as the teams tried to outsubstitute each other to gain a mismatch. "You're better than they are," he told his players. "But they hide their inadequacies well." A particular Patriot strength was the slant patterns run by Wes Welker and other receivers. Pettine showed the defense film of Patriots low crossers being diverted and the sacks that resulted.

"Going with the untucky!" Ryan said, walking out among his coaches in the locker room to model his black short-sleeved game shirt. It was a warm Indian summer day, and during a messy game filled with penalties and Jets punting, the Jets defense kept things close. It was 10–7 Patriots at the half. Later it would be clear to the Jets coaches that the Patriots people up in their own coaching box had seen something that they'd passed along to Brady during the break. Early in the game, the Patriots used a bunched-receivers formation, and in response Eric Smith had crept up to the line from his safety spot. The Patriots were betting that if they gave the same look again, they'd get the same response from Smith. On the first play of the third quarter, Welker lined up in that bunch formation, Smith indeed came creeping forward, and then Welker, master of the quick-developing pattern, ran a route no Jet could recall the Patriots using out of that look. He went deep. Down the seam Welker sprinted, blowing by the surprised Revis into open space for a seventy-three-yard catch and run.

In addition, the Patriots were rushing the ball well against the Jets' usually formidable run defense. It was especially deflating to have a perceived Patriots weakness obviate a Jets strength. Late in the game, with the Patriots ahead by six points, on third down, the New England running back BenJarvus Green-Ellis took a direct snap and swept around left end. Rather than holding his ground and forcing the play back toward the middle, Cromartie seemed to disappear. Three plays later, another third down, and this time Brady threw to Rob Gronkowski. The tight end had run a standard Patriots wide receivers' pattern. Before the snap, all the Jets coaches had recognized what was coming. They screamed at the safety Brodney Pool, warning him. The coaches could see it all: Pool jumping the route, bringing the ball back, winning the game! But because New England tight ends hadn't run the route out of that formation before, and because Pool's responsibility for the game was covering the tight end, he knew the tight-end routes and wasn't familiar with Patriots receiver routes. Pool cautiously fell back into deeper protection, and Gronkowski made the catch. First down. Field goal. Insurmountable lead. The Patriots prevailed by nine, 30–21. Until it was over, the Jets had thought they would win. Ryan was calm afterward in the locker room, saying how "encouraged," he was. "Stay together," he urged.

In football, visitors' locker rooms are designed to promote defeat. They are small, bare of amenities, decorated in sullen colors. (The University of Iowa notoriously painted everything in its visitors' locker room "puke pink" because the former Iowa coach Hayden Fry had studied psychology and believed pink floors, sinks, and toilets would undermine the opposition's aggression.) It doesn't smell good in a visitors' locker room, it doesn't look good; there's a garish glare to some of the lights and gloom in other places, not enough light. The percentage of backed-up toilets tends to run high. After a loss, the cramped spaces with their slick concrete floors and ugly paint make the sad, large men filling them seem sadder because there's nothing pleasant to distract them from the unpleasantness that just took place.

Afterward in Foxborough, the Jets coaches were almost bent with frustration. Schotty kept wiping his forearm across his eyebrows. Some players quietly derided themselves. One of them threw something hard toward a trash can, missed, and cursed. There were two bus rides and an airplane flight to look forward to. How did the song go? "There's something in a Sunday that makes a body feel alone." In football, the life was so insular and demanding, so focused on these critical moments, that when things went wrong, the whole world for many coaches became fruitless and grim. There was the stated belief that if you'd truly given your all, that was enough. That wasn't enough. The point was to win, and all the games were closer than they seemed, which meant that losses were easy to reimagine as wins if only...It was maddening. The coaches had been thinking about the Patriots for months.

Reviewing the game film back at the facility the next day, the Jets coaches saw many questionable officiating calls, and as Pettine nominated plays to be given to the league office for review, he sounded world-wearier and world-wearier—"Send it in. Send it in." Not that he was blaming the loss on the officials. And not that the league office could provide anything more than an explanation or, at best, agreement without recompense. Today the defensive coaches were mourners because thirty points were on them. Sutton kept thinking about the crucial third down when the Patriots had snapped the ball directly to Green-Ellis, the running back. That play was right there in the tendencies Sutt had prepared, and in the moment, he'd failed to remind David Harris to watch for it. There was only one way for everyone to feel better. "We need a win, boys," said Pettine at the end of the meeting. "Let's go get one." The next opponent would be the Miami Dolphins, and the Jets third-string quarterback, Kevin O'Connell, had recently been with them. Pettine spent much of the next two days running ideas by the lanky O'Connell, trying to find an advantage.

Meeting with his quarterbacks Wednesday morning, Schotty seemed no different than he'd been after the two early victories. Mason was gone, suddenly departed for Houston via a rare NFL in-season trade, and in the team meeting Ryan had asked the players to respect his long career and speak well of Mase. Then Ryan chided Cromartie for playing off the line. The head coach insisted that a player with Cro's speed and ability needed to "show up a little." Next, he turned to Sanchez and told him, "Son, we got to find a way to come out of the gate." You couldn't keep conceding sizable early fractions of the game without scoring and still expect to win. He asked them all to "put a little fucking chip on your shoulder for the week."

In the defensive meeting, Ellis Lankster, re-signed from the street, was welcomed back as Lancaster. He sat up front listening to Pettine explain, "There's nothing magical in football. It's a game of a million little things. Once you show a weakness, that's what you'll get from most teams." Then Pettine clicked up onto the screen film of a down against the Patriots where no play call had come through to Harris. "This one's a hundred percent on me," Pettine confessed. "Technical issue." The sun had been in his eyes and he didn't see that he was on the private headset channel rather than the main line, so DT could not hear him speaking. That had never before happened to Pettine. He ran on through the game film, and when Pettine got to the direct snap to Green-Ellis, everyone watched Cromartie retreat and appear to turn his back on the approaching rusher. "You got to show up," Pettine said. "You got Dave coming across to make the tackle."

Three straight losses had many players so frustrated that Thursday's practice felt like a rodeo—all noise and dirt and blood and thudding contact. As Westhoff pointed out, right in the middle of it all, scrimmaging with such furor he gasped for air, was Nick Bellore. Bellore's practice and special-teams play had been consistently excellent. As a white middle-class kid from the Midwest, Bellore had been regarded skeptically by some of the defensive players, but Westhoff said he'd proven he belonged. Scott agreed. "That big head can hit!" he said. Scott himself had been seeing fewer plays and generally had become more reflective and withdrawn. "Sometimes I go for long drives, listen to my music and I just drive," he said. "If there's traffic, I don't worry about it."

Watching film with Revis, Cro discussed one of the Dolphins receivers, Brandon Marshall. Cromartie said that because Marshall had been a safety for most of his college career, he played more physically than most offensive players. Revis was the one who'd cover Marshall, but he kept silent the whole time, and when Cro tried to engage him, he just kept staring at the screen.

By week's end, Schotty had yet to shave, and lately he'd forsaken his usual banter as well. The newspapers had been trotting behind him with wolf's teeth, assessing his competence, and that constant scrutiny was a part of the job the coaches never got accustomed to, since they had yet to meet a newspaperman who they believed knew enough technical football to judge them fairly. Schotty didn't seem perturbed, just deeply in it. He took the quarterbacks through the progression of throws on each passing play, quizzed them all on the various protection schemes. Sanchez was subdued. The team was losing and he hadn't been practicing well or playing well. Cavanaugh told me that part of being a young quarterback was learning how your attitude affected your teammates, even the much older players. What part of yourself you projected to others was an aspect of the primary offensive position that took time to master, just like any other.

At practice, young Ellis Lankster, who had no technique, was a Rough Rider out there, charging up and down the field, making mad, fearless dashes on every play, ecstatic with energy and toughness, trying so hard that both his legs began cramping. The sight of him made people shake their heads at "that great kid."

Antonio Cromartie, who had all the technique you could ask for, was a man in professional crisis, and the whole NFL was watching. Looking at the practice film later, the defensive coaches could see him on his heels, could see Leonhard cheating over to help him. Leonhard was as worried about Cromartie as the coaches were. Cro so detested criticism that he often shut down in response to it. Something in Cro could never trust that all anybody else on the team wanted to do was to help him. In Baltimore, Leonhard said, the best defensive players—Ray Lewis, Haloti Ngata, Terrell Suggs, Ed Reed, Jarret Johnson—had been the ones most diligent about improving their technique. Cro, like Sanchez, possessed all the obvious skills to dominate at his position. The lesson again was that part of football was temperament, and while the classic corner-back was thick-skinned and fearless, Cro was a sensitive guy. How to raise the confidence of such a player? As Leonhard put it, "If you're a little tentative as a DB, if you lack even a little confidence, you're fucked."

While the coaches watched the film, an O'Jays song came through the radio. "Great one!" said DT.

"Panty-dropper," Pettine agreed.

"Panty-dropper!" DT laughed, and then they were all laughing for the first time in what seemed like half a month.

During the defensive-backs' meeting, DT was encouraging of Cromartie. "Keep working at it, Cro! Keep working at it! Good coverage." All his criticisms of Cro were delivered obliquely. DT said it was up to the room what kind of a secondary they wanted to be. Afterward, walking past the coaches' kitchen, DT saw that someone had sent over gourmet cookies for the pleasure of all. "I don't want gourmet," he growled. "I want ghetto!"

Watching film late in the day with Revis, Cro analyzed the Dolphins. He was, as usual, vivid and precise, and it interested me that he described the nature of offenses with some of the same phrases DT and Pettine liked to use, such as "They'll do what they do."

Sometimes, said Revis, Ryan would come to him before an important team meeting and say, "I'm gonna bash you in the meeting." "He knows I can handle it," Revis added. At the Saturday team meeting before the Monday-night game with Miami, Ryan told the players he wanted to talk with them about being a good teammate. Brandon Moore and the other linemen continued to feel antipathy toward Holmes for chiding them after the Ravens game. Moore was out there while still recovering from bilateral hip surgery. Mangold had played against the Patriots on an ankle that hurt to walk on, and now he was on the practice field again, preparing to center the line against Miami. They were giving all and here was this receiver going at half speed and then jabbing at them. Ryan told the team that being a great teammate was Eric Smith publicly taking the responsibility for the seventy-three-yard Welker reception that was really Revis's fault. "Right, Rev?"

Down in his seat near the front, Revis nodded. His view of such matters was "I'm not hurt to be criticized. Nobody that plays football's perfect. I mess up, I'm, Dang! The team. Me, I always take the blame." But in the moment the team had been losing and a Revis mistake had cost them against the Patriots. His family down in Aliquippa, Pennsylvania, had been hearing in detail about how upset he was. "He remembers everything that went wrong," Revis's grandmother Aileen Gilbert told me after the season. "Everything."

The weather had turned cold and windy, the year's first real chill. At practice, Revis was, as usual, out there competing against Patrick Turner, Sanchez's former USC teammate. Turner was tall, wore an Abraham Lincoln beard, and had a friendly, unassuming way about him. He would have been a fine NFL receiver had he been faster. Since he wasn't, he owed his position on the team to the fact that he was an excellent blocker. Not many wide receivers were. "Blocking is a lonesome thing," Turner said. "You have to want to do it." He played exceptionally hard, especially in practice against Revis. When Turner blocked, he tried to give Revis a very physical time of it with his hands. Normally Revis understood that Turner was making him a better player, but today he was not in an understanding mood. Turner was supposed to be mimicking Brandon Marshall's pass routes, but Revis believed Turner was breaking them off to get open. The right look was everything to Revis. In response to these perceived improvisations, Revis was increasingly aggressive with Turner. Soon the aggression got to the point of fury, and Revis made no attempts to play beyond smashing into Turner as soon as the ball was snapped, swinging Turner around, shoving him. Everybody could see that something had to give.

Suddenly the two were fighting. From Revis, there was an onslaught of blows so savage he seemed momentarily berserk. His knuckles kept crashing against the hard plastic of Turner's helmet, the sound like a man pounding the top of his uncooperative television set. "That's the Aliquippa coming out," Sutton said as he watched. "It's a hard town. Nothing left." There was initial silence from the other players and then tremendous excitement. DT was screaming something about Turner knowing his role, which Turner surely couldn't hear, much less take in, because of all the shouting from the other players and the fact that he was trying to fend off someone who wanted to kill him. Westerman got between them. Perhaps he was thinking what Ryan was thinking: that if Revis kept it up, he'd break a hand. I remembered suddenly what Revis's uncle Sean had said about football players and their switches, that there was a madness to football.

They led Turner off the field and a few players stood and watched with him while Revis continued practicing. If football could be compared to real estate, then Revis was beachfront property; Turner was subletting out near the shopping center. Had it been Sanchez fighting with someone, Sanchez's opponent would have been similarly escorted away. "I have no problem with PT," Revis explained later. "We made up. It's preparation. If it's training camp, okay, you're trying to get on the roster. During the season I need your help to get the right look. If it's the wrong look all week, I'll be surprised in the game. It irks me, irritates me. Why should I be there if it happens wrong all day? I got to work hard. I'm big on technique and I *do, not, like, them, to catch a ball.*" He also did not like giving Ryan reason to call him out in a meeting; he did not like that DT had put the Welker play in the practice script for him to see again; he did not like teammates picking at each other; and he did not like losing. And because he was the team's best player and not given to speeches, he'd expressed his disapproval with his fists.

The guest kicker that Friday was the broadcaster and former quarterback Ron Jaworski. Ryan centered the ball, Tannenbaum held, and Jaworski, wearing elegant slacks and suede boots, sent the ball fluttering just over the upright and scraping inside the post. Booting an extra point in suede was something to see, but all anybody wanted to talk about was what Leonhard had dubbed "the donnybrook." Football fights last for brief moments, but they feel much longer because the experience of time slows, especially when it expresses the emotions of so many witnesses. In the circle after practice, Ryan told the Jets, "We'll be all right if we don't kill one another first."

Turner was circumspect. "That's my guy," he said of Revis. "But it's competitive. It's O against D. I'm a physical receiver. He's a physical corner. I'm doing whatever's on the card, and if he felt it wasn't a good look, that's how he felt. It's tricky to run somebody's route unless you're watching his film."

A day or two later the two spoke: "You good?" Revis asked Turner.

"I'm good," Turner told him.

"Okay!" said Revis. "We're cool."

Turner said yes, they were cool.

In the defensive meeting the Sunday morning before the Monday-night game, the players and coaches reviewed the practice film. When they reached the Revis/Turner fight, Pettine began narrating—"Feels him out with a jab! Loads up with a right! Devastating punch!" At the sight of Westerman wading into the melee, Pettine asked, "What's the rule?" Westerman had grabbed a green defense jersey instead of a white offense shirt. "I grabbed a white guy!" Westerman said and even Pettine couldn't stop laughing. "Hey," said Westerman, looking a little confused. "I got a lot of white friends!"

During the pre–game-day walk-through, there were the usual conversations among the players. MTV recalled his experiences as an incorrigible seventh-grade brawler in Hayward, California. The reserve nose tackle said that everybody he ran with then was a juvenile delinquent. "We all had to struggle, none of us were set. We were in the streets." His father was "gone," his mother worked three jobs, and so his informal gang of friends were the people he relied on. "Gangs and football teams are similar," MTV said. "They both are like family environments." One day at school, MTV punched an eighth-grader. On the way home, a Mustang full of kids pulled up beside him, and he was saved only because a man from the neighborhood saw what was happening and ran the kids off. The next thing MTV knew, his older brothers intervened, and he was sent to a group home in a wine-country town of fewer than a thousand people. One brother was there too. He'd broken some kid's jaw. At the local high school, MTV had a wonderful teacher who interested him in books—especially the *Iliad*. He began dating the class president. She had a 4.0 GPA and suspicious parents—"Rightfully so. I was really thug." The high-school football team had only thirteen or fourteen members, but twelve were from the group home, and "we bombed on the football field!" Almost every kid he met there was from a single-parent family, "just like football." He was now twenty-three and still dating the class president.

Julian Posey was talking about the draft process, why it had taken him so long to come around to the Jets on signing day. The Bears, he said, had been in touch all the way through the lockout. But he preferred the Jets for all the reasons DT had told him he would. Said Posey, "If you can play Jets style, physical press corner, you can play anywhere. I say it, 'If you can do the grill work, you can cook anywhere!'" After college, the NFL-rookie life of getting up at five in the morning, lifting weights at six thirty, and then attending football meetings and practices until at least six at night was grueling for Posey. He said he sometimes found staying awake for so many hours in the dark meeting rooms "more than hard." Before he'd been cut, in his free time Posey had shopped and gone to movies, restaurants, shows, and clubs. No more. He realized "how serious it is. It's *very, very* serious and you're respected only for what you do in here." In meetings now, to keep himself alert, he drank lots of very cold things like water and Gatorade and ate sunflower seeds. And he went to bed early. "You can't burn the candle."

Posey remained quite literally wide-eyed, and the veteran players, especially Cromartie and Leonhard, liked and felt protective of him. Out at practice they were always pulling him over to pass along tips and encouragement. You'd see them talking, Posey's helmet bobbing in agreement, those eyes urgent behind the mask. "He so clearly wants to be good," said Leonhard. "It's like watching a little kid trying to mold himself into his parents. He's so innocent. He hasn't been jaded."

After the Dolphins, the Jets would play the San Diego Chargers. The Sunday afternoon before the Dolphins game, most of the coaches tended their yards, played with their children, or caught up on sleep, but Smitty spent the sun-drenched autumn day alone in his windowless office, carefully drawing plays the Chargers favored for the following week's practice cards. After the Chargers game would come the Jets bye week, and Smitty would rest then. As he sat at his computer and drew, Smitty imagined Devlin's reaction when he saw the cards: "I hope Dev will think, That's a really good one! And what if it's that one play that makes a difference? Nicky," he counseled, "precision takes time."

The stretch of hours alone for Smitty was welcome even if they were spent at the office. Pettine's town house had been visited by Pettine's sister, and she had unbachelored the joint. There were fresh towels, fresh sheets, freshened air, bright décor. The dead tree had been banished. Much as Smitty revered Pettine, Pettine was still Smitty's boss, and Smitty's home was still his boss's house. His father's illness weighed on Smitty. And so did the losing. In a meeting during the week, O'Neil had teased Smitty and managed to do the near impossible—get Smitty really mad, mad enough to tell O'Neil, "You have the worst laugh I've ever heard." When everyone in the room cracked up, Smitty looked surprised. Then he smiled in spite of himself and joined them.

"Hi, Worm," Brunell said when I walked into the quarterbacks' meeting that evening at the hotel.

"Can I have a promotion?" I asked. They'd been calling me Worm now for two weeks; being around them was beginning to feel like the worst part of seventh grade.

"How about Creep!" Sanchez said. He wore a ski hat with a pom-pom, a hoodie, and a watch almost as large as an alloy wheel and just as shiny. I knew how it went. The point was to make the new guy feel foolish. In the oil fields, the least experienced roughnecks were all called Worm. In the Vietnam War they were cherries. Later Callahan told me the bad news: "Once they give it to you, that's it, it's yours, you're it." I couldn't blame them. If I was going to come in and sit with them and watch them lose, I deserved to prove to them that I could handle something too.

It was Schotty's birthday, and Sanchez had ordered pizza for all. Schotty scarcely seemed to notice. He was reviewing the openers, the new sheet of plays he planned to use at the beginning of drives, and even creating such a document made him anxious. He told the players several times to put the sheet somewhere safe—"This is valuable stuff, men." A pass to Holmes, "hauling ass to get to the far pylon," had the coordinator very optimistic. "If there's ever been a call ready to get dialed, it's this one," he said. "It was gonna win the New England game for us."

At the game, Ryan made a symbolic gesture to address team unity that others called "typically Rex." Each week the head coach chose game captains to run out to the middle of the field for the coin toss. For this duty, Ryan tended to select players for whom the game might have personal significance—players from the state where the game was being played, or a player who'd formerly been a member of that day's opposing team. This week, he sent Santonio Holmes and Brandon Moore out together. This did not immediately yield offensive solidarity. "Rhythm!" Tannenbaum kept pleading in his box. Alas, there was none of that, and also no tempo, no syncopation, no backbeat—and thus no first-quarter first downs. Many seconds disappeared from the clock before Sanchez ran each play. It was, to use a favored phrase of Carrier's, bad ball. After a quarter, the Dolphins offense had accumulated 173 yards; the Jets offense only 10. "How can that be?" Tannenbaum asked. At the end of every game the GM went home with a migraine headache. Now he already felt the aura. Miraculously, the Jets were ahead in the game, all because Revis had returned an interception one hundred yards. Later Rev picked off another, leading the Jets to a 24–6 victory and leading his coaches to wonder why anybody would throw anywhere near him. To Ryan, it was a football axiom. The "Revis Rule" held that on whatever side stood Revis, the throw should go to the unequal and opposite side.

On Tuesday, in his office with his assistants gathered around him like courtiers, Tannenbaum made a flurry of roster moves. MTV, who had been in the middle of a goal- line stand against the Dolphins, was demoted back to the practice squad. Eron Riley, a receiver, was brought in. Scotty McKnight remained. Taking in the situation, Scott Cohen said thinly what many were thinking: "Scotty McKnight must have pull around here." Out the window, the practice-worn fields were being reconfigured and relined; the new arrangement rotated the gridiron by ninety degrees, so the less trampled grass near the end zones would now form the middle. A few player agents were checked in with, and the medical people gave their reports of who among the injured Jets was likely to play on Sunday against the Chargers. Then Tannenbaum began musing about Sanchez's present state of mind. "Mark is twenty-five," the GM said, "and he's human. The owner says this to him. The head coach says this. The coordinator says this. He hears a snippet of ESPN radio on his way home. If you were twenty-five, your mind would be swirling a little too."

Downstairs, Ryan, wearing a "Dear Lord, If You Can't Make Me Skinny, Please Make My Friends Fat" T-shirt, was eating peanut butter and chocolate while Pettine, in a black Foo Fighters T-shirt, was considering the color and the shape of success: "When you win, the food tastes better, the beer tastes better, and the sex is better." Then the defensive coordinator looked at the head coach and summarily banned all foodstuffs from his office. At 8:43 in the evening, O'Neil told Smitty, Sutton, and DT, "Boys, we got to get Pet going. Only two calls up!" True, some additional calls in the plan were known as lemon juice. These were the ones the players knew so well they weren't written down. The origin had to do with the old children's spy trick of using lemon juice as invisible ink. By four thirty in the morning, the lack of rest was acute, but the game plan was finished.

At the Wednesday quarterbacks' meeting the next morning, Sanchez was buoyant. Maybe he was savoring the Miami victory or, more likely, a long-carried weight had been lifted. Sanchez had heard Tom Moore would be coming for a visit from South Carolina. "Field trip!" the quarterback cried. "I'm smoking cigarettes with him." Schotty was also feeling better. When Brunell answered one of his questions correctly, Schotty said, "Way to go, Bru! Gold star! Have fun at Benihana tonight!" McElroy's cast had been removed, leading the others to mock him for all the typing Schotty would now get out of him. McElroy was spending his time studying football and lifting weights five days a week. In college, McElroy had bench-pressed nearly four hundred pounds. When the swingman Josh Baker heard about this, he took in McElroy's red hair and said, "No ginger could do that." Among the players, Baker's line was repeated and repeated. They couldn't get enough of it. Not playing was wearing on McElroy. The rookie was thinking of avoiding practice because just watching made him "depressed."

As usual, Schotty took every available second, so the quarterbacks had to hurry down the hall to be on time for the team meeting, where they heard Ryan announce that Revis was the AFC's defensive player of the week. As for the offense's perpetual poor starts to games, the head coach looked over at Sanchez and advised him to take the field at the beginning of the game and "pretend it's the second quarter." Afterward, in the defensive room, Pettine congratulated his recrudescent players for becoming again "ourselves." Then he took them through the game plan like a lawyer making his case, every call's intent explained with care.

At practice, the air was mellow, the spirits same. Bart Scott was back to cheerfully calling white-shirted offenders slapdickmotherfuckers, and in Mo Wilkerson's direction he cried, "Hootie Hoo Temple Owl!" BT arrived on crutches, his first visit to his teammates since his injury. BT said he was lonely at home, needed the company.

Nobody played harder than Aaron Maybin. Maybin was one of the only players on the team I'd ever heard talk about what he would do after football. He'd studied art and hoped to paint, draw, write, and illustrate children's books. Maybe it was that he had a visual, not numerical, mind, for something about football plays failed to achieve purchase with Maybin. He was a bright, interesting person who simply couldn't remember Xs and Os. So Smitty made him a wristband with everything written down on it for him. But Maybin still had gone the wrong way on a couple of calls, mishaps that led Pettine to suggest two wristbands.

At the Flavia coffee machine before the morning defensive meeting, Marcus Dixon assessed the various choices of brew. "'Dark and intense,'" he read. "Just like me!" In the meeting, everyone was treated to another sampling from the Pettine cache of young Mike DeVito photographs. Today's exhibit was DeVito in full pirate regalia. "Mike must have had a great childhood," said Maybin. "I never had a pirate hat or nothing." Suddenly Pettine looked out at Wilkerson. "What game number are we playing, Mo?"

"What game number?"

"Yes."

"Seven!"

"Seven means time to stop being a rookie."

A big question for game planning against the Chargers was whether San Diego's seven-time Pro-Bowl tight end Antonio Gates would play. Pettine had heard that the Chargers were building a second, contingency game plan in case Gates couldn't go. Carrier spoke up, warning his linemen to stay aware of Kris Dielman, the Chargers All-Pro guard, who was known for very physical play. There were two types of players: those who played to the official's whistle, and those who played through it. With Dielman, if you could hear the echo of the whistle, he was still coming at you. Carrier didn't want anyone letting up early and getting trucked.

Afterward, they all divided into positional groupings, and Pettine went to his office. Pettine no longer attended the outside-linebacker meetings. He'd ceded the room to Smitty. The senior coaches believed that Smitty was progressing so well because, unlike most former players who'd decided they'd like to coach, he didn't ever lament his vanished playing career, and he no longer thought of himself as a player. Instead, he willingly accepted that he had a new profession that required even more of his time than playing had and for which he was paid a tiny percentage of his previous income. The game was about the players. A coach's perspective had to shift so that everything he looked at, he saw through the prism of the players' experience, the way a father would see a seaplane and become excited because his young son was interested in them. Smitty understood the game, both the practicalities and the spirit of it, and he was also generous, a man who wanted the best for others. That was a coach.

During practice, DeVito fell to the ground, rose, and fell back.

As he was helped off the field into the facility, the sidelines were quiet. Twenty minutes later DeVito remerged, wearing a knee brace. Po'uha ran over and hugged him. Dixon gave him a relieved head rub. "He's back for morale," said one coach, doubtful that the injury was minor. Countered Pettine, "In a game they would have braced him up and he would have returned. Mild strain."

During the break, along the sidelines, Leonhard and the veteran linebackers reviewed sports movies. *Hoosiers*? "Too boring," said David Harris. "Too many white people?" countered Leonhard. Then came *Lucas*. "Never heard of it," offered Calvin Pace. "You been watching PBS?" Harris asked him. The all-linebacker panel agreed that some of the most entertaining sports movies were *The Best of Times, The Program,* and *Blue Chips.* None of these films was deemed terribly realistic, but life was not a movie.

The football existence, however, meant that documentary film dominated your days. At that afternoon's defensive-backs' meeting, included among the Jets/Chargers film that DT showed the players was two-year-old footage of former Jet Lito Sheppard not having his best day against the Charger receivers in the playoffs. As the film rolled, Marquice Cole narrated DT's in-game response to the situation. First, said Cole, DT gave Sheppard a nod of the head that Cole said meant "Son, come stand by me." Sheppard offered his coach a solemn gesture in return that Cole called "the TV nod." This Sheppard immediately followed up with the "Coach, I'm ready to go back in" nod. To which DT responded with the "Son, you stay right here by me." Cromartie had still been a Charger during the playoff. "This game was so funny," he said. Speaking of the San Diego offense, he remembered, "They'd come to the sidelines and say, 'They're coming from everywhere! I can't see shit!'"

For Chargers week, Don Martindale, the former Broncos defensive coordinator, again visited the Jets defensive coaches. He offered an analysis of the Jets struggling offense. Martindale said that if you really pushed Schotty and Cav, "they'd say they don't have an acceptable quarterback right now." No matter how many different plays Schotty developed for Sanchez, Martindale said, in years past, the Jets had never felt like a complex opponent to him. He always had a pretty good idea what Sanchez would do. Schotty, Martindale guessed, badly missed having Brad Smith this season. "He put me on my heels. I had to think about him and I couldn't think about the rest as much." Martindale thought Ryan was frustrated with the offense's inability to establish the running game but wouldn't intervene because he would have hated someone doing that to him. Martindale, like Tannenbaum, wished Ryan would intervene. "You don't get many chances to be a head coach," Martindale warned his friend.

Friday was a typical NFL day, a lot going on at the facility. In the morning newspapers, Pettine was quoted expressing the defensive coaches' exasperation at the inconsistencies of Cromartie, explaining that early in each game, he and DT would assess which Cro they had that week, Good Cro or Bad Cro. It was unusual for the coordinator to speak publicly in the terms he used in coaching meetings.

When Pettine met with the defense, he told the players that Antonio Gates would play and Mike DeVito would not. The Chargers starting quarterback, Philip Rivers, was six-foot-five, but he threw from such a low release point it was possible, Pettine said, to swat down his passes and make him very frustrated.

During practice, Bart Scott fondly remembered a Bengals lineman who'd been holding him on play after play during a game. Finally Scott said, "You keep holding me, I'll poke your eyes out." The lineman replied, "But Bart! I'm old and fat and slow. I have to!"

Because of DeVito's injury, Kenrick Ellis would see more time in the game. So at practice Tannenbaum strode over to him and asked, "Hey, Kenrick, what are San Diego's top three runs?" The rookie was unsure. Tannenbaum told him, "They're on a plane right now watching movies and eating snacks. Take advantage of this time."

In that morning's special-teams meeting, Westhoff had called Aaron Maybin Andrew, and when Maybin didn't respond, Westy gave him hell: "Andrew! I'm talking to you." Throughout practice, from deep in the scrum, you could hear, "My name's Aaron!"

Ryan yearned to innovate, and in that frame of mind, he fixed on LaDainian Tomlinson. In his prime with the Chargers, Tomlinson had become one of the NFL's highest career rushers, a football fusilier behind his famous dark-visored face mask. Although Tomlinson was now finishing his career with the Jets as a part-time back, he remained a stunning athlete. At practice Ryan could see the way Tomlinson still accelerated almost instantly to his fastest gear. He could see that Tomlinson retained his keen, instinctive spatial understanding of himself in relation to the mass of players around him. Ryan had also noticed that Tomlinson could backpedal at a rapid shimmy. Running backs didn't need to backpedal, but defensive backs did. Ryan envisioned a safety with rare closing speed. When he mentioned this to Tomlinson, the running back was game to try defense against his old team. So whenever Ryan saw Pettine, he brought up his idea. Pettine always refused.

After practice, in his office, Ryan hosted an "ice-cream social" for Holmes, Burress, and Sanchez, an informal chewing of the butterfat with the players. Sanchez's after-ice-cream report was "It's like therapy in there!" The offensive linemen, meanwhile, wanted to know why they didn't get to eat ice cream with the head coach.

At the hotel on Saturday evening, Tom Moore walked into the quarterbacks' meeting, and immediately everyone seemed happier. After the offensive guru received embraces, back claps, and felicitations, Sanchez told him, "Coach, you should stay! I'll rent you a room in my house!" Moore gave the (handsome, young, model-dating) quarterback a slight raise of the (bushy, wizened, white) eyebrow. "I don't think I could stand all the traffic I hope is coming in and out of there," he said.

Holmes arrived, saw Moore, cried, "Coach! How are you?" and buried him in a hug.

Waiting for the rest to arrive, Moore regaled the players, in his deep, warm voice, with yesteryear stories of Terry Bradshaw on the ice at Rockefeller Center with his girlfriend, the figure skater JoJo Starbuck, and how this had played with Steelers head coach Chuck Noll. "Chuck about had a heart attack. Terry won four Super Bowls in six years. Course, a *rouge* could have won the first two, the defense was so good. In one Pro Bowl, eight of the eleven defensive players on the field were Steelers." The present irony of this as it related to the Jets was not remarked upon.

In the defensive meeting, however, the offense's struggles were very much on the coordinator's mind. It was another week, another declaration that the D would have to win it for the O. The experts were favoring the Chargers, Pettine told his players, doubting them on their own field without BT and DeVito. Give me a signature game, he requested.

Tom Moore would watch the game from Tannenbaum's box. Up there as well this week was Terry Bradway, man of a million past and present protégés. He had one of them on his mind—Schotty. "Ultimately," Bradway said, "coordinator is a thankless job."

The larger-than-usual cohort in Tannenbaum's box also included Don Martindale and Brendan Prophett, as well as Tannenbaum's doppelgänger. When things were going against the Jets, Tannenbaum took it out silently on his yellow legal pad. Today the pages suffered, as the Chargers led much of the way. The game turned in the second half when, off a Cromartie tip, Revis made yet another big interception. As that welcome event happened, Tannenbaum erupted into his other self. He bull-rushed Martindale, embracing him in a simultaneous tackle, noogie, and fist-pound. "You all right, Don?" he yelled at the astonished coach. "If it's too big for you, we can get you to Newark Airport before the end of the game."

When Tannenbaum went to the restroom, everybody expressed concern for Martindale, who, embarrassed, brushed it off. "No problem," he said. "It's because he can't do anything to help." Soon Tannenbaum was back; the Jets continued to thrive, and Prophett absorbed a heavy shot to the shoulder. By now I myself had bravely taken permanent cover beyond Bradway. It was a tense, close game, and the GM remained at full Watusi as Burress caught three short touchdown passes and Greene ran well, in part because he received crucial blocking from Holmes. Revis and Cromartie were far better than good, holding the Chargers fine receivers Vincent Jackson and Malcom Floyd to two catches combined. (Gates caught five, one for a touchdown.) After Tannenbaum headed downstairs to the locker room to greet the players, Bradway smiled ruefully at his departing disciple. "I tried to train him," he told Moore and Martindale. Bradway supposed some people might object to a GM behaving that way, but, really, this wasn't a boardroom, it was a box in a football stadium. Football was the national passion, and Tannenbaum was a passionate guy. He was being true to himself or, maybe, as Prophett had it, "He's not himself. He's in an altered state. Another person. He's Mikey, not Mike!"

The Jets won, 27–21. Ryan said he had hankered "in the worst way" to play Tomlinson at safety for one play against his old team, but LT had the flu, and, anyway, Pettine was incredulous at the idea of putting the great running back out there in harm's and reputation's way. If a player hadn't repped something, Pettine wasn't going to allow him to try it on an NFL field. "Rex!" he howled, as he'd been doing for so many years, and that, finally, was that.

In the morning DT walked into the dining hall, spotted Cromartie eating breakfast, and went over to him. "It ain't magic," he said. "That's the best game you've played with your hands and feet since you've been here." When the coaches watched the film, Pettine noted that "Cro's putting on a clinic." There was much talk about what foul epithets the Chargers receivers had been yelling at their quarterback Rivers as the game went awry for San Diego. "Gates was *hot!*" reported O'Neil. Martindale watched the film with them and pointed out how quickly Revis could find a ball already in flight when he looked back at full speed. For Revis, that was three picks in six days—and three since his bout with Turner.

The coaches began to discuss some of their opponents coming up after the bye week. One would be the Broncos, whose quarterback Tim Tebow they considered "the world's best-throwing fullback."

At the Monday team meeting, Ryan announced—to applause—that Tomlinson was now the fourth back in NFL history to catch six hundred passes. Then Ryan congratulated them all once again on owning a winning record (4 and 3), told them to get a lot of sleep, drink plenty of water, and enjoy their days away.

When Pettine reviewed the game film with the defensive players, he paused on a hit Pace made to the side of the lowered helmet of San Diego guard Kris Dielman. Because Dielman had delivered many a staggering blow at the whistle in his time, nobody was sorry that Pace had "ear-holed him." Dielman returned to the game, and eventually he went low on Pace, a dirty move that Pettine called "the ultimate sign of respect." The Jets would learn that Dielman had suffered a grand-mal seizure on the airplane home. He would miss the rest of the season with a severe concussion, and the lingering symptoms were such that he retired from football. Nobody said much about this. Such things happened in football.

Only some final Tuesday meetings separated the coaches from a few bye-week days off. At noon the senior coaches and the front office met in the defensive-coaches' conference room for the "self-scout" midseason reports. Thick binders containing the team's internal evaluations were distributed. The cover of each one said "Good vs. Evil" and had a photograph of Schotty looking patiently off toward the horizon while Pettine glowered at him. Everyone considered this to be some inspired artwork.

The Jets players were all ranked best to worst at their positions relative to their teammates, and then each man's performance was reviewed individually. The defensive coaches were especially pleased with Wilkerson, felt he was a future star, and were very happy as well with Calvin Pace, who was quietly having a dominant season. Maybin amused Ryan because "obviously there's issues, but the guy makes plays and we lack playmaking ability." Nick Bellore, Tannenbaum said, was the player he received the most calls about from other teams. "Every year you get me one Nick Bellore, and we got it made," said Westhoff. Revis, they agreed, had won them three games all by himself. "Best player in the league not named Brady," Ryan said. Everyone applauded the reserve cornerback Ellis Lankster's enthusiasm, and they all worried about Cromartie's consistency. Posey they thought had been "scared straight" and was, as Westhoff said, "heading in the right direction." It was crisp, efficient, and nothing was said that wasn't completely consistent with the opinions that had been expressed day by day.

Westhoff went through the special-teams personnel in rapid order, and then came the offense. The big concern remained the quarterback. The coaches and front-office people worried, as they always did, about Sanchez's poor decisions and his ability to lead. The strength coach, Bill Hughan, who'd been with the Falcons, was asked how Sanchez compared with Atlanta's quarterback Matt Ryan. "Matt's more focused," he said. That word, Schotty said, summed up what Sanchez lacked. He was plenty smart, but didn't yet have a brain for professional football. They discussed how badly they missed the complement of Brad Smith. It was clear they thought that Sanchez still had too many ideas of who he was supposed to be, didn't yet have football self-knowledge.

Santonio Holmes they predicted would have a terrific second half. Schotty thought the receiver wasn't a bad kid and was "wow! A great player." As he said this, I thought, Wow! There is a man incapable of bearing a grudge. Brandon Moore was still recovering from surgery and should now steadily improve the line at guard. Wayne Hunter was the Cromartie of the offense: immensely talented but a different player every week. Scotty McKnight's name never came up.

And with that, they scattered. Tannenbaum was off to surprise his wife with a lavish birthday party and to turn away more inquiries concerning the availability of Nick Bellore. Schottenheimer visited his family in Nashville. David Harris headed for Grand Rapids, Michigan, lugging an ice machine with him so as to heal his bruised body while drinking a little family-recipe restorative. Cromartie flew to the Bahamas and forgot about it all. Pettine went to see his children in Maryland. Aaron Maybin visited his child in Maryland too—he had a daughter—and said upon his return, "If I don't see another diaper, it won't be too soon." Only one player continued to come every day to the facility. That was Mike DeVito, whose sore knee benefited from the daily treatment but whose pleasure in football was such that had his knee been well, he would have come there anyway.

Eleven

SOFTNESS

First—Chill—then Stupor—then the letting go.

—*Emily Dickinson, "After Great Pain, a Formal Feeling Comes"*

Like most members of the organization, Bob Sutton returned from the bye week with the belief that the Jets had momentum and that momentum in team sports was real. "What do you say," he greeted the younger coaches, "let's get after it!" Pettine was reviewing film of the week's opponent, the Buffalo Bills, who'd defeated the Patriots in September by scoring and scoring. Watching the film damped down Pettine's own sanguine post-holiday mood. He said often that he believed in "farming my own land," and he knew that he could not allow his discontents to rend the bonds between offense and defense. Yet the recent memory of seven three-and-outs from his own offense against the very Patriots defense that he was now watching the (modestly accomplished) Bills pick apart could aggravate a man and turn him away from his better agricultural angels.

Out on the practice field, Scotty McKnight fell untouched to the ground with a loud scream. He pulled off his helmet, cradled his knee, and was surrounded by Ryan, Tannenbaum, and Sanchez. In football, there are said to be more noncontact knee injuries than tears caused by hits. Sanchez was nonplussed. "ACL?" he asked a medical staffer. After a couple of minutes, with McKnight still lying there, all the other players and coaches moved to the opposite end of the field and resumed the practice. Eventually McKnight was carried off.

Dave Szott, the player-relations director, told me that Sanchez and McKnight's relationship wasn't unusual in the game. It was common, said Szott, the designated players' confidant, for players to develop a best football friend forever. DeVito and tight end Matt Mulligan, fellow fundamentalist Christians and former University of Maine roommates, wore matching T-shirts, each imprinted with the same line of scripture, to the Jets pregame Saturday-night meetings; they made up new shirts for each game. The two were so close that they'd seek each other out for a hug following a fine play. Szott said that after a game in which a player had been injured, Jets would call the player-relations director to ask if their buddy was okay, "even when it's not a bad injury."

Such as a dislocated little finger. Strickland was now absorbing sideline ribbing from Revis after he'd been caught consulting a trainer about his pinkie. Revis was like DT. He was friendly with his teammates, and he treated Kyle Wilson as his advisee, but that was because Wilson sought him out. Rev didn't seem to require close football friends. Everything about him, including his position on the field, made it clear that privacy was his nature.

And then there was McElroy, a position-group loner, though not by choice. Of the other quarterbacks he said, "They don't like me but I like them." It was more that he was a rookie third-stringer and injured, two qualities that, in such a brisk business, the others couldn't see past to notice that he'd do anything to help them. "All of us work really hard, and we want Mark to be successful," McElroy said. "It's so fun when he has a great week." I was reminded of a factory job I'd had during my college summers. The first summer, I was a college boy, beneath the other workers' contempt. When I came back the next year, I was one of them. As for McElroy, when he made the Jets team again a year later, he would seem different to the others, they'd treat him differently, and he would be different.

*   *   *

Drafting the Buffalo Bills game plan on Tuesday in Pettine's office, the coaches came up with several brand-new calls, which then needed to be named. The goal of new call names was to make them instantly memorable. First, Pettine named a blitz call after Strickland. They were playing the Bills, and Strickland had attended the University of Colorado, whose team's nickname was the Buffalos, so, easy!—Buffalo. Then Brodney Pool was the source for some call etymology Pettine considered a little more inspired. People often thought Pool's first name was Rodney. This annoyed Pool. That annoyance naturally led Pettine to drop the occasional "Rodney" on Pool after he made a mistake. Now came the pièce de résistance—Bug Rodney!

Looking up from his laptop, at his usual Tuesday-night place across Pettine's conference table from O'Neil, Smitty said he'd been thinking all day about the Chargers lineman Kris Dielman. "He played on the verge of a seizure? That's tough."

In between these reflections, the three coaches worked as hard, O'Neil said, as they'd ever worked on a single game plan. That was because they were adjusting their calls for nine different personnel groups, protecting against mismatches, taking care that Jim Leonhard wouldn't be isolated one-on-one with a fast receiver and that David Harris wouldn't have to cover Bills running back Fred Jackson all by himself on pass plays out of the backfield.

The most substantial work of this kind was undertaken to keep Aaron Maybin from doing anything but pass rushing. The new Niner personnel package, for instance, had been created to counteract the Bills' penchant for spreading out four wide receivers in formation with Fred Jackson also in the backfield. If a defense responded to that spread with a package featuring extra defensive backs, the Bills would run Jackson. If the defensive coordinator chose not to supplement his secondary, the Bills would throw. So Niner reinforced the backfield, with four cornerbacks and two safeties, and reinforced the line—four down linemen with only one linebacker.

As the defensive coaches built their game plan, Mike Devlin came by Pettine's office, as usual taking everything in with one penetrating glance. He told the defensive coaches about one of his early coaching superiors, who'd informed him, "Mike, you know how to use computers and that's good and bad. Means you'll always have a job, but also means you'll be up all fucking night." Dev looked meaningfully at O'Neil and Smitty and left. Start to finish, the plan took them eighteen hours to complete.

In the team meeting, Ryan said that everyone had to contribute if the Jets were to have success because "this is the only sport with a one hundred percent injury rate." He compared the Jets to the St. Louis Cardinals, who'd just won baseball's World Series because unheralded understudies like Jason Motte and Allen Craig had stepped forward when their teammates faltered. Then he reviewed the Bills. Fred Jackson was, he said, "the real deal," but the starting quarterback, Ryan Fitzpatrick, had gone to Harvard and "you know what that means. Number one, he can't play. He'll throw a book at you." Number two, said Ryan, Fitzpatrick had married his Harvard girlfriend, another devastating mark against his football. In the defensive meeting, Pettine referred to Fitzpatrick as Big Brain.

The collective-bargaining agreement permitted each team only fourteen padded practices during the seventeen NFL weeks. Today, the Jets held one of theirs. Three new practice-squad players took the field to join in. New players always meant hard hitting; on their first day, they all wanted to show what they had. It was now November, and the contact, heard from the sideline in the colder time of year, had a new sound to it, the loud and dull thuds bringing to mind a heavy drift of snow falling from a roof.

On the sideline, Pettine was astonished to learn that Wilkerson, MTV, and the other young linemen standing with them had no clue who Lee Harvey Oswald was. Pettine simply had no idea what to say. Jimmy Leonhard leaned in to help his coordinator bridge the generation gap. "He's the guy who shot Tupac," said the sly safety.

At the late-afternoon defensive meeting, after the mostly sleepless Tuesday night, Smitty was "struggling," and I was right there with him. Sometimes on Wednesdays I was so tired I thought football had given me narcolepsy. Sutton advised us both to "make a commitment to enthusiasm that'll get you through the meeting." Revis, too, was weary. In the defensive meeting, DT ribbed him, the coach pretending to pick up a phone and saying, "Hey! What up! What time you get off? Midnight. Okay! I'll be there. Ain't got nothin' to do but practice."

Watching the Bills receivers on film with Cro, Revis wore his hood tight as a snood, and he departed for home earlier than usual, leaving Cro and me alone. In practice, Cro had been teased along the sidelines for being sensitive. Actually, he said now, he was just "sluggish" on Wednesdays. (Cro was sensitive about being sensitive.) In general, he'd decided he was overdoing it with the film review. DT had been telling him this for some time, but it always seemed important to Cro that he come to his own conclusions. "I've been overloading my brain. If I watch too much, I play the play before it happens. For the San Diego game I didn't watch as much." In football, he said, the danger was always the temptation to try something new and different instead of just refining what you already did well. There was something koan-like in this observation. Coaches and players made it often, and yet each time they did, it hit me like a revelation.

In the Thursday-morning quarterbacks' meeting, Schotty was thinking refinement also. "Trying to do the things we do well," he said to Brunell; Kevin O'Connell, who was wearing a fashionable new scruff of beard; and McElroy. Sanchez was five minutes late. This occasionally happened and such was football time that those minutes passed like little generations. Today Schotty was considering locking him out. It was impossible not to feel fond of Sanchez and equally impossible not to throw your hands up sometimes. There was a still-teenage quality about his relationship to clocks and calendars that I would think about as he opened his morning Megatron energy juice by repeatedly stabbing the seal with a pen instead of just pulling the tab; as he sprawled in his chair, then stretched, then gargled the Megatron, then startled up from his slouch and looked around, bright-eyed, ready to pounce on the next pounce-able remark.

"Buy stock, men," Schotty said. "Jeremy Kerley! Cav and I have." Schotty was in a fine mood, and when Sanchez arrived, Schotty didn't even rebuke him. Instead, Schotty amused everyone by narrating our inner monologues—"Greg's thinking about sunny Alabama, Mark's thinking about his Megatron juice!" Circled on the board was "Rex's play." Joe McKnight would take a direct snap and run. It was named 38 Special and had been triggered by something Seth Ryan's high-school team ran. There were plays drawn everywhere in the office, plays on top of plays, even plays covering the thin escarpment of whiteboard under Schotty's wall cabinets. A room without a view didn't trouble Schotty. He found blandness in his surroundings inspiring—wanted to fill it in with vivid football ideas.

By the middle of the meeting, Sanchez was saying "Yes!" to every point Schotty made. He was telling McElroy to shut up and asking me, "You get it, Worm? Freak!" When Cavanaugh began to review some Bills film, Schotty told him, "Go ahead, Cav! Coach your ass off," and Sanchez chimed in: "Get 'em, Cav!" He was waking up.

That evening Pettine and the defensive coaches did not rest as they normally would after building a game plan. They stayed at work on three hours of sleep and spent another lengthy night building a Wildcat game plan to respond to those snaps when Brad Smith replaced Fitzpatrick at quarterback and might run, pass, or hand off. Smith had recently been a potent part of the Jets offense, but the Bills scarcely used Smith, making it a mystery to the Jets why Buffalo had signed him. Still, whatever the Bills had done to this point, the Jets defense had to be ready for Smith. The basic idea for Wildcat deterrence was, as Mike Smith put it to the outside linebackers, "Don't be in a hurry. Slow play—feather it." He meant that, yes, you pressured the ball carrier, Smith, but not until you'd set the outside edges. As Smitty detailed the paths forward Brad Smith could offer the football, I had a sudden flashback to Schotty's wall, all those blank spaces filled with little drawings of dramatic, well-ordered future events just waiting for someone like Smitty to drag a thick, black marker right through them.

Scotty McKnight would have knee surgery when the swelling went down. He'd been hurt on Monday. On Thursday, he said, "I was depressed. But then I just decided to focus on getting better." McKnight was receiving ample sympathy from the other players. The feeling among them was that he'd joined the team under difficult circumstances and handled himself well. As for his knee, it was no secret that around the league many injured players used human growth hormone to help them heal faster. McKnight had heard as much, but he said he had no idea what HGH looked like or where to get it if he wanted it, which he said he didn't. One of the most challenging aspects of injuries for players was filling the sudden surplus of hours. BT had begun stopping by the facility more frequently, and he was the first to say he wasn't handling so much time at home well. It was a good thing, he said, that his wife had an accounting job. A player without a team to go to didn't know what to do with himself.

During the Thursday practice, Revis tipped a pass in the back of the end zone and kept his feet inbounds while he found the ball in the air and caught it, and then, as his momentum took him across the end line, Rev whipped a no-look, behind-his-back pass to Brodney Pool. The long, live tracking shot continued with Rev now confronted by a tall pile of equipment someone had stacked back there. Still in the same motion, he hurdled over the entire pile. The plays Revis made in practice led even men like Westhoff and Devlin, who'd seen it all, to talk of feeling privileged to watch him. Terry Bradway walked up to Revis later. "That was the kind of play I used to make at Trenton State," he told Revis.

"Did you?" said Rev.

"In my dreams!"

"Dreaming is good!"

Nobody could one-up that, but Cro came close. During a field-goal block drill, he vaulted over the entire offensive line.

Coaches, like players, had their good and bad weeks, and Schotty was, it suddenly came to me, running his best week of meetings. There was an art to it, creating a relaxed yet focused room, managing the shifting young personality currents, ignoring the wide receivers when they spaced out, quietly changing your speaking timbre when you were going to ask the room for something different. Schotty was also responsible for the players' weaknesses; he had to assess them and protect their flanks without admitting to anyone, most of all the players, that he thought they had any weaknesses. The quarterbacks' meeting had never felt more confident and high-spirited and close. Sanchez even asked McElroy if the rookie hazing was wearing on him. McElroy looked pleased to be asked and demurred. When Schotty reminded everyone that, in his Jets-specific field geometry, "The money zone starts at the twelve-yard line, not the fifteen-," Sanchez said, "At the twelve! Oh no! *That's* why I throw all those picks down there!" In such moments, it was possible to see how Sanchez could become a genuine leader.

*   *   *

In the defensive-line meeting, Marcus Dixon noted that one of the new Jets scout-team players, tight end Shawn Nelson, had begun the year with the Bills. "He got some line stuff?" Dixon asked Weeks.

"No... I don't think so," answered Weeks.

"Got to check," Dixon said.

"Whatever," Weeks replied.

"Whatever," one of the players repeated.

To lighten the mood, Po'uha pointed at rookies Wilkerson and Kenrick Ellis and said, "Fresh money in here! We got a number-one draft choice and a number-three. Hammer: what do you want for Christmas?"

"New iPad," said Carrier instantly.

From the back of the room came Wilkerson's low, easygoing voice: "iPad *Nano!*"

Wilkerson was going to be a terrific player. The upside of the relaxed demeanor that had worried everyone before the draft was that nothing seemed to ruffle him. His mind was uncluttered out on the field, leaving him free to relish the game. When Wilkerson made fine plays, the other players saw his uncomplicated happiness in what he'd just done, and that enthusiasm, coupled with his great ability, kept the first-round draft choice from being resented.

During the previous Friday's practice, O'Neil had taken an accidental hit and the team had played well, so Cavanaugh told him to go absorb another one today, just for luck. Which O'Neil did. There was far less superstition in football than in many other sports, but the appeal of what there was made sense because it emphasized both the necessity of repetition in football and the fact that anything could happen, that it was all, on some level, out of your control. No matter how good your habits were, you needed the luck. Following the loss to the Ravens, Greg McElroy, aspiring as always to contribute, said that he and I should switch chairs in the quarterback meeting—"Superstition," he explained. So we had.

After practice, while playing the crossbar game, somebody threw a ball back toward me, and as I reached for it, Revis decided he wanted the ball and was instantly in front of me, abruptly, violently intercepting it by grabbing the ball and pivoting off my extended index finger. There was a splintering sensation. The index finger quickly resembled a tie-dyed sausage casing, a swirl of red, green, yellow, and purple. I didn't tell anyone. Given the culture, keeping it to myself seemed the thing to do.

Maybin's role had increased in the defensive game plan from ten plays to forty. That afternoon, Smitty created a new wristband for him that held so much information it looked like a stock-market page. The two of them now spent entire defensive meetings whispering back and forth, albeit Maybin's whisper a rumble. The coaches were expecting big things from him against the Bills, the team that had drafted him in the first round and then cut him.

By Saturday morning, my finger was a line of Adirondack mountain ridges. I went to the training room, where I was given a cup filled with ice and slush. The cup attracted attention. Soon all the players in the training room were showing me their digital manglings. Rob Turner had a finger bent into a left-turn arrow; it turned out Scotty McKnight had been catching passes with curled tree-sloth claws. At the walk-through, these demonstrations continued. Carrier came bearing semaphores. Matt Slauson had dislocated every finger at one point or another and said he had fingernails torn off "all the time." Devlin, who in retirement reserved half his desk surface as a staging area for bottles of Advil and Aleve, said that over the years, he'd suffered so many injuries playing on the lines of Iowa, Buffalo, and Arizona that sometimes he'd overlook a new one and his wife would discover it, like something under the couch cushion. Devlin had once entangled a finger in an opponent's face mask. It rotated completely around so that "I was staring at the point." Alas, Brandon Moore informed me that proper NFL hand protocol was not to ice anything short of a ruptured tendon or ligament. I hung my head. "There's a difference between being hurt and being injured," Pettine added.

Others were more forgiving. Henry Ellard recalled that when he was a collegian, a freshman quarterback threw a short pass at him so hard that "I got a compound fracture. No blood. Just a bone sticking out. It was pearl white. The trainer told me, 'Don't look.' I got a lot of stitches and played Saturday." Then Ellard warned me not to believe everyone about fingers, especially linemen. "They're a bunch of teddy bears!" Revis agreed. He explained that the lineman's tactic was to walk into the training room on some pretext—"Ahhh, my leg hurts!"—and then, said Rev, casually mention, "There's this funny thing with my pinkie. Take a quick look at it?" Head trainer John Mellody was with Revis. "They need their hands," he said. "They come in with what you did."

On Saturday the team flew to Buffalo and that evening, Tannenbaum and Scott Cohen invited me to join them for dinner at a steak house. Tannenbaum pointed out how many couples were on dates at the restaurant. He then expertly evaluated how each date was progressing, who had sufficient desire, who was a player. In his own single days Tannenbaum himself had been very strategic about dates. For example, he had a first-phone-call rule stipulating that it should last no longer than ninety seconds. The point was to make a date. Why waste further effort? You might not like each other. Life was short. The one occasion when he had violated this protocol involved a friend of an old friend, a woman he began talking to only so as to arrange their blind date. But before Tannenbaum knew it, over an hour had passed. He enjoyed the conversation so much, he decided that there was no way he was going to like anything else about her. But at least they'd be friends. Which he and his wife, Michelle, remained, in addition to everything else.

In season, during the week, Tannenbaum considered his job to be problem-solving. On Saturdays and Sundays, the GM said, he was "the last person who can help. By then I can't do anything." Now

Burress had an ailing back—the rare weekend opportunity for Tannenbaum. He found a well-recommended Buffalo chiropractor and also had a special mattress delivered to the receiver's hotel room. Tannenbaum said that when Burress learned that the Jets had bought him a bed, "in his face you could see where he'd been and where he was."

Before the evening defensive meeting, I got another cup of ice for my finger. As I walked toward the meeting room, O'Neil intercepted me. His voice rising, he told me to get rid of the cup. "You're not bringing ice into a team meeting and spreading your softness." It hit me that you never saw an NFL injury report with a player listed as "Doubtful—Finger."

All week, it had been difficult for the coaches to get the team sufficiently worked up about the Bills. It was challenging to demonize a team who year after year lost more than they won. Hence Ryan's Harvard angle. Now in the defensive meeting, Pettine gave it his own college try, noting the Bills' fast start, telling the Jets the world loved an underdog, calling the Bills "the darlings of the NFL." He predicted the first Buffalo play would be the Woody boot.

In the team meeting, Ryan selected players to stand and give their thoughts about the upcoming game, assess for everyone else what needed to be done. Tight end Dustin Keller said, "The big thing is ball security." That was a very offense thing to say. The defensive take was offered up by reserve safety Emmanuel Cook, who asserted, "This week we want to bounce some motherfuckers out!"

That night, Maybin dreamed of touchdowns scored by himself. Bob Sutton, however, joked that he'd been kept awake by thoughts of Maybin failing to set the outside edge. In the morning, during a special breakfast meeting with Smitty, Maybin was so overexcited that when Smitty quizzed him on his calls, he became instantly stricken, like a kid in a spelling bee. Gently, Smitty reminded him about the wristband he was wearing and then told the high-strung linebacker that Buffalo was a dish best served cool.

In the locker room before a game, I always made it my business to dress and clear out as quickly as possible. This week, I walked in with Smitty. He paused to speak with David Harris, who wanted to know what music Smitty was listening to. I didn't know where to go in the visitors' locker room, so I waited. They began discussing the songs of Brother Iz, the Hawaiian singer. After a couple of minutes of waiting, I said something about how big Iz was and immediately heard a shout: "Don't talk to the players on game day!" It was Tannenbaum. He grabbed my arm. I was stunned. The whole team was watching. What I had done was inappropriate, of course. But still.

Out on the field, there was the usual relaxed pregame pageant of men playing catch and greeting one another. Kotwica and Brad Smith met on the field and hugged up as former coaches and former charges often did before and after games. Back at the bench, Kotwica said he'd told Smith, "I understand you guys are running a lot of Wildcat today." Smith had denied all before saying, "What does it matter, you guys'll just blitz it anyway."

I was still preoccupied with Tannenbaum and could not locate my armadillo skin. And though I reminded myself that none of this was about me, and I said nothing about it, I was grateful when Smitty leaned back on the bench and said to Kotwica, O'Neil, and me, "I'd rather be with you three guys right now than anybody in the world." I was also grateful when O'Neil, distributing pregame candies, asked, "Who needs a pick-me-up?" and then, without waiting for an answer, handed one to Smitty, looked at me, and said, "Nicky, take three! And the next time Tannenbaum puts his hands on you, jack him up!"

Down in the end zone, Ryan was determining whether DeVito's knee was well enough for him to play by lining up opposite the player, putting his hand down, and testing for himself DeVito's movement off the snap. DeVito could scarcely budge Ryan. DeVito was impressed by Ryan's technique. Ryan wasn't impressed by DeVito. He told DeVito he'd play next week. Nearby, Cavanaugh and O'Connell were throwing Burress passes for the same evaluative purpose. It was decided the mattress had done its job.

Up in his box, Tannenbaum had plainly forgotten all about what had happened in the locker room. During the coin toss he talked of "the angst running through my body." The game began, and Kyle Wilson dismantled the Woody boot; "Just how we drill it," as O'Neil said later. Almost everything went the Jets' way. They won 27–11, and the Bills' only touchdown came at the very end. The defense was physical, with David Harris especially on point, making an interception, defending another pass, stuffing the run. Calvin Pace faked a blitz, dropped into what had looked like single coverage, and intercepted a Fitzpatrick pass. Even 38 Special worked, going for twelve yards, whereupon Ryan announced his retirement as an offensive play-caller. Brad Smith had been telling the truth: the Bills seemed to have given up the Wildcat. One of the privileges of charter flights was that you could keep your eletronic devices turned on while up in the air. En route to New Jersey, everyone around me followed the progress of the Patriots game against the Giants, and when New England lost, there was much happiness. The Patriots and Jets were now both 5 and 3 and would play again on Sunday night.

As the coaches watched the Bills film on Monday, their favorite plays all involved Maybin. First Pettine froze the film to reveal Maybin checking his wristband while in his three-point stance at the line. Nobody had ever seen this happen before. Many NFL players had been diagnosed with attention deficit hyperactivity disorder. Maybin was taking ADHD to a higher level. After the game had come another first. There were always five team airport and hotel buses. Each week Maybin rode on bus three. Leaving the locker room, by mistake, he stowed his bag on bus one and boarded it. Realizing his error, he got off and boarded bus two. Wrong again. So Maybin found his way to bus three. Sinking into his seat, he remembered his bag was still back on bus one. Off the bus again to retrieve it and place it on...bus four. Back onto bus three. Oh no!

Once more unto the breach. At last bag and Maybin came to rest on bus three. Sutton gazed at Mike Smith. "Coach," he said. "There's only one solution—wristband!"

The film advanced and everyone cringed as Fred Jackson blindsided Marcus Dixon with a crack-back block. Later, when Jackson complained to the officials about a noncall near the Jets sideline, the Jets coaches could be seen communicating residual indignation. "We were all talking a gang of shit to him," said Carrier. "Even Sutt was talking shit." Proclaimed Sutton proudly, "I told him to go back to Coe College!" What probably made them happiest was that Bart Scott earned a game ball. Much as they sometimes "dog-cussed" Scott's film, they loved the man.

At the Monday team meeting, the players gingerly lowered themselves into their seats. They would play the Patriots Sunday night and then, on Thursday night, face Tebow and the Denver Broncos in Colorado. "Take care of your body and lay it on the line the next couple of weeks," Ryan told them. Then, after two punishing games in succession, he announced, would come the rest and reward. They'd have Thanksgiving off, "because, quite honestly, I want some green-bean casserole!"

Thanksgiving was a workday in the NFL. There were coaches who'd never once celebrated the holiday with their families. It was, after Super Sunday, the most prominent date on the league calendar, and if you weren't playing, you still had the big Thursday practice prior to your Sunday game. Just like Ryan, the players said, to give them that day off and to do it far enough in advance that they could make plans for how to spend it.

In the defensive meeting, Pettine was still chortling over Pace's interception of Ryan Fitzpatrick. "Old Harvard," he said. "Guess he didn't see that coverage in the Ivy League! Now next time we play them, we line up three strong and bring them all." Maybin was praised for his play and questioned about his wristband checking. "I was just being sure," he said, sounding almost shy. Then he told Smitty, "This was the most fun I've had since high school."

*   *   *

DT said he'd heard that I'd been "jumped" by Tannenbaum in the Buffalo locker room and he was delighted by the little situation, stifling mirth and brimming with manufactured outrage. "Man, it makes no sense," he said. "I played a lot of years in the league and everybody handles anxiety differently. If he can't handle it, go sit his ass in a corner. *You!* Nick, *you* can't affect anyone because what affects a game, where it can be won or lost, is in the preparation that goes on all week." Carrier approached me with similar sentiments and others did too. I appreciated their kindness, but these overtures embarrassed me. I knew that it hadn't been personal with Tannenbaum. It was a blunt-force-trauma world, and the boss had a lot going on in it.

Tannenbaum was not Ryan, but he was a charismatic person himself. In the interests of winning, he was willing to cede all that to the cause, to be the authority figure while Ryan sailed on the good ship bonhomie. Yet I thought, as I had before, that it must be challenging for Tannenbaum to work with someone who was as self-confident and good at making other people love him as Ryan was. All season, it inevitably seemed to slide to Tannenbaum when trouble arose. When I asked him about this, Tannenbaum nodded and said he'd spoken of this bind with Ryan. "I told him, 'I can't always be the villain. You're always recess!'" Tannenbaum often seemed lonely to me during road trips. He'd just won his fiftieth game as a GM. The only person who had thought to congratulate him was Michelle. That was exactly the sort of detail Tannenbaum himself would never have overlooked if the issue at hand was someone else's success. He was the rare GM who sent notes and gifts to other GMs when their teams did extraordinary things.

It occurred to me that it would have been easy for the Jets coaches to make me a pariah: the GM had yelled at me. They did the opposite, maybe because everybody's against the boss in life and for sure because that's how the team worked. People were always having at each other and then finding a way to console each other, which made the group stronger and the skin thicker. Jeff Weeks, however, seemed pleased at what had happened to me. "I'm always in trouble," he said, explaining that it was a relief to have someone else in the chop. I felt what he was saying. I could never shake the idea that it must be painful, no matter how much money you were making, to hold a job many colleagues believed you had because your friend loved you and wanted you beside him. Or maybe it wasn't painful. With Weeks, it was difficult to tell.

The thirty-four-call Patriots defensive game plan took the defensive coaches twelve hours to produce, from 3:45 in the afternoon on Tuesday until 3:45 a.m. on Wednesday. Much of that time was spent re-creating established calls for personnel groups that had not previously used them. This gave the very familiar a fresh look and was more or less the defensive version of what the Patriots did every week with their offense. There were new personnel groups, including Trojan, which used only one linebacker, Bart Scott. If the Patriots ran, "Bart plays football." If they threw, "Bart chooses somebody and hits them." It was a long day into a long night, but not unlike other game-plan sessions.

Before I began spending time with the team, I might have expected the Jets coaches to fill the week before they played the Patriots with an unusual amount of preparation, commensurate with the importance of the game against their primary rivals. Now I'd seen that football didn't work that way. For every game, the coaches did all they could within the context of the established schedule. They had to eat and they had to sleep a little, and other than those inconveniences, the coaches were committed to whatever was the current cause. Football fans thought of the games as infrequent and awaited them impatiently. For the coaches, it was sometimes all they could do to keep up with time's rapid passage. To them a game, any game, was inseparable from what came before

it, the actual hour of play merely the conclusion to the latest install-
ment of the serial narrative they were creating all the time.

"All right, men, Patriot week," Schotty began the Wednesday-
morning quarterback meeting. He said he would first show them
some film because "gotta learn to swim before you go into deep
water."

"What about swimmies?" asked Sanchez. Soon he was referring to the Patriots linebacker Rob Ninkovich as "my Russian
friend." The man was loose.

Schotty played film of the Patriots defensive backs reading the
quarterback's drop, how once he took a fourth backward step, the
backs fled into deep-zone coverage, willing to bend, not break. In
this way, they were the opposite of the Ravens. "Expect disguise,
disguise, disguise," Schotty said, because Bill Belichick thrived on
calling something different from whatever he displayed. Schotty
urged Sanchez not to get caught up pre-snap when the Patriots
tried to mess with him by showing dummy formations, false
coverages.

The Patriots, Schotty told his players, had cut the talented lineman Albert Haynesworth. It was just like Belichick to do that. At
the beginning of the season, he'd let go Brandon Meriweather, a
Pro Bowler whom Ryan had then considered Belichick's best defensive back. Haynesworth had a history of poor conditioning and
confrontational behavior. Belichick was always willing to take on a
hard case, but if you didn't reform, you were history. "Nobody
picked him up?" Sanchez asked.

"Not yet," Schotty told him. "Lot of baggage there, brother."

Ryan, who lived for big games, walked into the team meeting and
approached his lectern with a purpose. He carried a wooden baseball bat roughly the size of a loblolly pine. David Harris, he

announced, was the AFC defensive player of the week. Then Ryan said, "This is the game! They're pissed off. We're pissed off. You want to know how to be successful in a big game? It's all preparation. Do the little things." To beat a team as good as New England on a Sunday, the head coach said, you had "to beat them every day." Sutton leaned toward me and whispered, "Both teams will be ready. One team will be prepared." Then Ryan said, "Both teams will be ready. One team will be prepared." Sutton grinned. "I'm telepathic," he said. (Sutton occasionally helped the head coach with his speechwriting.) "This," Ryan concluded, "is a bring-your-bat game." (The flourishes were all Ryan.)

Pettine told the defense all he cared about was that they played fast, physical football. Question: How had the Steelers defeated the Patriots two weeks ago? Answer: "It was violent." The thirty-four-call plan might soon become twenty-four calls. Whatever it took. "Physicality," Pettine said, echoing Ryan, "is not something you just turn on come Sunday." He urged them not to make anything easy for Tom Brady because even when life was hard for him, he was "still fucking Tom Brady," and he'd hurt you some.

Pettine was methodical as he reviewed the calls, explaining not only what he wanted but also each new call's relationship to previous iterations. Everything was a version of something they knew well. A few calls he'd been saving for weeks. One call had been created for the first New England game but never used; there'd been a pre-snap penalty, after which Pettine changed the look. To counter the Patriots' many horizontal routes, the defensive coordinator showed precisely where along the grid the Jets linebackers could expect to intersect with the low crossers. He peppered his descriptions with what the players' thoughts would be: "David asks, Whose helmet can I knock off? Whose ribs can I damage?" It was very exciting.

Afterward I bumped into Sutton upstairs, where he had just hunted down a Diet Pepsi. It wasn't yet 11:00. "Getting started early?" I asked. "Big one!" Sutt said, gesturing to his drink. "Got to do the little things."

At practice, to join the scout team and play Wes Welker for the week, Tannenbaum had brought in off the street Dexter Jackson, a small, quick receiver who'd once been a Tampa Bay second-round draft choice. But although Sanchez shouted "Boom!" each time he completed a pass, and although Revis made three interceptions, the play was generally ragged. Why? Nobody could say. It was one of the cryptic aspects of the sport: good practices could not be willed. Afterward, with the team circled around him at midfield, Ryan was as angry as I had ever seen him. Usually he preached the need for balance in the players' lives. Not now. He spoke a philippic about "nothing, I mean nothing in your life this week" being more important "than this game."

Reviewing the Patriots film together, Cromartie and Revis were as struck as Pettine was by the contrast between Brady under pressure and Brady with excellent protection. "He gets ready to feel the pressure," said Cro, "and when he doesn't, he gets calm." Brady had, Cro thought, "that nervousness in him." Most quarterbacks did. It was just that Brady was usually so icily poised that the vulnerability in him was more striking when you saw it. Revis was still lamenting Welker's big catch in the first game: "I don't know how he caught that. I saw it and thought, Pick! and then it went"—with his hand, he made a parabola. "Okay," he said. "I'm out. I've already seen all this ten or twelve times." Cro said he could understand how Rev felt. On film, the Patriots were doing "the same thing over and over. It's not even different formations. It's just different personnel groups. The exact same thing with different people running it." He shook his head. As a football purist, Cro admired the effort that went into doing a few things well and here was the essence of the condition.

Julian Posey appeared. He'd decided after walk-through he would try "creeping into that room to soak up a lot of that knowledge." Cro welcomed him and soon was tutoring Posey as the film ran. "Watch: any time two release outside, one's coming inside." Then he was comparing the Patriots offense to his own. "This is what makes them so good. They put everybody in the quarterback's vision. He can see where everybody's gonna be. Our offense, if they run two posts, they run the other guy coming back. Mark can't see him—it's not in his vision."

Posey was fascinated by Brady's skill. "He's so smooth, so subtle with it," Posey said. It seemed to Posey that Chad Ochocinco, the flashy veteran receiver the Patriots had traded for, "isn't the same on the Patriots."

"He's confused, man," Cro said, agreeing with Posey. "He doesn't know what to do!" Cro packed his things into his patent-leather backpack, gave Posey a hug, and left.

Posey began talking about Revis. Revis, he felt, had "changed the game. In a game that's all passing, in a league where passing's deemed unstoppable, he's the one stopper. You can't coach a player not to feel rushed or feel beat. You feel beat and you rush yourself, but Darrelle knows there's always time. Everybody spends money to be fast and strong. What he has are the priceless things: eyes, feet, balance, awareness. How often do you see Revis fall?" I said that, come to think of it, I never had. Posey nodded. "People say to me, 'You just say he's the best because you play with him.' No! I see a simple catch made on him in practice and everybody says something. LT too." He went on, now speaking of Tomlinson. "You can really tell what he was. It's that great balance. I don't know what he sees behind that visor, but he always makes the right moves. He's got a great sense of a crowded space. And if LT was right here running and I threw a dime at his feet, he could cut off that dime."

We spoke for a while longer. The rookie cornerback told me about his brother in Brooklyn who worked for an artisanal pickle company and had also researched questions for the TV show *Who Wants to Be a Millionaire*. His brother was in Williamsburg— hipster heaven!—a neighborhood teeming with fabulous youth, fabulous eats, fabulous hangs, fabulous kicks, and fabulous threads, a fabulous place to be young and wide open to the world, as Posey was. But Posey didn't really plan to see the brother until after the season. All he wanted to do now was become better at football.

Meeting with his quarterbacks on Thursday, Schotty was completely engaged. During one call discussion, he suddenly left his feet and tackled two chairs. From the rug, still riffing on the coverage, the coordinator looked up, saw a maintenance man passing by outside in the hallway, said, "There's Juan!," and kept going, concluding, "It's textbook 1935 Bill Belichick football. Just sayin', he reads a lot of books, men."

There was a lot of energy in the room. Sanchez called me Worm and then, mimicking my voice, he said, "That's not my name!" Having gotten me to laugh, he then addressed Cavanaugh as Cavvy, the way Schottenheimer often did, and Cavanaugh told him evenly, "You can call me Coach." O'Connell was teased about his unmanly love for drinking low-fat chai lattes, leading him to challenge Brunell to meet him on the fifty-yard line, which led Sanchez to cry, "Show 'em your blitz eyes, Kev!"

Pettine had told the other offensive and defensive coaches he believed he'd had an off game the last time against the Patriots and he was determined to make up for it. In the defensive meeting, Pettine had a new delayed blitz to show the players that featured so many coverage rotations, fake overloads, hesitations, and compensatory drops, it looked like severe weather on the Doppler radar report.

Once again practice was ragged. Afterward, Ryan sternly said that everyone needed to step it up and that Marquice Cole and Donald Strickland were being counted on and needed to do better. The two singled-out defensive backs were standing beside each other, and as soon as Ryan spoke their names, David Harris went to them and put a hand on each of their shoulder pads.

*   *   *

How hard was Sutton working? In the morning he made coffee, forgot that he'd made it, and made coffee again. "Big game," he said. "It'd be a big one in a parking lot!"

In the Friday quarterbacks' meeting, Sanchez told of how every Thursday night he went by himself to a local restaurant to eat a late dinner and study the flashcards that he always made to memorize the week's game plan. Last night, the waitress had come to take his order just as Sanchez flipped to a new card and discovered that— oh no!—somebody had slipped in a card decorated with an enormous red dong. So, was it Kev? Not Kev. Bru? Not Bru. Cavvy? Him neither.

Later in the morning DT met with the defensive backs and told Posey he wasn't moving well, saying, "You look like you're carrying a picnic basket out there on your way to Grandmother's house." As a practice-squad guy, Posey wouldn't be playing in the big game against New England, but if you were sitting in front of DT, he was going to coach your ass.

After practice, while the defensive coaches were watching the film, Sanchez stopped by the meeting to inform Pettine that he should call me Worm. Then, with an evil glint in his eye, the quarterback said joyously, "The nickname spreads!" and scampered off.

Pettine crossed everyone up at the Saturday-morning defensive meeting by putting up on the screen a photograph of a baby that was not Mike DeVito. Nobody, not even Garrett McIntyre, recognized who it was, which was amusing since it was little Garrett McIntyre. Then there were two pictures of DeVito after all, one of him flexing tiny arms and another of him sitting in a wicker chair gazing out at the distant future. The existential DeVito just killed them. Pettine smiled. "Never gets old."

During the walk-through in the field house after the meeting,

Revis used his hands on the receivers he covered, a Saturday walk-through first. Rev didn't even want you walking your pattern against him.

Marquice Cole, who wore his hair in many braids, recalled his days at Northwestern, which he'd considered too much of a "country club." When the school recruited him to play football, he had the braids, as he did right up until the first college game, when he was suddenly ordered to cut them. He didn't want to. "They didn't take kindly to me," he said in his unusually deep voice. "And I didn't take kindly to them. They knew what they were getting." Cole was, Leonhard thought, "very complex. He knows how talented he is, but with all that talent and your role not increasing — it's not a good sign. Worst thing you can be as an NFL player is getting comfortable. He's got comfortable. Possibly a bigger role makes him nervous."

News about Penn State football coach Joe Paterno's role in concealing the sexual abuse of children by one of his assistants, Jerry Sandusky, was beginning to circulate, and a number of players and coaches were talking about how troubling they found it all. Maybin, a former Penn State player, said there'd always been something odd about Sandusky, but no players he'd known could ever quite identify what it was. For Pettine, a loyal son of Pennsylvania, the present situation was not ambiguous: "You blew it, Joe," he said. "I used to have so much respect for him. Not no mo'. He enabled a monster."

Samson Brown, an offensive assistant, had a glow about him at the walk-through. Brown lived in Manhattan, where his wife was a medical resident. Given that, and given that Schotty kept his assistants on sixteen- to eighteen-hour call with work, something astonishing had happened the night before. The couple had shared dinner together at their apartment. "Staying home is going out for us," Brown said. "We order in. We haven't had a home-cooked meal in five months." Not that Brown was complaining. He knew that most men in America spent their workdays counting down the hours, talking about all the many things in life they wished they had. Brown worked at an office where all anybody wanted to discuss was what he did for a living. Brown felt lucky. Lucky, and tired.

That night at the hotel, in the 7:45 quarterbacks' meeting, Sanchez was reading from the big and colorful call sheet like someone happily perusing a bistro menu when Schotty asked him if a particular call confused him. A similar call, the coordinator said, had given the quarterback problems against Miami. Suddenly Sanchez looked like he'd eaten a bad snail as he frowned and reflexively told Schotty, "I messed that up."

"Worked out great, dude," Schotty told him. "Tone double move gets a PI [pass interference]. You decided, 'Hell with this short stuff, Schotty, we're opening it up!'" Sanchez looked at me. "Put *that* in the book," he said. I thought again about how challenging it was for a coach to bring along an emotional young person in such a public and pressured job and felt that Schottenheimer was making progress.

The receivers arrived, and Schotty told everyone, "Sooner or later they'll get tired of giving up those eight- or nine-yard routes and then you can go deep." As he spoke, Sanchez made a succession of funny faces and finally said, "Unnhh!" When the others gazed at him curiously, he said, "Just getting excited!" This seemed to be his way of demonstrating DT's postulate that everyone handles football pressure in his own way.

Before the game, Dave Szott and I were talking. "The great thing about football is you have to face your fear," he said. "Any player that ever played this game has felt fear and if they say no, they're lying."

In Tannenbaum's box, I sat to Terry Bradway's right, again shamelessly using that congenial man as a GM shield. Tannenbaum was immediately upset at the way the Jets receivers came out of huddle, their body language betraying run (they'd seem disinterested) or pass (there'd be a bounce in their step). "It's obvious to me!" Given the many injuries in the Patriots secondary and the low number of Jets completions, one could almost understand the receivers' frustration.

The defense's plans for matchup substitutions were being thwarted by the Patriots shift to a no-huddle, hurry-up offense in which Brady lined his offense up again at scrimmage right after the tackle and shouted out his coded instructions from under center. He ran play after play so quickly the crowd couldn't even organize a roar to drown out his voice. "Look at the pressure no-huddle puts on opponents," said Tannenbaum. "Shouldn't we do that to them?" Still, despite the Jets offense's latest slow start, the Jets were in excellent position because the defense had given up only two field goals and then harassed Brady into a safety. Near the end of the half, Sanchez led a touchdown drive. Unfortunately, he had called a time-out right before the score, stopping the clock and leaving Brady and the Patriots eighty seconds—enough time for them to traverse the entire field and retaliate. With nine seconds left in the half, New England regained the lead, 13–9. Tannenbaum didn't even have to say it. "The little things," everyone thought.

It was the job of those in the box to be responsible for the irresponsibility of others. When Cromartie fled north as his man went south and west for a huge play, it was ultimately on them. Nobody on the Jets could cover the hulking New England end Rob Gronkowski, and that redounded to them as well. There were several other people in the box besides Bradway, Tannenbaum, and me, and at halftime, a couple of them shook their heads and quietly seemed to doubt that the team could win games like this with Sanchez. The Patriots had second- and third-stringers, including a receiver, playing defensive back. How could Sanchez not be taking advantage? Of course, the Jets had won a playoff game with Sanchez on the road in New England. But that was long, long ago in football time—ten full months.

The Jets defense played well for a while in the second half, but gradually they tired and the score became 23–9. When the offense scored to make it close, the Patriots then took it "eighty-four yards right down our throat," as Tannenbaum said. After Sanchez threw a denouement interception to Ninkovich, which his Russian friend returned for six more points to make the final score 37–16, Tannenbaum, thinking about defensive rosters, asked, "How can they be out there with thirty-seven points with the players we have and we have sixteen points and the players they have? Can anybody explain this?" One answer seemed to be Belichick's decision to emphasize offense, a practical assessment of the times and also perhaps an indication that the Patriots coach, a defensive specialist, was disciplined enough to build his team around Brady even though offense was not the part of the game he himself was most drawn to. Another explanation was the no-huddle. "No-huddle is the hardest thing," Leonhard would say later. "Everything speeds up. For us, we try to do so many different things, it makes the game simpler, and for us, we try not to simplify."

The morning after any loss, the facility was a desolate place. The wide hallways were like downtown streets in a Rust Belt city, the loss pervading in such a strong way that I half expected to confront fallen trees, broken windows, overturned garbage cans, wrack-strewn puddles. Steve Yarnell, whose job was to observe everything that went on at the facility, said simply, "Monday here after a loss fucking sucks. It's like death." Football was just athletics, and only a game had died, but nonetheless, men were pouring their whole lives into something, and they were hard hit. For Westhoff, a win lasted an hour; losses kept him up all night. After this week's loss, Callahan experienced the near inability to speak. "I'm gutted," he said. "Gutted. Just devastated."

The way they moved past the great pain was by seeking a formal understanding. All around the building, they gathered in groups to watch the film, to ask themselves if Sanchez could learn to read the coverages more astutely, to ask if he could get through his progressions faster. "After a game," said Bradway, "everybody identifies what didn't go well and you can correct it. But then you can lose what you did do well." Figuring into all this was the knowledge that there was a difference between moving on and forgetting.

In a late-Monday-afternoon team meeting, Ryan said he couldn't lie to the Jets. They probably wouldn't win their division. There was much else to play for, the coach said, and then he placed a chip of wood on their shoulders and knocked it off. Had they heard what Belichick had done after the game? Walking off the field, the Patriots coach had turned to his son and said, "Thirty-seven points on the best defense in football, suck my dick." In his meeting-room seat, Revis was horrified. "I think that's a jerk," he said to me later. "Maybe some people think he's a good, collected guy off the field, but then why say such things? It's degrading. Suck my *what?* Say it to my face. That's not great character."

The fact remained that the Jets had lost, so what could Revis do except look to the next opponent, another difficult game. They'd play against Denver and Tim Tebow, the former college phenomenon who was now a portent of NFL things to come, a starting quarterback who won games by running. To Pettine, the Broncos represented about as abrupt a stylistic shift from the Patriots as he could imagine. He compared moving from Brady to Tebow to transitioning from a Ferrari to a truck.

Part of the challenge was scheduling. NFL teams hate playing Sunday-night games. Football men are up-in-the-morning people, and here you had to wait all day, and then, even if you were the home team, you didn't get to bed before two. If you were on the road, it was a missed night of sleep. Thursday-night games were loathed even more than Sunday-night ones. There was insufficient time for physical recovery from the beatings of the previous game and insufficient planning time for the next one. To play on Thursday night after playing Sunday night, with, moreover, the second game on the road, and at altitude, was tearing out the sutures before the wound was healed.

Given the brief interval at the facility between games, not quite three days because of the long flight to Colorado, triage would be in order. Opposing Tebow required extra rehearsal, meaning there would be no two-minute practice for the defense, and that would prove costly.

Don Martindale had been right back in the summer. After beginning the season on the bench as Denver went 1 and 4, Tim Tebow had led the team to three wins in their last four games, two of them miraculous comebacks even by secular standards. To the nation, the quarterback was becoming a flesh-and-blood kouros, with his conspicuous practice of sinking to one knee and placing his head to his fist in prayer after a notable moment—Tebowing. That he was willing to remove his shirt to advertise underwear but was saving himself for marriage only increased his fundamental fascination.

Professional football players prepare so obsessively for each game they often don't know the names of the players on a future opponent's team until the week before the game. As Maybin once said to Smitty about a running back, "He's just a number. Who gives a fuck who they are as long as we do what we're supposed to do." Because Tebow had been, until recently, a reserve NFL player famous for his college career and his religious good works, he was a football specter to most Jets. They were *aware* of him but they hadn't gone ahead and *seen* him.

Greg McElroy had opposed Tebow in college. Talking on Monday afternoon, he recalled the Alabama defensive game plan against Florida. The Alabama coaches didn't think Tebow read defenses well, McElroy said, so they showed Tebow complex looks and created a pass rush that emphasized containment rather than their usual high-pressure dashes toward the quarterback. That was because Tebow's most devastating skill was his ability to circumvent blitzers, creating drive-bys, pass rushers veering past as he went thundering downfield.

Later, Pettine was in his office studying Tebow. Because Tebow had played so seldom in his Broncos career, there wasn't much NFL game tape on him. Thinking of what McElroy had said, I asked if Pettine had ever reviewed a player's college tape as he prepared a professional game plan. No, Pettine said. The two levels of play and scheme were sufficiently different that it wouldn't be helpful.

Tuesday was usually the players' day off, but in this short week they had a full day of classroom work and practice. At the morning defensive meeting, Pettine further introduced Tebow to a roomful of yawning men clutching coffee cups and spit bottles for tobacco. Tebow, Pettine said, was erratic, and streaky, and a winner. As a passer, he threw three in the dirt and then, the coordinator said, he threw "a laser beam on the money." When he ran, he broke many tackles, was deceptively fast. The idea was to force him to make quick decisions. "He can make you miss," Pettine warned. "Bit of a Houdini."

Everyone seemed still exhausted from the Patriots game as they headed out to practice. "This field's a prison!" yelled Dustin Keller. After leaving the stadium following the New England game, Smitty had worked on the Denver game plan until three in the morning and last night he'd been back at it until three a.m. again. "I'm light-headed," he said to Sutton. "It's just an attitude," said Sutton. "Now I'm better," said Smitty.

It was a cool New Jersey fall day with a high slate-blue sky and soft breezes, yet somehow it seemed overcast, with so many people walking around dog-faced and hurt. Revis, his knee sore and braced, was glum. It was at times like this that Ryan shone. During his first season with the Jets, the team had at one point lost six out of seven games. The Jets players expected retribution. Instead, one afternoon Ryan promenaded through the locker room wearing only a black vest. Here he was everywhere, telling jokes, relating anecdotes to lighten the mood, bucking people up. Devlin, too, was full of cheer, calling, "Nice rack, fellas. Nice tempo," as the starting offense came off the field after a series of plays. When Burress made like a tollbooth gate, raising his long arm improbably high to snag a pass, everyone yelled, "Whooooaaa!" Last week at this time it had seemed reasonable to talk about the Super Bowl. Now one loss had thrown all into doubt.

After practice, Revis and Cro watched film of Tebow, observing with incredulity the length of time it took him to wind up and release his passes and the frequent inaccuracy of those throws. "Man, I don't understand it, man!" Cro said. On the screen, balls were geysering everywhere. "What in the hell!" Cro said. "That's crazy."

The Jets planned to run and run and expected the Broncos to do the same. Runs didn't stop the clock the way incomplete passes did, leading Sanchez to say on Wednesday morning in the quarterbacks' meeting, "Men, this game's gonna take like twenty minutes." For the rest of the meeting the quarterback continued to employ stock Schottyisms. Everyone was addressed as "Men," and many things were prefaced with "the ole," which was, in fact, a Rexism appropriated by Schotty. Schotty, in turn, was referring to Sanchez as Coach. Looking at me, Schotty said, "Nick, we're dealing with maturity issues this side of the room!" It was the only time all year he voiced aloud something I was sure often ran through his mind. As for McElroy, Schotty said, "Greg, you know he's thinking, I go from winning a national championship to dealing with this shit!"

"Gonna be one of those days," McElroy said.

"Every day is one of those days," Schotty told him. But in fact, Sanchez was on top of the playbook today, dialed in. As Kevin O'Connell once told me, every week was a new series of problems, and the secret to football was trying to identify them and solve them. The big one they'd just quietly overcome in the meeting was the heartbreak of the loss to New England.

In the Wednesday team meeting, Ryan told the players, "Be comfortable on the plane. No suits unless that's you!" Most chose to fly in sweat wear, some in sweat suits of Baskin-Robbins colors.

To his defense Pettine stressed that in a short week, nobody knew what the other team would allocate time to prepare for and that all football teams felt vulnerable when they believed they were underprepared. It would be good to worry the Broncos in that way early. "Give them conflicting looks," Pettine said. "Move around. Make them think."

In Colorado that evening, at the quarterbacks' meeting, the players discussed Tebow's propensity to sail balls toward the stands and nose-cone them into the firmament. Like Cro, they'd never seen anything like it in an NFL starter. Brunell kept receiving texts. His youngest child had recently been given her first cell phone and was treating her father to the convert's inevitable initial flurry— the rare sign of the outside world infiltrating the web of the game. Sanchez, wearing a Chi-Com gray fur hat, was looking exhausted, and Schotty treated him with particular solicitude, telling him, "You're doing a really good job with a lot of stuff." The coordinator urged Sanchez, "Say uncle! Protect the ball and move on with your life." It was not a game in which to try anything rash, Schotty said. "Just get points. They're at a premium because I don't think they score on our defense."

The next morning the quarterbacks met again at 9:45. Their room was just down the hotel hallway from the team dining area. Nick Mangold stuck his head in. "Guys," the center said in his usual even tone, "it's that awkward time when there's about a minute left on your waffle and you're not sure whether to stare at the guy making it or..." He offered an enigmatic smile and vanished.

I was cold at the walk-through, so I wore a green ski hat. "Nicky!" said Ryan. "That hat! That's the kind of hat we used to wear to play pond hockey in Toronto." I was instructed to lose the hat and "put a hood on!" Ryan told the team he wanted passion, but the most passionate Jet, Bart Scott, was looking morose. Since his role in the defense had been reduced, he'd worn a snug hood in meetings, and during the New England game, he'd sat on the bench, woebegone. Ryan warned the defense not to be taken in if Tebow pumped a throw and then ran, which the coach called "the ole dog-and-tennis-ball trick."

On the bus to the stadium, there was a faint odor of anxiety. Well before we reached it, the stadium was visible in the distance, a big shimmering new-world building. Out on the field before the game, Tebow soared errant practice throws so far and high I kept noticing the downtown skyline.

Callahan's young, bearded son Brian was a Denver offensive coach. When he came over to say hello, his father introduced him around to the young Jets coaches. They asked him what it had been like to work for Josh McDaniels, the former Belichick assistant who'd been the Broncos head coach the year before. Brian said McDaniels was a relentless taskmaster; at night there was always the feeling you shouldn't go home. But it had been a terrific "apprenticeship." This was exactly the way these Jets coaches talked of their own former-Belichick-assistant-turned-head-coach Eric Mangini. Just then Brian was called away for a photograph with a Broncos cheerleader. Could this be his girlfriend? The young Jets coaches who had had nobody but Schotty in their datebooks stared as the young coach and the young beauty posed together. Brian came back to say good-bye.

"That your girlfriend?" he was asked.

"Yeah," he said. The Jets coaches shook their heads. He even said "yeah" the way they would want to say it.

Up in the coaching booth, before the game, Pettine sat silent with his multitude of pens and markers, then he fist-knocked with Devlin, O'Neil, and the other Motorola-headset-clad coaches before kickoff. Prophett was there with a pair of binoculars so he could call out Broncos personnel groups. Early on, Pettine kept careful track of the positioning of the edges and his deep safety. "I can't stress it enough, edge guys, don't chase until you see the QB give up the ball," he said into his microphone.

The game involved much punting. The Jets defense often was left to work from poor field position; five Broncos possessions started from the Jets side of the fifty. On these possessions, the Jets held Denver to only three points. The Denver backs were having no success, Tebow wasn't running much, and Cro had been right; the quarterback's big windup brought to mind a gantry crane boom as he swiveled before he threw. Pettine was on his game. "Watch the screen," he'd call and it would be a bubble screen. Schotty and Sanchez were having less success. "Unbelievable," said Pettine after every drive-killing offensive penalty or run for a loss. The offensive coaches seated to Pettine's left were very quiet. When Sanchez imprudently burned a time-out, one of them muttered, "Schotty might kill him." The Jets got the defensive formation they wanted for a 38 Special—reborn!—direct snap to Joe McKnight, but the ball rocketed way over Little Joe's head. "Un-fucking-believable," said Pettine.

Suddenly, in the third quarter, the offense was at the Denver one-yard line. Pettine was begging, "Please don't fuck this up." Bilal Powell fumbled into the end zone, and lineman Matt Slauson recovered for the touchdown. "Un-fucking-believable." Pettine sighed. "Line drive in the box score," said Devlin, eyes front. The Jets led 10–3.

Pettine played personnel chess with the Broncos, sending one group out a few steps and then withdrawing them: "I want to go big sub—not yet!" Denver changed to a running set. "We've got big people in. We're okay." Tebow heaved a pass that appeared bound for a snowdrift outside Aspen. "Oh!" cried the coaching box in wonder. But it was Sanchez who made the crucial mistake. On a third and six, instead of saying uncle, he threw an interception that was returned for a game-tying touchdown. "Fuck me!" roared Pettine. "And he's got Joe McKnight one-on-one with the linebacker."

They had contained Tebow so far, but as the third quarter ended, Pettine asked Ryan, "Want to heat him up, Rex? Just asking." Instead they went with extra coverage. Devlin, meanwhile, took it to heart every time Sanchez didn't see open receivers in his progression, especially when the open man was a tight end. A nifty one-handed catch by Joe McKnight led to a Jets field goal, making the score 13–10 in the Jets' favor with nine minutes and fourteen seconds left. Then Harris stuffed the Broncos on third and two. "Let's go up two scores," said Pettine hopefully. But the problem all year, Brandon Moore would say after the season, was a lack of offensive "energy." What he meant was they were professionals, fine professionals, but like a band, they needed hits, calls that in the crucial moments, on a big stage, they could fall back on because they always worked.

The offense punted all the way to the Bronco five. To this point, eight of the eleven Broncos possessions had lasted three plays. On their third downs the Broncos were one for eleven. Tebow had run twice for eleven yards. Passing, he was six for fifteen. It was difficult to imagine any team playing better defense on short rest than the Jets were. There was five minutes and fifty-four seconds left. On first down, a Tebow pass in the right flat to Denver's Eddie Royal found Leonhard with a clear goal-line shot at the receiver. Royal juked a hip and Leonhard missed him. "All we got to do is keep the edge," said Pettine. They couldn't. Tebow began dropping back and either completing passes or working the dog-and-tennis-ball.

"Tell these guys to stop flying by the quarterback," Pettine cried. "Our guys are gassed," O'Neil told him. Tebow had become a football Sherman, leading an inexorable march. Into Jets territory he went, the crowd chanting his name.

With the Broncos across the Jet thirty, again Pettine considered the blitz, which he had yet to call. "At some point we got to come after him. Is now the time?" At third and four at the twenty, with three Bronco wideouts in formation and nothing else showing signs of stopping the Broncos, Pettine asked Ryan, "Want to come after him, Rex?" Ryan did. The call was Comcast, meaning Eric Smith was to blitz. The safety charged, Tebow eluded him, and with the edge now uncontained, the Colorado plains opened up vast and unpopulated. In the end zone Cro lingered behind Bronco receivers as Tebow heavy-hoofed toward the goal line for the lead.

The game ended at 17–13, Broncos. Tebow sank to a knee as up in the booth Pettine said, "Oh, this is a kick in the nuts, boys." In the locker room Schotty was slumped, speechless. "Job's not for the faint of heart," he told me later. Ryan looked at his players, who had just lost twice in four days, and spoke them a threnody: "It stings. It hurts. I believe in this team. Am I the only guy who believes in this team?"

Twelve

REVIS ISLAND

We were a very small group and it was as though I was directing Rashomon *every minute of the day and night. At times like this, you can talk everything over and get very close indeed.*

—*Akira Kurosawa on living with the cast and crew while making his film* Rashomon

After the regretful flight home from Colorado—If Jimmy could've made that tackle, Ryan kept thinking—the only true comfort to be had was the familiar paregoric: to go straight to the facility and look back at what had happened. And so Ryan sat in front of the film screen in Pettine's office, the two old colleagues accompanied by a few of their assistants, watching the well fires burn. Every so often, one of them would say, "How did we lose this game?"

The defense had been magnificent. On the film, the coaches found clinic moments for so many defenders: Wilkerson, Po'uha, Kyle Wilson, Kenrick Ellis—"The big boy was rolling!" Ryan raved. Of Tebow, Ryan said, "Kid's a fucking winner." Then he said, "This guy can't throw a lick against us and they beat us!" When the film showed Cromartie failing to leave the end zone as Tebow made his game-winning run, the entire room was mortified. Ryan always wanted to think the best of people, and so he reminded himself that Cro had a damaged sternum, that it was not for one man to judge another's pain.

At nine that morning, the defensive coaches sat down together in their meeting room. "Our guys played their asses off," Pettine said. "Handled a very difficult set of circumstances: a unique offense, a unique scheme, unique travel. I don't understand how they can rise up and others can't. That's what frustrates us all, I think."

"Yes," Sutton said. And nobody else had anything to add.

All the coaches met with Ryan. Schotty was feeling completely exasperated. At one point in the game, Sanchez had completed eleven consecutive passes. He could do it! Then, on the crucial pick-six, he had failed to notice what Pettine had seen, Joe Mc-Knight alone in space against the much slower linebacker, had read his progression poorly, and had thrown late to Burress. How could a coach help a player overcome such patience-exploding inconsistency? "Just sloppy, the whole performance," Schotty said, which was as close to Pettine-like ire as he got. He knew that Sanchez was frustrated and also, as Sanchez himself had said, "embarrassed." What Sanchez would never say, and what Holmes had earlier in the season tried to say for him, was that it was difficult to make your reads when you were under withering attack in the pocket.

Callahan wanted to take the blame for the line's sagging play, but Ryan pointed out that Moore's and Mangold's spirits were willing, but their bodies were listing.

"I'll take the bullet for the call at the end," Pettine said. "We put Eric in a tough spot. I tried to force Tebow into a mistake. We hadn't done it the whole game. I'll take the bullet. It's a shame. Guys played their hearts out."

"I want to throw the fuck up," said Westhoff. "Monday I'll be different."

Ryan nodded. "Monday, as a coaching staff, we got to be so enthusiastic."

Back in Pettine's office, with a free weekend ahead and my family

372 • NICHOLAS DAWIDOFF

away, Smitty and I were considering going to see a movie. We didn't know anything about any of the current features. *Crazy, Stupid, Love*—that sounded intriguing. Pettine had never heard of it either, but he said if we went to something called *Crazy, Stupid, Love*, we couldn't ever come back into his office.

As the defensive coaches left the building, they could see Schotty in his office with his assistants, having another meeting. Was it the line? Was it Sanchez? Was it them? The offensive coaches would have given anything to make things better. Sutton was the same way. Over the weekend, he reread *As a Man Thinketh*, James Allen's short tract on self-improvement.

How consuming was football? "All my real-world knowledge has been replaced by football," Leonhard said. When you put that much into something only to be disappointed, maintaining your spirits was difficult no matter how well you were paid. Mindful of this, Sutton sent a text message to BT. For some time, Sutt had been urging the injured linebacker to come sit in on the defensive meetings, telling BT his presence in the room helped the other players, telling BT the team needed him. On Monday, BT appeared. "BT! You been away too long," Pettine told him.

Pettine began by apologizing to the defense for the blitz he'd called at the end. Then Pettine showed them the Broncos-game film. At the end, when Cro remained rooted in the end zone, Pettine said something anodyne about the need to play like a Jet. "That last play was bad," BT whispered to Pace. "I don't want to talk about it," Pace replied. Smitty gathered the outside linebackers and told them about his experiences being on a Ravens team with a weak offense. He warned them, "You can't get frustrated. Just do your job."

Afterward, BT visited Pettine's office. He was upset about Cro. Why hadn't Pettine said anything to the room? Pettine told him he didn't want to humiliate Cro. BT was unconvinced. Pettine shrugged.

He didn't think, at this point, it would do any good. BT argued that you had to try.

At practice, under low November sunlight, Revis covered Patrick Turner close as a pocket sewn onto a shirt. "I love that," Sutton said. "It's my favorite thing in life. What would make me think I could do it in a game if I can't do it in practice?" Cro too was all over the field. Sutton shook his head. He sighed. "It's hard to erase that image."

Burress wasn't at practice and Jeremy Kerley had been hurt, so the offense might need bodies at receiver for the home rematch against the Bills. Schotty told the quarterbacks Cro had volunteered to help the offense. The plan for him as a pass catcher, Schotty said wryly, was very complex: Cro would "run by the guy!" What number was Cro? Sanchez asked. "Thirty-one," said McElroy.

In the defensive-backs' meeting, DT told Cromartie, "Cro, I see you working at your job and you're getting better."

Cro was not the only defender to cross the line of scrimmage. During practice Ryan stood with the offense, receiving many jeers from the green-shirted defense. But among the white shirts, the mood lightened, as it did among the defenders when Po'uha intercepted a pass and ran with it for several yards, during which the earth vibrated, before pitching it to Revis.

Pettine had been without sleep so long he suddenly grew ill, spiking a high fever. After spending a couple of hours curled up on the floor under his desk, he'd gone home to sleep it off for the rest of the day. During the coaches' film session after practice, DT sat in Pettine's chair and decreed that no music could be played "because we've been getting our ass kicked." Later, in the secondary meeting, Julian Posey brought in his dessert from lunch, a slice of pie, and DT took it away from him. Then DT put up some film from the first Bills game and told Cro that "the new Cro" would destroy the Bills receivers by pressing them. "Are you the new Cro?"

*   *   *

Schotty began the Wednesday-morning meeting by telling the quarterbacks, "Words! Enough words!" And then as they gloomily watched the Bills defense play the Raiders offense, Schotty suddenly became expansive after all: "There's Denarius Moore! Loved him for the draft coming out of Tennessee. One of the best rookies in the league. But I'll take my man JK! Might get my favorite slot receiver back today. Men, where's he want to spend Thanksgiving? With his favorite coordinator!" Some clips from the Broncos game against the Bills came next. The Broncos slot receiver was Brandon Stokley. "Who knows Brandon Stokley's nickname?" Schotty asked. "Come on, men! This is essential. Slot Machine! But I'll take my man JK!" Then he showed the quarterbacks a fake reverse to Santonio Holmes and told them the fake would set up the real reverse because "they're not even looking at him!" And then: "The ole sprint option, men!"

"Yes!" cried Brunell, who'd made his name in the league running the ball fifteen years back.

"Easy!" said Schotty, settling Bru down with the flick of a syllable. "You and Cav go have a dip somewhere, maybe in the shitter, and talk about Bill Walsh!" Now the coordinator ran a cut-up of the Bills playing Cincinnati. "Hey, nice catch, Jermaine Gresham! Who is from—Kev?"

"Oklahoma!" shouted O'Connell.

"Ahhh! *Football Almanac.*"

And finally another Raiders cut-up: "Hey! Great catch there by my guy Denarius Moore. Read my report on him!"

On the TV monitors around the facility, Ryan had posted a message: "Don't Let Anyone Rob Us of Our Dreams." HBO's *Real Sports* had filmed a segment about Marcus Dixon's teenage travails in and out of prison in Georgia. Pettine had seen it and been so moved that he'd wept. He asked Dixon if he could tell the room about it, and Dixon thought that would be fine. So in the defensive meeting, Pettine said that if they wanted "to know what kind of man and teammate" was among them, they should watch. Dixon's reaction to that was "I was proud. Some people might be ashamed. To me, on and off the football field, I'm a great guy, and for him to mention that in a meeting, I was proud." After football, Dixon planned to return to his Georgia hometown. "I didn't do anything wrong. My hometown is where I'm born and raised. I won't let anything run me out of my home."

BT began prodding Westerman to dream big, live large, go get himself a pick-six against the Bills. Maybin, who'd seen Westerman dance, told Westerman if he did make one, he'd "get fined for excessive gyrations!" Westerman was indignant: "I don't gyrate, man. I wiggle."

At Wednesday's practice, the day before Thanksgiving, the offensive scout team was so depleted that Posey was needed at wide receiver. At the end, as the Jets came together around him at midfield, Ryan asked Bart Scott to break down the team by saying a few words pre-holiday, and the linebacker struck an evanescent tone. "Be thankful," he said. "It doesn't last forever."

Posey's younger brother DeVier was a well-regarded Ohio State receiver. In the defensive-backs' meeting, DT reviewed Posey's performance at the position that day against the defense. "Nice route you ran on Revis, Posey," DT said. "You remind me of your brother."

"You mean he reminds you of me!" Posey sparked back. "Where you think he got it from?"

"From your parents! You got robbed!" Before he dismissed them for Thanksgiving, DT said, "You watch this game long enough, you'll see all kind of shit."

In the Friday quarterbacks' meeting Schotty was all business. He had stopped shaving, ostensibly because he didn't want to take the trouble, though maybe also because at times like these, it was good to have extra protection. The newspapers had been rough with him lately, and even if he didn't see them, they still sometimes found their way under a football man's skin. "Don't read the newspaper" was DT's advice. "You got enough people picking you apart." Eric Smith, too, had been receiving sports-page censure for losing containment along the edge when he blitzed Tebow at the end of the game, and so, at his weekly press conference, Pettine made a point of explaining that his own call was at fault, not the player.

Absorbing criticism was such a big part of being a football professional that learning how to take it was a valuable skill. What the coaches told the players in meetings could sound blunt, but, Ryan said, "It is never, ever personal. You just want to fix the problem. What's personal is the problem. These are rare dudes. They're mighty men. It's easier to win a lottery than to play in the NFL. You'll be criticized. The old gladiators. Thumbs up. Thumbs down."

In the team meeting, Ryan called for tempo, an admonition not received by Revis, who was late. Revis was an upset man again these days. Ever since Holmes had chastised the linemen, there had been bad feeling within the team. Holmes was respected by all for his ability, yet when Ryan had named him a captain, many players winced, because Tone had made it out of the sugarcane mostly by relying on Tone. In the past, veteran and inspiring offensive players like Tony Richardson and Brad Smith and Jerricho Cotchery had been adept at keeping the Jets' collective offensive outlook tight and bright, but in their absence, Revis felt that more fell to him, not a natural role for the cornerback. "I don't know everything," Revis would say, looking back, "but I know a team that's not together. Players were coming to me every day in the locker room. I'd say, 'Just chill,' but too much negativity." When Revis finally arrived in the middle of the defensive meeting, he received a big hand.

After the players split off into positional groups, Smitty asked Westerman what he would like the outside linebackers to watch from the archive of Bills film. Westerman chose Buffalo's recent game against Miami—"Unless anybody wants to watch something else. I don't want to monopolize."

"It's all right, Jamaal," Maybin told him. "Your world and we just live in it."

"It's Revis's world," Westerman riposted, "and we all just live in it."

Breaking down practice, Ryan praised Sanchez's throws, declared that everybody had done well, except for one thing: Revis had been late. "You know nobody loves Revis more than me," the coach said, "but I'm gonna fine the shit out of him. I want to make sure all of us are pointed in one direction. You were wrong, right, Rev?" Revis conceded that he was.

Then DT skipped the weekly crossbar game. He said he was jilting everyone because he didn't have it today. "Got to know when to fold 'em," he explained. "So medieval!" said Jim Leonhard, who vowed not to let that pass. DT of all people! This wasn't tennis, where you walked off the court in the middle of a match that wasn't going well and people said, "He withdrew."

From the outside, the Jets, at 5 and 5, appeared to be an eddying team. From within, the experience was vortical, their attempts to achieve a smooth football flow constantly interrupted by turbulence. Anxiety was such a big part of football, and every NFL game was so difficult, each player's health and status were so tenuous. All a player or coach really had to fall back on was himself.

All of which was to say, thank goodness for Brodney Pool's new haircut. Pool's hair went several inches high and was rounded off on the top like a stovepipe, and seeing it at the Saturday-morning meeting, Revis laughed and laughed. Revis's laugh didn't sound like anyone else's. It was a deep, hearty, guttural, open-mouthed, head-back, boisterous, all-of-himself guffaw. How had Pool described such a look to his barber? "I pulled out my iPhone and showed him the picture my sister sent." Because the cut made Pool resemble the Steelers hyperintense coach Mike Tomlin, famed for his Death Star gaze, Pool spent the meeting fielding requests to "make your eyes big!"

At the walk-through, DT was handed a contract from the Crossbar Brotherhood that stated the Missing Man would never again skip crossbar, or else no soap operas, no solitaire, no California lollipops, and no barbecue-flavored 10:00 a.m. sunflower seeds for him. DT signed. Cro signed. Leonhard signed. Eric Smith signed. All the other participants signed, except Revis, who announced, "I ain't signing without my agent." Everybody looked perplexed. Sutton came to the rescue: "He's got more at stake than the rest of you," said Sutt.

As this went on, the offensive coaches across the way were standing in a line looking like a council of concerned elders. Nodding toward the perpetual object of offensive fretting, Sanchez, Sutton said a quarterback had to be free, loose, and confident, "a tough thing with so much in your head."

In the quarterbacks' meeting that night at the hotel, Sanchez was free, loose, confident, and also accurate, nailing every game-plan question Schotty threw at him, and Schotty moved the meeting along at no-huddle tempo. Afterward, everybody seemed in a good way, until out in the hall, heading off downstairs to the unit and then team meetings, I was startled when Burress said loudly to Holmes, "Waste of time."

Ryan looked out at the entire team, irate. He said that if the defense still wanted to be considered an elite unit, they needed to finish games. Then he went one by one along the offensive line, telling each player what he expected of him. "Son, I know, two hip surgeries," he said to Moore, "but I need you to be you." The frank urgency in the coach's voice was experienced by others the same way Revis's laugh was, as something physical. It shook into you. Ryan said little about the Bills, the point seeming to be that too often, his team's real rival was itself.

On the stadium field before home games, some of the coaches frolicked with their sons. Devlin now had his redheaded son Zachary working on long snaps. Zachary was getting very good grades in high school and was an excellent high-school center, but he was undersized by collegiate standards, and so the long snapping was a fallback, a football sinecure in case he failed to grow. Every team these days needed a long snapper. There was one other "problem" with Zachary, said Devlin: "My son's such a good kid. I just need him to be a prick on the football field."

Ryan, meanwhile, threw bombs to one of his own progeny, skinny, sunglasses-wearing Seth, whom Ryan fondly called Slugs, even though Seth could really run. Seth had it in mind to someday attend a school like the University of Alabama or Clemson, a school where he could play and study football at the feet of a sophisticated college coach—as Schotty had done at Florida under Steve Spurrier.

Meanwhile, Schotty's father, Marty, winner of two hundred NFL games as a head coach, was over on the sidelines talking football. He said that he became a coach because it enabled him to keep playing "vicariously." His playing position had been linebacker, and he thought that watching over everything from back there as it developed and then came toward him had been excellent coaching training. He talked of coaching Bernie Kosar in Cleveland, not much of an athlete at quarterback but intelligent enough to devise a means to succeed within his limitations: "His passes were puffballs but they floated in perfect alignment with wide receivers, so catchable and yet elusive to defenders." As I was thinking about those smart little puffballs finding their way, a Bills player, Ruvell Martin, came by and thanked Marty for encouraging him to stay with football when he cut him from the San Diego Chargers. "The next year I had that confidence," Martin said.

To all of them, football was the family business, and it interested me that these sons, who doubtless saw less of their fathers than most kids did, were attracted to the lives the fathers led. That made sense; football had such obvious importance for the fathers that of course the sons would be drawn to it. Either that or repelled by it, as Ryan's other son had been as a teenager. How much of a guy's guy was Ryan? "If we had a girl, it wasn't mine," he once joked.

The scene was what you'd expect from a bunch of football coaches on a field with their sons. The air was full of instruction, advice, and encouragement. Into my mind came Ellis Lankster, so beloved among the coaches, and his description of growing up with his mother and sisters in Prichard, Alabama, the roughest part of Mobile County, where the air base and the paper mill had closed, where sneakers dangled from the wires. "I stayed in a house, older dudes on the corner shooting dice, smoking weed, drinking, weed all day. People get drunk and end up just shooting. There were gangs. The Crips. You had to wear blue. At eight years old I wore white and red to school and the older dudes told me, 'You better go home and change or you'll get in trouble.' It was rough, now." Lankster's father was a roofer in Detroit. His mother, Sayinka, had worked twelve-hour days at an Alabama chemical factory and then at a Coca-Cola plant. Eventually she married a truck driver named Billy Jackson. When I asked Lankster how he chose his junior college in Mississippi, Lankster said, "Because it's in Ellisville."

The locker room at MetLife Stadium never felt very familiar to the coaches and players because they visited it so seldom. In the coaches' dressing area, the TV was on and the crawl asked, "Do the Jets need an offensive identity?" Callahan paused, read this aloud, shook his head, and said, "Brutal." On the shiny coffee table beneath the television was one magazine. On the cover was the beatific face of Tim Tebow.

In the game, the Bills and Jets traded touchdowns. And then, with the Jets backed up near their goal line, as soon as Tannenbaum said, "We can't win the game down here but we can lose it," Sanchez threw an interception leading to a short Stevie Johnson touchdown against Revis. It was 14–14 at the half, and in the GM's box, the conversation had to do with why every last thing seemed to be so hard for the Jets right now.

Early in the third quarter, DeVito led the line in denying the Bills on third down and he received a massive hug from Matt Mulligan as he came off the field. Tannenbaum, noticing, said, "I wish somebody cared about me the way those two care for each other." A touchdown to Dustin Keller led to a Tannenbaum boomer fist-knock coming my way up in the box, a real red knuckle-splitter. A moment later the Bills punted, a punt that Cromartie muffed and fumbled. Ryan Fitzpatrick, an economics major, thought he knew a soft market when he saw one, and he went right at Cro on the next play with a scoring pass to Brad Smith. Cro's coverage was actually too good. He was in position to make an interception, and Smith was trying to prevent that. Smith swiped at the ball; it popped into the air and settled serendipitously into the receiver's arms.

Both the Jets cornerbacks had trying days as Stevie Johnson ran slants for short, productive gains against Revis. "Stevie Johnson is the shiftiest motherfucker there is and so Rev can't come up and press him" was Posey's analysis. DT said that Johnson's "herky-jerky" way of running was difficult to read. On the Jets bench, the joke was that Stevie Johnson was in a beach chair with a lime in his Corona and his feet cozy in the toasty sand on Revis Island.

The whole team seemed out of rhythm. Ten Jets were on the field during one play; for another, there were twelve. The Bills took the lead. A dreary facility Monday seemed imminent. And then Sanchez played some of his best football of the season. Burress made one of those tollgate one-handed plucks and Holmes followed it up by catching the touchdown with a minute left. A big drop by Stevie Johnson, open again, saved the day at the end. The final score was 28–24.

After Holmes's touchdown, he and Sanchez didn't even bother to congratulate each other. The year before, when a similar late throw to Holmes beat the Browns, Sanchez had gone running down the field to celebrate with the receiver. Tannenbaum saw them turn away now and was so upset he stayed awake thinking about it deep into the night.

The locker room was subdued. During the customary reciting of the Lord's Prayer, I knelt beside Sanchez. He looked forlorn, as though the team had lost and he'd failed. What more could an American athlete ask for than to throw the game-winning pass and earn millions of dollars for doing it? Everyone wanted to throw the game-winning pass. Later on for the ice-cream socials, I thought. These guys need some Outward Bound. Put them in a canoe together.

DeVito was on the training table. He'd reinjured his knee and was in considerable pain. Mulligan arrived to bury him in a long embrace.

"Wins and losses come in all shapes and sizes in the NFL," said Pettine on the way home, "and it's hard for us when Rev has a bad week. Everybody has matchup difficulties. This is his."

Revis was far too competitive to see it that way. "He caught like five slants!" the cornerback protested. "We can live with that. He's good at jerking a lot. Lot of herks and jerks. But I'm playing zero coverage with no help. I'm not concerned with people catching a ball on me. I have some games, my guy gets one catch and five yards, but the game's too good. These guys study me too."

Against his former team, Aaron Maybin had played his best professional game. He'd hit Fitzpatrick six times, sacking him twice. His sack celebrations were a one-man cancan. Cro, however, remained adrift. When he was supposed to press at the line, he retreated, allowing so many yards of cushion it looked terrible on film. Even worse was the contact he avoided. His heart right now didn't seem to be in all that football required of a player. Ryan and Pettine agreed to leave it to DT to decide if they should bench Cro and start Kyle Wilson. "No problem," said DT.

At the team meeting, Ryan told the players he'd begin shortening the practices to keep them fresh for the final quarter of the season. Then Pettine met with the defense. Their fundamentals were slipping, the coordinator said. "This isn't going to be a bitch session," he went on. "This is being men. Treating you like men. But the tape doesn't lie and we're gonna put the best guys out there. Sounds cold. That's the business we're in." Lest they forget they'd won, he said, "We did some great things. And," he added, "some horrific things."

Bart Scott was told to be in his stance and ready when the ball was snapped. You could talk to him that way. Scott was sensitive, but he was also a pro and a realist, knew how it all worked. Cromartie's defenses were thinner, but Pettine tried. He praised Cro's coverage on Brad Smith's fluky touchdown. Soon enough, on the film, Cro was four yards off the line of scrimmage with his back turned to his man. When Pettine chided him, Cro said, "Shut up." Then he said, "Fuck you." Pettine told him quietly, "Don't lose your cool. We're all in this together." DT spoke up. "Players play and coaches coach." The rest of the session was quiet.

As soon as Pettine left and the defense split into positional units, Cro said loudly that Pettine was "a high-school coach" and declared he wasn't "gonna take it" from him. The other defensive backs were tense. It didn't help that Emmanuel Cook, a popular player, had been released earlier in the week. DT again urged them to stay together as a team, not to pick at one another. He told Cro to go talk with Pettine if something was bothering him. "If I talk to him, I'll punch him in the face," said Cro. On the other side of the room, O'Neil looked shocked. DT told Cro that Pettine had a job to do. Revis raised his hand. He said he wanted to play receiver. Everyone laughed. Marquice Cole raised his hand. He looked at Strickland and said, "Fuck you!" Then he went into a long riff parodying DT: "I done things in this league..." This did not lighten the mood. It was strange, as though Cole had started out trying to be funny but then gave way to his desire to release a little of his own rage. Revis could understand that. Cole had lost a brother that summer. "I think he was just trying to find some joy in his life. He was close with his brother. Losing his brother was deep for him." The meeting moved on deathlessly. The subject under discussion was the Washington Redskins' passing game. Nobody could concentrate on that. After a while, Pettine sent word that Cro should come by his office. The team needed Cro.

Right afterward, O'Neil marveled at Pettine. "I would have lost it," he said. "Pet was perfect. He handled it perfect." When the season was over, Leonhard said he still thought it was the "craziest thing I ever saw. Cro's not mentally tough, and if he feels attacked, he flips out. He felt attacked. Everybody in the room agreed with Pet, but Cro felt attacked. All they're trying to do is help him. They see that, physically, they don't make them like that. He fights what's good for him. It's obviously a core issue with him. It may hold him back his whole life."

Revis thought the same. Revis's childhood appeared to bear similarities to Cro's, but it was different in crucial ways. Revis grew up poor in a single-parent family with a working mother in the boarded-up city of Aliquippa. "It was a rough town," he told me after the season, when I visited him there. "Mills closing. Then just the corruption of the people. The violence. The drug dealing. Probably prostitution. Politics. Anything you think of in a negative way. Gangs. I was never part of that stuff. My family kept me out of it. But I've seen some harsh things. I always ran away from that. One reason is my family finding God. Another is I wanted to be a Michael Jordan, a Sean Gilbert, a Mark Gilbert, who instilled in me if you sell drugs, you can't be a professional athlete."

We were in the home of Aileen Gilbert, Revis's grandmother. Gilbert for a while had worked in the steel mill, first operating a jackhammer and then serving as a bench man, in steel-toed boots, helmet, and shield. Later, she had jobs at Head Start and in a women's shelter. She was a force of accountability for her children and grandchildren. Aileen Gilbert said now, "Darrelle was never a bad kid. We hovered over him to make sure he was good, and if not, there was consequences."

"Two big uncles!" said Revis.

"Jamal probably took you places you didn't belong," Gilbert said, giving Revis a long look.

"He did. The ghetto!" Revis began to describe the fate of kids he'd known from the heights housing projects: "Some got shot. Some on crack. Some now just getting out of jail. There was some stuff. I never got into it. My uncle would say, 'No. Go shoot hoops.' Or we'd play football with the bigger guys, and they'd rough us up, make us tough. I used to be around those guys until high school, then they'd get guns and I'd be, 'No, thanks. I'm cool.'"

"Darrelle's always been polite, he's always listened," said Gilbert. "I never had to whup Darrelle." Revis spent boyhood summer vacations with his father, who lived in another state.

Revis had his family, and he also had football. "Growing up, you loved to have a team," he said. "All together, a lot of passionate people working for a goal." And although Revis described Aliquippa as a place where there "ain't a lot going on," he always went back, which was not at all the way Cromartie felt about Tallahassee.

Revis began talking about Cromartie. Since October, Revis said, when Pettine had made his comments to the newspapers about Good Cro and Bad Cro, Cromartie had been brooding. "It was building up in Cro," Revis said. "I told him, 'Don't worry about it.' But it was building up in him and we were losing and he went off in the meeting. Crazy day. Shouldn't have happened. Cro can't take authority. DT'll tell him something and it's 'Got you, Coach.' Sometimes it's 'I *said* I *got* you, man. Why you keep coming at me?' You have incidents with Cro from time to time." Revis noticed that some days when Cro came into the dining hall at breakfast, even though all his teammates were seated at one of the round cafeteria tables, Cro would go find his own table and eat by himself. "He's got five or six baby mamas, nine kids. You don't know what goes on with him when he leaves work. Nobody knows what he deals with on the day-to-day. He could be the best corner in the league. I just gotta be positive with him."

As with everything else that upset him in his line of work, Revis talked over the meeting with his family. His grandmother said that she'd seen Cro on *Hard Knocks,* sitting there on camera naming his many children, and she agreed with Jim Leonhard that the moment, like the incident with Pettine, spoke to qualities that were fundamental in Cro. "It comes from childhood," she told Revis. Revis said that the only man Cro really trusted was Ryan. "He has a lot of respect for Rex."

Just because Ryan preferred tough men with "armadillo skin" didn't mean he couldn't see virtues in more fragile people. "Cro has a big heart," Ryan believed. A problem, said Ryan, was that "it became too much Pettine's defense. It all comes from me. They think I have the serial number of the Unknown Soldier. They do. Pettine downplayed that, and there's guys who don't believe in Pet. Cro. Bart Scott. Pet's telling them the truth, but they thought he was disloyal to me. Pet is my chosen guy and I thought I was being fair to Pet by not being in there as much."

The older defensive backs worried about the effect of Cro's outburst on young Posey. Leonhard told Posey, "Now that you've seen that, you've officially made it to the NFL." The day after the meeting, Cromartie himself sought out Posey and apologized to him. He said, "It's not what I want to show to young guys and not the person I am." Then Cro asked Posey what he'd thought of it all. Posey told him, "I thought you're crazy! Tripping out!" Cro told Posey, "There were a lot of pent-up things and I snapped." As Posey pondered it all, he said, "I thought, Why's Cro so sensitive and high-strung?

He's in a high-stress situation. That's why he's so unpredictable day-to-day."

After the season, Cromartie remembered the day essentially the same way. "You get tired, fed up. You can be holding something in and it bursts out. Like I told our rookies, that's not something they want to do. It was a mistake to do it in front of them. It happens more in other places than here. Pet can be sarcastic. Rex is more of a guy, you understand where he's coming from. They both have a good heart."

With people like Cro and Tone, I occasionally found myself imagining what their lives would be like now if they'd had it a little easier as children, had childhoods like Revis's. I noticed how many of the best NFL quarterbacks came from stable families. When a little less fell on you early, it seemed you could take more later. Cro could appear so fierce and sound so harsh and dismissive. But at the facility, he was generous to young players, and to me, watching film, patiently explaining the game. Then, too, there were times on the practice field when he was feeling relaxed and he looked so soft-faced and tender. Guys would come up behind him and tap his shoulder and then run away laughing. Or they'd find something innocuous to tease him about. They wanted to hold him there, didn't want him to go off into himself.

In football, maintaining order is part of the culture. When both units of coaches met later in the same Monday afternoon as the incident, Pettine described Cro's "meltdown" but emphasized, "The room is strong." Meanwhile, Holmes's attitude was imposing a sullen drag on the offense. Even on his touchdown, Holmes wasn't running full speed. He and Sanchez were barely speaking. Pettine suggested that Ryan make them game captains in Washington, and everyone laughed. Then Pettine offered to walk out to the coin toss with Cro. Ryan said, "It's easy to me. 'Tone, you're not giving it to us on the practice field, you don't play.' "

The problem wasn't the system. Tone knew his routes and everyone else's. The problem was that successful football teams are a random family of people, a bachelor's cutlery drawer of personalities. Whether individuals successfully found common cause or not depended on what football men classified as chemistry. Every team had moments of toxic reaction. The best teams ventilated them by winning. Schotty shook his head and said he admired Sanchez for getting angry with Holmes: "I like Mark when he's pissed. He's not afraid of anybody. Fucker's not afraid of the devil." Ryan thought it was "all in a day's work." Looking at Callahan, he winked and said, "Bill, you never had any of this in Oakland, did you?" Then he said, "Hell, we won!"

Before leaving the facility on Monday, Pettine and Cro met in Pettine's office for a heart-to-heart. Cro explained his inability to get past Pettine's remarks to the newspaper. Pettine apologized for them and urged Cro in the future not to wait when something bothered him—the door was always open. He reminded Cro of the spirit in which football criticism was given. It sounded personal, but it wasn't personal. The team needed him. It was decided that on Wednesday Cro would apologize to the defense, and Pettine would "ease his way, make it easier for him." Nonetheless, the plan for Sunday's game with the Redskins would feature a Boise personnel group with a series of calls in which Kyle Wilson replaced Cro.

On Tuesday, in the field house, the front-office staff held an audition. The off-season roster would expand in the long run-up to training camp. Players in their midtwenties who'd starred for schools like Concordia–St. Paul and Cal State–Sacramento arrived. This was their NFL moment and they'd do anything to impress. The particularly muscular were shirtless; the particularly slow-footed spatted their shoes with white tape; the particularly Texan worked full cheeks of chaw. "They all have dreams," said Tannenbaum. One of the eleven who came, University of Massachusetts running back John Griffin, would be invited to the Jets training camp. A few of the current Jets players walked past these proceedings, conspicuously aloof.

In the Wednesday quarterbacks' meeting, Schotty explained that the Redskins defensive coordinator Jim Haslett once coordinated the Pittsburgh Steelers and had brought to Washington much of the Steeler philosophy, which Sanchez then neatly summarized as "Blitzberg." Schotty looked around at the breakfasting players. "You guys are slurping a lot today," he said. "Settle down!" Said Sanchez, "We're excited!"

During the team meeting, Ryan told the Jets they had to practice better. Looking at Holmes, the coach said, "Tone, it starts with you. You have to lead from the front. You're the number-one receiver on this team. You have to run full speed. He needs to know where you'll be."

There were five games left, but Sutton leaned over to say that, really, only one of the six AFC playoff positions was still in doubt: "Nick, it's like the NCAA basketball tournament. All the brackets are set, everybody knows where they're going, except there's one spot to play for and we're playing for it."

At the defensive meeting, BT eased into his seat, wearing a T-shirt emblazoned with the words "Play like a Jet." Right behind him was Maybin, who was drinking carrot juice with wheatgrass, not the typical meeting-room eye-opener. Cromartie stood and faced his teammates. "I want to apologize to the defense for Monday," he said. "I let some stuff linger. I should have been man enough to go talk to him. Especially to the young guys; don't ever do any shit like that. Thanks."

Everyone applauded and Maybin yelled, "Way to be a man!" I asked him how his juice tasted. "Need to feed my moneymaker," he explained. By now everyone had come around to Maybin. He was the enthusiastic, rambunctious in-law who, over time, had been welcomed, his quirks now virtues.

Pettine faced the room and said, "Don't let things fester. Get it off your chest. Come see me. We're all in this together. If there's an issue, we'll have an answer. Might not be the one you want to hear. We're here to help you. Nothing's personal. I like everybody in this room except BT. Now no hugs. We did that on Monday." Then he moved on to another category of temper, the Redskins, a team with players so eager to mix it up that they got into fights with opponents at the coin toss. Reviewing the game plan, Pettine directed many positive observations in Scott's direction. On Monday, you were put on notice. On Wednesday, they built you up.

"Football's a hard game," DT mused afterward. "Tom Landry used to tell us that by the time you really learn to play it, you'll be too old. Quarterbacks improve as they get older because they stop relying on their physical gifts and they compensate with preparation and study. That may happen to Cro," he reflected. "Cro may have to start playing the game a different way. Cro grew up in a rough part of Tallahassee. No father. Never knew him. Just his mother. That's why he's resistant to criticism from male authority figures. He never had it."

Cromartie was not unaware that his childhood might have cost him as an adult. The previous off-season, Cro's business manager, Jonathan Schwartz, invited Cro to stay with his family in Southern California while Cro trained for the season, and Cro enthusiastically accepted. Schwartz had been married for eighteen years and had three children and a dog at home. "He saw a family environment," Schwartz said. "You sit down, have dinner together, have conversations, you clear your dishes. We're all converging at similar times in the morning. He really took to that. He saw people go off to school, go off to work, he saw us discipline the kids. He walked my son to school." Schwartz knew that many football players never had "a strong, positive parental support group. Not to make an excuse, but you have to understand his challenges."

Cromartie said he was trying to do that. Of his stay at Schwartz's home, he told me, "I saw the importance of a husband and a wife in the household." Cro said his wife, Terricka, also came from a single-parent family. Of his many children, Cro admitted, "It wasn't meant to be like that. Something that happened. I love my kids to death. I could care what anybody else thinks. It's just up to me to take care of them." He and Schwartz had arranged Cro's finances so that Cro could always provide well for all of the children. Said Cro, "I'm getting a better understanding of what I'm supposed to do as a father and a husband."

December arrived, and with it a cold for Sanchez and then that time-tested elixir Tom Moore. Cavanaugh told Sanchez that the Redskins defense was a secret system that Sanchez could decrypt if he only took the time: "When you see enough of the tape, you'll think it's easy. Look at it again and again and suddenly you'll realize you're gonna kick their ass."

Sanchez then told the others, "Cav made me stay here until one last night."

"Cav's such a grind," said Brunell.

"All for you, Mark," Schotty said magnanimously. Then he told the quarterback, "Cav's point is, as we sat and studied this thing for ten hours, it's really easy once you see it." Then he asked Sanchez many questions and Sanchez didn't miss one of them. "Man on a mission," somebody said.

Things flared and then they receded. During practice, Sanchez and Holmes drifted off alone to work on a play together.

In the defensive backs' meeting, DT asked, "What do we need to do?"

"No deep balls, tackle, and communicate," said Cro.

"I'm gonna get you a whistle!" DT told him.

When Ryan distributed the game balls for the Buffalo win, he told the team, "Sanchez throws four TDs and gets booed. Everybody boo!" Dutifully, the team booed. Sanchez received his ball. Then Ryan awarded balls to all the youngest coaches.

Before practice, Ryan was in Pettine's office discussing the day's guest kicker—himself. The team's owner, Woody Johnson, would snap, and Tannenbaum would hold, which made Ryan worry about the possibility of a kick getting no lift and hitting the boss. "If I get let go, I'll say that it wasn't that we underperformed. It was that I booted one into the owner's butt." On Monday Tannenbaum had been talking with Ryan about soothing the rift between Sanchez and Holmes "or we'll be gone." Less than a year ago, the Jets had been the team of their time. Now job security was on their minds.

Out on the field, Johnson asked Ryan about his accuracy, and Ryan told him, "You'll be fine." Ryan laced up his old Lou Groza 1950s-style square-toed kicking shoe, which he referred to as Lethal Weapon, and then he "snuck one in" over both owner and crossbar. Pettine watched these proceedings with MTV, who wore his hair in long dreadlocks. With them was Jamaican-born Kenrick Ellis, who was clean-cut. "You bringing back your dreads?" Pettine asked him. "What would people think of me?" said Ellis, whose court case was still pending. "With all the things I've been through? That was the young Ken." Ellis was twenty-three. After the season, he would resolve his legal problems by reaching a plea agreement to serve a forty-five-day prison sentence on misdemeanor assault-and-battery charges. Woody Johnson, Tannenbaum, and Ryan would all visit him at his Virginia jail.

During practice, Eron Riley caught a long touchdown against Cro. Afterward, Sanchez broke the team down at midfield and everybody booed.

*   *   *

In the Saturday defensive meeting, Pettine asked David Harris this: "Dave, of their first fourteen screens, how many went to the boundary?" Replied Harris, "Twelve." If Harris had answered a question from a coach incorrectly that year, I couldn't remember it. During the review of Friday's practice film, Cro got up and walked out of the room just before Riley's touchdown catch against him.

Instead of going to Washington with the team, I decided for the first time that season to stay behind so I could watch on TV with BT, who invited me to his house. (Injured players did not travel.) Given the mess BT left behind after meetings and given his ravine of a locker, known to Pettine as the Science Project, I was surprised to find that the home BT shared with his wife and children not far from the facility was spacious and impeccably neat.

BT wore black sweats. An ice machine was working on his injured foot, and he had an iPad on his lap. "Wake up, fellas!" he called when the Redskins took a quick 7–0 lead. Then he began discussing Cro. "I wanted to get in a fight with a coach my rookie year," BT remembered, "but a veteran told me, 'It's not worth it. They just want to help you.'" Cro was playing well today. Boise would scarcely be seen.

Unable to participate himself, BT had become an avid Fantasy Football GM. That was what the iPad was for—update checking. When Rashard Mendenhall scored for the Steelers, BT groaned. He'd decided to sit Mendenhall for the week. "That clown! I play him, he does nothing. I sit him, he's got two TDs."

Turning his attention back to the Jets, he said, "We should do more no-huddle. New England does it to us and it's so effective." I asked him how much the success or futility of the offense really affected the defense. "It pisses you off when they don't do well against a defense they should be doing well against," he said. "And you can get fatigued if you're on the field too much. But other than that, it doesn't change anything because when you're in that meeting room watching the film, you're not watching the offense."

He began talking about life after football. "I couldn't sit home all day," he said. "I'd go crazy. My wife'd go crazy. I have rental properties and stuff, but I need something to fulfill me." He said he thought he'd make a good football scout. "What about Mendenhall?" I said. He laughed, but the pathos of it struck me, this big powerful man with his wounded foot on ice whose career might be over. Football brought so many little deaths so early in life.

Sanchez had figured out the Redskins and was playing well. He'd finish the afternoon 19 for 32 with a long touchdown to Holmes. The Jets defense was intimidating the Redskins quarterback Rex Grossman into a 19 for 46 day. Maybin had another sack. Gradually, the Jets pulled ahead to win, 34–19. As they did, BT raised his arms. "But why y'all got to make it so close?" he wanted to know.

Grading the Redskins-game film the next morning, the coaches were worried about Scott. "The Bart I know would be goring that guy like a heat-seeking missile," Pettine said at one point. "Head-scratcher." Scott seemed logy to them. Later Scott made a pass deflection and thereafter was seen racing from sideline to sideline. "This looks like the Bart we know!" Pettine said as they all rejoiced.

In the Wednesday-morning quarterbacks' meeting, Sanchez looked at Tom Moore and said, "You're mine today." Moore gazed back at Sanchez with steady eyes and told him, "I hope you have a long career." Sanchez was wearing a red and gold sweat suit. Moore asked him if that was Stanford Cardinal red. "Mission Viejo!" replied Sanchez, whose loyalty to his old high school was a powerful thing. "Vince Ferragamo was from around there," Moore, the old Steeler, remembered. "He took the Rams to a Super Bowl, then Jack Lambert picked him and he was never worth a shit after that."

On Schotty's desk was a boxed toy truck. These were distributed annually at holiday time for the coaches and other employees to give their children. Sanchez began unwrapping Schotty's truck. Then he drove it on Brunell's back. "Well, my son won't be getting that now!" said Schotty blandly. To which Sanchez said, "I'll rewrap it!" And then he did, after which he said, "Now it's a Mexican present."

Schotty shook his head and fell back on football. Of this week's opponent, the Kansas City Chiefs, he said, "Men, they win games because the corners make plays."

At the team meeting, Ryan had difficulty describing the Chiefs as a formidable offensive opponent; they'd scored two touchdowns in their last five games. So instead he talked at length about the Chiefs linebacker Tamba Hali, one of the game's "premier players." Ryan really did admire Hali. He also enjoyed saying "Tamba Hali," making the name sound a little like "Timber!" It was, Ryan thought, a perfect football name.

The defense was never as giddy in the meeting room after a win as it was glum following a loss. That Scott had played well, however, restored his wit. At one point he began describing himself as "an old-ass Toyota Camry. A hundred and thirty-seven thousand miles on me. Dead carburetor."

Then came the last padded practice of year. Revis, too, was in revived spirits. He threw a ball at Mo Wilkerson and then hid behind some other players. Later he performed a hilarious spoof of DT driving along in his BMW sports car, singing a song, happy and free of care, until he encountered an SUV in his facility parking space, which ruined his day.

At safety, Brodney Pool and Jim Leonhard were playing their best football of the year. Pool was a safety because nothing made him anxious. Leonhard was a safety because everything made him wary.

* * *

Sanchez arrived at the Thursday quarterbacks' meeting carrying treats from Starbucks. "What did you get the rest of us?" Schotty asked him. "No *I* in *team!*"

Sanchez smiled. "There is in *win*."

"Wife's coming in tonight, men," Schotty continued. "Be out of here at seven. You figure out the money zone on your own!" Schotty, it turned out, had gotten some sleep.

Afterward, out in the hallway, Sanchez beckoned to me with a conspiratorial gesture. I walked over. He showed me the hand-warmer he wore at his belt during practice. It looked like a two-sided tube pocket but was, in fact, Mr. Sanchez's Cabinet of Wonders. From it he proceeded to extract ChapStick, cough drops, tissues, cold medicine, nasal spray, vitamins, pens, a spare electric cord, and small, disposable hand-warming devices. "Resourceful, huh?" he said, with a raised eyebrow.

Football players carried all sorts of things on their persons. Things they kept in their helmets while playing: ChapStick, inspirational sayings, photographs of loved ones, swatches of wool (for warmth).

Walking down the hall, Schotty said of the newspapers that continued to rake him, "You haven't made it as a coordinator until you got killed and they're calling for your job."

Later I ran into Callahan. The offensive line hadn't allowed a sack in the two weeks since Ryan had told each of the players that he needed more. Callahan was thinking ahead. He divided football seasons into four-game blocks. There was now only one of those seasonal quarters remaining. "It goes fast, doesn't it?" he said.

With the days and the season waning, many people were feeling nostalgic. Devlin said that more than playing football, he missed the friendship—the locker room and the practice sideline. "The jokes, the funny stories, the camaraderie. That's what I miss." Wayne Hunter was anticipating identical regret. "I can already see myself missing the locker room," the tackle said. "What other job can you have and be with men all day just talking?"

At the defensive meeting, Pettine projected on the screen a photograph of a youthful Bart Scott in Jheri curls. "I used to be a pimp," Scott told everyone.

Smitty had been training hard, losing weight, getting fit. "How does it look to be coaching these guys, they're running around, and their coach is huffing and puffing after them?" he said. "You're either getting better or you're getting worse every day. Nobody stays the same."

Out at practice, Leonhard made a flurry of picks. On the sideline, Sione Po'uha discussed the biography of Steve Jobs he'd been reading. Once he'd established that I, too, liked to read, Po'uha had been giving me enthusiastic reports over the past couple of weeks. Now he was turning against Jobs. "I think of Ben Franklin and Thomas Edison as anchors," Po'uha explained. "Jobs was a buoy. He floated along with the times. When there was a storm, he might go under. Not strongly anchored."

That afternoon, Pettine was melancholy. Smitty had gotten a remunerative offer to coach at Washington State, where his old college head coach Mike Leach had been hired. Smitty earned an entry-level Jets coaching salary and was doing a position coach's job as well as his quality-control work. Pettine was pretty sure some of the younger coaches also planned to leave at year's end and he blamed Jeff Weeks. Weeks made more money than three junior coaches combined. Pettine could have let it slide, except that just wasn't in him. He said he knew the grass wasn't necessarily greener anywhere else, and he knew that he probably ought to be more political, yet in matters like this, he didn't want to be. He was likewise aware how it might appear to others, that his aversion to Weeks had to do with his and Weeks's relative roles in Ryan's life, but to Pettine, this was purely about staff morale and the principle. Principle was what Pettine most liked about defensive football. The game was direct, tough, and bound by a ligature of rules and plans

that felt like ethics to him. He thought he would have to speak to
Ryan about the situation, a prospect he did not relish but did not
fear. He planned to do so after the Chiefs game. "Monday will be a
big day," he said.

Friday's was a lighthearted practice. Sanchez entertained the quarterbacks during their morning meeting with an imitation of Tom
Moore's deep, quavery Southern voice. Out at practice, Westhoff
was wearing heavy boots rather than the usual sneakers, and Joe
McKnight was concerned. "Sutt!" he told Sutton. "You got to *do*
something about Coach Westhoff. He's wearing some Rocky Mountain boots. You *got* to, Coach! Swag him up!"

Cro reported that he'd been doing extra lifting and suddenly
was feeling healthier. So was Leonhard. Last year's leg injury fully
healed, he was playing, as Ryan noticed, "really well."

On Saturday morning, a *Daily News* article appeared portraying
Smitty as the intern who was the secret to Maybin's success. "Without him I'd probably be a fish without fins in the open sea," Maybin
said. To the defense, Pettine praised the offense's week of practice:
"They did a nice job and so did you."

Tim Tebow had continued to win games for Denver, and
around the building he was a topic of conversation. Ryan thought
Tebow's sui generis national popularity had to do with personality:
"Tebow's a straight arrow. The boy next door. The kid you want
your daughter to marry. He's still a virgin!" Sutton said that the
importance of Tebow's religion to his fellow Christians could not
be overstated, and neither could the importance of his narrative,
the person everybody said couldn't succeed in the NFL doing just
that. People liked the many improbabilities in Tebow's story, that
he'd defied the current football trend toward multidimensional

offenses with an ultra-conventional, old-school running-and-jump-passing style of play. They liked how emotional Tebow was. He got to people. That Tebow was a slow-looking, big, handsome white guy in a mostly black sport might also have had something to do with it. As for Pettine, he refused to discuss Tebow. He said the subject was still too painful.

That night at the hotel, Schotty had an entire section of calls ready if Tamba Hali was too much pass rusher for the Jets base-line protections. Pettine told the defensive players that most big plays against them were not caused by the superiority of the opponent but by Jets mistakes. In other words, they were good enough to control their fate. As usual, Ryan sat in the back of the meeting jotting down a few quick notes for his speech to the team. His oratory, like so much about him, was most effective when it came extempore. Suddenly Posey got up and left. As a rookie, his day of initiation had come, and he'd been told to try chewing tobacco. The poor fellow was now green as a can of Skoal.

DeVito and Mulligan walked into the team meeting wearing their shirt of the week. It read: "For I am not ashamed of the gospel of Christ: for it is the power of God unto salvation to everyone that believeth." Romans 1:16. Ryan told the gripping story of how his old dog Winston, named for the 1960s Jets lineman Winston Hill, defeated all the other big dogs on his father's Kentucky farm.

At the game-day breakfast the next morning at the hotel, Bart Scott and DT watched a TV report on baseball star Albert Pujols, who had recently signed a free-agent contract with the California Angels. "Two hundred and fifty million for five good years!" Scott exclaimed. "DT, we picked the wrong sport. That's why I'm making sure my kids don't make the same mistake. Soon there's gonna be the word out. The brothers are back! And they're stealing bases like crazy!" You could find plenty of players and coaches who weren't sure they wanted their children to play football, but this wasn't a subject anybody besides Scott really wanted to get into.

Ryan had urged me to spend the game this week on the sidelines rather than upstairs. "You can't believe how big and fast and violent it is," he said. "The collisions! It's the difference between watching boxing on TV and standing next to a fight." Leonhard urged the same. "There's so much energy in a stadium on a sideline," he said. "It's just so cool." So in the locker room I put on the required khakis and, because it was December, a green Jets parka and a green Jets wool hat.

The game began inauspiciously. Sanchez was forced to call a time-out before the first play, when only ten guys showed up in the huddle. The fullback John Conner had gone missing. That head-scratcher aside, I was impressed by how orderly everything was. There were no defensive penalties and not a single group personnel error. From the practice sidelines, I was used to the violence of the contact and to the trash talk. Here they all stood together but existed in efficiently separated little worlds. There was a *Rashomon* quality to how differently everyone experienced much that went on in football. The daily interactions and even the games had alternate versions for the various players and various coaches. When the defense was on the field, Cavanaugh and the quarterbacks studied still photographs of the just-completed series of plays, and they could have been in Marina del Rey, so oblivious were they to what everyone else was doing. They didn't for instance watch Jim Leonhard's interception or notice that he failed to get up afterward. I could see the safety clearly, his face drawn, slush-colored with pain. Leonhard looked younger and smaller even than usual. He'd ruptured a tendon, and for the second consecutive year he was lost for the season. Out on the field Revis was very upset. "Both years at crucial times," he said he was thinking.

At halftime the Jets had gained nearly two hundred and fifty total yards and allowed four. The Chiefs offensive stat sheet showed one first down. "Keep your feet on the gas," Pettine told the defense.

"Don't let them leave with any dignity." Ryan reminded everyone that they were "the big dog!" The final score was 37–10. Sanchez threw for two touchdowns, ran for two, and was cheered. So was Brunell, who got into the game. Tamba Hali did not require an extra layer of protection. The Jets were now one game ahead in the standings for the last AFC playoff spot. Afterward, in the parking lot, Pettine smoked an enormous cigar but said, "I'm sick about Jimmy Leonhard. I can't enjoy this because of it."

Thirteen

FOOTBALL IS MY FATHER

*God, it's so painful, something that's so close, is still so
far out of reach.*

— *Tom Petty, "American Girl"*

The Monday-morning defensive coaches' film session offered those football cinephiles a little dark art-house escapism starring Jim Leonhard. There stood the little big man reborn, playing traffic patrolman as he organized the defensive crosswalks, acting as the cavalry as he arrived at full gallop to fill in for the positioning oversights of others, and then, finally, appearing as a last-stand martyr, making the interception, only to be done in by such a blue-moon injury none of the coaches could figure out from the film what had happened to him on the fatal play.

The Chiefs quarterback Tyler Palko said after Sunday's game that with so many Jets defenders in motion, he'd felt as though there were thirteen opponents out there against him. With BT and Leonhard absent, the Jets coaches had now lost the two smart players who allowed them to exert this maelstrom of looks and calls. And with Eric Smith gimpy at the knee, Pettine worried that the team wouldn't have enough back-end speed left to cover the Eagles whippet receiver DeSean Jackson on Sunday.

To Sutton, Leonhard was "a perfect last line of defense. He's also got character. This team has lost a lot of character." Sutton, like many others, believed the ongoing problems with the receivers never would have happened with Cotchery in the receivers' room. Burress often seemed disaffected; he didn't have to say a word for everyone to know when he wasn't getting the ball. Sutton was also sad that Leonhard, not especially fast to begin with and now grounded with leg injuries in consecutive seasons, wouldn't get the set-for-life Eric Weddle contract he'd been waiting for. Last season, when the Jets lost Leonhard on a Thursday, it stung the team and they'd been defeated on Monday night by the Patriots, 45–3, and then lost their next two games. This year, Sutton thought, they'd miss him again.

The beginning of the NFL year meant hope for every team, but the end of the season left plenty of bodies in the spillway. That afternoon, as both senior coaching sides were getting ready to sit down together in a meeting room, word came that the Chiefs had fired their head coach, Todd Haley. In photographs of Haley from Sunday, his hair was scraggly, his face was lined and sallow, his eyes blank. The year before, the Chiefs had been 11 and 5, had made the playoffs. Now, said Pettine to the other coaches, "He walked into the GM's office and there was a plastic sheet on the floor." Callahan nodded. "Hard league," he said. "I got fired the year after I went to the Super Bowl."

Pettine suggested that Ryan award a game ball to Cromartie. Then he returned to his office. "I'm tired of being tired," he said. The younger coaches had taken to snapping photographs with their mobile phones of any fellow coach who fell asleep at his desk or while eating a meal.

The next morning, a front-office assistant toured the senior facility offices, removed Leonhard's name from the depth charts, and put in its place a card for Gerald Alexander, a journeyman safety. It was going to be O'Neil's job to teach Alexander the Jets defense. There was also the Eagles game plan to be written. O'Neil was trying to organize his time. How long would Alexander remain a Jet? How much course work could he master by Sunday? The moment could have felt futile; Leonhard had run the defense. But the coaches talked often of how in every football crisis there was opportunity. Sometimes it was just more difficult to see what that might be. They checked Alexander's Wonderlic test score. Twenty-five, they discovered. Alexander the Wise! "Good!" said Pettine. Scott Cohen, Tannenbaum's deputy, stopped in. O'Neil asked him how serious an addition Alexander was. "Full speed until you hear otherwise," Cohen told him. "Of course, he barely passed his physical."

"What's the problem?" O'Neil wanted to know.

"Heart."

"It's just a muscle," Pettine said.

"Great," mused O'Neil. "I'll make him a four-page tip sheet and you guys'll cut him!"

Cohen was a person all the coaches liked because he was a hardworking straight shooter who revered football information. Even Cohen's son knew the forty-yard-dash times for dozens of college prospects. Cohen's son was ten years old.

The game plan amounted to one long conversation about how to force Eagles left-handed quarterback Michael Vick to his right. Vick had become so infamous for sponsoring dogfights that people who knew nothing about football could nonetheless name him as the torturer of pit bulls. In his prime, Vick had played football like Tim Tebow even before there was a Tebow, only Vick had been a far more electric runner and thrower. "The only person I've ever seen who could win a football game by himself was Michael Vick in his heyday," said Calvin Pace. Vick had run for more yards than any quarterback in NFL history. For the Eagles game, Pettine wanted to design a cup to contain Vick and then create what Vick would think was a crack in the cup but that was really a way to funnel Vick rightward for the pursuit to find him. "He can be ridiculously accurate," Pettine said, "but with pressure in his face, he isn't very accurate, and on the run to his right he's less accurate." The new trap for Vick they named Pit Bull Bonus. The ensuing conversation about the full-call inventory in this first week without Jim Leonhard featured many sentences that began "How about…" followed by many that ended "we can't run it."

The offense would face its first four-down-linemen, three-linebackers formation since the second week of the season. Schotty told the quarterbacks on Wednesday that for the Eagles, "one of the benefits of having a line coach as D-coordinator is he understands protection."

Tom Moore looked at Sanchez and proposed a Peyton Manning–style special-review session. "Mark!" he said. "Seven o'clock Friday morning."

"Yikes!" said Sanchez.

"It's good luck," Moore explained.

"We don't need luck if we work hard enough," Sanchez said reflexively. Then he told Moore, "I'll be there."

McElroy delivered Schotty's standard six-egg sausage-and-cheese omelet to Sanchez and Sanchez's vegetable-filled omelet to Schotty. Schotty looked horrified: "Dude!" he told McElroy. "I almost ate spinach. That's a concern."

The Eagles were among the more talented teams in the league, but they had played poorly and were 5 and 8. Several times Schotty and Sanchez described them as a "selfish" team, and the way both said it made it clear that there was no more despicable quality in football.

In the defensive meeting, Gerald Alexander sat in his seat listening to Pettine describe Vick as the "most explosive athlete we'll face at quarterback." The coordinator said that there would be a "big street-ball element," because no NFL player was better at darting around making free runners miss. So mesmerizing were the quarterback's improvisations that players got caught up in watching him, allowing receivers to slip into the open, and then Vick would throw to them.

In entrancing contrast at practice was the sight of Po'uha scoring a practice touchdown. "It's a win-win, Bo," Pettine told him. "You scored and you took two minutes off the clock."

Along the sidelines, Eric Smith said that he'd hurt his sore knee when somebody stepped on his foot at the same time another player hit the side of his leg. "It's a torn chunk of meniscus. It can lock up on me."

This was a Wednesday of many challenges for DT. He was minding his own DT business, critiquing the defensive backs as he always did, when Kyle Wilson suddenly asked him, "My brother, why must we put one another down?" DT had no idea what to say to that. Then, when DT sought an explanation for something from Ellis Lankster, Lankster wrinkled his brow in the funny way he had, said, "I ain't got time," and disappeared to meet obligations back on the field. I was wearing a cap. The cap was yet another affront to DT. I defended my "perfectly nice cap." Said DT, "Some people can look good in a hat, Nick. Others put on a perfectly nice hat and they look like they work at a gas station." After that, DT referred to me as Gas-Station Man.

It could have been much worse. The temperature was warm for December, and as Bart Scott watched Cro high-stepping around in shorts, leg sinews rippling, Scott told him, "You a specimen. A top-ten slave. You'd work the lower field. You'd pull the plow." Cro just laughed.

Revis and Cro watched Michael Vick play on film with more excitement than they'd displayed for any other player. Said Revis, "Look! He just threw sidearm around the rusher. That's talented!"

"You want to see somebody who really believes in his arm strength," Cro said, "Vick really does. He'll try and fit it in anywhere."

*   *   *

It was a good Wednesday afternoon for Smitty. Pettine had post-poned his talk with Ryan, moving it from Monday to Wednesday. That morning the defensive coordinator had awakened in a sweat at 5:00, filled with anxiety. But, from Pettine's perspective, the talk had gone well. After he informed Ryan that Smitty was planning to leave, Ryan said he would officially offer Smitty the outside-linebackers job. Ryan also told Pettine that Weeks wouldn't be returning. Then Smitty received an e-mail from Tannenbaum telling him, "You've done an incredible job for us." Washington State had offered Smitty twice what Ryan told Pettine the Jets could offer, but Pettine wasn't worried about that. If need be, Pettine said, he would restructure his own contract, taking less so the team would have the money to keep Smitty in New York.

Sutton's persistent texts finally worked, and BT limped into the Thursday defensive meeting. The room applauded. BT looked over the skinny free-agent safety Tracy Wilson, who'd vowed not to cut his (frazzling) hair until season's end. "Got a crackhead," said BT. The room laughed. BT opened his playbook. The room concentrated.

When the defense broke off into position groups, in the outside-linebackers' meeting, BT told the others, "Big fantasy week for me, boys. Don't let Michael Vick get shit!" Then Smitty detailed the unit's Secret Santa rules. Everybody participated. Nobody could spend more than $250. And no Rutgers gear, Westerman. And put some thought into it, Westerman. "Mike," said Westerman. "What do you want?"

"Sacks for you guys and BT back," said Smitty.

"I want you guys to go to the Super Bowl so I can be in on field-goal block," BT announced.

"You *stank* at field-goal block!" Maybin recalled.

"Don't matter," BT said affably. "I want that one Super Bowl play."

At practice, Joe Yacovino, one of the retired officials the Jets had hired to work their practices in stripes, flagged the offense for a penalty. Revis nearly leaped out of his six layers of sweats. "Hey, Joe! Hey, Joe! My man *Joe!* That's right!"

On the sidelines, Cole, a lithe cornerback, and DeVito, a three-hundred-pound lineman, were discussing their knee injuries in too much detail for Pettine. "You're comparing a brontosaurus knee with a jaguar," he told them. Po'uha walked over. "I quit Steve Jobs on page four hundred and thirty," he announced. "I decided he wasn't innovative."

The *Rocky III* theme song, "Eye of the Tiger," was pumping through the huge practice speakers when boxing broke out. Aaron Maybin had been getting a quick jump off the snap, and in response, Wayne Hunter had been offering what Maybin later called "some extra shit." So Maybin returned the lagniappe. Bad idea. "I'll break you in half," Hunter screamed. An unwritten rule in the NFL was that you never backed down from a fight—unless your opponent was Wayne Hunter. When Hunter got angry, "better bring a knife and a stun gun," advised Steve Yarnell, the security director. Two years ago, the Jets kick returner Justin Miller was teasing Hunter for having to run punishment laps after being called for a practice penalty. Hunter asked Miller to cut it out. Another Hunter penalty and more argy-bargy from Miller and suddenly Hunter wanted to maim him. After Hunter was sent off to run his laps, Ryan told Miller to return to the locker room, grab his stuff, and not even bother changing, just leave for the day. This time it took several men to subdue Hunter. Said Joe the ref, "That's one guy I never seem to throw flags on."

For the rest of practice, an uncracked cup of players and coaches formed around Maybin. At one point, Sanchez came over and gave Maybin a pat and then stood quietly for a while with the defense. Tom Moore joined him and the two chatted about the great Lions running back Barry Sanders's legendary pregame meal, which Moore said consisted of one apple. After practice Rex told the players not to fight, that they were a team, and though they didn't have to like one another, they did have to respect one another.

In the ice-cream social that afternoon, Holmes was reflecting on Asante Samuel, who would cover him. Tone said Samuel was "big." To which Tom Moore countered in that deep, quavery voice, "He's five ten!" So Tone told him, "But he plays big."

On Friday morning, Schotty was firing questions at Sanchez and slyly worked in "Try not to use a time-out on this one!"

"Try to have the right personnel group out there!" Sanchez retorted, referring to the John Conner mix-up against Kansas City.

"Ohhh!" cried Schotty.

"First play of the game!" said Sanchez. "A-Lynn was so crushed."

Walking down the football-field-length main facility hallway could be awkward; you might find yourself facing off with someone for seventy or eighty yards. Today Wayne Hunter and I came slowly together. "*High Noon!*" I said, and, thankfully, he smiled. Later I asked him about fighting. Hunter said that the grind of the season could wear on you, make you so tired and irritable you might behave under a helmet in ways you almost immediately regretted. "Everyone has days you don't want to practice, don't want to go to meetings, go on a field and have to be aggressive," he said. The Maybin confrontation was, he said, "one of my days. I try so hard to keep it at bay. I'd been doing so well and that was the day for me. Maybin is so loud, talking so much. He was coming so hard, I snapped. But me and Maybin are cool. Maybin's a unique and special guy." That playing good football could occasionally seem almost an overwhelming challenge for a man as huge, strong, fast, and intelligent as Wayne Hunter sometimes made me wonder how anyone could expect to excel at it.

*   *   *

Pettine kept "tweaking" the game plan all week. He took out edge blitzes because he wanted to "pincer" Vick, and in one call he placed an outside linebacker at nose tackle. At the Saturday meeting, he detailed all this for the players. Then he showed the room a photograph of DeVito asleep in front of his locker. Next came an image with Mully napping beside him in the locker room.

At the walk-through, Julian Posey told of going ice-skating at Rockefeller Center the night before. He affected a blasé tone. "Just chillin' with my lady," he said. But he couldn't fool anybody.

Scott was describing himself. "I got two modes," he said. "Stop and go. I don't jog. I walk lazy. When I come home, my wife hears me come in and first thing she says is 'Pick your feet up!' " Scott was wearing a T-shirt that read "I'm Wearing My Angry Face."

Every week, the defensive coaches created hand signals for their new calls in case the Motorolas failed. Dime Spike 1 (Vegas), for instance, was a shake and a roll of the tumbling dice. Now Pit Bull Bonus, it was decided, would be a tug on a restraining leash. During the walk-through in the field house, the team seemed loose. A pass play had been designed for the eligible lineman Vlad Ducasse. His big walk-through moment came: a pass was sent to a completely uncovered Ducasse, and he dropped it. Sanchez threw his hat. Holmes rolled on the turf in dismay.

Speaking to the team on Saturday night at the hotel in Philadelphia, Ryan informed them that when Nnamdi Asomugha interviewed with the Jets, he'd asked Ryan, "What would you do special for me?" This was typical of the current Eagles, Ryan said. They were a white-collar team in a blue-collar town.

The game was one long Jets downsizing. Ryan had been sure the Jets could run on the Eagles, and right away that ATV of a halfback Shonn Greene was gashing through their linebackers. Then came a routine completion to Holmes, which he inexplicably fumbled after making the catch. The ball was run back for a touchdown. Later in the quarter, after an Eagles fumble deep in their own territory, a short Sanchez puffball to Holmes floated through the receiver's hands and Samuel intercepted. On the sidelines and in the box everyone was wearing his angry face—except Holmes, who, weirdly, was smiling. He seemed in some kind of bizarrely altered atmosphere. In short order, the Jets edges crumbled, their discipline frayed, Pit Bull Bonus was blocked, the secondary without Leonhard appeared off compass, and when Pettine called blitzes, his subsequent refrain was "We flat fucking missed him." Soon Vick ran for a touchdown. And then came a Sanchez fumble. It was 28–0 midway through the second quarter. The Eagles were swollen with emotion. For the Jets, the game had burst like a pillow; there were feathers everywhere. Up in the box, you could feel the disappointment, the mortification, and the blame.

A Holmes touchdown catch made it 28–10. And what was this? Tone placed the football on the ground, put his foot on it, and flapped his arms. An Eagle. The Jets were assessed fifteen yards for using the ball as a prop. By the end of the first half, the team had been called for eight penalties and had committed three turnovers.

After the half, Pettine's and Ryan's tempers shortened: "Rex, you tell me to come after him, so I come after him. Now we give up a play, so you say zone. Which is it?" So Ryan took over the play-calling. That had never happened midgame with them before. Down on the field, listening on the main defensive radio channel, Smitty was horrified. Pettine had made the plan and Ryan didn't know it well, so now Pettine had to guide him. Pettine's tone remained even, composed, as he told Ryan, "Can't call that, Rex, because..." and "Closest thing we have, Rex, is..." The game ended 45–19. On the bus back to New Jersey, there was silence up and down the aisle except for the sounds of eating and tinny fuzz from headphones. Jim O'Neil leaned in to say to me: "Two years in a row, we lose Jim Leonhard and in the next game we give up forty-five points." I suddenly recalled something Sean Gilbert, Revis's uncle, had told me about how it was "too easy to let down in football."

On Monday, Smitty went from office to office saying farewells. He was moving on to coach college football, "because of the way he treated you," he told Pettine. But Pettine counseled him, "If I went by the way I feel right after a loss, I can't count the number of times I'd have handed in my resignation." In fact, as they had on many mornings-after, Pettine and Ryan had it out. Pettine told Ryan, "Look, if you have that little faith in me, I'll resign now," and Ryan told him "No, no, no," and they discussed Ryan's propensity during games to revisit what had just happened when the need was to move forward.

The good news was that if they won their final two games, they'd still make the playoffs. The Jets would play the Giants on Saturday, Christmas Eve, so today they needed to build another game plan. Ryan and Pettine decided to join forces: Pettine would make the first- and second-down calls, Ryan would handle third-down calls, and together they'd get back to their old blitzing ways. Immediately they began cooking up some new things for Maybin. After each idea, Smitty would say, "I'll get with him right away to make sure he understands!" The others began to tease him—"Oh, but Mike, you're leaving!" They worked him over about his "last night in the NFL" and his future "on the other side of the rope," how he'd be like the rookie who gets cut, goes to a game, calls out, "Hey, Darrelle!" from behind the security barrier, and Revis has no idea who he is. "Look," Pettine told Smitty, "you're a young guy, barely begun coaching, and you're about to be making pretty damn good money already. You're young and the NFL's emotional. But once you leave, you'll realize what you let go." Then Ryan took Smitty aside and praised him, told him his salary would be made "right," and Smitty suddenly was snagged back, suddenly couldn't imagine himself in Pullman, Washington. For the first time in many weeks, Ryan stayed all Monday night with Pettine, O'Neil, and Smitty, making the plan. When Ryan did that, there were more old stories and more new calls. When Ryan did that, to Smitty he was again the forever guy.

On Tuesday, everybody still seemed so sapped from the road trip, the loss, and the night of game-planning that even if the team did qualify for the playoffs, I couldn't see how they would have anything left to give. When I asked around about this, I learned about the greatest energy drink of them all—making the playoffs. There wasn't, everyone said, a second wind that could compare.

In Schotty's office, the coordinator had his old leather Bible out on his desk. Sanchez had been hit numerous times during the Eagles game and he sat there swathed in wires and beeping machines. Cavanaugh asked him how his neck was. Sanchez was coy. Cavanaugh told him, "I hear they tried to make you go to rehab and you said no, no, no." I always wished there was time for Cavanaugh to say more in those meetings. He was an ideal cabinet member for Schotty; the old quarterback had a natural toughness, unpredictable bite, and unflappable composure, and he could take the been-there, done-that long view. Everyone in the room was so tired that Schotty let them leave early for the first time all year.

In the team meeting, Ryan praised the Giants defensive line and then he stepped back: "In a nutshell, here's what we got in front of us. We have six workdays left in the regular season and two business days. But you got a lifetime of memories. You'll remember those games all your lives. Don't do this game a disservice and say it's just another game. These guys think they're better than you." He went on to describe the way wealthy kids looked down on poor kids. Then Ryan said it would be special to beat the Giants. He wanted to do it by running the ball.

Pettine told the defense that because Nick Bellore "is having a

Pro Bowl year on special teams," he'd earned a personnel grouping. Chippewa would feature two outside linebackers, two linemen, and four inside linebackers.

At practice, Brodney Pool was teasing Eric Smith, so Sutton told Smith to ask Pool about his first NFL play. Smith did. "I was knocked out on teams," Pool confessed. Then he added, "But I knocked *myself* out."

Carrier and some of his linemen stayed on the field after practice for further work. Tannenbaum had sent word he was displeased with the lack of development from some of the young players, specifically Kenrick Ellis.

At the afternoon defensive meeting, the players and coaches learned that when Pettine grew truly weary, he lapsed into erudition. Speaking of a Giant receiver, the coordinator referred to Newtonian law, saying that unless there were unbalanced forces acting on a receiver, "an object in motion tends to stay in motion."

This week Revis and Cro watched film together with aggression in their hearts. Of the Giants receivers' release, Revis said, "They're going to have to do better than that because I'm gonna be up on the line hitting them." When the film from a Giants game against the Eagles showed Asomugha beaten on a fade, Cro, whom the Jets had re-signed after the failed Asomugha courtship, allowed himself last-laugh satisfaction: "He's getting embarrassed this year."

Revis left and Posey arrived. Said Cro, "I look at these films and it's ridiculous. Nobody puts their hands on them. You have to disrupt their timing." Then he told Posey and me, "See, here's what they do. They put all three receivers on this side so Eli can read them, one, two, three. Our offense doesn't do that. They distribute them across the field, and it's impossible for Mark to look at them all."

"Why don't you say something to the O?" I asked Cro.

"They'd never listen."

* * *

Sanchez arrived at the Wednesday quarterbacks' meeting, and instead of the usual fist-knock greeting, he faked a knock then engulfed my entire hand in a grab and said, "Starfish!" None of that today for Kevin O'Connell, who had a sore finger. For this he received much abuse, until he was bailed out by a film clip of Green Bay quarterback Aaron Rodgers bursting into a sprint against the Giants. "Mark, can you run that fast?" Schotty asked Sanchez.

"No way! I'm caught there. But Bru could!"

Brunell demurred: "My calves would fall off."

"If we gave you the right supplements?" inquired Sanchez, who, despite his Golden Grahams, was a big proponent of healthful nutrition.

"Kev could!" said Brunell.

"Except for his finger," concluded Schotty.

The defensive-line meeting resembled an army infirmary, all the wrapped knees, heat pads, casts, sacks of ice. The list of players who needed off-season surgery was not short.

At practice, MTV was speaking of his longtime girlfriend, Leah, the former class president. On her birthday, he'd sunk to a knee and offered her an engagement ring. Which was accepted. "Got to be traditional," he explained.

"Rookie mistake," said Calvin Pace.

That afternoon, the defensive coaches were visited by Plaxico Burress, who helped them review his former team's pass routes, cadences, signal checks, and snap counts. Football teams are in such constant personnel flux that coaches don't usually change such things from season to season, the reasoning being that most players are too busy learning their new playbooks to summon up the old. Burress, however, had superior recall. "I watched the Dallas game," he told the coaches. "They hadn't changed a thing."

After Burress left, DT said, "Coaches are arrogant. They think, 'He was in jail for two years. He won't remember anything.' They give him no credit."

In the defensive-backs' meeting, DT asked the younger players how long they'd studied their Giants playbook. "Scrappy?"

Trufant told him, "Forty-five minutes!"

"Posey?"

"One hour twenty minutes!"

"Brodney?"

"Long time!"

"How long a long time?"

"Two hours!"

"Where do you play on Fifty-One Hole?"

(Sounds of uncertainty.)

DT was incredulous. "Do you just float through life? We're getting ready to play the most important game of the season because we fucked up some other ones. We have to communicate. We have to study. Communication makes you confident. Get your own defense down. Tomorrow we'll be going to the board, gentlemen."

"Can I be first?" asked Cromartie.

The meeting ended and, as he left the room, Posey burst into song: "Ain't too proud to beg!"

"What are you doing to the Temptations?" cried DT, who loved Motown the way Jim O'Neil loved Tom Petty.

"I was in the church choir!" Posey told him.

"They must not have had good choirs in Ohio," DT said with a huff, trying, and failing, not to laugh.

Revis didn't smile. I asked how he was. "Frustrated, man," he said. We watched some film of the Giants against Redskins. "Oh, pick!" Revis cried. Interceptions always made Rev happy.

The defensive backs met on Thursday to cast their Pro Bowl ballots. Voting value was divided evenly among the choices made by the fans (online), the coaches, and the players, who did not vote for teammates. There was some freedom within each NFL team to decide how votes would be cast. Schottenheimer and the offensive coaches, for instance, voted only for defensive players they'd opposed in games, making their choices collectively, in a unit meeting. The Jets players' part of the system limited each position group to voting for the opponent position group whose play they knew best. Hence the Jets defensive backs voted for quarterbacks and receivers, and vice versa. The DBs' first two picks were unanimous, Brady and Welker. For the second-team quarterback, Matt Schaub being injured, Revis proposed Tebow. Around the room a superstorm of oratorio began:

"You sellin'?"

"You're haters!"

"It's his team, not him!"

"You a Christian?"

"More than five hundred yards rushing."

Eventually they agreed on Andy Dalton of the Bengals.

Pettine was so weary, he looked years older than he had at the start of training camp, but he was still at it, playing cartographer, mapping Eli Manning's most frequent paths of pass-rush-pressure avoidance. Manning, he found, preferred to move forward and slide right. So Pettine designed a call making Isaiah Trufant a 165-pound defensive end. From that spot near scrimmage, Tru'd run to the accustomed Manning slide spot. Trufant fascinated Pettine with his ability to change direction in confined spaces at high speed. "Look at that!" said Pettine. "How many people on the planet can do that? I'd be getting my hip flexor surgically reattached."

By now the fog of loss had lifted, car windows were defrosted, the sun was up, clear December skies. The linebackers were exchanging their Secret Santa gifts. Pace gave McIntyre large sunglasses. "Tryin' to put him in the game," said Pace. There followed large watches, cunning little cameras, Italian wallets, various non-Nano iItems, and soft cashmere. Bob Sutton, who had spent his off-season missing Bart Scott, took the opportunity to show the player how he felt about him. He handed Scott three packages and instructed him to "open them in order." The first contained a toy helicopter. The second was a book of aerial photographs of New York City. The third was a gift certificate for a seat on a helicopter tour of New York. Scott was overwhelmed. "Let it out, Bart! Let it out!" cried the others. Scott picked up the book. With feeling, he promised, "I'm gonna put this in my *gallery*." Westerman looked at McIntyre, who was modeling his shades. "You can go to a black club now," he told him.

The only person who didn't receive a gift was Mike Smith. Maybin had forgotten it. When Pettine heard about this, he told Smitty, "Should have put it on the wristband." (Maybin later gave Smitty a Louis Vuitton briefcase that, like so many of the gifts chosen by the players, cost many times the spending maximum.)

The defensive players never watched film of opposing defenses, but the Giants defensive line was putting a lot of pressure on quarterbacks, and, out of curiosity, the outside linebackers pulled up some Giants film. Concluded Calvin Pace, "You know, one common theme of these guys getting sacks is that there're four people who just go—no other responsibilities. We're so conditioned to doing other jobs."

At practice in this chillier time of year, the coaches favored gray sweat suits that were a size or three too large, and since they were bulky men to begin with, in these billowy swaths of gray, they resembled armored cars going through battle exercises. Westhoff was an anticipating armored car. He thought that so far as regular-season games went, "they don't get much bigger." Players were now playing in significant pain. Joe McKnight was hiding behind a barrier so nobody outside the team could see the agony he was in trying to get a shirt over his shoulder pads. Ropati Pitoitua's finger had been jammed straight back so violently he had a spiral fracture. For him to play, the trainers had to fashion the lineman a protective club of tape, but any contact still hurt him. "They'll numb it up," he said, meaning for the game. "Be all right."

On the tackle-eligible play, which allowed a designated lineman to become a receiver, MTV, subbing in with the white shirts, shambled briskly across the field, and made a nice catch. All these months later it was still remarkable to me what nimble athletic maneuvers men well over three hundred pounds were capable of. MTV's green-shirted defensive brothers didn't see it this way. They gave him the silent treatment for having too much fun with the offense.

Along the sideline Revis was doing his Tom Brady imitation, scanning the defensive set and then changing the call based on what he'd deciphered. "It's very frustrating when Tom Brady gives you the Look," Rev explained. The Look meant, said Rev, "Oh! Okay! I got it." Then he imitated Peyton Manning peering out at the defense and noticing a weak man-coverage defender like Lito Sheppard on the field. "Peyton, he's up there, sees Lito, says, 'Okay!'" Revis might play off to himself, but he loved the banter, the groupness of football. This was not the first time he'd done his Brady. The Look, like any other skill for Revis, had to be practiced.

Sutton, who kept track of everything, noted that when DeVito led the Jets pregame prayer, the team didn't win, whereas Mully was 3 and 0, so, he said, "I told DeVito, 'Mully's doing the prayer. He's 3 and 0, and the Lord's not taking your calls.'"

Over on the offensive side, the coaches watched practice in upright, alert, hopeful stances, as if they were the Wright brothers at Kitty Hawk wondering, Will it fly?

The defense received a postsurgery visit from Jim Leonhard on Friday. "I finally got two hours of sleep," he said. Not only had his leg been operated on, but Leonhard's wife had given birth to their first child.

Ryan, due to call third downs, spent more time speaking in the defensive meeting than he had all year. He'd created an eight-man blitz look, except that this wasn't the 46, and not everybody blitzed. "Pet and I wouldn't have put this in unless we thought we'd kick their asses with it," he said, and then off he went to see the offense.

Walk-throughs the day before the game were uninteresting to most players, but not to Cromartie, who could never spend enough time on a football field. Cro had recently submitted to a vasectomy—"I got snipped," as he told me. Eric Smith surveyed the jubilant, excised cornerback and said fondly, "I wish it had calmed him down!" After-ward, all the players scattered except Sanchez. A terminally ill little girl was there to meet him through the Make-A-Wish Foundation. Long after every other player and coach was gone, the quarterback was still talking with the child.

At the hotel Friday night, Schotty instructed Sanchez, "Early in the game I don't want you standing up there taking a lot of time with kills. So whatever it is, go with your gut and we'll make it happen, and if something isn't right, we'll live with it."

Pettine told the defense that losing should make them "physi-cally ill." He said he'd thrown up after losses. Then he chided him-self for being "negative" about the offense in the heat of headset passion and advised them that the way to think about the offense's three and outs was "More TV time for us!"

Around the NFL, the Giants had a reputation as a family orga-nization that treated and paid people well. Ryan said he was tired of hearing how classy the Giants were. No Giant ever said nice things about the Jets. He began talking about how the Giants seemed to believe they were not only "better players" but also "bet-ter people." Now he was weeping. Every week, it was Ryan's job to inspire his team by turning the opponent into the enemy. Most of Ryan's players had heard a lot of pregame speeches. I'd seen Ryan give nearly twenty of them, and every week, in the moment, I was convinced he meant what he said. Whatever the team's problems, they did not include resolve. The Jets gave Ryan what they had. He really was a masterful motivator.

Game-day morning, Ryan and Pettine reviewed their calls. "We're all in this together," Ryan told his coaches. "Let's go kick some ass." Were they all together? The game began and Ryan and Pettine were sharing the game-calling and bickering per usual. Said Pettine, "Rex! You're asking me my opinion. You like it, call it. I don't like it." Then Sanchez threw to Josh Baker for a five-yard touchdown and I imagined the elation of Baker's discoverer Terry Bradway up in Tannenbaum's box.

The Jets defense was more intense than ever. When Eli Manning, as predicted, stepped up and to his right, David Harris was waiting there and sacked him, leaving the coaches making visceral noises of pleasure. They vowed to soon get Trufant involved. After several three and outs, the Giants reached the Jet two, and then the Jets held. A Giants field goal cut the Jets lead to 7–3.

Ryan and Pettine had experienced some further early static—"Rex! We never repped it out of that grouping!" (When Ryan chose plays that weren't in the game plan, that hadn't been repped in practice, O'Neil sat there and felt "panic" surge through him.) Pettine was a paragon of preparation, whereas Ryan's nature hewed more toward the Napoleon dictum *on s'engage et puis on voit.* (You enter the fray and then you see what to do.) The combination invited discord, yet when Ryan and Pettine were clicking together, you could see that calls would work before the snap. "This is gonna be good," O'Neil would say, and indeed it was. "He threw it so quick, the routes didn't develop," approved Brian Smith. Something had to have worked really well for B-Smitty to say something.

What was holding down the offense right now were penalties, and the score remained 7–3. With the first half nearly over, the Jets punted to the Giants' one. Pettine got Ryan to third and ten with passes defended by Revis and then Cro, and then he turned the call over, saying, "You got it, Rexer!" Ryan chose that tempting character actor Max Blow. A short Manning throw went to the receiver Victor Cruz. Revis, on the other side of the field, was thinking, We're about to get a safety. But it was Denver redux, only worse. First Kyle Wilson and then Cromartie missed tackles. Eric Smith had an angle, but he could no longer run at full speed. Brodney Pool was nowhere to be found. And just like that, Cruz sprinted for the thirteenth ninety-nine-yard touchdown in NFL history. It would be, along with the late Tebow drive, one of the two signal moments of the Jets' season. Sutton had been watching Smith. "I saw Eric on the bench and I thought, by the look of pain in his eyes, there is no way he can get through this. I am awed by what people like Dave Harris and Eric put themselves through." As had happened frequently this season, the defense had dominated the Giants. The Giants had six yards rushing. Manning had completed seven passes. And yet the Jets were losing 10–7 at the half. "We're kicking this team's ass," Pettine told them. "We just can't give up the explosive."

In the second half, against what was perhaps the NFL's best pass rush, Sanchez threw and threw. He had open receivers, the booth could see them: "There's Mully!"; "Was anybody on LT in the flat? Nope." But Sanchez wasn't finding them. He seemed befogged out there. The defensive coaches, in turn, were baffled: "Why don't they run the ball?" Where was the run? Brandon Moore was so upset after a three and out on three straight passes that the guard lost his temper and screamed at Schotty to run. By the end, Sanchez had dropped back to pass more than sixty times, an exceptionally high total. Even the offensive coaches later would say, "That was weird."

In the big game, Revis was all over the field. The one reception made against the cornerback, Pettine would describe as the perfect NFL throw and catch. Slowly the game withdrew from the Jets' control. A Sanchez interception led to a field goal and a 20–7 Giants lead. The coaches thought he was just not reading coverages. As they spoke these criticisms, Tom Moore sat silent. He'd known the young Terry Bradshaw, about whom worse had been said. Quarterbacks—you could never tell.

There were more chances; it was the NFL, there were always chances. The Giants knew they'd won only late in the fourth quarter as Ahmad Bradshaw ran over Brodney Pool, making it 29–14. "Ford over rooster" as the defensive coaches called it.

In the locker room Ryan looked at his team and told the offense, "Pretty simple, guys. Too many turnovers. Four of twenty-one on third down ain't gonna get it done. And the D can't give up the big plays. It'll be on my shoulders. Let's go kick the fuck out of this team next week." What had Bradway been thinking in the box? "I'm worried about us" is what he had been thinking.

Part of the problem this season, as I saw it, was that Ryan wanted what he wanted—which was fair; he was the boss. But he didn't like forcing what he wanted on reluctant people, didn't even like cajoling them, and so he created friction, and then, with his aversion to professional confrontation, he fled from it instead of reaffirming his demands. He was a young head coach, and it seemed to me, going forward, that he would need more directive clarity, had to tell people what his wishes were and then hold them to them, and himself, to it. He had so much self-confidence, so much confidence in others. And all that was fine, until what he promised didn't come to pass and he acted betrayed—as he had recently with both Schotty and Pettine. Ryan was such an endearing and seductive man; people would do a lot for him—especially if he was more present, right there with them all the way through.

Some of the coaches, like Pettine and O'Neil, made quick out-of-state trips to spend Christmas Day with relatives. Schottenheimer hosted a gathering for both sides of his family to which he also invited young coaches and players who had nowhere else to go.

Others dined at Ryan's home. All of them were brooding, spoke later of spending the holiday lost in the same football moment.

On December 26, the coaches were back in their offices reliving that nadir on film, watching Cruz's ninety-nine-yard play many times. When the coaches met, Pettine told them, "Guys, we gave up nine completions and got blown out. We had fifty plays for ninety-one yards, and five for two hundred and forty-one. It'll make you sick." The system depended on unblocked linebackers making tackles. Scott had missed some big ones. On the ninety-nine-yard play, why had Brodney Pool frozen? "Wow," said Pettine as the film ended. "'Bleak' ain't the word." DeVito, Carrier said, had a plus grade on every play until the final touchdown, when his injured knees betrayed him. "I feel so bad for him," the coach said. So many players were hurt that Pettine went to see Ryan about canceling the day's practice.

In the team meeting, Ryan spent most of his address criticizing the play of the defense. This enraged some of the defensive players, though not Maybin, who later visited Ryan's office "bawling like a child," said Ryan, "because he felt he let us down by not doing enough."

When Pettine met the defense, he told them that the season's last game in Miami would be an audition for those who wanted to remain Jets. That he and Ryan "weren't always on the same page" and created play-calling confusion, he apologized for. To Pool he said, his effort was "a head-scratcher, Brodney. That's unacceptable." Pool would sign with Dallas as a free agent in the off-season.

To the defensive backs, DT spoke with passion: "What you put on that tape is who you are. I want you guys to have long careers in this league. Don't take it personal. I want to help you make a lot of money and play in the league a long time. I'm coaching for perfection. I may never get it, but I'll never stop trying." He asked if anybody had anything to say. Nobody did. As DT left the room, Cole, who didn't play against the Giants because of his sore knee, yelled, "I have something to say. I played a lot of years in this league."

Cole would remember the year as incredibly trying because he'd lost the brother with whom, as a child, he'd "gone through all the many same troubles with together." Bart Scott had been right. In the days after the murder, just as training camp was beginning, much had fallen on Cole out in Illinois with his family. Although Cole said, "I was able to handle it and keep going," the year had completely drained him. He was grateful to Ryan, who'd stayed in touch and consoled him when he was away from the team during training camp, who'd made the Jets feel like "a second family." For some people, Cole said, "it's a first family. I know people who played football instead of joining gangs." Cole would sign a free-agent contract with New England after the season.

At the end of the long Monday, Ryan sat in Pettine's office with Smitty and O'Neil. They discussed, yet again, the burden placed on a defense when the offense didn't score often—and scored so many points for the opposition. Brandon Moore's fit of temper as Schotty called pass after pass during the game reminded Ryan of the great Raven Jonathan Ogden, that six-foot-nine hillside of a man who moved with rare agility. Ryan thought he was probably the best left tackle in history, an intelligent athlete "with a locker full of books." The Ravens head coach Brian Billick respected Ogden so much that when Ogden felt the team wasn't running the ball enough, Ryan said, Ogden would glare at Billick, make a pounding signal, and Billick would call a run. This Ogden later confirmed. "I'd throw my helmet halfway across the sideline every now and then if we got too pass-happy," he told me. "You got to pound into them. This is a physical game." Everything that was happening to the Jets had already happened to other NFL teams before and would happen to other NFL teams again.

The Jets coaches discussed their slim remaining hopes of making the playoffs. The subject was changed to the North Carolina beach house Ryan rented and invited everyone to in the off-season.

And then Ryan left for the press conference he always gave the day after games, promising "to be nice and humble."

There were so many people involved with a football team, and so much happened that most knew nothing about. Eventually the coaches learned that after the first play in the Giants game, Brodney Pool had lost the vision in one eye. What had happened to him, I asked O'Neil later. "Big hit," he answered. On the bench, Pool seemed to his teammates to be completely out of it, but Pool insisted no coaches could be told because the team had run out of safeties. "He's in misery right now," said O'Neil. "The Bradshaw run is all over *SportsCenter*. He's crushed. Just crushed." Jim Leonhard and I discussed the situation and Leonhard explained that to the players, Ryan "is like a dad," and Pool "wouldn't tell him because he knows Rex wants guys to be healthy. He knows it's bigger than football. He doesn't want to put people in harm's way."

To Nick Mangold, the end of an NFL season felt routinized; by now, the center said, he was "programmed." Ryan was not that way. As the season slipped away, the coach grew more emotional—filled with sentiment. He was a person who had benchmark stories, stories he enjoyed returning to. Like any excellent storyteller's, his stories were present for him when he told them. He relied on them in times of trouble.

As the Tuesday-evening game-planning for the season's Sunday finale on New Year's Day in Miami began, Ryan arrived in Pettine's office and soon was regaling them with tales from happier times. Ryan recalled Bart Scott's frantic hitting as a rookie. He recalled MTV's first day as a Jet, when he got off a bus after two and a half days of constant travel from California, refused the offer of a hotel room and sleep, and, at over three hundred pounds, instead took and passed the team conditioning test right away by running twenty forty-yard dashes in under six seconds each. This story led Ryan to recollect his own svelte days in Arizona, when he weighed two hundred and thirty-five pounds, not his current three hundred and fifty, and ran three miles before he went home, no matter how late he worked. "My jogs might not start until three or four in the morning." Cheered, Ryan left to go ask Schotty about a blitz the offense hadn't been able to stop, in case there was something there for Ryan to adapt for the Jets defense. But not before allowing Pettine to tease him about some of Ryan's calls during the Giants game—"Stop it! Stop it!" Never was Ryan more appealing than when he laughed at himself—which was one of the two qualities he most prized in Jeff Weeks, the other being his nonnegotiable loyalty to all Ryans.

In the Wednesday-morning quarterbacks' meeting, Schotty explained that the Dolphins used so many coverages, "it's almost impossible to summarize." Then he looked at Sanchez and warned him, "Take care of the football; we'll win the game. That simple."

At the team meeting, Ryan told the players how good he thought they were—"There's not one team I don't think we can't beat"—and how proud and grateful he was for how much so many of them had sacrificed: "Guys who can barely walk, guys who need shoulder surgery," had been there "for each other." He congratulated Revis for making the Pro Bowl and told Harris he would send the linebacker to dancing school so Harris could call better attention to himself and be chosen as he also deserved to be. Harris blushed.

Mostly the defensive game plan consisted of adjusting familiar calls so that the Dolphins wouldn't recognize them. Because the Dolphins were susceptible to nickel blitzes, Pettine had drawn up a new one. For a name, he had chosen Nicky Read Tracy. Afterward, Kyle Wilson, who had overcome his freshman falterings to become a solid pro at the nickel, told me to have faith in him for "your" call because he'd been working on his blitzing technique, and "I really want a sack!" To have a call named after you, I saw, made you feel more invested, responsible for it.

At Wednesday's practice, Tannenbaum was grave, still upset about the Giants game, upset about his quarterback and his offensive coordinator. The GM considered the loss "a microcosm of the season. We were the better team and four or five plays cost us the game. Some of it was coaching. Something's not working between Brian and Mark. Mark's getting worse."

DT looked at the ragged practice film and saw "little hangover, little malaise. You got to fight it or you'll get knocked off the following Sunday."

Late in the afternoon, I watched film with Revis and Cromartie. Still with us in the linebackers' room was a small Christmas tree spangled with lights, and beside it sat Posey, himself a little lit up just by being there. Revis didn't think the Dolphins had significantly changed their passing approach since the first time the two teams had played, in October, so he left pretty quickly and Cro soon followed. Posey stayed on.

For Posey, finishing college in Ohio and coming to the Jets was, he said, "like the Indians leave the tribe and go to the woods and spend a couple of weeks out there in the wild with all the skills you've learned, and you come back with a bear. I definitely caught a bear this year and I am tired. But I love it here in this building."

Innocent as he might seem to the others, Posey had seen his share of life. At Ohio University, he had majored in health-service administration so that after football he could care for the sick and also so that he could, in retrospect, better understand his father. His father had been a heroin addict; he'd contracted HIV from a dirty needle and died in California when Posey was ten. "Crazy," he said. "Really crazy. You know what it's like, being the son of a guy who had AIDS? That word speaks. People look at you differently." But not on a football team. His mother, Julie, moved the family from California to a poor neighborhood in Cincinnati when Posey was four. When he was older, he tested into Saint Xavier High School—"It's the Harvard!" Posey said. The all-boys predominantly white Catholic prep school was "too much of a culture shock for me. Poor kid in the neighborhood doing his thing in the streets. Too much of a jump." So Posey left for La Salle, another Catholic high school. He kept Saint Xavier in mind: "Seeing those rich kids with their dads. I didn't have one. It motivated me."

Football, he said, "has been my father in life. Not exactly each coach, but football has replaced my father. It's taught me to be disciplined in whatever I do, be tough, be physical, be mentally tough. It taught me what is a man, because there are so many men within it. You decipher who is a good man and who puts on a front. Football is my father." He mentioned his respect for Brandon Moore and for Revis and Cro and Scott and DT and then he began talking about Jim Leonhard. He admired Leonhard for being "a walk-on at Wisconsin, wasn't drafted, defies the odds at five eight, a buck ninety-eight with wet nickels in his pocket. It's perseverance that makes him play ball with the best of them. You lose Jimmy Leonhard, you lose the confidence in the back end."

Posey said he had come to feel "appreciative" of his father. Although he never really knew him, he knew what his father's life had been like, and so "what he did, I did the other. I had a negative example." That was why the rebuke the Jets had given Posey, cutting him, in part because he seemed to be enjoying the nightlife too much, had so affected him. He feared he was throwing away what he most wanted out of the world for the sake of pleasures that meant nothing to him.

Later, Posey and I got a copy of the movie *Undefeated* and watched it in a meeting room. It was about a group of Memphis high-school football players whom Posey described as "hood as hell, all hooded up." The film's premise was that football doesn't build character; it reveals it. A kid in the movie had a pet turtle, and Posey said, "In a second life I'd be a tortoise." I asked him why. "They live a hundred and fifty years!" But, I said, they also live in shells. "We all live in shells, Nicky."

My own childhood had some similarities to Posey's—single mother, little money—and I told him about it, told him also about how, as I was walking in from a practice one day, Ryan had asked me about my father, who had suffered from such severe mental illness that he'd wander the streets before another stay in the wards. I rarely saw my father, and when I did, I was always afraid of what he might do. That day, Ryan wanted to know if this had made me nervous about having children of my own. Few people I knew well had ever taken this subject up with me, but in football, so many of the players came from troubled families that Ryan was used to having such conversations. And, as Sutton once said, Ryan was fundamentally "kind and generous"—he concerned himself with the aspects of life that were difficult for other people. I said to Ryan that conceiving children had made me nervous both because I didn't know what I might pass on and because I had no firsthand knowledge about what a good father did day after day. After relating all this to Posey, I told him how fine a thing I thought it would have been to be a part of a football team when I was young.

The last of the regular-season game weeks passed the most quickly. The Jets could still make the playoffs if they won and if several other games went their way. They yet had something to play for. "Good plan, really good plan," Schotty told the quarterbacks on Thursday. "Just got to execute third-down completions, stay manageable." He looked at Sanchez. "And just so you know, couple of guys went to Rex about what happened with Tone in the meeting. And so Rex is meeting with him. You should be prepared to play with him or without him." In a players-only meeting, there had been a spat between Holmes and Sanchez, the sort of thing that "happens," as Ryan later said.

At practice, Eric Smith was unable to run and Brodney Pool received a new nickname. Ryan was calling him Ole One Eye. During the afternoon defensive-backs' meeting, Lankster and Trufant were called to diagram plays at the board by DT. They did well. In those small triumphant moments, everybody could tell what a sentimentalist DT was underneath the coat of mail. It shone all over him.

To the last Friday-morning meeting Schotty wore a battered ball cap, a rumpled sweat suit, sneakers, graying socks, and a "positive energy" band on each wrist. Behind the huge tankard that held his energy drink, he looked small. He had ink blotches all over his hands and creases all over his face. The man had essentially eliminated sleep. Of the Dolphins he said, "They have absolutely nothing to lose. This is playtime for them. They can do whatever they want." They looked at some Miami film, and in reference to a woofing defender on the screen, Schotty said dryly, "I love it when a guy makes a tackle and then feels a need to tell everybody all about it."

Sanchez was nodding enthusiastically. "He says, 'Excuse me, gentlemen! Everyone! Did you notice that it was I who made that fine tackle!'"

On the field, when the offense suddenly shifted to a no-huddle, hurry-up mode, Revis quickly lined up the whole secondary and then broke up a pass play. He was, as someone observed, "better than a movie."

During the defensive linemen's last Friday-practice buckboard competition Pitoitua became distracted by an insect that had alighted on the football and lost his round without moving his hands. Then, in the finals, Wilkerson finally defeated Po'uha; his hands leaped from ground to board. Then the rookie toured the field declaring himself the new champ, and was undaunted when Po'uha claimed to have been bored into defeat by so many consecutive victories. I could see, in the moment, how I'd always remember both of them.

Eric Smith remained in such pain that, to kneel, he had to place his helmet on the ground, clamp a hand to it, and lower himself.

Along with the disappointment of how the last games had gone, there was a feeling of unraveling. I asked Wayne Hunter if I was seeing an unusual season. "This is the way it is," he said. "Nothing out of the ordinary." He compared all football seasons to roller-coaster rides. This year, he said, things were especially volatile—"Nothing seems cohesive, in sync. I was with the Seahawks for three years," he said. "We went to the Super Bowl. But we weren't as aggressive or as passionate. This is the perfect team for passion and aggression. Some teams have passion, but it's not as authentic as it is with Rex. He's pure passion."

In Miami on the New Year's Eve Saturday night, the team hotel hallways were crowded with revelers. At the quarterbacks' meeting, Schotty didn't require a copy of the call sheet as Sanchez read from it. Schotty lived the plays. He also now drank strong coffee at 8:00 p.m. Sanchez, wearing a white sports jacket, a black T-shirt, and gray linen trousers, was teased for affecting *Miami Vice* clothes. On the whiteboard was written, "Kevin drinks his own pee." Sometimes Sanchez gave you the feeling that he was an old-souled guy watching some goofier version of himself do puerile things just for the fun of seeing how they hit everyone. For unknown reasons, several portable IV machines were lined up against the meeting-room wall. Property of Brunell, it was suggested. The next day, Bru, the classy old pro, who'd been in the league since 1993, would dress for an NFL game for the last time.

You could hear the sound of exploding New Year's firecrackers somewhere outside as Pettine told the defense, "Tomorrow has the makings of a very emotional day." He said he suspected all the games tomorrow would break the way the Jets wanted.

The last Sunday was instead yet another day to regret. I stood on the sideline, and when the offense scored the game's first touchdown to take a 7–3 lead, you could feel the defensive spirits rise. Soon the Jets were back to punting, and after one of his kicks traveled only twenty-two yards, TJ Conley was disconsolate. "Don't worry, TJ," said Ben Kotwica, a realist. "You'll have many more chances." Alas, one reason for this was the offensive line's lack of

COLLISION LOW CROSSERS • 433

harmony; there were many false starts. When the offense was flagged for their fourth, Marcus Dixon got up and told himself, "Better walk around." Then the offense was called for a fifth. Just before the half, Sanchez threw an interception to Randy Starks, a three-hundred-pound defensive lineman, and a Dolphin field goal made the score 10–6, Jets. A lineman making a pick was rare to see. Schottenheimer spent much of the break telling the offense, "The penalties have to stop."

Late in the third quarter, the Dolphins began a twenty-one-play, ninety-four-yard touchdown drive that consumed more than twelve minutes of playing time and that felt to those on the sidelines like the embodiment of what the season had come down to. All year, the pattern was that the defense would hold off trouble for a long while and then at last that retardant would give way to the burn. It was 13–10, Dolphins. Then Starks made another interception, leading to a field goal and utter disbelief on the Jets sideline. Why did these things happen to Sanchez? With three minutes left, and the Jets behind 16–10, Sanchez drove his offense to the Miami ten. Holmes had still not made a catch. He had glided through the game in what looked like a trance of personal remove. Maybe now he would come through and redeem himself. He had never gone through an NFL game without making a catch. Great players, Ryan and Tannenbaum both liked to say, made big plays in big moments. "We're gonna win!" shouted a coach.

Sanchez threw his third pick. Quickly came a Dolphin field goal and it was 19–10. Miami won 19–17. The Jets would lead the NFL in opponent points scored off their turnovers. Afterward, Callahan reflected on the killing sequence of plays. "That late drive in Miami," he said, "typified our season. We're coming down the field. There's hope. There's energy. We're rolling. We're gonna beat the Dolphins, end the season on a positive note, and then doom! Death! Again! When you live this life, the highs are higher and the lows are lower. They are *low*." That night when he finally reached his home, Callahan poured himself a tumbler of Jack Daniel's and sat in silence for a long time: "I was numb and number." He would leave the Jets to become offensive coordinator of the Dallas Cowboys.

All manner of strange things happen in football huddles. Players told of spotting enormous bugs in the grass, of players puking, of players saying they couldn't feel their asses after absorbing big hits. Nobody had ever before seen a player evicted from the huddle by the other players, however, and when, in the waning fourth-quarter moments, this had happened to Holmes, it took a moment to register that the linemen were sending him off. He sat by himself on the bench, head up. Looking over at him, a lineman said, "He's a selfish pussy and it should have been recognized a long time ago." The only reason I saw all this was that it happened right in front of me. There were so many people on the sideline, each absorbed in his own responsibilities.

In the locker room Ryan praised those who had played "not just hurt but injured." He asked the players to take a good look inward. "Did you give everything you had? Are you a good teammate? That," he emphasized, "should be the easiest thing." Then he told the press, to whom he'd promised a Super Bowl many months ago, "I'm not a loser." Revis said later he found the whole thing dismaying, most of all because this was the first time in his Jets career the players didn't stick together as a team. "One article gets out. Santonio says the linemen need to block. That was our season. The linemen bark back. It happens again. Then it starts with Mark and Tone and we couldn't ever get out of it. You can't be negative. Come together. Be supportive."

The quiet bus, then the quiet airplane. Beside me, Brendan Prophett was watching the comedy *Old School* on his laptop. The laptop had only one headphone jack. He offered me one of his earbuds "because everybody needs a little laughter after a day like this." Then there was the quiet ride to the facility parking lot, where people fled, some car tires screeching, toward the exit. Several of the defensive coaches went out together for a beer, and I accompanied them. The defense had again finished in the top five in the NFL. They were proud of this. But winning was what they really cared about. It was now very late. O'Neil, not drunk but not wanting the season to end, returned to with me to Pettine and Smitty's house, and we all went to sleep. Early in the morning, O'Neil awakened, drove home, and climbed into his own bed beside his wife, Stacy, where his three-year-old son, Danny, confronted him. "Hey! You're in my spot!" said the boy. O'Neil told his son, "It's the off-season. I'm home now."

PART III

After

Fourteen

REX IN WINTER

I attended the burial of all my rosy feelings.

—*A. R. Ammons, "Transaction"*

At the final team meeting on Monday, Ryan, in a vast cowl of hooded sweatshirt, raged against the dying of the light, telling his players that if they could force themselves to watch the play-offs they would see the Jets had more talent than some of those still competing, "but we didn't have as much of a team." Blaming himself for misunderstanding the levels of group tension, he talked about the corrosive effects of "selfishness," the word he had so often used to describe opponents. His voice cracked as he declared, "I will get better. Will you?" Overcome, he left in tears. After a full year with the team, I suddenly found myself thinking back across all the strenuous sixteen-hour days that go into the sixteen weeks of a football season. Almost every person in that room resembled a man whose fiancée has broken up with him without warning. They were limping, red-eyed, and spent.

Then a walk across the hall, past the many dispensers of Purell along the wall, to see Pettine say good-bye to his room. He was brief. He looked out on one of the NFL's five best defenses and told the players, "It's been a rough year physically, mentally, emotionally. Take some time to enjoy your families, watch the playoffs, and get pissed off knowing we should be there. We played our asses off. We were put in some ridiculous situations. Yesterday typified the year."

Sutton and others had warned me at the beginning that the end for a good team that didn't win the Super Bowl was inevitably so abrupt, the season would seem to have vaporized. Now, in the still shocking moment, DT took the opportunity to offer his defensive backs one last life lesson, emphasizing his strong feelings about how to unite a team. His long view was that in football, the vanishing point was always near. For that reason you had to be candid. "When you play a sport by yourself, tennis, boxing, that's you," he said. "But when you play a team sport you rely on other people. At the end you have to grab the person you count on and hold them to the standard you hold yourself to. Champions hold people accountable to a championship standard. It's hard to do. Winning the Super Bowl will be the hardest thing you'll ever do in your life because everybody wants the same prize." DT had never won the Super Bowl as a player or a coach. The previous September, like Ryan and the others, he'd thought this might well be the year.

It was an unnerving time. Nobody on the Jets had expected to lose and certainly not amid so much discontent. On a Rex Ryan team, mutual goodwill was supposed to be a given. Before the Miami game Bart Scott had cleaned out his locker in dismay. The others now did the same job, filling up garbage bags and cardboard boxes with their belongings and carrying them out to their pickups and SUVs in the parking lot. Holmes was escorted from the locker room by a team official; that way nobody would give him too hard a time. To Holmes, the problem was that Schotty had treated his players like "robots." As he saw it, "Schotty gave us no freedom to have fun on the football field."

I had become accustomed to the exaggerated moments of strong feeling that pervaded football, the way it concentrated daily experience. Because there were few guaranteed contracts in the sport, all teams were annual teardowns, and with the arrival of the year's last meetings, some of the players had the sudden, chastened feeling that they were orphans. Every player I spoke with said he hoped the Jets would want him back. Posey planned to work out all winter and maybe also take a songwriting course. "I rhyme from time to time," he explained.

In fact, Posey would become a member of the Dolphins practice squad. In Florida he rented a furnished apartment and then proceeded to move the couch, tables, and chairs out of the living room so that at night, after practice, he could perfect his technique at home. The young cornerback could feel himself getting better, he said, and his new team could see it. Toward the end of the season, the Dolphins would promote him to the game-day roster. Happy as Posey was in Miami, he found his time with the Jets stayed present with him. "I went to Defensive University," he said. DT, Revis, and Cro had been "my professors" who showed him the attitude and the approach necessary to successfully compete in the NFL.

Lankster was going to receive an award from a foundation that helped stutterers. Most people on the team had no idea that he had a stutter. As a kid, he said, "I was laughed at a lot. It *was* funny. I never let it get to me. I never had a fight. Yes, sir, I can read aloud without stuttering. I can rap a song without stuttering." Upstairs in the management offices, Lankster and the others all knew, changes were already in motion. Lankster wasn't going to sweat it. There was a quality of inner peace to him that, if combined with aggression, was ideal in a football player.

Tannenbaum sprang into action. How had this happened? One of the GM's many praiseworthy qualities was his desire to bridge the usually independent football worlds of upstairs and downstairs. Accordingly, he now met nonstop with veteran players, catching them before they left town, showing them a calm, sympathetic face but inside so angry and upset, so driven with vengeful purpose to make it all better, he could think of nothing else. In the hallways, people asked him questions about tangential matters and he'd say, "I haven't given it a moment's thought."

The search for control of things gone completely out of control possessed him: "We fell short—I fell short. Now I could have real impact for the first time." He upbraided himself for the ways the team's lack of depth at positions like center and safety had cost it. The moments of sectarian locker-room strife had been unexpected with Ryan at the lead. But they too would be addressed. The GM also thought that "maybe some complacency set in."

The final event of the season was an after-action postmortem during which the team's senior coaching and personnel people sat in the defensive coaching staff's film room and evaluated the roster one last time. Everybody in the room was coughing and sneezing. They discussed the veteran lineman with "old-man knees" and the younger lineman who "will go to Burger King and then come and eat salad in front of us." Tannenbaum, hearing that, said, "We're not asking you to be autobiographical, Rex!" When Pettine opined that Wilkerson had exceeded expectations, Tannenbaum zapped him too: "Of all people to say he exceeded expectations, your college report had him as Deacon Jones!" The coaches considered Marcus Dixon to be the most improved member of the defense. He'd been given the team's award for character. By the following September, Dixon would be on the street.

Moving on to the linebackers, the staff compared Bellore to Mike Smith, which led to the telling again, by Ryan, of the "you won't be able to cut him" story, with Smitty smiling and looking at the floor. "Thank God we got him," said Bradway of Bellore. Nobody spoke critically of Bart Scott. The only villain there was change, said Tannenbaum. It was now a league for linebackers who could thrive in pass coverage. Scott had achieved everything in life by believing in himself. How did a man like that adapt?

Now came the defensive backs. The coaches and others affirmed their love for Ellis Lankster, of how he expressed the raw, wild pleasure they all took in the game. They talked also of the fascinating way Cromartie could be shaken when what he'd seen on tape didn't appear before him on the field. They wanted Leonhard to know how much they prized him. What more was there to say about Revis? Inevitably, there was more. He had revealed he was studying his own hamstrings, experimenting with weight loss to see if it helped his speed and health. Trufant too had shed a few pounds. "One hundred and sixty pounds and watch him run into two huge wedge-type guys and make a tackle," said Westhoff, shaking his head at the valor of it all.

The defense finished, and it was the offense's turn. It was a dreary conversation. The coaches were people who got into the profession because they were optimists, celebrators of the skills of others. The offense hadn't been good enough and they all knew that Schottenheimer's job and those of others were under the blade because of it. Still, there was no recrimination and no attempt to justify. Sanchez had abundant physical ability and competitive spirit, but the turnovers and the poor reactions under pressure were going to cost him his job unless he improved. Sanchez himself agreed. Cavanaugh had written out an evaluation and showed it to the quarterback, who hadn't disputed a thing in it. That's what made it so hard to assess Sanchez; lodged in every deficit there were virtues.

And that was also at the foundation of football—what made the game so popular. Nothing was ever sure; anything could or couldn't happen. Around the NFL, there was acknowledgment that a quarterback's fourth year was perhaps his most critical, the bellwether season. Members of the Giants management had publicly criticized their slumping quarterback Eli Manning's abilities during his fourth season, before it all came together for him and he rallied the team to a Super Bowl. As they contemplated Sanchez's upcoming season four, the Jets still had hope that Sanchez was more than "just a guy," that with improved focus he would excel.

This was something Cavanaugh thought was certainly possible. The quarterbacks coach always emphasized how challenging it was to be an NFL quarterback. "Mark is young, he's still right on pace with the greats," he said later in the spring. "You need to be patient with quarterbacks, and it's an impatient game today." In Cavanaugh's years as a player, in the 1980s, he said, nobody would have expected an NFL quarterback to master his position so quickly. People were always trying to defeat the inevitable cycles of football, but rarely could it be done. Cavanaugh had won a Super Bowl as the offensive coordinator with the Ravens, and later a division title; the next year he was fired.

Since Sanchez had arrived in the NFL, people around the Jets facility had treated him protectively, emphasizing his virtues, posting that media-relations staffer by his locker whenever he gave interviews. All this reinforced an impression that Sanchez, though playing the leadership position, was still a student. Now they wanted him to grow up. The real question seemed to be how to direct his whimsical personality to advantage on a field. Sanchez, I knew, felt the responsibility of their expectations, and yet he was who he was.

In the meeting, the urgent practical question had become how to accelerate the most important player's maturity in time to save him. And save themselves; their careers were tied to his and if Sanchez remained an unfinished work, he would finish all of them. The solution seemed to be the classic one: the goad of competition. "We have to bring somebody else in," said Ryan. Schottenheimer agreed. "Guys will come here. They see him, they see an opportunity."

And what to do about Holmes? "It's not us you have to worry about," Schotty told Tannenbaum and Ryan. "We're grown men. We can roll our sleeves up. In this room we have soldiers. We'll fight on. It's the guys in the locker room we have to worry about. It'll be del-i-cate." Or maybe not. "People might have crowned him the villain but he's not that type of guy," Revis would say later about Holmes. "The frustration of the year was when you're not winning. This was just an upsetting year for a lot of guys. When I'd talk to him every morning, he'd say, 'All I want is a couple of touches, I want to make plays for the team.' He wanted to make things happen." The coaches all knew what Tannenbaum now said, that in the NFL you won with talent, and Holmes had rare talent.

Tannenbaum took copious notes on a yellow legal pad. Then he went back to his office and reflected further on how organized chaos had lost its fragile balance. Among Parcells's analects was the belief that "You are what your record says you are." The Jets had been 8 and 8. The Giants, who'd finished at 9 and 7, were in the midst of a galvanizing late-season run that would end with them winning the Super Bowl. Many of the issues that afflicted the Jets had touched the Giants as well. An unpopular draft choice, rancor among players, rancor between coaches—they seemed to matter only when the team wasn't winning. It wasn't possible or necessary to change everything. You just had to fix the right things.

With the meetings done, with the future uncertain, the coaches' days now quieted. They were often alone in their offices, suspended in states of rumination and rue. "This time of year we have the realization of how challenging it is to get a group of people to truly believe in one objective," Sutton said. "I'm not sure how you quantify what a unified team is, but when you have it, it's electrifying—it pulsates through your whole organization. And when you don't have it, it's like carrying around a sack of bricks. There's always something weighing on you and what happens is you get tired. All the things that came up at the end," he went on. "They're typically bubbling below the surface on most teams."

It was impossible not to think about how the year had treated Ryan. Bart Scott thought that "Rex was a little more distant, more disconnected." The effect of that on the team was "we leaned too much on what we'd done before. We didn't have a sense of urgency." Had Ryan been distracted by sudden fame, had he misplaced his connection to what brought him fame in the first place? He was always a vibrant presence at practice and when running team meetings, but otherwise during the long football days, the meetings were rarely inflected by the head coach's personality. Ryan himself freely admitted that he'd "lost" the team's "pulse." During the year, at times he'd seemed drifty to me; when he sat working alone in his office with his television tuned to the Discovery Channel to keep him company, I imagined him engaged in searchings of his own. It was also in those partially removed Ryan moments that I sensed people wished for more of him. Tannenbaum knew it. He was always pressing Ryan to help Carrier with the linemen, to visit more with Schottenheimer. But Ryan liked to let people perform their roles; hands-on supervision did not come naturally to him. Pettine's careful opinion was "becoming a head coach changes every man. The good ones are those who can recover their former selves—recover what about them made them successful to begin with." What did Ryan think? "Our season shows how hard it is to get there year in, year out, consistently," he told me. It also showed the difficulty of getting the outside world to validate one's own internal narrative.

For the moment, the coaches were left with the losing. January was the restless time of year, when other teams played big games and the leaders of those teams that didn't sat in their offices, working desultorily on the upcoming February Combine, but mostly waiting. Since every team save one was going to lose, some just more slowly than the others, NFL coaches should have been masters of losing. And in a way they were. They were all trying to control the uncontrollable, and losing was the inevitable result. They lost their sleep, they lost their pleasures, they lost their homes, they lost their cities, they lost their children's childhoods, and they lost their marriages. And for all that, they also lost their players and their colleagues and their jobs. All they kept was the satisfaction that, while everyone out there in America was headed for defeat, they knew defeat and could stand it. In America, land of happy endings to feel-good films, this was the truer entertainment; to fail is human.

Some of them now were going to be fired. There were times that season, as I sat in the tense meeting rooms after the big losses, that I'd wanted to disappear into the fabric of my seat. No matter how much experience a person has with losing, he'll find it hard to be observed in his adverse moments. That was the entire team, however, a shared disappointment. This was personal, out of mutual context. Accompanying people who were waiting to discover whether they still had jobs felt almost lascivious. I couldn't bear to do it, so I got a garbage bag and filled it with already fading green and white clothes. Carrying the bag to my car, I ran into Devlin, who smiled and said, "Isn't it a shitty feeling, cleaning out your locker?"

I had been with the team for what everyone seemed to agree was an emblematic NFL season. "You saw how much goes into it," Patrick Turner said. "The highs, the lows, the drama, the mental aspect, the cerebral aspect is really what you saw. It's a grown man's business at the end of the day. A grown man's business. There's nothing like it. It exposes you like nothing else." In my year, they lost as many as they won, experienced a crushing finish, and had an abundance of little autumnal moments of vision along the way. Revis would tell me, "You probably saw some things this year that were surprising to you, maybe even upsetting, but what you have to understand is what an emotional and passionate thing football is." I saw all that, saw also that those old coaches Joe Gibbs and Bill Callahan were right, that football was a game of process and the arrival could never be as meaningful as the approach.

Now it was going to get much worse for the Jets. Ryan would spend his days behind closed doors and drawn curtains with Tannenbaum. For them, there was no full stop. Life was enjambment with one season immediately becoming the next, the day-to-day a relentless unfolding of events. Personnel decisions would be made. Delicate phrases such as "will not return" and "won't be back" would be used, and Pettine would tell me, "This is the cruel part of the business. It's very strange here. Some guys who are secure in their jobs are just sitting in their offices, and others, guys you've worked with for years, are getting called into Rex's office for a talk with the shades down. They come out and begin packing their offices up." Then they'd look in on Pettine and tell him, "Hey, I just wanted to say good-bye."

Henry Ellard would become the New Orleans Saints receivers coach. From Texas, where he had gone to become the Dallas offensive coordinator and line coach, Bill Callahan would tell me, "You just jump in. I haven't thought about New York. When you take a new NFL job, you don't ever look back."

At the facility Ryan would look back. He was optimistic for himself and those he cared about and in that way suffered when the world did not conform. Warding off the wistful winds was one of the reasons Ryan kept so many people so close. For him, forgetting was a hard art to master. Of the NFL teams that had interviewed him and then failed to hire him as their coach, he would say, "Of course you never get over it. You remember everything and you let it drive you." November's loss to Denver—"We beat the fuck out of them…you never get a game like that back"—and the unbalanced pass/run ratio in the Giants game would likewise refuse to recede. As a result, Schottenheimer would move on to St. Louis, hired by the Rams as their offensive coordinator. (He would bring along with him Wayne Hunter and Matt Mulligan.) In St. Louis Schotty would work with twenty-four-year-old Sam Bradford, a former number-one draft choice at quarterback with dark features and bright eyes that, from a distance, made him resemble Mark Sanchez. When I would say to Ryan, "But Rex, you were the boss! These guys weren't open rebels. Why didn't you simply tell him to do it your way?" the coach would explain, as he had many times before, "I wanted to treat Schotty with the same respect they treated me in Baltimore." And after talking again about "freedom and trust," he would admit, "I did a poor job of saying, 'Listen, you motherfucker, run the football.'"

Schottenheimer was still not yet forty, though his many big life experiences made him seem older. During the off-season, when we spoke, he said that of course the defense's caustic attitude had penetrated: "I'd be lying if I said it didn't piss us off. But we used it as motivation." Then he would assess his own strengths and weaknesses, all but eliding the strengths and going straight to the weaknesses, concluding: "At times I overdid things, overthought things. It's a game. It needs to go on instincts." He added, "I could have given each coach more individual time with his players by ending meetings sooner. I had a good staff." He was the good soldier who also wanted to be true to himself—a man with qualities. It's rare to come upon someone, especially someone so young, who is capable of accurate self-criticism. If anybody could come through this bruising part of the profession well, I suspected, it was him.

Back in the narrow office beside the more spacious one where Schotty had spent so many nights, and where a new offensive coordinator, Tony Sparano, now sat, Cavanaugh would sigh and say he was sorry good men lost their jobs because Sanchez was slower to develop than the times required.

Mark Carrier had been given complete freedom and trust to coach a position new to him. Now it was decided he hadn't done well enough. Carrier learned indirectly that he would not be returning to the Jets; he and Ryan never spoke of the decision. Even in such a devastating moment, Carrier was not vindictive. His players often remarked on what personal probity the Hammer had. "I don't know what happened," Carrier would say from Ohio, where he moved after being hired as the Cincinnati Bengals defensive-backs coach. "Honestly, I don't. I didn't see it coming. It's never a smooth, clean break. Sometimes this is the way it happens. It was an odd situation, but it's part of the business and we all accept it." One advantage, he said, was that "my wife's closer to her family in Chicago." Ryan, Carrier said, had recommended him to the Bengals, and between them, "It's all good."

And then Ryan would brace himself, walk into Jeff Weeks's office, and tell him, "Look, man, I can't bring you back." Weeks,

Ryan would say, "was pissed. He wanted to beat the shit out of Pettine. I was like, 'No, I have to do it.'" In the moment, Ryan would be angry and defended, oscillating with blame. As soon as they all were gone, their offices empty, the head coach became distraught, telling people, "I just fired my best friend of thirty years." He hoped it would be a good thing for Weeks, that it would allow him to better order his life. But he would mourn his absent friend. Speaking also of Carrier, he would say, "It's the worst. It's like I failed. I talk to my wife. To Tannenbaum. It's brutal. I failed. They're all good people."

Ryan saw beyond football, thought about the happiness of those who played and coached for him. Of Weeks he would say, "If I was gonna get a head-coaching job, Weeks was gonna be on my staff. We were gonna have fun. I want to get back to being me. I want to get back to having fun. That was actually the purpose he served. I never realized how it would bother people. Pet was my twin in Baltimore. I need that twin. 'How can you go to lunch without me?' That all wasn't fair to Weeks. Pet can't be the twin because he's coordinator."

I would find all these partings dramatic and unsettling and would think about what a man who severed professional ties with his ultimate comrade, his ultimate wingman, might take from such an event. Weeks was irresponsible in the sense that he scorned the grind, was not committed to the hard-drive details of modern professional football. And yet he was filled with spontaneity and always freer than anybody else. Now he could be truly free.

As for Ryan, his job was to enthrall others, draw them to him and to his cause, and nobody in the NFL could do it better. And yet for Ryan, perhaps this moment signaled the end of his apprenticeship and would make him realize that a great leader can't please everyone. A leader has to be a little ruthless. As Bart Scott put it, "The game's always evolving. You have to evolve with it or else you're a dinosaur. You adapt or you die." When Bill Belichick was a young head coach with the Cleveland Browns, he was a difficult, driven man with a 36 and 44 record. Given another chance by the Patriots, although he remained disdainful to the world, Belichick, according to people who knew him, became more open to those he worked with.

Ryan would spend the winter consulting "my sensei," an executive counselor whom Tannenbaum hired. Ryan would describe him: "Chinese guy. Old dude. He's helpful. I'm an extrovert. Now I've realized I pull away from introverts. I'm learning to be more inclusive." Ryan would also talk with Steve Young, a former 49ers quarterback, about the difference between offensive and defensive players. Among his findings: "Defensive players like to be told they're gonna kick your ass. Offensive players don't like it. The defensive attitude doesn't necessarily work for the whole team."

Ryan would also eliminate "Rexican" meals in which he ate as many as twelve tacos at a sitting. Now he'd call for a single plate of nachos and finish only four. (To help, DT would remand his desktop stash of See's peanut brittle and lollipops to his car trunk.) By the end of summer Ryan would have lost 106 pounds and cast off last season's weight of another sort, confessing he'd been "down almost the whole year. It was a brutal year. Especially at the end." He said he'd felt "pulled in so many ways. Now I'm doing nothing but football. I got away from it a little bit. I love coaching. I love teaching. I wasn't doing enough of it."

Wanting an offense that would stand up to the defense, the team hired Tony Sparano, who'd recently been the Dolphins head coach, to be its offensive coordinator. Sparano grew up in the Hill, the toughest neighborhood in New Haven. His father poured steel at a foundry and drove a liquor truck, a combination that seemed to describe Ryan's preferred style of offense. And with the coaching situation resolved, Ryan and Tannenbaum would turn their attention to improving their quarterback.

Out in Denver, the Hall of Fame Broncos quarterback John Elway, who now ran the team, was unsentimental when it came to his position, and in a passing age, Tim Tebow's throws brought to mind shells wobbling over the trenches at Passchendaele. The Broncos would sign Peyton Manning to replace Tebow. The Jets, meanwhile, would give Sanchez a contract extension that, if he did become a fine pro, would represent a relative bargain for the team. Yet even as they were betting on Sanchez, Tannenbaum and Ryan would reflect on the memory of Tebow on the run, shedding exhausted Jets defenders, and Tebow would join those he'd vanquished. The Tebow trade would leave Santonio Holmes, like most of America, bewildered. Immediately Holmes would telephone Sanchez and find him "lost for words. Didn't understand it. I encouraged him. Tebow's only a teammate." Out in Missouri, Schottenheimer would root for Sanchez, hoping the presence of Tebow would motivate him to grow up as a quarterback. Sanchez, he thought, "has all the ability. Tebow might be the best thing in the world for him." The Jets had believed that Tebow would add depth and nuance to the narrative. In profile, however, Tebow was a leading man. It was testament to the hermetic nature of football teams that the Jets had not foreseen that bringing such a celebrated presence to a New York team might prey on the team's energy.

In the NFL, all men are optimists. Schottenheimer believed his Rams, who'd finished 2 and 14 in 2011, "can win the whole thing." In 2012, Ryan thought the same of the Jets, of course, but post-sensei, discretion was an art of war. It was wise restraint. In their first 2012 game, the Jets would score forty-eight points and Sanchez would throw three touchdowns in a defeat of the Buffalo Bills. Among the defensive standouts on the field that day were Wilkerson, the number-one draft choice who was now among the best linemen in the sport, and Cromartie, who at year's end would be selected to the Pro Bowl. About the rest of the season, probably the less said the better. In the third 2012 Jets game, against Miami, Revis, who'd never had surgery of any kind, sprinted in open-field pursuit and fell untouched to the ground, his left knee ligaments sheared, his season over. The next week, all the sharp cuts seemed to catch up with Holmes, when he, likewise, fell to the ground untouched with a season-ending foot injury. BT, his Achilles still troubling him, played again, only to tear a tendon in his shoulder. "He wasn't," said Pettine, "the same guy." The horror of the body-annihilating game was that its most valuable resources were so ephemeral.

It would get worse. On Thanksgiving, during a loss to the Patriots, one of the Patriots touchdowns would involve the year's most ignominious play: Sanchez, after a backfield miscommunication, ran toward the pit, collided with Brandon Moore's posterior, fumbled on impact, and then pawed the ground as the ball was returned for a touchdown. This demoralizing episode became known as the butt-fumble, and the flummoxed, scatological ineptitude of one man whanging into another like a dairy farmer colliding with the hindquarters of his milk cow would become a cultural meme, the avatar for the team's rapid declension from unexpected glories to absurdity.

The cruel nature of things in the ultimate team game was that a disproportionate amount of blame would fall upon the quarterback. Sanchez was plainly affected by the presence of Tebow, even though Tebow, curiously, was as negligible a change-of-pace quarterback in the Jets scheme as Brad Smith had been the previous year for the Bills. Sanchez played even more poorly than he had in 2011, staring down receivers and throwing off his back foot on the way to leading the league in the most crucial statistic of them all—turnovers. Turnovers inspire the opposition and deflate your own team. Each game, supporters watched Sanchez with unease, waiting for the next one. Said a member of an opposing team, "Everybody knows Sanchez throws money to the defense." Sanchez lacked the presence in the pocket that allows quarterbacks to sense the onrush of the basilisks; he still did not seem a prescient decoder of the defense's intentions; he didn't move through his progression of receiver pass routes quickly enough; he made capricious decisions. Worst of all, he did not improve the play of others. Football was a difficult game. Sanchez made it look too hard.

They would finish at 6 and 10, apparently back where they'd started before Ryan's arrival, a doomed enterprise, the fated street corner on which store after store has a grand opening that quickly ends in shutters. Ryan's bravura approach had, from the first, earned the Jets plenty of detractors. That enmity was fine when the team was winning. Now that they were at a loss, the Jets were again the loathed football team, a victim of sporting schadenfreude that I would find painful because it canted so far from the resolute and inspiring professionalism I'd experienced, that I knew still existed in Florham Park, as it did across the NFL, a strange multibillion-dollar world where men gave their lives to make a violent, dangerous sport beautiful to watch. To talk in 2012 with Tannenbaum, Ryan, DT, Sutton, A-Lynn, Bradway, Smitty, and the rest was to hear the times trying their hardworking souls. "How's life outside football?" I'd ask Pettine, to change the subject, and the reply would come: "What's that?"

Tannenbaum, after sixteen years with the Jets and many short nights spent sleeping beside a fish tank, would lose his job. That long a stay with one NFL organization was rare, and leaving it would be "really tough" for Tannenbaum—"It was sixteen years. Those feelings can't leave overnight. It meant a lot to me. " For a while every piece of Jets news hit him hard, the feeling each time like seeing the new owner's car in the driveway of your foreclosed dream house. Out in the world he would resolve to speak only grace notes about the team, taking all responsibility and leaving things at that. Changing careers, he became a sports agent; coaches and broadcasters would now benefit from his fastidious attention to their details, and so would his family. Some hiring people in the NFL had reached out to him, but right now he wanted to stay in the same town with his wife and kids.

And Ryan, who a winter ago had promised to deliver Super Bowls, a thrill of a presentiment he said he regretted, now would suffer. Disconsolate as he was, in defeat he would meet his other, quieter ambition. In January, when the For Sale signs appeared outside the houses of NFL coaches, in the suburban New Jersey towns around Florham Park some of those properties were empty because the occupants had been offered better jobs elsewhere and Ryan had not stood in their way.

Pettine would move on to Buffalo to become the defensive coordinator of the Bills. For Pettine, the Bills were his opportunity to become his own coaching man, to show he could run a first-rate defense without Ryan. And to help him do it, Ryan allowed Pettine to take with him O'Neil, now to have his own "room" as the Bills linebackers coach. And to coach the Bills defensive line, Ryan also let him have Anthony Weaver, the former Ravens player who'd been a promising assistant Jets coach in 2012. Smitty could have gone to Buffalo as well, but he got married and returned instead to Lubbock to be the co–defensive coordinator at his alma mater, Texas Tech. There he would be in a better position to help his ailing father, and he and his new wife would live close to their families. A football coach's wife, Smitty knew, needed a supportive community nearby when she began to have children. Sutton would be hired by Kansas City to become the defensive coordinator of the Chiefs, and joining him there, on the defensive line, would be Mike DeVito. DT would rise to become the Jets defensive coordinator, Ryan pledging to help him build the plans and call the games. From Ryan's 2011 staff, including Schottenheimer and Callahan, there would now be six offensive and defensive coordinators working in football. Ryan's other guarantee had been to create a "coaching tree," with his former assistants running their own teams, and the pinecones had been scattered.

At the facility, Westhoff would retire and Kotwica would be promoted to replace him. Brian Smith would receive O'Neil's former job. Some of the offensive coaches were offered more senior positions by other teams; Ryan asked them to fulfill their contracts with him. A-Lynn would become the Jets assistant head coach as well as the running-backs coach, making the experience of sitting in a window-less office while teaching men to run to daylight a little brighter. Devlin would become the Jets offensive-line coach. Tony Sparano would not be asked back and would move on to Oakland to be the Raiders line coach. In the facility hallways there, he would pass Joey Clinkscales, beginning his second year as the Raiders director of player personnel. In professional football, for a proven coach, if the circumstances were no longer amenable at one branch office, there was usually a job waiting at another—which was how Matt Cavanaugh ended up in Chicago, presiding over the Bears quarterbacks. And eventually, if you were fortunate and could stand an itinerant life where you were always on the verge of exile, a proven coach might win the Super Bowl—as Don "Wink" Martindale had in 2012 with the Ravens, who'd hired him to coach their linebackers.

Thin at many positions and building for the future, in the depths of the winter of 2013, the Jets' prospects for a flourishing fall did not seem likely. Everyone in Florham Park talked about the new GM, John Idzik, as a deliberate, disciplined person. One of Idzik's obstacles was all that extra salary now tied up in Sanchez. Two of his early decisions were to cut Tebow and trade Revis to Tampa Bay for the draft choices and salary relief he would use to begin the latest reconstitution of the Jets. (Among the team's new defensive backs was the former Temple safety Jaiquawn Jarrett, signed off the street after an unsatisfactory professional debut with the Eagles.) True, the breaks of the ultimate team game had lately been against the Jets, and such was the random element in pro football that there might be triumph in the offing. But only a spectacular optimist would have thought so. A spectacular optimist (and loyalist) Ryan yet remained. He rehired Jeff Weeks. With so many of the others leaving, he needed his friend, and, anyway, the first two years with Weeks they'd won. "He's kicking ass," Ryan told me happily in the spring. "His life is dramatically changed." Ryan was aware that Weeks hadn't performed well in 2011, but the coach said, "Everybody deserves another opportunity. He needed help. He went and got it. He's a different guy." Another old Ryan comrade and football lifer, Sam Pittman, who would gladly travel halfway across the country if Ryan needed assistance building a fort for his kids, who had known Weeks and Ryan for many years, thought, "He just loves Weeks. Sometimes with Rex it's blind love, but that's who he is. Part of it makes him great, part of it gives him flaws."

As the Jets I had known in Florham Park dissolved, only to reanimate in these far-flung places, I followed all their teams. The map of the country had been transformed for me; I saw it in dark silhouette with a series of small, bright beacons designating football coaches. But it was also true that as they spread around the United States, the coaches remained fixed in place and time as Jets for me, still voices in the same headset wire. In unexpected moments, I would find myself thinking about them.

I would think about how, during games, when emotions ran high in the coaches' box, I knew that it was difficult for Devlin to hear the defensive coaches' dismay, but I never saw Devlin show it. I would think about how Weeks liked to talk about the outsize popularity of football in his native South; if you came from less, he said, whatever you did have meant more to you. I would think of how every morning Carrier would ask me about the traffic I'd confronted the night before on my way home. The thirty-mile drive could take me as long as three hours, and he'd always want all the details of the various snarls and impediments because he knew, better than most men, what they meant to the people at the end of the journey. I would think of how Pettine would not allow any father to use the term "childcare" or "babysitting" in reference to his own children because "it's called parenting." I would think of Smitty, who had never in his life seen a lazy Susan until one night at the O'Neil family table. He'd asked what that round little thing was called, and now, when any of the others saw one, they'd text out to West Texas a picture of it, a way of saying all the things that most guys don't say to each other. I would think of how, during the season, when Ryan was going through his lowest times as a coach, Sutton would find occasion to talk about Ryan's gift, how he, Sutton, could watch the same film five times through while Ryan would look at it only once and still Ryan saw more there "than I ever could." I would think of Ryan in abstract relation to all of the departed, how they were all his graduates now, spreading his message and their own, filling up a league with their hopes for the coming season, how if their plans were good enough and they had the luck, any one of them might earn a jewel for his finger.

And I would think about that last day of my season when I'd driven out of the gated community of the facility into the half-light of the world. Immediately I'd been downcast. I missed the big, bright facility, had wanted the year to go on for them, wanted for them the success they had pursued through so many hours to the exclusion of all else. I thought of how often football players struggled after they left the sport, how their marriages ended and their finances went into arrears, how life as part of the crowd in the outside world undid them. Although none of his coaches yet had any idea of it, BT was beset with such domestic miseries. The police would visit his tidy home and he would be charged with domestic violence and possession of drug paraphernalia. With his wife's encouragement, BT was admitted into special counseling programs. "I blame myself and I regret it," he'd tell me months later. "It's much better now."

Leaving the facility, I could see how such tragedies happened. It was the gravity of the place. In football the facility was designed to be difficult to leave. Everything was there for you. A barber came in regularly. So did a dry cleaner and a car washer. Three meals a day were served. And best of all, there was the built-in coterie of brothers and fathers and uncles and a mutual sense of binding purpose. "It is a pull," said Revis.

Driving home from the facility with a garbage bag full of work-out clothes in the trunk, thinking back across the year, my mind had returned to Miami, to something I saw out the team bus window in the parking lot after the final game of 2011, on New Year's Day 2012, as I waited for everyone to board. It was Ellis Lankster in crisp jeans, a polo shirt, and shiny new high-tops standing at the barricades that separated the visiting team's buses from the public. Lankster was talking with two women whose resemblance to him was so close it was obvious they were his mother and sister. It turned out that they and Lankster's stepfather had driven nine hours from Alabama in a pickup truck to watch Lankster play special teams. That was nothing; when Lankster had been a college football player in Morgantown, West Virginia, they'd driven fifteen hours for those games. And even then his mother had been back in Alabama to work her Monday shift. "A lot of turnarounds," as Sayinka Lankster put it. Lankster had his mother's face, a face that made you like a person right away, a face full of sunny personality and easy affection. His sister also had that face. Looking through my window, I saw both women were tender with Lankster, patting him, resting a hand on his shoulder, and he was that way with them. I sat on a bus full of wounded, crestfallen men older than Lankster, and it was easy to see how much the two women cared about him, easy also to see how shadow could veil what was going on in the light.

Through the bus window, Lankster was neither wounded nor crestfallen. He looked so young. The night before every game, his ritual was to pray, to call his son and his mother and his high-school coach. After high school Lankster had planned to "get a job, help my mom," until the high-school coach intervened and urged him to go to college: "He told me, 'You have a gift. God's blessed you. Try it out.'"

For some people, the American football Sundays have the quality of holidays. There are even those who revere the game as a kind of national religion. It was Sunday, New Year's Day. All around Lankster and his family, crowds of people were passing, heading home, many dressed in the festive costumes and uniform shirts fans wear to football games, some of these costumes already a little dated, the numbers on the shirts now remnants from another year.

And suddenly, looking past Lankster, there on the bus, I had thought of this day of celebration that seemed to be inadvertently marking an occasion different from the one ordained, that instead of welcoming the new bade farewell to a place and a time, to all those facility faces and all those facility hours, to people who had shared something as one and now would be forever linked even as they dispersed. There was a sense that they had been through something transformative together, something powerful and unexpected, something easy to remember for what it hadn't been. When football was falling, not glory, the disappointment was so everyday-public you could almost forget how difficult it was.

Afterword: Not For Long

Looking back now, nearly three years later, what I was least prepared for was how fleeting the NFL would be for those inside. Rex Ryan had warned me that a third of every NFL roster turns over annually, but hearing the coach say that was one thing—watching them all disperse to Buffalo and Kansas City and Oakland and off the football grid (and onto the street) was something else. It was the essential NFL contradiction: the necessity of achieving a deep, self-abnegating unity among teammates, and then, a few months later, the population scattered, every third man for himself.

Relocation could happen to anyone. In 2011, the most valued Jets players were Mark Sanchez and Darrelle Revis. Come 2014, while recovering from shoulder surgery, Sanchez, and his costly contract, were released by the Jets. He signed on to play a reserve role in Philadelphia, and perhaps to discover advantages in this backward turn, as had those vaunted late-to-bloom quarterbacks of

Super Bowls past Jim Plunkett and Rich Gannon. You could never tell about quarterbacks.

As for Revis, following a lavishly compensated year in Tampa, the Buccaneers allowed him to set sail. Revis browsed his suitors and this time the corner did not press for the most money. Instead, he joined the heretofore-reviled Patriots. Was it love thine enemy? Was it keep your enemies closer? Here's what it was: Revis wanted to win and, mindful that in football the fourth quarter is always nigh, he calculated that his championship chances were better with Brady and Belichick than against them.

Meanwhile, in late January, Mike Pettine, the former Ravens third video guy, was hired away from coordinating the Buffalo Bills defense to become head coach of the Cleveland Browns. (Pettine made his orderly protégé, Jim O'Neil, the Browns defensive coordinator.) In Northeast Ohio, Pettine would inherit a devoted fan base, a first-class team facility, a promising roster (six Pro Bowlers), and a team that had just tied an NFL record for consecutive seasons with double-digit numbers of defeats (six). Even if you'd been down that long, the future always looked like up to an NFL coach, and many people liked Pettine's chances—if he could find himself a reliable quarterback.

To address that necessity, come the May draft, Cleveland selected Texas A&M's Johnny "Football" Manziel, an improvisational dynamo on field and at fountain. Given Pettine's prior experiences with Ryan and Sanchez, and Pettine's ability to invest others in his strict expectations for them, it seemed to me that he stood as good a chance as any publisher at keeping this particular football freelancer out of the Warehouse District. If nothing else, the Browns would be colorful.

How did Pettine think back upon his years with Ryan and the Jets? "It all runs together, blurs," he said. If you aspired to remain in the NFL, your compass pointed ever forward. Except, perhaps, on the day a man accepted his dream job. Pettine's previous head-coaching experience consisted of terms at two Pennsylvania high schools. When he learned he was now in charge of an NFL team, he telephoned his parents. Whereupon Senior surprised him: "For the first time ever," Pettine said, "he used the words 'I'm proud of you.' Typical Italian father!" And what did Pettine himself do to mark the momentous life occasion? Did he jump around? Did he drop that Nae Nae? I could feel the familiar hard gaze through the telephone. "Nicky," he said. "Before I laid my head on the pillow that night, I might have grinned a little."

When Ryan was given a contract extension by the Jets after an 8–8 finish in 2013, his players reacted with what news reports described as an "an orgy of love." The head coach's dismissal had been a near thing, and publicly Ryan was now a more subdued figure, which made me wince. I missed the old rousing Rex, and muting such a joyfully charismatic man seemed to me something like requiring James Brown to mind his stage manners. Football is a big business that isn't supposed to feel like a business.

Say what you will about Ryan, emotional attachments were never a contrivance in him. It laid Ryan low each time a Sanchez, a Revis, and so many other Jets players he'd nurtured in the hallways and meeting rooms of Florham Park left town for good. "I got close to all of them," he said. "The toughest part as a coach is you build those bonds and then watch them walk out the door and play for other people. It's a contradiction, no question about it. The sad truth of the league." When a former subordinate flourished elsewhere, Ryan said he thrilled for him: "How great is it that Pet has a head-coaching job? Unbelievable! We had that goal together forever. Fuck, *I* tell him I'm proud of him!" Ryan's capacious Jetly optimism remained durable—"I believe it's gonna happen, it sometimes doesn't, but I believe it"—as did his sense of professional fulfillment. "It's been the best," he said. "Even through the hard times, it's the best. I got a great life. I get to compete. This is all I ever wanted to do." He thought for a beat. Then he said, "One day it's going to be taken away from me."

June 2014

Appendix I

Principal Characters — 2011 New York Jets

Woody Johnson, owner

The Coaches

Rex Ryan, head coach

Defense

Mike "Pett" Pettine, defensive coordinator
Bob "Sutt" Sutton, linebackers
Dennis "DT" Thurman, defensive backs
Mark "Hammer" Carrier, defensive line
Jeff Weeks, assistant defensive line
Jim O'Neil, assistant defensive backs
Mike "Smitty" Smith, assistant outside linebackers
Brian "B-Smitty" Smith, quality control
Clyde Simmons, intern

Offense

Brian "Schotty" Schottenheimer, offensive coordinator
Bill Callahan, offensive line
Anthony "A-Lynn" Lynn, running backs
Matt Cavanaugh, quarterbacks
Mike Devlin, tight ends
Henry Ellard, Receivers
Tom Moore, consultant
Lance Taylor, quality control
Samson Brown, quality control

Special Teams

Mike "Westy" Westhoff, special-teams coordinator

Ben Kotwica, assistant coach

The Front Office

Mike Tannenbaum, general manager

Scott Cohen, assistant general manager

Joey Clinkscales, college scouting director and draft
coordinator

Terry Bradway, senior personnel consultant and former general
manager

Brendan Prophett, director of pro-personnel

JoJo Wooden, assistant director of player personnel

Dave Szott, director of player development

Sara Hickmann, sports psychologist

Michael "Mr. Mike" Davis, assistant director of college scouting

Jeff Bauer, scout

Matt Bazirgan, scout

Jay Mandolesi, scout

Joe Bommarito, scout

Dan Zbojovski, college draft coordinator

Steve Yarnell, security

The Players
Defense

Darrelle Revis, cornerback

Antonio Cromartie, cornerback

Jim Leonhard, safety

Eric Smith, safety

Bryan "BT" Thomas, outside linebacker

Calvin Pace, outside linebacker

Bart Scott, inside linebacker

Davis Harris, inside "Mike" linebacker

Mike DeVito, defensive end

Muhammad Wilkerson, defensive end (rookie)

Sione Po'uha, nose tackle
Kyle Wilson, cornerback
Dwight "D-Lo" Lowery, cornerback
Ellis Lankster, cornerback
Julian Posey, cornerback (rookie)
Marquice "Quice" Cole, cornerback
Donald Strickland, cornerback
Isaiah "Tru" Trufant, cornerback
Davon Morgan, safety (rookie)
Andrew Sendejo, safety
Gerald Alexander, safety
Josh Mauga, inside linebacker
Nick Bellore, inside linebacker (rookie)
Aaron Maybin, outside linebacker
Jamaal Westerman, outside linebacker
Garrett McIntyre, outside linebacker
Ropati Pitoitua, defensive end
Marcus Dixon, defensive end
Vernon Gholston, defensive end
Kenrick Ellis, nose tackle
Martin "MTV" Tevaseu, nose tackle

Offense

Mark Sanchez, quarterback
Mark Brunell, quarterback
Greg McElroy, quarterback (rookie)
Kevin O'Connell, quarterback
Shonn Greene, running back
LaDainian "LT" Tomlinson, running back
Joe McKnight, running back
Bilal Powell, running back (rookie)
John "Terminator" Conner, fullback
Santonio "Tone" Holmes, receiver
Plaxico Burress, receiver

Jeremy Kerley, receiver (rookie)

Derrick "Mase" Mason, receiver

Patrick "PT" Turner, receiver

Jerricho Cotchery, receiver

Scotty McKnight, receiver (rookie)

Josh Baker, receiver (rookie)

Dustin Keller, tight end

Jeff Cumberland, tight end

Matthew "Mully" Mulligan, tight end

Nick Mangold, center

D'Brickashaw Ferguson, tackle

Wayne Hunter, tackle

Brandon Moore, guard

Matt Slauson, guard

Colin Baxter, center

Rob Turner, center/guard

Vladimir Ducasse, tackle

Matt Kroul, guard

Others

Buddy Ryan, former NFL coach and Rex Ryan's father

Rob Ryan, defensive coordinator Dallas Cowboys and Rex
Ryan's twin brother

Eric Mangini, former head coach, New York Jets

Joe Gibbs, former head coach, Washington Redskins

Bill Belichick, head coach, New England Patriots

Tom Brady, quarterback, New England Patriots

Don "Wink" Martindale, former defensive coordinator, Denver
Broncos

Steve Shafer, former NFL defensive-backs coach

Jonathan Ogden, former offensive lineman, Baltimore Ravens

Mike Pettine Senior, former high-school coach and Mike
Pettine's father

Sean Gilbert, retired NFL player and Darrelle Revis's uncle

Aileen Gilbert, Darrelle Revis's grandmother

Haloti Ngata, defensive tackle, Baltimore Ravens

Ed Reed, safety, Baltimore Ravens

Ray Lewis, linebacker, Baltimore Ravens

Terrell "T-Sizzle" Suggs, outside linebacker, Baltimore Ravens

Brad Smith, quarterback/receiver, Buffalo Bills

Tim Tebow, quarterback, Denver Broncos

Appendix II

Schedule for a Typical Week During the Season

Monday
- 10:00   defensive and offensive coaches' meetings (game-film review)
- 1:00   team meeting
- 1:25   offense and defense meetings (game-film review)*
- 3:20   offense and defense walk-through
- 4:00   after-action meeting (senior front-office officials and senior coaches)
- 5:30   game planning begins

Tuesday
players day off
coaches game planning

Wednesday
- 7:45   special-teams meeting
- 8:00   quarterbacks' meeting
- 8:45   team meeting
- 9:10   offense and defense meetings (game plan installed)
- 12:00   walk-through
- 12:35   practice
- 3:30   offense and defense coaches' meetings (practice-film review)
- 4:00   special-teams meeting
- 4:20   offense and defense meetings (practice-film review)*
- 5:20   offense and defense walk-through (Revis and Cromartie excused to watch film)

*On Monday and Wednesday, position coaches might meet briefly with their players after the unit meetings.

Thursday

- 7:45: special-teams meeting
- 8:00: quarterbacks' meeting
- 8:50 offense and defense meetings
- 10:00 offense and defense positional group meetings
- 11:45 walk-through
- 12:20 practice
- 2:30 offense and defense coaches' meetings (practice-film review)
- 3:30 special teams meeting
- 3:50 offense and defense meetings (practice-film review)
- 4:50 offense and defense positional group meetings
- 5:30 offense and defense walk-through (Revis and Cromartie excused to watch film)

Friday

- 7:45 special-teams meeting
- 8:00 quarterbacks' meeting
- 8:50 team meeting
- 9:05 offense and defense meetings
- 10:15 offense and defense positional meetings
- 10:50 walk-through
- 11:05 practice
- 1:00 offense and defense coaches' meetings (practice-film review)

Saturday

- 8:45 special-teams meeting
- 9:15 offense and defense meetings (review Friday practice film)
- 10:15 walk through
- afternoon off or travel
- (evening, team hotel)
- 7:15 worship
- 7:45 quarterbacks' meeting; special-teams meeting
- 8:30 offense and defense meetings
- 9:00 team meeting

Sunday

- 11:30 pregame meal
- 12:30 early bus to stadium
- 1:15 late bus to stadium
- 4:30 kickoff

Source Notes and Acknowledgments

The New York Jets allowed to me spend the 2011 year with their
football team in order to write something deeply reported
about this country's most popular sport. I carried a pen and notebook paper everywhere I went in Florham Park and made over
eight thousand pages of notes as I witnessed most of what takes
place in this book. (A few events and conversations took place in
the spring and fall of 2010, when I spent a number of weeks with
the Jets.) What I didn't see, I did my best to validate with those
involved. When events required it, I talked about them later with
the participants to achieve clarity. After the season ended, I visited
from time to time, but I mostly kept in touch by telephone and
e-mail. It was obviously essential that I remain objective. One way I
did so was to pay for my hotel rooms on the road as well as for everything else that could be paid for. When someone told me that a
conversation was off the record, I put my pen down. That happened
only a few times. The Jets placed no particular restrictions on me.
They simply showed me their world.

Jets owner Woody Johnson very generously permitted me to
immerse myself in the day-to-day life of his football team because,
as he told me, "people don't know what it's like. They want to know
what it's like." The Jets players seemed to feel similarly. Bart Scott,
the bright, ebullient linebacker, advised me to "be sure to give the
raw, uncut truth. Football is not always pretty." And Patrick Turner,
a receiver who backed down from nobody, including Darrelle Revis,

said, "Keep it exactly what it is. Show how much goes into it." I tried on all counts to follow their advice.

It was really Mike Tannenbaum and Rex Ryan who welcomed me to Florham Park so I could see how everything worked and who then took the time from their highly involved lives to help me to understand what I was seeing. They treated me with great patience, kindness, good humor, and consideration, for which I remain appreciative.

I had no special knowledge of football when I began to seek to write about it, and all the Jets coaches did their best to help me overcome this liability—"Just trying to make you football-perfect," as Bob Sutton would tell me.

My day-to-day life was spent with the defensive coaches led by Mike Pettine. It can be difficult to have an outsider walk into your world, but the coaches weren't defensive with me. Thanks to Pettine and his staff: Dennis Thurman, Bob Sutton, Mark Carrier, Jeff Weeks, Jim O'Neil, Mike Smith, and Brian Smith. Thanks also to Sean Gilbert, Clyde Simmons, Anthony Weaver, Karl Dunbar, and Mark DeLeone.

Brian Schottenheimer and his offensive coaching staff, Bill Callahan, Mike Devlin, Anthony Lynn, Henry Ellard, Matt Cavanaugh, Lance Taylor, Samson Brown, and Andy Dickerson could not have been more welcoming. Thanks also to Tony Sparano.

The special-teams coaches Mike Westhoff and Ben Kotwica were a privilege to talk football with.

When I ventured upstairs, the game broadened for me because of Scott Cohen, Joey Clinkscales, Terry Bradway, Brendan Prophett, JoJo Wooden, Ari Nissim, Dan Zbojovsky, Jacqueline Davidson, and Greg Nejmeh, and the scouts Michael Davis, Jeff Bauer, Jesse Kaye, Matt Bazirgan, Joe Bommarito, Jay Mandolesi, Jim Cochran, Brock Sunderland, and Cole Hufnagel.

Tim Tubito, Ryan O'Heir, Sal Aiello, and Mike Giuliani had the videotape.

Bill Hughan, Kevin Stewart, and Bryan Dermody showed me strength.

Injuries and physical health are a crucial part of the life of a football team, which I came to better understand because of Dr. Kenneth Montgomery, John Mellody, Josh Koch, and Dave Zuffelato.

Peace of mind is likewise vital in ways David Szott and Sara Hickmann helped me to grasp.

Gus Granneman, Vito Contento, and Brendan Burger were always nice about an extra man going out to Blake Hoer's practice fields in hunter green and white.

Robert Mastroddi, Rich Bedell, Aaron Degerness, Montelle Sanders, Casey Lane, and especially Clay Hampton and Steve Yarnell kept me out of day-to-day confusion.

My presence meant more work for Lauren Reed, Laura Young, and Kathryn Smith, and they were kind about making it not seem that way.

That was also true for the Jets media-relations staff of Bruce Speight, Jared Winley, Meghan Gilmore, and Nikolaos Filis, who treated me with exceptional courtesy.

I am also grateful to Matthew Higgins and Thad Sheely.

I met and talked with well over two hundred football players and coaches during my time with the Jets. Many of them are named in the text. To a man, they were helpful as I tried to learn about the game. In some cases, they put me in touch with members of their families, conversations that broadened my understanding of what it takes to play or coach professional football. Many thanks in particular to Aileen Gilbert, Sayinka Lankster, Joyce and Mike Pettine Sr., Julie Posey, Michelle Ryan, Michelle Tannenbaum, Stacy O'Neil, and Emily Fitzpatrick.

As I worked, I kept up with the daily Jets coverage published by the Associated Press; *Newsday*, the *Star-Ledger*, ESPN New York, the *Record, New York Post, New York Daily News, Metro New York, Wall Street Journal*, and the *New York Times*. I read Peter King's *Sports Illustrated* column "Monday Morning Quarterback" and Austin Murphy's sterling coverage of college football for the magazine. I depended also on Pro-Football-Reference.com, NFL.com, ESPN.com, and back issues of the *Baltimore Sun*.

Rex Ryan and a few others suggested books about football that I should read. The most edifying of these for this project were *The Last Coach: A Life of Paul "Bear" Bryant* by Allen Barra; *About Three Bricks Shy of a Load* by Roy Blount; *Bringing the Heat* by Mark Bowden; *Bear* by Paul "Bear" Bryant with John Underwood; *End Zone* by Don DeLillo; *A Fan's Notes* by Frederick Exley; *Great Football Writing: Sports Illustrated 1954–2006,* edited by Rob Fleder (especially helpful was Jeff MacGregor's Jets piece, "Muddied But Unbowed"); *This Was Football* by W. W. "Pudge" Heffelfinger as told to John McCallum; *Run to Daylight* by Vince Lombardi with W. C. Heinz; *Out of Their League* by Dave Meggyesy; *The Fireside Book of Football,* edited by Jack Newcombe (especially helpful was Herbert Warren Wind's piece, "On Any Given Sunday"); *Paper Lion* by George Plimpton; *Meat on the Hoof* by Gary Shaw; and *Finding the Winning Edge* by Bill Walsh with Brian Billick and James Peterson. The best account of how football coaches think that I've encountered is a book about the making of a painting—James Lord's *A Giacometti Portrait*. A football team is, in some measure, a surrogate family. Anybody interested in contemplating that enormously consequential subject ought to read Ian Frazier's masterful book *Family*. There is a grave, complicated, mortal, holiday feeling to the end of a football season and as I experienced this firsthand, I thought enough about Philip Larkin's poem "The Whitsun Weddings" that it would be remiss not to say so.

The Brooklyn Arts Exchange offered me an inspiring place to work.

I received crucial assistance from Greg Bishop, Kevin Byrne, Wendy Herr, Cindy Mangum, and Michelle Schmidt.

I'm very indebted to my friend Gerry Marzorati, a writer's

editor, who, with help from Ilena Silverman at the *New York Times Magazine,* in 2010 told me to consider the idea that football was a big, important subject in our time and then urged me on all the way through. David Remnick, with help from Willing Davidson and Michael Spies at the *New Yorker,* gave me the ideal way to measure my progress. Michael Spies later reviewed this book's manuscript for factual accuracy. Any errors are, of course, my responsibility alone.

At Little, Brown, the meticulous, sore-kneed, bright-eyed catcher John Parsley and Michael Pietsch have been (my) champions since the beginning. Many thanks as well to Amanda Brown, Fiona Brown, Malin von Euler-Hogan, Heather Fain, Chris Nolan, and Tracy Roe. And I'm beholden in so many ways to Ben Allen, who always brings his (Louisville) bat.

I am that fortunate man who never lacks for excellent counsel and thoughtful readings because of my loyal agent David McCormick. Bridget McCarthy at McCormick and Williams did me a thousand benevolences.

Even as I spent most of my waking hours in Florham Park, I was sustained by a number of friends and family members who took an interest in the project and offered me advice and encouragement and criticism as I worked. Thanks to Alexandra Alter, Kathy Chetkovich, Heidi Dawidoff, Mike Desaulniers, Ian Frazier, Jake Goldstein, Estelle Guralnick, Jake Halpern, Larry Harris, Tom Hjelm, Richard Howorth, Ben Koren, Greg Lyss, David Means, Amelia Mirsky, John Pitkin, Catherine Sheehy, Charles Siebert, Freddy K. Trois, Colson Whitehead, and Kevin Young. Vijay Seshadri read the manuscript for me with unusual care. Throughout the course of the project, no matter how busy they were, Jonathan Franzen and Jan Pantucky always found time to talk it through with me, often in the small hours, and then they read the completed manuscript, indulgences that always made me feel fortunate in their warm friendship.

The most enthusiastic Jets fan I ever met was my friend of thirty years John Solomon, the very picture of a lovely person whose big, good heart stopped far too young.

I got some sense of the personal sacrifices that go into a life in professional football because of all the time I spent away from my own family. Ozzie and Bea will soon be old enough to read about what besides missing them very much their dad was up to all the days and nights. My beloved wife, Kaari Pitkin, is my safety and my center.

Index